Competing in the New Capital Markets

Competing in the New Capital Markets

Investor Relations

Strategies for the 1990s

Bruce W. Marcus

and

Sherwood Lee Wallace

HarperBusiness
A Division of HarperCollins*Publishers*

Printed in the United States of America

Library of Congress Cataloging-in-Publication Data

Marcus, Bruce W., 1925–
    Competing in the new capital markets: investor relations strategies and tactics for the 1990s/Bruce W. Marcus and Sherwood Lee Wallace.
        p. cm.
    Includes bibliographical references (p.   ) and index.
    ISBN 0-88730-409-5
    1. Investment analysis. 2. Capital market.   I. Wallace, Sherwood Lee.   II. Title.
    HG4529.M37 1991
    332.6—dc20   90–22265

91 92 93 CC/HC 9 8 7 6 5 4 3 2 1

To
Lucy
and
Lois, Adam, Core, and David

Contents

Preface

The business of seeking capital to build, sustain, or grow a company is as complex and multifaceted as a well-cut diamond. The result of the effort, when it's well done, can be just as valuable.

Once it was relatively simple and straightforward. Not easy, necessarily, but that's not quite the same thing. One either borrowed money to start a business, or sold a portion of it—*shares*—for capital. If the business thrived, then the investors benefited handsomely, either through dividends or by being able to sell the stock to somebody else at a profit, predicated on future profits for the company behind the shares of stock.

The innocence of the system began to erode when it became institutionalized, in the sense that there grew a market for buying or selling stock.

We are a long way from simple beginnings, in the stock market as in everything else. We are at an era in which some 32,000 brokers in more than 9,000 brokerage houses, 50 million individuals, and innumerable institutions trade stock in more than 18,000 public companies. Add to that the effects of the new SEC Rule 144a, in which stock can be issued for institutions only—stock that is not available to the general public.

Where once the stock market consisted of a few hardy souls (or were they hustlers?) buying and selling stocks under a Buttonwood tree on what is now Broad Street in New York City, we now have major stock-trading institutions in every large city in the world. We have companies issuing stock and selling them directly to major institutions, such as insurance companies and even leveraged buyout firms. We have electronic markets that turn the world itself into one big stock market, and we are on the cusp of new structures in which stock will trade around the clock, and that may eventually eliminate the concept of the stock exchange as we know it today. The success of trading by computer on the NASDAQ network makes clear, even to the exchanges, that the real estate on which an exchange is located doesn't contribute much to the process of trading, as it did in the days of the Buttonwood tree.

What's more important is that the sources of capital, once relatives and friends, are now worldwide pools that begin in a hundred currencies, and then cross borders as easily as the winds. And for at least convenience, the interlocking relationships and ownerships of banks and other financial houses is so multinational that the Japanese participate in ownership of American firms, the Americans participate in ownership of Dutch and British firms, and so on. In the several hundred years since the beginnings of modern capitalism, the sources of capital, and the shape and configuration of the capital markets, have become so complex that only computers, with their millions of calculations per second, can keep track of what's happening, and where, and to whom.

To the company seeking capital, it's a dynamic process, somewhat like trying to board a train that's moving at a hundred miles an hour. And the size of the company is irrelevant—the problems are generally the same, and only the magnitude is different.

In a sense, it's a two-edged sword for the company seeking capital. The sources of capital have proliferated vastly, bringing into the arena capital from such disparate sources as Asia and the Middle East and Europe. In the 1980s, Japan and West Germany supplied some $80 billion and $60 billion respectively. This is expected to change in the next decade, however. In Japan, internal growth and such factors as a rising middle class and increased social spending will likely curtail the capital available for investment outside its own borders. In West Germany, the need to invest in resuscitating the eroded East German industry—it will take hundreds of billions of dollars—will turn their vast capital pools inward as well. The number of sources may have proliferated, but the pool is clearly not bottomless.

At the other edge of the sword is the complexity of the process, the increased number of participants in it, and most significantly, the increased competition for capital. For all that and all that, capital, no matter how large the pool, is finite. The needs for it, it seems, are infinite.

A corporation is a peculiar entity, with a life of its own and an insatiable appetite for capital. By a corporation's very nature, and the nature of our economic system, capital is the fuel for generating profits.

That means that for the company that wants to thrive, or even merely survive, the need for capital transcends the exigencies of the moment. A company that needs capital, whether debt or equity, needs it when it needs it, and so must compete for it in foul times and fair. Indeed, it often seems that the need for capital is often greater and more urgent when the equities markets are at their lowest ebb and the interest rates at the highest tide.

Perhaps that's why the competition for capital must have a running head start; it must begin well before the need for capital. And that, to a large degree, is what this book is about—the long and arduous competition for capital that must begin well before it's needed.

The context of the competition for capital is as inconstant as that point at which the past meets the future. What happened in history is at much a guide to the future for those willing to watch and learn, and a clue to its mystery, because nothing in an economy ever repeats itself in quite the same way. The economic context changes almost daily, reflecting the broader context of governmental and administrative economic policy, combined with human reaction to it. World events impose themselves on the best-laid plans. After half a century, for example, in which capitalism fought with, and was so absorbed in, the competitive nature of communism, how startling to be taken by the admission of the world's communist leaders that they were wrong all along. So startling was it, in fact, that almost two years later, the world hasn't fully absorbed its impact and meaning. How do you anticipate economic tides in a world in which this kind of surprise can happen?

On a somewhat smaller but no less consequential canvas, the policies of an American administration hover constantly over the capital markets. In the 1980s, we were treated to Reaganomics, a simplistic form of primitive monetarism. It left us with a vast federal budget deficit, the effects of which are by no means described by common agreement. But yet, the effects of eight years of Reagan were so profound as to alter economic structures of long standing. And with an activist Supreme Court dominated by Reagan appointees, the economic impact of the Reagan years will be with us for the working life of some very young conservative justices. Even the relatively moderate conservatism of George Bush can't quickly mitigate nor leaven eight years of Reaganism.

On a less grand, but no less important, scale there are the everyday effects of economic life on the capital markets. It can be as whimsical as a change in popular taste for a particular brand or style of automobile, or the economic effects of a raging epidemic such as AIDS on the health care system, or the effects on the meat industry of a national growing awareness of the dangers of cholesterol—each or any of these can alter the best laid economic plans of a nation, and thereby, its equities markets.

These economic events, both large and small, are given greater velocity in today's society by both the technological speed with which they race through a nation's or a world's economy, and by their ability to reinforce or alter one another to increase or change the impact on the economic and business world, no matter how random.

This is the arena in which the competition for capital is fought. It's fought, of course, with many weapons, the best of which is still the sound and well-managed company. Nobody wants to invest in any company that doesn't readily project the ability to appreciate invested capital.

But in a world in which the competition for capital is not only keen, but loaded as well with competitors, few companies, no matter how sound at the core, can depend upon being discovered serendipitously by investors. Serendipity is great, but a poor vehicle upon which to build a career or a company.

Which is why investor relations—well and thoughtfully practiced—is so important a tool in competing for capital.

Here, investor relations is the mechanism by which companies marshal and orient those facts about themselves that can be projected to the capital sources to lead to a judgment of corporate operational ability. It then communicates those facts, through a number of very well tested devices, to those who are most concerned with making or influencing investment decisions.

And today, more than just communicating facts, investor relations has itself become a complex practice, incorporating the most contemporary techniques in marketing and advocacy in behalf of a company. Like the equities market, investor relations was once a simple process. Today, it's complex and multifaceted, requiring a multifarious configuration of skills and imagination and experience.

The primary targets for investor relations are the professional investor and investment advisor, on all levels, who inform or influence buyers of stocks or who themselves buy stocks. Competition for the attention and fealty of these analysts, brokers, money managers, and others, through direct appeal, through visibility in the financial press, through myriad devices, is the main substance of most investor relations programs. When stock prices rise, and their true value is accepted by the marketplace, it's most often due in large measure to the success of investor relations in directing attention to the company in the center arena.

Which is not to say that a stock's price can be inflated without a strong base of legitimate earnings, return on investment, and promise of continued and sustained growth. While there are some spectacular exceptions, the acoustics of Wall Street are magnificent, and too good to allow a poor stock to be touted for more than a brief period. Investor relations can give a company and its stock visibility and focus. Flagrant misrepresentation is the exception, not the rule. But given two stocks of equal value, the more visible one—the stock of the company best known to, and understood by, the investing public—is the stock that gets the higher price/earnings ratio, and the greatest value in the marketplace.

That is what this book is about—how a company can compete for capital in diminishing or aggressively competitive capital markets. The book's primary purpose is to apprise the corporate executive of some of the techniques available to compete effectively and successfully in the capital markets.

It's a how-to book as well, in terms of the day-by-day mechanics used by investor relations professionals. For both investor relations professionals and corporate executives, it's designed to delineate the options available to perform the competitive function, and to define the arena in which the competition is fought.

The book's aim is to serve the financial professional by helping him or her to understand and evaluate those options and that arena, so that skill may be profitably applied to serve the specific needs of the company.

Acknowledgments

We are still friends.

Now, that's something to be said for mutual respect and strength of character—when two collaborators who've never done it before are still friends when their jointly written book goes to press.

We should say, at the outset, that we've been friends for years, starting back when we were both partners in one of the first major investor relations companies. And because we come from essentially the same professional roots, and have the same sense of perspective, we see investor relations pretty much in the same way.

Add to that the experience derived on the road to the success of The Investor Relations Company (Sherwood Lee Wallace, founder and proprietor), and the input of its marvelous and very vibrant people, and you have the source of keeping this book cogent and *au courant* with the latest fashions, practices, skill, rulings, and art in the strange field in which we ply our trade and craft.

Because this book is so rooted in experience, then, our first thanks go to clients, past and present, who unwittingly (perhaps to both of us) served as a laboratory to test many of the practices delineated in this book. First among equals, in this context, must be Pat Patrick, of Patrick Petroleum, whose faith, trust, and encouragement were the good steed on which to surmount the horrifying hurdles of the first days of The Investor Relations Company. As for our debt to all clients, past and present—for IRC and the old Bruce W. Marcus Company and all predecessors and successors—no practice, no device, no strategy we've described is untested. This is not academic exercise; we've actually done, or seen done by professionals we respect, everything we've written about.

Which means, of course, that our second thanks are due the Street—those analysts, brokers, portfolio managers, money managers, investment bankers, traders, and other assorted stock handlers with whom (and sometimes in spite of whom) we've practiced our trade and craft these many years.

The thanks given to families in these sections of books are not plastic nor arbitrary. Books tend to be written at home, and often on family time. No such book is ever written without impinging on the good graces of those we live with. And so our thanks go to Mana and Lucy, and to Lois, Adam, Corey, and David.

The staff and professionals of The Investor Relations Company contributed time, effort, patience, and professional wisdom. A goodly lot are Carmen Berkowitz, Dixie Watterson, Gale Strenger, and the others in both the Northbrook and the New York offices.

A few random paragraphs were, as they say in the used car business, preowned—in that they appeared in other contexts in *The Marcus Report on Professional Services Marketing,* Bruce W. Marcus, editor.

The round of professionals who reviewed parts or all of the manuscript, contributed ideas and suggestions, and otherwise kept this book on the path of professional purity are too numerous to mention in entirety. But among those whose contributions were special are Ira Lee Sorkin, former director of the New York office of the SEC and now a partner in a New York law firm; Donald Aronson, a partner at Arthur Young & Co. and now at Ernst & Young; Ben Rosen, of Sevin Rosen, and chairman of the board of Compaq; Kenneth Lipper, of Lipper & Company; Kay Breakstone, senior vice-president of Burson Marsteller, a founding member of National Investor Relations Institute (NIRI), and its past president; Richard Cheney and Tim Metz, vice-chairman and vice-president respectively of Hill & Knowlton; Deborah Rothschild, Ken Wright, and Jan R. Book of Price Waterhouse; Edmund Kelly of Dominick & Dominick; Tim Powell of FIND/SVP; Richard Weiner; Angus Maitland of the VPI Group; and Laura Jajkowski and John Bajkowski of American Association of Individual Investors. Special thanks to Thomas E. King, Jr., president of King & Associates—one of the first investor relations practitioners who drew upon a lifetime in finance and Wall Street to move investor relations out of the office and into the Street. Both Tim and Earle Brown, the head of Investor Relations Consultants Inc., and an estimable investor relations consultant himself, contributed a lifetime of friendship and sounding board over many years, and Peter Horowitz, director of corporate marketing and communications for Booz·Allen & Hamilton, supplied logic, reason, warmth, and support. Much was learned—and incorporated in the book—from *Investor Relations Update,* the bulletin of the National Investor Relations Institute (NIRI), and its estimable editor, William F. Mahoney. It's a publication any organization should be proud of, and an organization that serves its members and its industry exceedingly well. Larry Rader of Merrill Lynch; Bill Witter of William D. Witter; Ezra Mager at Furman, Selz, Mager, et al.; Jim Kinney at CIS; Larry Udell at Bear Stearns; JoAnne Barnes at Howe Barnes; John Doss at Dominick & Dominick; and myriad other professionals in the several disciplines of finance and investor relations contributed to our knowledge and experience in a thousand different ways. You know who you are—and by golly, so do we, with gratitude.

Thanks, too, to the many journalists who helped and sustained us during our careers. Notable in this context, if we may say so without straining their sense of independence from those of us who beseech them constantly, are Ann Morrison of *Fortune,* and Dan Dorfman of *USA Today.*

For the spiritual aid so important to writing a book, our thanks to departed friends who inspired us at the beginning of our professional careers, who educated us, and who polished the greenness. Particularly special here are Winfield Green, one of the field's true pioneers and memorable personalities, and Richard M. Hexter, a prince of Wall Street, who knew more about finance instinctively than most people know in a lifetime of experience and education.

It's polite to thank your publisher and editor. In this case, however, we go beyond politeness to awe and gratitude to Martha Jewett, who added new dimensions and perspectives to this book without ever losing respect for its authors—a feat perhaps unmatched in the history of business book publishing; and to Mark Greenberg, president of Harper Business, whose knowledge of the context for this work may only be described as uncanny. The rest of the staff at Harper Business, including Barbara Wilkinson, Lee Watson, Susan Conn, and the rest, dwarf their counterparts at most other publishing companies.

Special thanks to Mr. and Mrs. Paul Wallace for original contributions to this effort, and to Sam Takiff, who impressed upon us that investor relations is a business, too, and must be run as one.

How nice for us that all these people labored so hard so that we could take credit for all that's included in the following pages. Our thanks to all of them.

Bruce W. Marcus
Sherwood Lee Wallace

New York City and Riverwoods, Illinois
July 1990

1

The Art and the Craft of Investor Relations

Things change.

Just a few years ago, in the early 1980s, the Dow Jones average was pushing 1000. As of this moment, it lightly flirted with 3000, only to drop several hundred points in response to Iraq's invasion of Kuwait.

In that span is more than just a few thousand points on the Dow— although those points are not insignificant. They represent more than inflation. They represent, in many respects, a whole new financial world that emerged in less than a decade.

There are changes both subtle and profound, all of which affect both the capital markets and the approaches and appeals to it. Certainly, they affect the reasons for, and the practice of, investor relations.

Some things, of course, remain the same. The stock market is still an auction market. Shareholders still buy and sell stock on the notion that the company behind the stock will either thrive or languish. There are still as many theories of what makes the market rise or fall as ever there were. And hope still springs eternal in the breast of the intrepid investor, who remains undaunted in the vale of the most consistent risk short of sky diving.

What has changed, though, is in many ways more significant than what has stayed the same.

There are many more financial instruments, and markets on which to trade them, than there were a decade ago. More than 600 new financial products can be traded, by last count. After generations of just stocks and just bonds, with a few variations, the number and variety of financial instruments is bounded only by the imagination of investment bankers.

Moreover, thriving new markets have arisen in which to speculate on

1

not just the value of the financial instrument itself, but on its performance in the market. Thus we have futures on indexes, as well as on commodities. And while it might be argued that these indexes and futures serve the trader a valuable function in hedging portfolios, the reality is that they are also purely speculative.

The financial world of the 1990s revolves faster, and on more axes, than ever before. For the company competing for capital, it offers a capital market with more complexity, more scope, more pitfalls, more competition, and more opportunity, than ever the world has seen. It's no place for the naive; to traverse it without a guide may be dangerous to one's financial health.

The New Capital Pools

Many new factors have caused this change, but the primary elements are the growth of capital markets in other capitals of the world—and the resultant internationalization of capital flows—and the increasing power of social factors, such as the institutionalization of retirement income security. These pension funds have created massive new pools of capital. Shifts in industrial focus have created new industrial power abroad. The small investor, a stranger in a strange land following a near crash on a bleak October day in 1987, has sauntered back into the market not as he or she once was, but on the bandwagon of the mutual fund. These small investors have made giants of the mutual funds, creating yet another pool of capital.

The internationalization of capital and the growth of pension funds are with us as factors affecting the capital markets for the foreseeable future. In the short term, the factors that affect the pools of capital are no less profound. They include the ups and downs of the initial public offering market, the effect of interest rates on capital pools, the whims of the individual investor, and so forth.

Dennis Weatherstone, chairman of J. P. Morgan, made the point most succinctly in his testimony on June 28, 1990, to the House subcommittee on financial institutions. He said:

"Today, sophisticated users of funds search the globe to find the most efficient way to finance their business. One day the Eurobond market might offer the best opportunity; another day the syndicated loan market; still another day a securities issue in the U.S. capital markets might be most attractive.

"These financial products are now so closely related that in the real world they cannot be separated. No one in the markets, and no client, treats them as distinct—except when forced by U.S. law to do so."

The sheer volume of trading, and the way in which it's done, of such institutions as pension funds and mutual funds have substantially changed the nature of the stock market. Within the lifetime of many readers the average number of shares traded each day has risen geometrically. Where once the individual investor dominated the market, now it is the block trade by the institution that matters in both the volume and texture of the market.

The emergence of the computer as a dominant factor in the marketplace has served to do more than simply facilitate trades. It creates juggernauts in which millions of shares are traded almost instantaneously, in which the marketplace has become a truly global market, and in which investment decisions that once took hours or days on a slide rule now take moments of electronic calculation. The computer also moves capital, and executes trades, at lightning speed to and from any part of the world. Today, even the small individual investor can make trades by computer from his or her living room. The speed that's now part of capital flows is like the loss of innocence. Nothing will ever be the same again.

Meanwhile, the art and craft of investor relations has become clearly one of advocacy. It does no good to argue that the practice of investor relations is still simply that of communications—of just a conduit of information from company to investor. In a more competitive capital market, only the advocate competes successfully. In fact, for many public companies, the investor relations professional, in his role of advocate for the company, may be the one best guide through the investment world, as we shall see further on.

And finally, the need for investment capital has increased. Corporate debt/equity ratios are at all-time highs, and at mostly untenable levels.

The Changing World of Investor Relations

All this and more of the same add up to a substantially changed world in which chief executive officers, financial officers, and investor relations practitioners must function.

Fifteen years ago, in the infancy of investor relations, the financial community was infinitely simpler. Investor relations then was primarily a communications function to an audience that was comparatively simple to define. In fact, most investor relations was practiced at the time by a few public relations people who had a financial bent. The concept of marketing a company's capability to the financial community, of advocating that company as a potential investment, was a relatively new one.

Almost a decade later, we began to see substantial changes. The orientation had been refocused in two ways—investor relations was more a financial than a public relations function, and the orientation was on marketing, rather than on simply communications.

One other element applied in both cases. The rationale for investor relations, just a few years ago, was probably as much theoretical as it was realistic. We simply didn't know for sure. There was some strong evidence that communicating to the investment community those factors that could persuade an investor of the potential growth of a company would result in increased activity in its stock. Investor relations activities seemed to make a difference, in some cases, in bringing notice to stocks that otherwise might not have been noticed and, in fact, sometimes improved the price of the stock. Today, we know considerably more about the effect of investor relations activities on stock investment, liquidity, and stock price. At the same time, we know that in order for investor relations to be effective, the practitioner—whether it be the chief executive officer, the financial officer, or an investor relations professional—must be infinitely better trained and more sophisticated in its arts and craft than ever before. The competition for capital, in an infinitely more complex financial world, is more arduous than it has ever been.

But here, too, some things remain the same.

For all the craft of it, investor relations is ultimately an art form. That hasn't changed. Contained in the following pages are the elements of the craft, carefully and (we hope) encyclopedically delineated. But to think that one can compete in any marketing situation without art, with just a litany of mechanical practices, is to believe that one can learn tightrope walking from a book. To those techniques must be brought imagination and innovation—the creative effort that tailors the strategy to the situation, and gives unique practice to unique circumstances.

Competing for Capital

The title of this book is derived from a basic reality that transcends the mere mechanics of investor relations.

James J. Needham, a former chairman of the New York Stock Exchange, put it:

> Even if the equities markets are called upon to supply no more than 10 to 15% of the total, we will be asking American investors to pony up an amount roughly equivalent to the entire present federal debt to keep U.S. business moving forward during the next ten years!

In other words, the drive for capital for American and international business, most of which must come from equities, is at least a finite pool.

Except for proportions—in recent years slightly more than half of corporate capital comes from equity—that, too, hasn't changed. If no more than a portion of the total of American capital comes from equity, the major portion of the remainder of the capital needed to run even a moderate-sized company must come from either debt or retained earnings (real, not inflated). It must be noted that the profits from which come retained earnings are also the source of dividends. This distribution of earnings becomes an investor relations problem, incidentally, because shareholders must then be made to understand the balance between profits to be distributed and the need for profits to be reinvested.

Competing for this more elusive capital obviously requires infinitely more realistic and sophisticated skills, more intensively applied. With new and moving targets there must be new techniques of communication; new strategies in reaching the sources of capital; new ways for a company to demonstrate its ability to appreciate the invested dollar; and new ways for voices to be heard above the competitive din.

Given what we now know about the efficacy of skillful investor relations in attracting and helping to direct the flow of capital to a particular company, there is now an even more intensive need for investor relations than ever before. Frank marketing prevails. As the prey diminishes in number, so must the hunter increase his or her speed, skill, and cunning.

In earlier years, even in times when investor relations was simple communication, we knew that it contributed substantially by virtue of its ability to expose information and to focus attention on a company.

During the past two decades we've had an opportunity to see investor relations function under a large number of conditions. We've had several business cycles. We've had recessions, profound inflation, and stagflation. We've had massive shifts of capital, new European economic configurations, and perfidy on Wall Street. We've seen virtually every possible event that could attack the market, other than another world war and another bone-crushing, 1929-style depression.

We've seen staggering inflation and remarkable stability. We've seen as well new industries emerge, and once glamorous industries, such as steel, decline. And through it all, the need for capital has relentlessly grown, and the role of investor relations has grown—its value proven again and again.

Equity Capital

While it's true that the equities market supplies only a portion of the total capital needed by corporations, its contribution to total capital formation is infinitely greater than just its dollar value. First of all, the contribution by equity represents a significant segment of the total capital formation in terms of the way it's used. It acts more often as a base for all of the financing. Equity capital most frequently represents the capital used for significant growth or expansion. At the time it's acquired (and aside from some of the ancillary reasons for going public, such as the personal needs of individual owners, capitalizing on personal assets in a rising stock market, etc.), it's usually used to move a company from one level of operation to another. While normal operational growth can frequently be financed from retained earnings, equity capital is used for the spurt; for the significant expansion of either operations or markets; for the acquisition program that sharply increases the size of a company. Moreover, equity capital belongs to the company. It's not subject to credit crunch, nor is it a drain on cash flow.

Second, a company moving from the private into the public market finds itself with a visibility that enhances its access to other sources of capital—banks, private investors, larger debt issues, and so on.

Third, a public company is a regulated company, which implies that since its operations are publicly observed there must therefore be greater credibility in its financial reporting.

To the lender—banks, institutions, and private investors—this implication of credibility also enhances the sense of stability about a company and makes it a more attractive investment vehicle.

It's assumed that the local bank extends its line of credit solely on the evaluation of financial statements. Unfortunately, and to the surprise of many a corporate executive, this assumption is not universally and forever true. It becomes less true when the prime rate goes up and as the amount of money available from any institution goes down. Even granting the primacy of the balance sheet, the lending committee of any bank must make a final decision predicated upon an assessment of intangible factors—off-balance sheet factors that indicate a company's ultimate ability not simply to repay a loan but to maintain an ongoing strength. To more and more banks, the lessons of corporate decline and takeovers of recent years have become abundantly clear.

Foreign Capital

For an increasing number of corporations, foreign sources of capital enter the picture. A truism of economics is that capital knows no boundaries. Certainly this is true today.

Without considering the argument of whether or not the Japanese or the Germans or the English own too much of America, the reality is that foreign money, for the moment, readily follows our market, including the tide of interest rates, the Dow Jones average, and real estate values. The last decade has seen massive infusions of foreign capital into American business, including substantial changes of corporate ownership. For the company seeking capital, this may be perceived as an opportunity, just as for the susceptible company it's seen as a danger.

It's difficult to speak of foreign money without recognizing, then, that for many corporations a defensive position must often be taken, in that one of the results of this rapid flow of capital has been the frequency of tender offers for American companies by European or Japanese corporations. Many corporate executives have suddenly awakened to find tender offers for their company's stock from foreign companies. It is precisely at this point that a successfully informed, wooed, and won roster of shareholders is most necessary. It is also precisely at this point, as you'll see in Chapter 11, that informing, wooing, and winning shareholders is too late.

And so the mere size of the contribution of equity to the total capital structure belies its actual effectiveness. A corporation's position in the equity market is of far greater importance to the financial community's total view of the company than may be surmised from the proportion of equity to other financing. It is for this, as much as for any other reason, that the prime concern of an investor relations program never strays far from its focus on the equities market.

And yet the debt market, once able to be taken for granted because interest rates were generally stable, is now more susceptible to the ministrations of investor relations than ever before. Fluctuating interest rates have added a new dimension to the debt market, as have new debt instruments. Reliance on the rating service alone is no longer the rule, and while the nature of investor relations in the debt market tends to be different from that in equities, more communication than ever is clearly prescribed.

As for "the current market," it is best viewed as the current in a river—always in motion.

The Stock Market

The market is always the current market. It does not matter that it was once better or worse, or even that it will ultimately be better or worse. The needs of the public corporation—immediate, near term, and far term—must constantly be faced, regardless of the Dow Jones average at any given moment.

The stock market, for all its mystique, for all its implied wisdom by virtue of its self-imposed notion of fiduciary concern, is a vast, complex, and cumbersome structure. It is made even more so by the advent of technology, in which information and action flow and occur at a far greater rate than ever before. At best, it reflects not considered individual opinion predicated upon wise, conservative insights, but rather scantily masked emotional reaction. It is an auction market and functions like one. Stock market values bear no one-to-one relationship to facts, so much as they reflect an overreaction or an underreaction to the news at any given moment, or to a dream of possibilities of the future.

This is made even more complex by the ongoing, and sometimes successful, attempts to fathom the underlying factors that control the way the market reacts to events and circumstances. New theories, again aided by the computer, proliferate daily, and some of them even contribute valid information. What it does, nevertheless, is complicate—not simplify—the relationship between the investor and the market; between the corporation and the investor. And as we shall see further on, the diverse theories add varying degrees of spice to investor relations.

In viewing the stock market in this context, one other observation must be made. There's a tendency to view the market not in the perspective of the individual companies that comprise it, but as a whole. Stock market movement is reported in terms of an average. A Dow Jones average. A Standard & Poor's Index. A NASDAQ Index. A New York Stock Exchange average price per share. It must be recognized, surely, that while these averages in a down market represent more stocks whose prices go down than up, there are stocks whose prices go up or remain stable. This is a significant point in considering the possibility of upside performance in a down market for a successful company.

For the individual corporation viewing the possibility of improving the performance of its own stock in even the worst of the markets, certain basic facts must be recognized:

- Regardless of the price of a stock at any given moment, or the low to which the Dow Jones average—or any other average—may sink at any moment, there is still a market. It opens every morning and it closes every night. Granted, volume may diminish sharply, but liquidity—or at least the structure for liquidity—still exists.

- The number of firms in the securities industry fluctuates rapidly and wildly. But the industry doesn't cease to exist, even in the worst of times. Despite some severe economic downturns, and profound securities industry shake-ups, the number of firms doing business in the securities industry went from 4,470 in 1970 to 9,021 by the end of the 1980s. The number of security analysts, those people responsible for analyzing a public corporation's potential for success in the stock market, went from as many as 15,000 in 1971 to 17,000 by the end of the 1980s. Today, with the increase in pension fund management and other institutional analysts, there are 17,000 analysts registered with the Financial Analysts Federation. There were 8,000 fewer stock brokers in 1974 than there were in 1971, but there were still 33,000 brokers out beating the bushes for new buyers every day. And by the end of the 1980s, there were still 32,000 brokers.

The structure of the securities industry in all aspects is now in its greatest state of flux since the stock market began in the 1700s under the Button-wood tree on what is now Broad Street, but it still hasn't departed from its basic occupation of buying and selling securities. Institutions now seem to control the greatest thrust of stock trading—some 80 percent of daily trading is now institutional—with institutional assets, both pension assets and mutual funds, now in excess of $6 billion. Pension funds alone hold about a quarter of all U.S. stocks, half of the stock traded on the New York Stock Exchange, and 65 percent of the S&P 500. Furthermore, it must be recognized that institutional decisions about a stock are theoretically predicated, to a large degree, upon the company's performance over years, plus the prognosis for that stock's ability to appreciate in market price. Not the same thing. In an auction market, *liquidity*—the ease with which a stock can be sold or purchased—is a major factor that greatly determines the increase in stock price. The institutions themselves must face the reality of destroying the liquidity of their own holdings. If their purchases go too far into the total number of shares available for trading, it's like killing the goose that lays the golden egg. The new U.S. Securities and Exchange Commission Rule 144a, which allows stock to be issued directly to institu-tions without being traded by the public, may ease the pressure on publicly traded stock, but probably not for a long time, if at all.

As the securities industry changes, internal structures for evaluating, buying, and selling securities change. The simple separation of power to analyze, recommend, buy or sell a security is no longer simple, as will be shown in the next chapter. Now the research analyst, who went from lowly statistician to exalted status as a market prognostication superstar, is challenged by brokers, traders, money managers, and others. Large firms such as Merrill Lynch, which for years have had large research staffs that were relatively insulated from other segments of the securities industry, changed their operations by adding top-notch industry specialists, and analysts who can double as institutional sales people. And as brokerage houses attempt to reduce cost by reducing research departments, a greater burden for research falls upon brokers and traders. The picture changes. The old ways and the old approaches no longer apply.

With computers to crunch facts faster than a speeding bullet; with databases regurgitating facts like the sorcerer's apprentice; with online trading tapes to input in real time, information means different things than it once did. Analytic theories abound that would boggle the minds of Messrs. Graham and Dodd.

The focus of purchasing power continually shifts. When conditions in our capital markets—such as interest rates—warrant advantages to bankers abroad, capital flows from Europe and the Far East to the United States on computerized wings. The market never wants for massive blocks of capital, although the currency may be from strange presses.

What it comes down to is that the equities market is changing, shifting, and growing. And, so long as it merely exists, there is a necessity—as well as an opportunity—to represent and advocate the corporation to the market, not only to maintain that level of visibility necessary for success in all aspects of the capital market, but as a responsibility to shareholders as well.

The Rationale for Investor Relations

In view of the current structure of the capital markets—its changed configurations, its new sources and velocity of capital, what precisely is the rationale for, and what are the techniques of, an investor relations program?

Both a bull market and a bear market have one thing in common. They are both markets, regardless of texture, regardless of volume. Shares of stock are still bought and sold, and money from other sources is still being invested and lent. Under any circumstances, this capital must be competed for against hundreds—thousands—of other corporations.

If a corporation of any size has need for capital beyond its own cash flow, it must be prepared to compete for that capital.

In order to compete successfully for that capital, any corporation must be prepared to demonstrate—clearly, forcefully, honestly, and skillfully—those factors about itself that indicate that an investment in it is warranted.

Furthermore, the marketing effort in the capital markets is very much like a hoop—it keeps rolling only as long as you keep hitting it with a stick. The minute you stop, it stops and falls over.

Nor can it be assumed that a company's record will speak for itself. True, there are rare occasions when a company's superior performance is discovered, recognized, and rewarded in the marketplace. But for each such company there are dozens of companies whose presidents moan in frustration that the price of their stock in no way reflects the company's performance. Under the best of circumstances nobody is watching. Under the worst of circumstances there is a lethargy and a suspicion that precludes the independent investigation that might turn up a corporate gem and follow it, quarter by quarter, through superior performance.

Moreover, the printed record is only half the story. It merely demonstrates where the company has been—not where it's going. Nor does it ever adequately expose the management team—the people who made the record possible and upon whom the investor must depend to sustain the record.

An extraordinary study done a few years ago showed a direct relationship between investor relations activity and coverage by the financial community. Using membership in the National Investor Relations Institute as a valid assumption of investor relations activity, the study discovered that companies with NIRI members on staff have more analysts following their stock than do companies without NIRI members (and therefore, it may be assumed, without formal investor relations programs). It was also discovered that the greater the number of analysts following a company, the higher its price/earnings ratio. According to a report of the study in the NIRI publication, *Investor Relations Update,* an attempt was made to determine through regression analysis whether other factors—profit margins, better returns on assets, superior growth, etc.—might account for the results of the study. This analysis offered no other explanation than the investor relations program.

One of the most compelling reasons for an intensive financial relations program during a down market—as well as during an up market—lies in the basic nature of security analysis itself. The greatest part of analysis is based upon intangible and unmeasurable factors, such as management and the company's ability to plan and meet its objectives. The more precisely and clearly the elements that define these intangibles are projected, the more readily the company's ability to appreciate the invested dollar will be understood. The more readily this ability is understood, the more likely the acceptance—and investment—by a financial community that discounts for the unknown—for the risk.

The Aims of Investor Relations

Essentially, the successful investor relations program seeks to demonstrate three basic things. It's true that security analysis and the attempts to judge a company's ability to succeed in the future depend upon an extraordinarily complex structure of characteristics, but still they all evolve to three basic points:

- Earnings and financial soundness
- Management
- Plans

Earnings, cash flow, and sound financial structure are, after all, what a corporation is all about. They represent the return on the investment. They signify the company's ability to succeed as a corporation. But at best, earnings, and even cash flow at any given moment, constitute only a small portion of the measure of a company's viability, and they demonstrate not the near future but the immediate past. If earnings and financial performance were the sole measure of a company's performance, there would be no auction market. It would all be done by computer. One could very well have bought the stock of a buggy whip manufacturer in its last great year before the invention of the automobile. What's more to the point is not just the earnings record of a company, nor even the consistency of its positive cash flow and earnings growth. It's the degree to which the pattern of financial performance demonstrates the ability of the company to continue to earn that must be projected.

Second is *management*. A corporation may by definition have a perpetual life, but its ability to operate successfully is a function of its management during the tenure of the individual managers. This is as true of a $2-million company as it is of IBM, for all its vast size and greatness. If, during the next few years, the president of IBM makes a decision about the computer industry that differs from his predecessors', it will alter the entire structure of IBM for many generations to come. And what is it that must be projected about management? Not just the skill, intelligence, vigor, and clear-sightedness of its officers, but its ability to see the company, the industry, and the economy clearly. It's the ability of the management team to deal with the day-by-day problems of the company, and its ability to develop and implement realistic long-range plans. It's the ability to fathom all aspects of management—operations, administration, production, marketing, distribution, finance. It's the ability to deal with contingencies in changing situations. Is the management that brought the company from $10 million to $50 million in volume capable of dealing with the same company when its volume reaches $100 million, and therefore with an entirely new set of problems?

Third is *plans*. Not just what the company is going to do tomorrow or five years from now, but rather its long-range strategic programs. Where is it going? What are its objectives—long- , medium- , and short-range? How does it mean to finance its plans? Are its plans realistic in terms of the industry, the market, the economy, management's abilities, and the company's financial condition?

When all of the elements about a corporation that can possibly be compiled in these three categories are projected and understood by the financial community, and when they are projected believably and consistently, then that company can expect to compete successfully in the capital markets. In fact, there is a premium that accrues to predictability.

Measuring Investor Relations

And how is success in a financial relations program measured?

It is measured in a feedback of knowledge and understanding about a company by those segments of the financial community that are most important to that corporation.

It is reflected in the relative ease with which a corporation can deal with the capital markets, ranging from banks to the equities market.

It is reflected in a realistic price/earnings or price/cash flow ratio, in relation to the overall average price/earnings or P/CF ratio of the stock market in any given time and, more significantly, a corporation's own industry.

It is reflected in increased *liquidity*—the comparative ease with which sellers find buyers and buyers find sellers, even in a sparse market.

It is reflected in increased and enthusiastic sponsorship and more market makers and supporters.

Assuming a clear and honest reason to believe that the corporation's efforts are leading ultimately to success and greater profitability, there is no better way that a company can compete successfully in all aspects of the capital market except through an intelligently designed and skillfully executed financial relations program. As any modern businessperson knows, the theory of the better mousetrap no longer functions in a complex competitive economy.

Not to be overlooked is the fact that investor relations has itself contributed to its own process.

Investor relations is now a mature practice, where once it was done tentatively by a handful of enlightened corporations. The investor relations practitioner, once a public relations person with enhanced and interesting responsibilities, is now a sophisticated and well-trained financial practitioner with skills in communication and marketing.

This was an almost inevitable change caused by a number of factors:

- The market itself became considerably more complex, requiring more financial training and skill than could be found even in the above-average public relations practitioner. And while in earlier days there were indeed some retread security analysts brought into investor relations, early investor relations practice was still considered a slightly recast public relations person's domain.

- Competition for capital, and for the attention of the capital markets, increased tremendously. This meant that investor relations became a frank marketing function as much as a financial function. And so all of the elements of marketing came into play. Essentially these elements are . . .

- *Know your market.* This means understanding who your best prospective buyers are, what they really want to know, and what they are looking for in terms of investment opportunities.

- *Know your product.* This means knowing every aspect, and every perspective of that aspect, of what your corporation has to offer the investor. Key on the investable idea.

- *Know your tools.* These are the tools of marketing—including those of both communications and finance.

- *Manage your tools.* This is the actual marketing effort, in which strategy is fulfilled by skillfully and imaginatively using the tools of marketing.

- As in any competitive situation the competition for attention bred new techniques and honed the old ones. Where once investor relations was a matter of press releases, shareholder reports and analyst meetings, it's now a much broader array of skills, techniques, and strategies, which is what this book is about.

At the same time the practice of investor relations has made its contribution to shaping the market.

Effective competition works that way. As more imagination is put into play to compete, more imagination is needed by other competitors. The result has been that in the past few years investor relations has helped to shape the market by . . .

- Popularizing higher standards on the kinds of information necessarily disseminated to the financial community. Better formats for shareholder reports; more informative press releases; better written and oral communication between investor relations specialists, their managements, and the financial community, and so forth.

- Market research, which has become a standard tool in investor relations. Analysis of prospective markets for a company's securities has become intensive and sophisticated, going more deeply into motivation and investment needs than ever before. Today, the market functions on more knowledge about itself than it has ever had. Investment analysis by the investor is virtually matched by analysis of the investor himself.

- Communications techniques, in which information is moved from the company to the investor, have not only improved but have become standardized. Today's investor lives by the computer, which means rapid input of information; rapid action in investing. Printed material is proliferating. Advertising is used more effectively. Shareholder lists are played like violins.

And so where once investor relations was a useful tool applied by some very bright company managers and their equally capable investor relations agents, it's now an integral part of the investment process itself. It's a primary pipeline of information that's at the very heart of the investment process.

There has been very little revolution—and much evolution—that bred this new world. Now, it behooves the company that must compete for capital to learn to navigate in its many new dimensions.

2

The Cast of Characters

The primary commodity of Wall Street, even before money, is information. And all the world of Wall Street information, no matter how you slice it, is divided into three parts—the buyers, the sellers, and the enablers.

The buyers of information—the brokers, analysts, money managers—translate the information into investment advice and investment action. They are the ones who can turn information into capital.

The sellers of the information are the executives of public companies. Their ability to sell information, and its quality, is what leads to (or away from, unfortunately) increased stock trading, increased stock value, and a stronger position in the capital markets.

The enablers—the lawyers, investment bankers, accountants, and investor relations practitioners—facilitate the process, each in his or her own way. While the process of capital investment is a function of the buyers and sellers of information, the enablers create the instruments of the process and smooth the way for those instruments to do their work.

Today, vast amounts of information about most public companies—particularly the few thousand largest—are available, and even thrust upon investors. The traditional sources—Standard & Poor's, Moody's, etc.—are loaded with facts and figures, and the on-line computer databases have much more. And the on-line databases are not only instantaneously accessible, they are updated almost minute by minute.

Add to this the constant input from the companies themselves, either directly or with the help of investor relations professionals. Today's investment professional not only absorbs information as fast as it can be generated, and manipulates it with awesome speed, but also subjects it to a dazzling array of analytical techniques that range from regression analysis and modern portfolio theory to the classic hemline index, which somehow relates the rise and fall of the market to the rise and fall of the hemlines on women's skirts. There are, as well, a plethora of economic theories, such as the Kontradief Wave Theory, and other cyclical theories about the economy. Those who would fathom the stock market don't lack for theories. More of that in Chapter 3.

And since the stock market is an auction market, and stock market prices don't increase in a one-to-one relationship to earnings, what the professional investor is really doing is not determining those companies in which the invested dollar will appreciate at a reasonable rate. He's really trying to fathom which companies the market will bet on to increase stock price.

In other words, the professional investor or investment advisor, in whatever role, must try to fathom, in a very practical context, a great deal of emotional reaction that's tempered by facts, half-facts, half-truths, rumors, guesses, and in a few cases, shrewd judgment.

The Analytic Process

The analytic process itself, however, falls into two broad general categories—fundamental analysis and technical analysis.

The fundamental analyst deals purely with the facts and figures of a company, to which is added an assessment of how management will contribute to that company's success or failure. The factors that concern the fundamental analyst are dealt with in the following chapter.

The technicians, or chartists, as they are sometimes called, are concerned not with the company, but with the stock itself, almost as an abstraction. They believe that stocks behave in a particular pattern that may be charted to project their future behavior. They concern themselves with such elements as the history of the stock's movement, a statistical analysis of the market's behavior, volume, and so forth. They believe that by charting a stock's historical pattern, they can project the pattern for the future.

Naturally, there's a great deal of controversy among analysts and other observers of analysis about this approach.

There is, in fact, a great deal of peripheral viewing of fundamentals by technical analysts, deny it as they will, just as they tend to be persuaded by economic news.

Analysts, whatever cloak they wear, whatever theory they cherish, are people too. They are frequently as easily moved by emotional reaction to the events of the day as are the most rank novices. Perhaps that's a good thing. If there were no diversity of opinion, there'd be no auction in the stock market.

Whatever the means of analysis used by the professional investor or investment advisor, there are two considerations. He or she today has more information to use in analysis than ever before, and that analysis, aided by the computer, will be done faster and with more complex configurations and permutations than ever before.

These two factors have substantially changed the nature of analysis and who does it in just the past few years. They've also, incidentally, changed the nature of investor relations, as we shall see.

While the security analyst is the prime practitioner of corporate analysis, he or she is not, however, the sole font of information to the capital markets. There are many others.

Until recently, analysis was primarily the concern of the research analyst—the descendent of the statistician whose job it was to manipulate information, to come to a conclusion about a stock or the market itself, and to supply it to brokers, money managers, and others. There were perhaps a few diligent and seasoned brokers who did their own research, but only a few.

Today, there are fewer analysts who function solely in that capacity. Aided by computers and other sources of information, people with many other roles to play in the market are all participating in manipulating information to make investment decisions. This includes brokers, money managers, traders, investment and commercial bankers, and even venture capitalists. Venture capitalists, for example, tend to work closely with groups of investors for whom they supply a broad spectrum of investment ideas, primarily about early stage companies.

Where once the analyst analyzed and the broker sold, today more of both do both, and for an increasing segment, the difference in their roles is represented more in shading than in distinct coloration.

At the same time, no matter how immersed the analysts or investment professionals may be in the esoterica of the stock market, it's important to remember that these sophisticated technicians and financial wizards are part of a sales effort. They're either directly involved in selling stock (brokers, for example), or they're indirectly involved in the process as analysts or advisors. Most people in the investment business are also investors, so almost everybody selling stocks is also buying them. The broker, whose primary job was to buy and sell stock, is today involved in buying and selling stock for himself or herself as well as for others, and frequently, in analyzing the market as intensely as was once the sole province of the securities analyst.

In fact, a special situations analyst at A. G. Edwards was asked, "What's the worst thing that could happen to an analyst who issues a research report? That nobody would buy the stock?"

He said, "No, the worst thing is that the stock goes down." What's the second worst thing that could happen? "That we recommend the stock and nobody buys it."

It's important to understand this concept, as later chapters unfold the process, because it then becomes clear that the investor relations professional is part of the dynamic; is part of the marketing effort.

If we can separate each of the characters on Wall Street from his or her classic protective coloration, this essentially is what we find in each camp . . .

The Security Analyst

It's difficult to view analysts as a group and to draw too many generalizations about them. In 1971 there were 11,500 analysts. The exigencies of the stock market sharply diminished that number in 1974 to 10,000. It is almost reasonable—*almost* reasonable—to assume that those who survived the valleys of the business cycles of the past decade are all superb at their task. This is hardly so.

There are more than 17,000 analysts currently practicing in the United States. They do continuing research on about 2000 companies, with intense focus on only a basic 400—the group that comprises the majority of traded stock. As an example, a study in the mid-1980s showed that analysts at Merrill Lynch regularly covered 1117 companies; Salomon Brothers covered 679 companies; and Goldman, Sachs covered 679 companies. Wheat First, a regional firm, covered 197 companies.

Most analysts have a business school background and many have come up through the ranks of the securities industry. There was a time, during the bull market of the 1960s, when the need for analysts was so desperate that some of the larger brokerage houses were taking bright college graduates with degrees in other areas and training them in-house. That practice seems to have abated, and many of today's analysts are considerably more sophisticated than were their earlier counterparts. The number of new analysts being trained today has sharply diminished as well, leading to a great deal of interfirm raiding, and very high salaries for the more successful analysts.

Ideally, the analyst has trained for his or her job in terms of those elements that offer the best assessment of a company's ability to succeed and thrive; to appreciate the invested dollar. Naturally, a company's ability to do this includes a large number of variables and intangibles. For example, the best-run company can lose ground when economic conditions change abruptly and to such a degree that the company cannot correct its operations in time to cope with those changing conditions. Witness the effect of sustained high interest rates and foreign imports on automotive companies. Consumer purchases of automobiles dropped sharply. This will be discussed in greater detail in Chapter 3.

Analysts, like most people, tend to gravitate toward specialties, and in some cases, those specialties have become institutionalized. The specialists tend to form splinter groups and separate organizations.

In fact, specialization tends to be a bit murky. For example, some analysts call themselves *special situations analysts.* This implies that they follow only companies that don't fit in other categories, and that portend vast improvement in both performance and the stock market. On the other hand, the growth in recent years of the entrepreneurial company has created a new and parallel category, called *emerging growth companies.* These are companies that are relatively immature, and yet give reason to believe—by virtue of either their industries or their management and markets—that they are going to grow at least 15 to 20 percent a year in revenues, and comparably in earnings. Sometimes, but not always, price/earnings ratio makes the difference, with the lower P/E companies addressed by the special situations analysts. At the same time, an emerging growth analyst might not follow a turnaround company, while a special situations analyst would.

It's difficult to distinguish one from another. A superior emerging growth group would be Lawrence Rader's team at Merrill Lynch. His growth group further defines emerging growth companies, generally, as those that have seven years of 15% percent compound earnings per share growth. One down year is acceptable. Rader says that another major criterion is at minimum $3 million in after-tax earnings.

Which is not to say that *generalists,* who follow any company they think will appreciate in value, would not involve themselves in either special situations or emerging growth companies. They may, individually, have other criteria. Some, for example, will not follow firms in a specific (and probably more complex) industry, such as energy or insurance. Sometimes, by the nature of the firm, the generalists follow everything. In the larger firm, with larger research departments, there may be greater segmentation and specialization. Beyond size and interest, there's also the question of talent and instinct. Analysts, remember, are people. They have idiosyncrasies and proclivities and instincts.

Not to be overlooked are the *industry analysts,* who specialize in one industry or another. Here, the guiding factor for the analyst may be that each industry is so specific that specialization is the best way to become immersed in its characteristics, which makes it possible to better understand the performance and potential of companies in that industry. Some analysts are particularly versatile, and specialize in more than one industry.

Analysts may also be characterized by the companies they work for. An analyst for a retail house, for example, will look at companies that supply potential for the individual investor. This may be defined by size, float, trading reach, and so forth. An analyst at a firm that serves institutions, on the other hand, is less likely to be concerned with companies with smaller floats. Not a hard and fast rule, but a general approach. However, because of the nature of the market today, with its heavy institutional involvement, the lines begin to blur. It's difficult to find a retail analyst, for example, whose work doesn't go to some institutions.

The Broker

The broker is the direct contact between the customer—the investor—and the company. Stock brokers, or registered representatives, are primarily salespeople. They have passed a simple examination that determines the ability to understand the fundamentals of the securities industry. The broker's education beyond that need not be extensive, although some are highly sophisticated.

Brokers work either on commissions or, in some cases, on a salary predicated upon a sales quota.

Traditionally, brokers rely upon their firm's research department for basic information about a company and for the intensive analysis necessary to make a sound judgment about a security. Today, however, more and more brokers are doing their own research, and some are getting very good at it. They are getting better at looking at the numbers, and they meet with management. New brokers' organizations serve as platforms for companies to make presentations, as analysts' organizations once did exclusively. The quality of these organizations, though, varies substantially. The best of the organizations are those run by the brokers themselves, such as in Houston or Allentown, Pennsylvania, and not those run by promoters or public relations practitioners. The AMEX (American Stock Exchange) clubs can also be valuable.

Naturally, with brokers as the focal point for the customer, it's almost as important that brokers understand a corporation as do analysts, regardless of the degree of sophistication involved in that understanding. A knowledgeable and enthusiastic broker with a large following can place a substantial amount of stock, and brokers are forming informal networks throughout the country with other brokers whose opinions they respect. Thus brokers are as important a target audience for corporate information as are analysts.

There's been an interesting reaction to this trend by some of the larger wire houses, which appear to be discouraging broker research. This may arise from the danger of a firm's liability as a result of independent recommendations by younger and inexperienced brokers.

When fixed commission rates for stock sales were eliminated, a number of brokerage firms sprung up offering a "plain pipe rack" brokerage service—stock trading without any of the frills, such as research. They cut commission costs to a minimum, seeking profitability on high volume of low-profit margin trades. They are, in effect, stock discount houses. An increasing number of people work with these brokers by computer, from home to the broker's office or floor position. Virtually all of the discount brokers have computer trading, which helps sales and volume, but reduces the cost of trades. Some have even begun 24-hour trading.

More investors now make investment decisions based upon their own analysis. They then merely instruct the broker—usually a low-fee, no-frills broker—to execute the order. They are more likely to come to the broker with the name of a stock they believe, for one reason or another, to be a good one. The low-commission brokers usually don't give investment advice, but simply execute orders (although some of the discount brokers are beginning to offer some research). The full-service brokers may inquire of their research department or simply give their own reaction to the idea, based upon knowledge and feelings they've gleaned from their own research. They are less likely than their discount colleagues to just execute the order without some comment.

The brokers' job is the most precarious in the securities industry. Regardless of the general condition of the stock market, their job—and certainly income level—depends upon their customers' buying and selling stock. If the market is down generally and if the small investor is not investing, the average broker obviously does very little business. If the stocks the brokers recommend, based on whatever factors, do not go up, or the stocks they recommend to be sold do go up after the sale, they lose their customers. Since it's relatively easy to become a broker, and extraordinarily difficult for a broker to make a good living in anything but a bull market, the turnover in brokers is overwhelming. In 1971 there were 53,000 brokers functioning. In 1974, with the market down, there were 33,000 brokers. In 1980, there were 48,400—and not necessarily including a great proportion from the earlier group. Now, at the beginning of the 1990s, there are 57,000 registered representatives in the United States. Of these, there are no statistics on longevity.

The Trader

Changes in the configuration of the market have altered and somewhat diminished the traders' role in some respects. They are no longer the buying force they once were. However, the power surviving with the trader today is sufficient to allow us to look back upon his or her previous influence with nothing less than pure awe. Years ago that job must have been even better than being a commercial banker. That was before NAS-DAQ and the heavy reliance upon the computer network for trading.

In the past, most traders had substantial funds available to allow active trading by taking positions in a stock (going long). Those were the days when information was scarce, spreads were erratic, and big profits could be made from most trades. Now everybody knows everything immediately via computer. Spreads are too narrow to make money on active stocks and too wide on inactive stocks to be fair sources of trading income. More brokerage houses, seeing diminishing chances to make money, are now committing less money to OTC trading. The OTC markets are growing because there are more OTC companies and more participants in trades, but each participant is gambling a lesser portion of his or her total capital in OTC. The brokerage firms themselves seem to be reluctant to bet their own money for their own accounts. Most of the trading now, and the reason for growth, is to service the growing demand by customers.

Are the traders the profit centers they used to be? It seems to be less likely than in the past.

Frequently, over-the-counter traders will still take positions in stocks they like in order to make an orderly market. However, these positions are not as strong as they were in the past. To the company involved, the size of the trader's long or short position can make a profound difference in the success or failure of the stock in the marketplace. A good company can have four to six market makers. A very popular stock may have fifteen market makers, but that's exceptional, and today, few stocks have that many.

Because of the losses that traders have sustained in the last few years, fewer traders will position stock these days.

An over-the-counter trader who works with a lot of active smaller stocks can make or lose a million dollars in one trading day, which makes trading a tense job. A trader's survival is almost on the line almost all the time, and the pressure and speed they work under is phenomenal. It takes a very special personality to do it. You can't have a long conversation with a trader during market hours—"long" being defined as more than 15 seconds. If the trader is a close personal friend, you might get three minutes, and their spouses probably get even less.

The best kind of trader to have supporting you is one who has a retail brokerage staff in the company, because he or she can get some stock out at retail. Also, the trader is there to serve the retail operation, and so is subject to pressure from brokers as to what stocks should be traded.

If the trader is with a wholesale operation, then he or she is generally just trading with other traders, and that can go on just so long, and the stock can go just so high, before some of that stock has to get out into the retail channel. There is certainly little impetus for traders to bid a price up among themselves.

Traders don't care whether the stock is going up or down. They work off the action. They get paid on the volume and on the spread, unless surprises, sudden swings, catch them on the wrong side of the market and there are some really severe losses. The traders don't care so much, then, whether your company stock goes up or down as long as it provides them volume. In volume is their opportunity to make money. If they buy at $5 when the spread is $5 bid and $5.50 asked, they can sell at $5.50. If the stock goes to $4.75 to $5.25, they can still sell at $5.25 what they bought at $5. A sixteenth of a point is important to them. A quarter is a nice profit, on volume. If the market goes to $5, they might sell and break even, but that's a 10 percent move. And what if the stock rises?

These are traders who only want to trade *on the numbers.* They don't want to know anything about the stocks they're trading. They're going for just the small price changes, which is an art in itself, and they want to focus on that, and not concern themselves with what the company's actually doing. They're more concerned with who's trading what, and what positions they have, and making a profit on a very small price movement.

Their emphasis is on every minute that prices change, and where they put the spread, and how wide they make it, and when they mark the stock up an eighth or a quarter or sixteenth or whatever, and when they don't over a specific period of time. This is what creates a trading pattern and this is what makes the price go.

Frequently, traders are armed with no more than the information they are required to know by securities regulation, which is little more than the company's most recent financial performance. Most of the smaller trading firms don't maintain a research staff, and so the onus for keeping the trader informed must fall upon the corporation.

The younger, newer breed of traders are more likely to want to know about the companies they trade. They realize that it might help them to get a feel of where the stock might go, so that there's less chance for them to get caught on the wrong side. This is clearly a trend, and one on which investor relations professionals should capitalize. Get to know your market makers.

The Specialist

On the exchanges, the orderly market is maintained by the specialist, a member of the exchange dedicated to buying or selling stock for his or her own account to balance and offset extreme swings in prices.

The specialist is an extraordinary figure in the financial world. Specialists are responsible solely for specific stocks. They use their own money, which means they can either make or lose a great deal, depending upon their judgment and the swings of the market on any given day.

Specialists should be kept as well informed of a company's activities as should be analysts. There is no reason for specialists to be surprised by the action of one of the companies they represent and protect on the floor of an exchange.

The Institutional Salespeople

Institutional salespeople, while essentially salespeople like brokers, are dealing with an infinitely more sophisticated and knowledgeable customer. Many brokerage firms draw their institutional salespeople from the ranks of the analysts.

Institutional salespeople are being seriously affected by the terribly low commissions that institutions now pay, even on volume. It's possible, then, that during the next few years, either the institutional salespeople as a breed will be assimilated into other aspects of the industry or they're going to become the point for selling other brokerage house services to institutions. This may include responsibility for selling the research function or the research reports, or for selling bonds, or block trading. But they're going to have to make commission money from other products that the brokerage house offers.

The Money Manager and Institutional Portfolio Manager

A money manager is a firm or an individual retained by others to manage investments. Money managers have the broader responsibility of overseeing entire funds or segments of funds, irrespective of how those funds are to be invested. The money manager is frequently a portfolio manager as well.

The money manager may be the head of a mutual fund, or a bank trust department, or a pension fund, or hedge fund, or a small pool of private investment capital, or a discretionary account for a brokerage firm. Some stock brokers manage money for individuals, IRAs, ESOPs, Keoghs, or even small institutions, such as nonprofit organizations with small funds. More brokers are now listing themselves, even if without cachet, as "broker and portfolio manager."

Most money managers tend to use the basic research supplied by their own or other research departments, including research boutiques, to which they apply their own judgment. There has been a trend, recently, for more money managers to do more of their own research. The problem is, though, that money managers tend to be in positions where they have to make decisions quickly. They just don't have the time to research an individual stock as completely as might an analyst. They do, however, combine instincts and training with reading and computer screening, and more and more, they meet with company management. They also seem to consider market, industry, and general economic factors more than do analysts.

Like brokers and analysts, money managers function in many different categories. Typical categories might be companies with investments of $50 million and under, $50 to $100 million, $100 to $250 million, $250 to $500 million, $500 million to $1 billion, and over $1 billion.

Managing money, too, is a precarious job, since it is directly performance oriented, with very little margin for error. Thus the money manager tries to be as informed as possible in order to have a basis for judgment of the research factors.

The singular responsibility of the institutional portfolio manager—the person specifically responsible for the performance of all or part of the portfolio of securities for mutual funds, pension funds, banks, insurance companies, and so forth—is to choose securities that increase the value of the full portfolio.

The parameters of each portfolio are very different one from the other. Some funds have portfolios drawn to match an index, such as the S&P 500. Some portfolios are chosen for growth, some for rapid appreciation, some for income. Mutual fund portfolios are usually highly specialized by industry group as well as by financial consideration.

Funds are managed by fundamentalists, chartists, and subscribers to virtually every market theory ever promulgated. This poses an interesting problem for the investor relations practitioner, trying to advocate a client's stock.

There are no sure answers, but there are some rational approaches. For example, examining a portfolio will give some clues to the kinds of securities the portfolio manager might accept. Certainly, talking to the manager will help. For a mutual fund, the prospectus defines the fund's parameters, but not the techniques used by its manager to select stocks.

The best approach may be to choose the fund that best suits the security, in terms of size, distribution, industry, etc. Then, by examining the portfolio, determine the best approach to the manager.

This is further complicated, of course, by the fact that most portfolio management is fairly dynamic, and parameters change as market conditions change. This means that to deal with any institutional portfolio manager, frequent reexamination of requirements is necessary. Attention must be paid, but to have your stock accepted by the right institution it's worth the effort.

The Economist

A little-known factor in corporate analysis is the economist for the major bank, the larger brokerage houses, research firms such as C. J. Lawrence-Morgan, Grenfell, and the major corporation. While economists are primarily concerned with larger economic trends, they rely to a large extent on industry information, and the performance of companies within that industry, for major elements in making their projections. Their output then becomes an important framework for security analysis.

As the financial markets have moved from individual country markets to world markets, it's become more important for investors and their intermediaries to have some knowledge of economic conditions and currency and capital movements world-wide and in each country. As a result, the role of the economist has become more important in the last few years. A lot of the language of economists is now coming into the average financial person's daily diet, such as *M1* and *M2*. And today, the front pages of the newspapers are loaded with stories on gold, the value of the currency, inflation, and how business is in Germany versus England and the U.S.

Corporate Portfolio Managers

Where once the corporate portfolio manager was limited, in his or her responsibilities, to managing a corporation's investments of its surplus cash (other than the corporate financial officer's cash management responsibilities), the portfolio manager is now usually responsible for the firm's pension fund investments.

Most larger corporations, with cash surpluses, maintain extensive portfolios of stocks, bonds, and money market instruments as part of their cash management programs. Companies in the Fortune 500 are those in that category, for the most part. Some firms even use their surpluses as venture capital funds.

But today the corporate portfolio manager, under ERISA (Employees Retirement Income Security Act), has extraordinary fiduciary responsibilities. There are vast sums involved, even for smaller companies.

While most corporations depend on outside sources for advice, and even to manage the money in the pension fund itself, the corporate portfolio manager still participates in making final stock-purchasing decisions.

These potential investors are not to be overlooked in your investor relations program. Companies such as Amoco, Masco, and Borg Warner have excellent and receptive money managers who will look at appropriate and interesting situations.

Other Investment Officers

Two groups that have grown in importance in recent years, with greater responsibility for investment decisions, are bank trust officers and insurance company investment officers. For example, Northern Trust Bank in Chicago recently sent a security analyst to examine Federal Signal Corporation as a possible investment for some of the trust accounts for which it has discretionary authority.

Here, too, ERISA is largely responsible for these groups' increasing role in investment decisions. Prior to ERISA, trust investment, and much insurance investment, was limited to state-approved lists of investments. ERISA, which is the first federal trust law, does not limit investments by list. Rather, it responds to the Prudent Man Rule with much greater reliance on the investment officer to make decisions. The Prudent Man Rule, incidentally, says that fiduciaries must invest funds under trust ". . . as would a prudent man with his own funds." Under ERISA, the concept of prudence is fulfilled by adherence to investment goals, rather than to approved lists of investments.

Other Analytical Targets

Those segments of the financial community that have been described so far constitute the main body of specialists to whom the elements of a company's potential must be communicated. Naturally, nothing in this area is monolithic. While the bulk of investment decisions rest with analysts, brokers, money managers, and others, there are still fragments of the securities industry whose opinions and impressions are important. The role of such other means of communications as the financial press will be dealt with later. The concern here is with specific focal points of judgment within the securities industry.

There is, for example, value in having the head of the corporate finance department of a brokerage firm or investment banking firm be aware of a company's profile, since they are frequently people who are sufficiently respected within their own company to have their judgment considered.

The role of the commercial bank in investing is growing rapidly, as banks test the Glass Steagall Act that has kept them out of investing since the 1930s. Moreover, these investment officers are becoming increasingly sophisticated, a fact that is recognized by a growing number of individuals and pension funds that put money under management with the banks.

For the younger, growing company, access to venture capital—and therefore communications to venture capital firms—can be crucial.

The person in charge of mergers and acquisitions for an investment banking firm is frequently looked upon as a source of new investment ideas, since the nature of his or her work brings the M&A specialist into exploratory situations with a great many companies. Within this context the merger and acquisition specialist has another interesting potential value. A merger is a form of investment of corporate assets. The mergers and acquisitions specialists can frequently put corporate information to better use on behalf of a corporation than can many other people in the investment community. They must be particularly careful, though, not to trade on inside information—as anybody who read the front pages in the late 1980s should know very well.

Credit

While the largest amount of activity for the investor relations professional is on the equity side, the greatest source of capital in industry is debt—the bank loan, the debenture, commercial paper—the full range. Credit analysis will be dealt with in Chapter 3.

Those who deal with credit analysis, however, are essentially the same kind of analysts as those who deal with equity analysis. The exceptions are the bank lending officers and the analysts in the bond-rating services.

The Overseas Market

As recently as a dozen years ago, in the late seventies, the securities industry outside of the United States wasn't attuned to investor relations as we here know it. The way for Americans to go into Europe, for example, was through American investment bankers with branches or associates in Europe. Access was limited, and very few American firms Europeanized themselves enough to really make a dent in the market. PaineWebber might have been an exception, at least in London and Paris, but Merrill Lynch and most others made comparatively very little impact in Europe. Investor relations professionals who went to Europe and worked through a few local firms, such as Leonard Baker in London, fared much better, and maybe even have a little edge today. Currently, there are about 29 or 30 U.S. brokerage firms with about 100 offices in Europe. Slowly, slowly the wheel turns toward Americanization of the industry.

In the interim, tremendous strides have been made, and investor relations in Europe and elsewhere in the world, although still generally behind the United States, is now considerably more sophisticated than it had been. This is for very sound reasons that relate to established customs and traditions in each country. The gradual breakup of old club attitudes in the financial community in the United States allowed investor relations to develop. In Europe, the old school ties still exist to a much greater degree than in America, to the detriment of the professional investor relations practice. Such exceptional investor relations firms as The VPI Group's Vallin Pollen, based in London, have made the grade in comparable professionalism, but they may stand alone in Europe.

The investment arena is substantially different in each country abroad. For example, in most countries there is no retail market as such. There are no individual investors as we know them, except in Japan, which is a market very much controlled by the largest Japanese brokerage firms. England is just beginning to develop a retail market. You must work, primarily, with institutional investors or very large individual investors through intermediaries. In London private client brokers work with the investments of extremely wealthy individuals in Europe.

Since the deregulation of the British securities industry in 1986, it has undergone a vast readjustment. From the rush of the first days of deregulation—the *Big Bang,* as it was known—the industry moved to a high, then a low of disorganization, volume, and business. It seems now to be stabilizing. The securities industries of all European countries are girding for 1992—the year in which the borders separating European Community countries will fall, allowing a new era in international trade. It should also be a new era in financial market competition, as the financial communities of each of the countries compete for the investment dollar.

For the U.S. company seeking to sell stock abroad, there are some major considerations, not the least of which is in the relationships that exist between the corporation and the different European financial markets. Different legal and regulatory frameworks also exist from country to country, although they almost universally subscribe to the same rule of disclosure that obtains here—that potentially price-sensitive information be released as soon as possible.

The financial press in Europe, for example, is truly national in each of the major markets, and is more influential, in most countries, than it is in the United States. According to Vallin Pollen, "A symbiotic relationship exists between the press, stockbroking, sell-side analysts, and investing institutions. The press and sell-side analysts trade stories with each other, and in turn, influence institutional investors." This is particularly evident, they say, during mergers and acquisitions, where the importance of the press is at its most obvious. At the same time, there tends to be some skepticism about investor relations, particularly among British institutional managers. They do accept investor relations help to reach management for input, but not always gladly.

It's important, then, that American companies and their investor relations counsels functioning in European markets fully understand the workings of the financial communities in each of the countries in which they may choose to operate. Until now, this has been lacking, with most European appearances by Americans taking on the demean of a road show, rather than a thoughtful, consistent attempt to establish relationships.

Identifying target stockholders should be the starting point of any program. This can be difficult, because there's no legal requirement to disclose foreign shareholdings. Moreover, in countries such as Switzerland, Germany, and France, obsessive secrecy prevails, making shareholder identification doubly difficult. For larger American companies, for whom 3 to 5 percent of their stock is in foreign hands, the job becomes a bit simpler, since the shareholders abroad are usually on the company's lists.

Local European investor relations firms are frequently both knowledgeable and well connected, and can be invaluable in developing market intelligence.

It becomes clear that establishing relationships with foreign financial markets is a task that requires ongoing commitment. It's not a casual exercise. Nevertheless, it's important for the growing American company, because Europe and Asia are sources of capital that can't be ignored.

The Sell Side

Taking aim at the array of analysts, brokers, money managers, etc., is a battery of corporate officers, ideally supported by investor relations specialists. The investor relations viewpoint would hardly be complete without a look, however brief, at the mission of those on the sell side of corporate information.

The Chief Executive Officer

At the head of the team, of course, is the chief executive officer, who may have the title of president or chairman of the board.

While each CEO may have his or her own agenda and visions for the company, inherent in the CEO's role is the charge to sustain earnings at a high level, and to build the substance to keep the value of the company's stock high and, if possible, growing.

This simple mission is not without problems. Presumably, the CEO's job is to keep the company strong, and to keep it capable of coping with the changing exigencies of the economy. This frequently means that earnings that might go to the bottom line to support the stock price are better used by reinvesting in plant, marketing, or distribution.

It's clearly a paradox, because despite the fact that the CEO's primary responsibility is to his or her employers, the shareholders, fulfilling that responsibility is a business decision that requires great moral fiber. Should the short-term route be taken, the candle of stock price may burn bright, but without reinvestment, it burns out quickly in most cases. Should the long-term route of reinvestment be taken, the CEO's tenure may be foreshortened.

While no paradox of magnitude lends itself to easy solution, there is at least the option to separate the responsibility for running a successful company from that of maintaining the stock price. Perhaps the best solution, then, is for the CEO to be interested in the stock price and market action, but not to attempt to manage it. That, perhaps, is the role of someone who runs the firm on a day-to-day basis—a chief operating officer (either a president or an executive vice president, or the chief financial officer—the CFO).

The Chief Financial Officer

The power of the CFO varies from company to company. In some, the CFO is little more than an accountant, functioning at the whim of the CEO. In others, the CFO is powerful, creative, and if not the co-pilot, at least sits at the pilot's right hand.

The CFO's title is not as important as the function. It could be vice president-finance, or treasurer, or any of several other designations. The responsibility, however, is to watch the firm's money and financial structure. This includes overseeing all procedures regarding how money is taken in, used, preserved, and paid out; monitoring the levels of capital either in or needed by the firm; dealing with the capital markets, including banks and investment bankers; dealing with the outside independent auditors, and to a large extent, dealing with investors and Wall Street.

While no corporate role is so clearly defined as to preclude crossing lines for any responsibility—a CEO, for example, may assume any of the CFO's responsibilities, if that's a personal need or personal talent—these job descriptions are a good general guide to responsibilities.

At the same time, any responsibility may be delegated by a corporate officer. Large corporations, for example, frequently have, under the CFO, treasurers, controllers, chief accountants, internal auditors, and so forth—any of which may be assigned responsibilities beyond the textbook definition of a title. One such job, frequently delegated in larger companies, is the investor relations function. In those companies that recognize the professionalism of investor relations, that function is usually assigned to an investor relations officer. That role is more fully described in Chapter 10.

In an entrepreneurial society such as ours, the corporate face to Wall Street may be an individual or a team, and the size of the company is not the basis for choice of either. Some CEOs are so entrepreneurial, so energetic, so charismatic, as to preclude any other voice dealing with the investment community. Others choose support from their financial experts, lawyers and investor relations professionals. Some deal with Wall Street enthusiastically and some do it reluctantly; some skillfully and some painfully.

The important thing to realize in all this is that, as seen in the following chapter, the personality, skills, and texture of management are the crucial elements to be assessed in analyzing a company. The competition for capital is not one of numbers; it's a battle of people.

The Enablers

Such is the nature of our society and economy that specialists are required to guide us through the dark woods of finance and regulation. The simpler times when entrepreneurs could raise sums of capital, beyond start-up, by themselves are perhaps centuries away. Today, no one can deal effectively with the capital markets without the help of lawyers, investment bankers, and investor relations consultants.

The roles played by each of these enablers are not manufactured by the professionals themselves; they are mandated by the complexity of the system. Laws designed for the good and protection of the public have become so complex that they must be interpreted by lawyers. The sources of capital are so varied they must be accessed with the help of investment bankers and their various levels of skill and experience. The competition for capital has become so intense, and is fought in so many arenas, that only the skilled and professional investor relations consultant can be relied upon to lead the charge effectively and cost effectively.

The Lawyer

For the public corporation, the largest part of the lawyer's job is dealing with regulation and disclosure—subjects covered extensively in Chapter 6.

While lawyers have many roles and responsibilities in companies—a corporation is, after all, a legal entity and not a person—our concern here is the role of the lawyer in competing for capital.

Lawyers, whether internal staff or outside counsel, prefer to command the areas of their expertise, which can sometimes pose problems for others who must function in the same arenas. Lawyers, then, will occasionally find themselves in conflict with CEOs who want to take risky or daring action, with auditors who want to disclose marginal data, with investment bankers who want to move stock in any way legally possible, or with investor relations professionals, who want to disclose and inform effectively and in depth where lawyers tend to be reticent.

Some time ago, a company was in the midst of a lawsuit that threatened its credibility in the market. Every suggestion made by the investor relations consultant for dealing with the press or shareholders was vetoed by the attorneys. Finally, in exasperation, the investor relations consultant said, "Look—your job is to see that nothing is said in public that will come back to haunt our client in court. My job is to keep the client viable in the marketplace. I'll respect your job if you'll respect mine." In interdisciplinary relationships with lawyers, this may well be the best approach.

Which is not to say that competent lawyers are not an invaluable member of any corporate team, if only to bring legal perspective, and to find routes through the legal jungle. Lawyers advise, but business people must make business decisions.

The Auditors

The role of the auditor, visible as auditors may be, is rarely understood by even the most learned observers of the business scene. This includes judges who want to know why the auditors didn't catch the embezzlement.

The auditor didn't catch the embezzlement because it's not his or her job, nor is he or she in a position to do it even if given the job.

The auditor's job is to take the financial information given by the company, to review the procedures for managing that information, and to determine whether the conclusions to be drawn from that information are accurate. Not whether the *information* is accurate, but whether the *conclusions* are accurate.

This is possible because the auditor simply tests the procedures for reporting financial information to be assured that they are consistent with *generally accepted accounting principles (GAAP)*. The auditor can be lied to, given false figures, have information hidden from him. But if the material he's given is organized and formulated according to GAAP, he's got to give the firm a clean certificate.

There are exceptions, of course. In the course of testing to see whether GAAP is being used, the auditor samples information. This may include, for example, verifying the cash in bank accounts, or verifying that random samples of accounts receivable are indeed accounts receivable, or that the physical inventory is actually on the shelves. If, while doing that, he discovers something not quite right, he's obliged to report it in the proper place in the audited statement. This may be a qualification in the certificate, or a footnote to the financial statements. But it is all part of the audit.

The auditor's independence—freedom from any taint of subjectivity or self-interest—is a crucial factor in the auditor's existence. Lacking this independence, the auditor's attestations are worthless. Auditors, then, will go to great lengths to preserve that independence and integrity, even to the point of resigning an account rather than be persuaded to represent as fact something they don't see as fact. This independence, this objectivity, is the major currency of the auditor.

The potential conflict comes when the investor relations professional is trying to produce the annual report, and the auditor has his or her own ideas about how the information is to be presented. In most cases, the auditor is merely concerned with presenting information fairly and accurately, by his or her own lights. But auditors are not necessarily communicators, and their concepts of *fairly* and *accurately* may not be the same as the lawyer's or investor relations consultant's.

The answer to the problem is that there usually isn't an answer, other than the persuasiveness, experience, and expertise on either side. The only protection for the investor relations professional is to know his or her securities law and accounting—and that's why so much of it is addressed in this book.

And again, the role of the investor relations professional is covered in Chapter 10.

The Investment Banker

It's impossible to function in the capital markets without a clear understanding of the investment banker and the role he or she plays in them.

The role of the investment banker, which changes drastically, from era to era, in response to the changing needs of business, is dealt with extensively in Chapter 12. Here, we must be concerned with the investment banker's role in competing for capital.

Investment Banking Services

What exactly should the corporation expect in the way of investment banking services?

Essentially, it adds up to not only the supply of capital, but intelligence necessary to maximize the profits on that capital. It's a total range of financial services that embraces every aspect of corporate operation as it relates to capital.

Currently, there are really relatively few investment banking firms that are qualified to meet the full spectrum of needs of the growing corporation, although the number may be increasing as competition and need increases. Mergers and dissolutions of firms place the inventory of skills in different hands, if not fewer hands.

A typical example of one such firm is Donaldson, Lufkin & Jenrette, Inc. DLJ sees its role in relation to its clients as one that begins with a thorough understanding of the corporation and its needs, to which it brings:

- Business and industrial analysis
- Economic, social, and political research
- Knowledge of financial markets and timing
- Tax accounting and legal skills
- Investment judgments

Its list of services brings to bear on any of its clients' problems an extraordinary range of capabilities in the areas of capital raising, capital management, professional advisory services, and market-timing. It delineates at least the following services in each of these four areas:

Capital Raising
Public underwriting
    Equity
    Fixed income
Private placement
    Equity
    Fixed income
Lease/project financing
    Corporate equipment
    Real assets
Public finance
    Health care
    Pollution control
Mortgage brokerage
Divestitures
Creating companies
Venture capital
Real property development
Natural resource financing

Capital Management
Portfolio management equities
  Pension funds
  Profit sharing plans
  Endowments
  Corporate
  Individual
  Public funds
Fixed income
  Corporate funds
  Institutional funds
  Public funds
Real estate
  Pension funds
  Public partnerships
REIT management
Real property management
Personal asset management
Venture management

Professional Advisory
Securities—equity, fixed income, option
  Research
  Portfolio strategy
  Economic analysis
  Opinion research
Corporate development
  Merger
  Acquisition
  Corporate strategy
  Financial planning
  Communications
  Market studies
Investment advisory
  Personal assets
  Tax shelter

Real estate

Financial planning

Market-Making

Stock brokerage

Common stocks

Preferred stocks

Convertible securities

Bond trading

Government

Corporate

Municipal

Block Placement

OTC Trading

Arbitrage

Domestic

Foreign

Options

Stock clearing services

Real estate brokerage

Special corporate transactions

Goldman, Sachs & Co., another major investment banking firm, offers essentially the same range of services, but with perhaps somewhat stronger capabilities in such specific areas as international financing and commercial paper.

It should be clearly noted that the services of these two firms are delineated as examples of the several outstanding firms in the field. Nor does size imply superiority. What's most important is intelligence and the ability to grasp the full range of a corporation's needs, and the investment banker's ability to serve that range of needs. Furman Selz Mager Dietz & Birney and Janney Montgomery Scott are two medium-sized firms with exceptional investment banking capabilities. There are several smaller investment banking firms in which the focus of talent is so intensified or so specialized that they serve the needs of the smaller corporation or the specialized needs of the larger corporation. One such very small firm, Leonard Harlan and Associates, for example, is unexcelled in knowledge and facility in real estate investment and financing. Its size has not precluded its contribution to the very largest corporations.

Some firms are emerging on the basis of particular strengths in one or two areas. For example, A. G. Becker was a regional firm in the Midwest that became national, first through its mergers and acquisitions capability, and then through a merger of its own with Warburg, Pincus.

Obviously, this kind of service is not compensated for in the old way. The fee from an occasional underwriting cannot supply the investment banker the wherewithal to pay for the kind of talent, and to run the kind of integrated organization, necessary to serve today's corporation. More and more, then, investment banking firms are moving to a straight fee structure. More and more corporations, recognizing the value of a full range of services, are happily accepting the fee structure.

As a result of a lawsuit a few years ago, another element has entered into the picture. Shareholders of a company that ran into difficulty—Tidal Marine International Corp.—successfully sued Shearson Hammill & Co. Inc., on the basis that as investment banker for Tidal, Shearson should have informed its brokerage clients of problems to which the investment banking side was privy. Shearson claimed that to have done so would have violated the confidential client-investment banker relationship. Paradox. The judge ruled that Shearson should either have made the information known to its brokers and brokerage customers, or refrained from handling orders or recommending Tidal stock.

Assuming the further development of the investment banking firm as outlined here, how is the difference between the investment banker-corporation relationship and the broker-customer relationship reconciled? The court gave no answer. What remains from that decision, however, is the spectre of severing the brokerage function from the investment banking function. A knot yet untied, although the shape of new structures arising from the mergers of brokerage firms with nonbrokerage firms offers a clue to direction.

This spectre is neither intangible nor necessarily bad. More and more investment bankers are coming to recognize that the recycling of stock is not the major function of investment banking, and that it must never again be allowed to overwhelm the role of investment banking in capitalizing industry.

Thus the emerging investment banking firm is just that—emerging. As of the moment there are all too few investment bankers who function—or who are capable of functioning—in ways that serve the needs of the corporation. A talent here, a capability there—but very little total capacity. The answer has not yet caught up with the need, and the need is proliferating.

For the emerging corporation in need of sophisticated investment banking services, the search for it becomes arduous. As the competition for capital becomes keener, the spectrum of expertise needed to find and intelligently use the capital has not kept pace. It behooves the corporation, then, to search it out assiduously. Corporate management can no longer afford to be cavalier in accepting an investment banker relationship on superficial criteria—such as the number of retail outlets or even the prestige of the names found in its syndicate structure. Every aspect of investment banking must be reviewed, in the judgment of capability, including those for which a need is not immediately foreseen. Circumstances change. The corporation not interested at the moment in an effective real estate capability may suddenly find itself, as a result of a merger, in possession of several million dollars worth of real estate. That's hardly the time to go looking for outside real estate expertise.

More than just a conduit to the capital markets, the investment banker is a primary factor in any corporation's operations. No company begins without capital, and no company functions without capital. Not to understand the investment banking structure and its relation to the capital markets is a weakness that no company can allow itself in today's economy.

The fascinating thing about Wall Street is that there is no rigid structure of occupations, in an academic sense. While there are titles and jobs and roles, it's become abundantly clear, in the dynamic of the financial world in recent years, that roles change as opportunities present themselves or recede.

The roles played by the cast of characters are determined by one thing— go where the money is.

3

The Elements of Analysis

A significant role of investor relations is to supply those elements of information that go beyond the bare facts; that combine with the facts to produce a perceived wisdom that tells the prospective investor that this may be the stock to invest in; that this may be the stock that will cause his investment to grow.

The raw facts about any public company are readily available. This is so by law, which requires disclosure of company activities and performance. But if all the most pertinent facts about a company were known and readily available, as in such services as Standard & Poor's, you still wouldn't know enough about the company to invest in it wisely. The investor, or the investment analyst, must still understand considerably more before he or she can make a judgment about the potential success of the company.

The role of the investor relations practitioner is to help guide the investment analyst to the context from which the analyst can draw the additional qualitative, subjective, and interpretive material he or she needs to make a decision.

Sometimes that's little more than exposing the firm's executives to the analysts.

Sometimes it requires a more sophisticated knowledge of how analysis works. How are these decisions made? What's the training of the analyst and investment professional, and what does he or she look for?

Dealing with Analysts and Professional Investors

There are really two aspects of dealing with analysts and investors—formulating the essence and substance of a company, and executing the mechanics of projecting both that essence and the raw data.

41

It's here that the role of the advocate is really defined. Within the boundaries of ethics and truthfulness, the CEO who understands investor relations, or the investor relations professional who understands the company, moves the facts forward in a forceful and persuasive way. Which is not to say that the facts are moved forward to tell a one-sided story. A story that's all good is too good to believe. Corporate problems offer opportunities for analysts to analyze.

The capital markets are, after all, a competitive arena. The artfulness in presenting the company to the prospective investor resides in the ability to project and communicate the future—the ultimate success of the company in the marketplace.

Is that ability artfulness? Probably, in that the difference to the financial community between two companies with the same fundamentals is the degree to which it believes that one company can outperform the other. Because this is frequently a subjective view, the assessment is susceptible to persuasion. Persuasion, within the boundaries of credibility, can be an art.

But it's an art that must be energetically pursued, if a company is to succeed in the marketplace.

And significantly, since it takes two opinions to make a market—one that says the market is going one way and the other that says it's going another—what are the analytical theories that must be understood if the advocacy role of the investor relations practitioner is to be effective?

The Analyst's View

The analyst is taught to view a company in terms of some rather specific elements, some of which are measurable and some of which are questions of judgment. Among those factors that enter into the analysis of the company are

- The financial structure of the company
- The economic context in which the company operates
- The nature of the industry in which the company operates, and the market for its products and services
- The management of the company
- The company's own projection of its plan for growth

Perhaps the best delineation of the fundamental aspects of security analysis is found in the superb work *Security Analysis* by Benjamin Graham and David L. Dodd (fifth edition, by Sidney Cottle, Roger F. Murray, and Frank E. Block). Benjamin Graham is considered to be the dean of analysts, not only for his success as an analyst, but because his book was one of the first, and certainly the most masterful, to set forth the basic elements of security analysis. Even if his precepts are honored in the breach, they are still a standard.

Basically, Graham believes that no company should be considered as an investment vehicle unless:

- The company is prominent and conservatively financed. Current assets should be at least two times current liabilities, and debts should be not more than 110 percent of net current assets.

- The company has been a consistent dividend payer. The more conservative investor would want to see dividends going back twenty years.

- There has been no deficit in the last five years.

- The price-earnings multiple is low. In a soft market, and with high interest rates, he suggests a maximum price of eight times current earnings per share.

- The stock is selling at one half of its previous high.

- The stock is selling at a price that is no more than two thirds of net tangible assets.

Obviously, these are stringent factors. Under many conditions, this would eliminate all but the smallest segment of publicly traded companies. And while very little argument can be taken with any of the points he makes, it can certainly be argued that the spectrum of investment possibilities is much greater than companies that fall within his parameters. An example would be a company with a current ratio of 1.8 to 1 but no long-term debt, and strong earnings gain. Dodd and Graham's credit standards may be too tight for this company, which may still be a good investment prospect.

At the same time the realities of the stock market today, and the range of reasons for investments, dictate some rather more flexible considerations in analysis of a company.

Varying Analytical Points of View

Who does the analyzing often determines how it's done. Certainly the bank trust department, functioning in a fiduciary capacity, must be infinitely more conservative than the speculator who is going for high return and who is willing to take a greater risk for it. The individual investor views a company rather differently than does the fund manager who must recognize that he is dealing with other people's money and will be held accountable for the results. The pension fund investment manager, concerned with new legal concepts of prudence and working within the confines of specific return goals, builds a different portfolio than does the hedge fund manager. The tape watcher who looks to make his profit with every movement of the tape sees investment possibilities very differently than does the long-term investor who is willing to buy a stock at a very low multiple, but with long-term growth possibilities.

Analysts, too, face the problem differently. The analyst for a bank trust department considers companies somewhat more conservatively than does the analyst for the hedge fund. The analyst for the mutual fund functions in terms of his fund's charter. The hedge fund analyst is looking for companies that he thinks the market will become enamored with, and whose stock the market would drive up rapidly. The analyst for the growth fund is looking for substantial growth with long-term staying power. The analyst for the pension fund is looking for companies that will not only grow steadily and appreciate over the longer period of time, but have a measure of safety. The bank or institutional analyst may have another problem in that bank and institutional portfolios are often so large that the ability to liquidate in volume is strictly limited. Some funds are limited to one kind of investment, such as dividend-paying companies, and stocks selling for more than $5 or $10. Fixed-income analysts are concerned primarily with cash flow, and what it says about the ability to make debt repayments without strain.

Some years ago, an economist at a large bank identified a problem in the airline industry at a time when the industry was doing very well and airline stocks were flying high. He passed the information to the trust department, which then calculated that it had a year to get out of the stocks before the market turned. If they had sold off their entire holdings at once, they would have been the cause of a sudden and steep drop in airline stocks. By slowly and quietly cutting back their portfolio, they had managed, by the time the prophecy came true, to sell off only 50 percent of their airline stock holdings.

The analyst for the large retail house must deal with the broader spectrum of companies because the retail customers have different portfolio needs.

Requirements of Analysis

Essentially, the requirements of analysis of a corporation fall into three categories—financial data, management, and plans.

Financial data are, of course, the simplest to define. Although there are still areas of operating information that many companies seem reluctant to disclose, for a public company there is relatively little to which an interested observer cannot become privy. The corporation that tells less deludes itself. More significantly, it deprives itself of the opportunity to view the company favorably. It also leaves itself open to a serious credibility problem. Most analysts feel that if a company is reluctant to disclose and broadcast information of any nature that is relevant to understanding performance, the reasons for doing so must be negative. And since most analysts tend to recoil at the least bit of negative information, any attempt to hide anything causes an almost immediate overreaction.

Furthermore, the SEC has been absolutely assiduous in its efforts to increase disclosure.

The overriding factor remains—the more that is known about a sound company the more readily it will be understood, believed, and favorably viewed.

In analyzing a company at least the following financial information is essential:

The Earnings Record

Since earnings, and the ability to project earnings, are the ultimate aim of most analysis, earnings history is a basic tool. It should be clearly understood, however, that the numbers for earnings never stand alone. Earnings are relative to many other factors, not the least of which is inflation. Certainly, earnings are meaningless except in relation to revenues as a percentage of revenues. They are meaningless if the role of inflation isn't clear. What is significant in analysis, then, is not just the earnings figure, even when there is a steady increase over the years. It's more important, for example, to note the degree of consistency and growth in earnings and margins. And even this doesn't stand alone, since a growing corporation is affected by many different factors during the course of a year. A sharp growth in earnings may be the result of astute management and a marvelously improved production, distribution, or marketing structure. It may also reflect a merger or acquisition, or a change in accounting practices. The *quality of earnings,* an analysis of earnings predicated upon factors that are not immediately discernible, such as accounting changes that can alter the measure of earnings in ways that do not accurately reflect the company's actual performance, means more than the numbers themselves. Prime examples are changes in depreciation method, or capitalizing versus expensing certain expenditures, or the treatment of foreign currency. For example, the measure of loss or gain from the sale of a segment of a corporation's operation is a function of the reserve set up for the disposal of those operations—and there is virtually no way to determine from most financial statements the basis used for establishing the size of that reserve. Historical earnings in the pure sense are themselves of limited value in gauging the ability of a company to continue to earn at a consistent rate.

With inflation, the historical cost, for example, of raw material or finished products in inventory moves a great distance from current or replacement cost. How, then, can assets be valued on a comparable historic basis? How can today's earnings, if they're based on inflated costs and prices, be made comparable to the earnings reported two years ago? The fact is that without some significant changes in accounting practices, they can't be made comparable.

Properly analyzed, however, the factors behind a consistent earnings history are a measure of contributing elements to ongoing earnings growth.

Revenues

Revenues are a measure of the size of a company—a way of categorizing the economic sphere in which it functions. Obviously, it may be readily inferred that many factors about a $500-million company are different from those of a $25-million company. The large company is generally older and better established and would seem to have a greater potential for growth and survival. It probably has a better grasp of its markets. It probably has a larger number of shares outstanding and a greater market value and liquidity in the stock market. It probably has a greater ability to withstand broader economic difficulties. Yet it mustn't be taken for granted that a very large company has any greater ability to succeed, or for its growth to compound faster, than does a smaller one. The number of giants that have fallen on hard times in recent years is too large to take size alone as a measure of investment safety. Witness Campeau and Eastern Airlines.

Cash Flow

Because of some of the problems associated with earnings, many analysts are turning more often to cash flow analysis, which, they believe, gives a truer picture of how a business is being run. Cash flow, many analysts feel, levels all the accounting acrobatics that sometimes obfuscate the picture of a company. The concept is an old one in economics that says that the value of an investment is derived from its cash flow.

Basic cash flow is net income plus depreciation. But, depending upon their needs and personal concepts, many investors use other definitions and measures. For example, one group of investors prefers to look for *operating cash flow,* which is the money generated by the company before the cost of financing and taxes. According to analysts at one investment firm, Goldman, Sachs & Co., a portfolio of stocks with the best price to operating cash flow ratio would, in 1988 and part of 1989, have doubled the return of the Standard & Poor's 500-stock index.

Other analysts prefer to use *free cash flow,* which measures discretionary funds—money that can be taken from the company without jeopardizing it. It's measured by taking cash flow and subtracting capital expenditures and dividends.

Today, an increasing number of analysts and investors look to the cash flow before they analyze other factors.

Margins

Normally, *margin*—the percentage of net income to revenues—is relatively simple to measure. It's a major factor in determining both the efficiency of a company and its ability to cope with costs and expenses—a constantly changing factor. It becomes even more significant in a period of raging inflation or unstable prices, when margins reflect vast swings in the cost of raw material and labor. Under those conditions, the margins can be severely hit if the company is not able to pass on to its own customers the high cost of certain basic materials. The quality of earnings becomes a serious concern in relation to margins, when many companies must sell from inventories that had been built up at lower costs, and were reported at inflated prices. In many cases, this results in a distorted picture of the company's realistic margin, since it's difficult to discern the consistent level of future costs for the same items. When this happened in the past, many companies changed their method of depreciation to reflect accelerated deflation. Today, that inflationary factor is built into many corporations' financial structures, further distorting margins as well as earnings. Moreover, the potential of mitigating inflation. . or disinflation . . . generates a further distortion in many companies.

Return on Equity

This is the *earnings per share divided by the book value (the difference between a company's assets and its liabilities).* In terms of investment, this is a most significant measure of a company's success. It is, after all, what investment is all about. If the return on any investment in one company isn't as high as it is in another—and assuming that the difference isn't offset by dividend yield or that the achieving company isn't so highly leveraged that it is threatened by high interest rates—then what is the point in investing in the company with the low return?

Balance Sheet

The balance sheet still offers the best picture of a company's financial position—as of the date of the balance sheet. If the balance sheet of Penn Central, which revealed an extraordinarily heavy debt, had been heeded, then its favorable earnings reports issued immediately prior to its bankruptcy might have been viewed with a bit more skepticism. The balance sheet does—or should—tell the analyst a great many things. It also poses a great many questions. And it behooves the corporation to anticipate these questions in order to prevent misunderstanding or misinterpretations, as well as to clarify the position of the company. There may very well be justification for a high inventory or a substantial increase in inventory from one year to the next. For example, a major customer under a multiyear contract may have deferred deliveries from the fourth quarter to the first quarter of the following year. The balance sheet alone will merely indicate the size of the inventory. It will not explain it. A reduction of cash from the prior year against a reduction of debt implies that the cash was used to reduce the debt. Without explanation it is merely an implication. Certainly a disparity from one year to the next in accounts receivable or accounts payable warrants an explanation, even if it's an unfavorable one. The growth of pension fund assets poses an increasing balance sheet problem particularly under a new accounting treatment.

While the notes to financial statements usually clarify the debt structure, questions about debt—both long- and short-term—go beyond the balance sheet. The balance sheet, it must be remembered, is as of a particular date. Debt can be increased or decreased the day after the closing of a balance sheet, as can any element of the assets or liabilities. This is a prime example of why a balance sheet never speaks for itself in describing a company; the analyst wants to know more than it can show. And with accounting standards rapidly changing, the company must be prepared to defend its accounting methods.

Ratios

The analysts, with their computers or electronic calculators, can compute a headspinning number of ratios, many of which, like astrological symbols, can assume meanings of varying import for different people. Ratios without explanation frequently imply a picture that, in view of changing conditions and other factors, may not be accurate in terms of the corporation's actual operations. Ratios, like any statistics, are a still picture of a corporation frozen at the moment the picture was taken, while the corporation continues to move on. It's extremely important that any ratio that differs from the industry norm, either up or down, is a signal for the need for elucidation and explanation.

The array of ratios is imposing. The ratio of current assets to current liabilities, if it is less than 2 to 1, sends a red flag flying. If the debt/equity ratio is too high, the analyst immediately wonders about the drain on future earnings by debt payments. The ratio of return on total capital. The ratio of depreciation and depletion to sales. The ratio of earnings paid out in dividends to earnings. The price/sales ratio for smaller, high technology companies. And this is exclusive of ratios of various factors such as earnings, dividends, assets, and sales to the market price of the stock. Graham, in his book, *Security Analysis,* leans heavily on ratios as a measure of company performance.

Cost of Capital

Some aspects of the cost of capital, such as the prime rate, are fairly evident. The company that must function heavily with short-term borrowing, such as a leasing company or an importer who depends upon revolving credit lines, will find itself in serious trouble when the prime rate gets up around 20 or 21 percent. The company that is fairly heavily leveraged—has a very high debt in proportion to its equity—is also in serious trouble. The expansion-minded company is always viewed in terms of its financial ability to expand either internally or externally. Even in an atmosphere that allows for additional capital through equity, the analyst must consider the cost of a company's equity capital in terms of its price/earnings ratio. This whole area then becomes a matter of major concern for analysts, and therefore of major concern for the corporation that wants to explain itself.

The Industry

For a company to represent its financial situation as independent of the industry in which it functions, or even the larger economy, is to delude itself. Even the company that is outperforming its industry for one reason or another must still realize that in most cases it's being judged in terms of its industry. No company president functions without intensive knowledge of his industry. But too often companies are presented to analysts without a clear explanation of comparable performances, common and uncommon problems and solutions, costs of raw materials and distribution, potential markets, and so forth.

Specialized Industries

The evaluation of companies in certain industries such as banks, insurance companies, finance companies, leasing companies, public utilities, energy companies, and so on, requires analysis of some additional elements, and a different emphasis on common elements. Sources and uses of funds and revenues differ. Accounting methods differ. Nevertheless the same rules of communication apply. Because the same ratios mean different things in different industries, ratios and changes require explanation, and nothing should be taken for granted.

Problems with Industry Specialization

There is yet another problem in that the analysis of specialized industries usually falls on a small segment of analysts who specialize in that industry. This poses two serious concerns. First, the judgment of a company by industry specialists, no matter how well it is performing, is often given the same general market value as is the industry itself. If the industry is depressed, a superior company within that industry faces serious stock market problems.

Second, the majority of analysts who fully understand the ramifications of a particular industry rarely change the relative rankings of major companies within that industry. Moreover, they don't represent a sufficiently large number to warrant devoting a major portion of an investor relations effort to them. It therefore becomes necessary to deal with a larger group of analysts functioning in other contexts, and in other organizations, who are not as well versed in the ramifications of a particular industry as are the industry specialists, but who may nevertheless see other values. The communications effort then becomes more challenging. Not only must the company be explained and sold, but the complex specialized differences in dealing with the company and analyzing it must be made clear.

The problem of specialization also arises frequently in dealing with companies with large international operations. Few American analysts feel they have the broader international economic background to properly assess a company with significant international activity. Their tendency is to ignore such companies and move onto those easier to understand. There are, after all, more companies in the broader economic sphere than any one analyst can follow.

These are the significant financial factors that must be communicated in judging a company. It should be clear, however, that in dealing with analysts and others who judge companies, numbers shouldn't be presumed to speak for themselves. They never do. They require elucidation and explanation. This is why financial statements have footnotes. It can't be repeated too often a corporation's statistics freeze the picture as of the date of those statistics, and corporations are dynamic entities.

Analyzing Economic Conditions

When Eastern Europe changed the course of history, and the USSR started a round of disarmament that was quickly followed by President Bush's reducing troop concentrations in Europe, companies in defense industries became obvious candidates for a downturn. When smoking was banned in public places throughout the United States, it adversely affected companies with heavy revenues from tobacco. When Japanese and other foreign-made cars began to make substantial inroads into the share of market held by General Motors and Ford, analysts saw American car companies differently.

Analyzing economic conditions is an arduous and sometimes frustrating task, and rarely do two economists agree on the meaning of any one event. But unless the company itself supplies the guidelines for evaluating the effect of these external economic factors on its own performance, the judgment by analysts as events unfold will almost invariably be an overreaction. The responsibility for putting any economic news in perspective, even before its effect is felt by the company, resides with the management.

For all its apparent sophistication, economics is a most inexact science. Just when everybody thinks it's been licked, some new and unforeseen element enters into it. A war. Currency devaluations. Inflation. Political uncertainty, such as the glasnost. A savings and loan crisis. A decision by the Federal Reserve Bank to tighten up the money supply. A beef shortage. A drought. A bankruptcy by a major company such as Campeau. And on and on and on.

Everyone knows where the economy has been and sometimes people even know where the economy is. But nobody ever really knows where it's going, despite computer models, economic indicators, or the ability to read the future in the entrails of sheep. Obviously this throws even the best analysis into a cocked hat. It moves it out of the realm of the economic certainty of a balance sheet, and the historical value of the earnings records, into a vast world of major uncertainty. It's not without its charm, however, in that it offers analysis the excitement of prognostication that one rarely gets with the electronic calculator or even the computer.

The Economics of an Industry

Prognostication for an industry is somewhat easier, at least within a limited range of time. If consumer spending is down as a result of inflation or higher interest rates, for example, it's reasonable to assume that retail purchases in certain industries, such as appliances and apparel, will have trouble achieving earnings records. If there are basic material shortages, with no relief in sight, it's reasonable to assume that those industries using those materials will have problems. When transistors were invented, transistor manufacturers enjoyed a boom in those products that used the transistors, such as miniature portable radios and portable tape recorders. But then as the industry became saturated with transistor manufacturers, and technology reduced the cost of transistors, it became impossible for any company to compete successfully and with very high margins, and the transistor stocks fell on their faces.

On the other hand, when a new industry emerges, such as computers, there are a new set of problems and opportunities. At first, there was a shortage of analysts and investors who fully understood the nature of the industry and where it might go. Then, as it began to grow and mature in the United States, the Japanese entered the field, creating a new kind of competition. Computer stocks, such as Compaq and Lotus, were at first undervalued, and then, as the companies broke growth records, moved into new competitive contexts that few analysts really understood. By the time the industry had matured, shares of market had shifted, markets became saturated, new technology changed and challenged leading companies, and there were new economic configurations that were unfamiliar to most investors. By the time the financial community began to understand Compaq, it was a mature company. By the time the financial community began to understand Lotus, the company ran into marketing problems which, fortunately, they resolved before the Street had time to discount them. This, in microcosm, is how a new industry affected the financial community.

Industry analysis is not without its problems. It tends to minimize, for example, the company that is outperforming its peers. In the second half of the 1980s, for example, the insurance world was hit with a number of problems that rocked the foundations of that staid old industry. Malpractice and personal liability suits proliferated and were bringing in huge awards for plaintiffs. Insurance premiums skyrocketed. Health costs rose substantially, causing major changes in health insurance costs and structures. Consumerism created legislative attempts to limit insurance costs and increase government regulation. And in 1989, the industry was hit with major natural disasters—a hurricane and an earthquake. In the midst of all this were companies like Chubb, which, while it felt some of the problems, was not as seriously affected as were others in the industry. It took industry analysts a great many months to recognize that Chubb was in fact outperforming the industry, and to report those factors that would raise its P/E to a more appropriate point. Still, a company in another industry, with Chubb's performance, would have been awarded a higher P/E than it earned as part of the insurance industry.

Sometimes industry analysts find themselves susceptible to the same kind of short-term response to which the individual investor is victim. One of the groups to be hit when it was first announced that the plastic, polyvinyl chloride (PVC), was a factor in producing cancer in both the PVC industrial worker and the consumer was the plastics industry. Plastics analysts felt that most plastics manufacturers would be subject to regulation that would either curtail production or involve large capital investment in safety equipment. It took a considerable amount of time, during which plastic stocks were adversely affected, for the analysts to sort out those companies that were unaffected, or had already built safety factors into their production.

The problem of environmental pollution lends itself to a similar potential for overreaction. Many industries—paper, steel, chemical, utilities—are now subject to production strictures that will affect their processes, and attendant costs, to varying degrees. But there are relatively few facts available on how these strictures are to be defined or how to judge the costs for individual companies, much less specific industries, particularly with uncertainties as to the future of environmental regulation under the Bush administration. Very little research has been done in this area, and without facts, overreaction is found to be the rule.

In the arcane world of economic influences upon company analysis, the burden is on management—and by extension, the investor relations practitioner—to clarify, to explain, to define context. For example, when the price of the dollar on world markets changed abruptly a few years ago, it made it seem that companies with large overseas operations were losing revenues and profits. But given an understanding of foreign currency translations, those companies with better investor relations communications and marketing skills fared better in the stock market than did other companies in the same plight.

Projecting Management Capability

The intangibles of a company that must be judged are its management and its plans. There are in American industry today many large companies that began as small companies. There are also many small companies—and many that no longer exist—that were started at the same time as companies that are currently large. One difference between two companies that started small and of which only one thrived is capitalization. The other and major difference is management, which, given management's role in raising capital, may be in some measure the same thing.

Management is about as exact a science as is weather forecasting. The analysis of management can be difficult, not only because it's intangible, but because it's highly subjective. The elements of management may be definable. What is not definable is the way the configuration of those elements will function in terms of results.

The broad definition of management is the subject of a full library of theories, many of which conflict and none of which is definitive. What is of the essence in investor relations is the ability to project to investors, believably, a corporate management's ability to manage its company, to cause it to thrive and to grow, and to survive, especially in difficult times.

Perception, in looking at a company, is often very different from reality. The problem is that too often, the facts don't count—it's what people perceive to be the facts on which they make judgments. This puts a particular burden on the company, and a particular responsibility on the investor relations practitioner.

Management Skills

A good management team must have a grasp of a great many things— finance, marketing, administration, production, distribution, the economy in general and its industry in particular. And even within the context of these elements, abilities are limited and alter with changing conditions.

A person who invents a cure for the common cold may be a thoroughly bad manager in terms of marketing, production, or finance. The entrepreneur who invents a useful and valuable item in his garage may be capable of managing the company he develops with his invention until sales reach a level of $10 million a year. As his company continues to grow, the shape of the company alters, his production needs change, and so, then, do administrative needs. A company in transition is at its most vulnerable point. The entrepreneur who is capable of building it to $30 million may not have the capabilities to build it to $100 million. The management of a one-product company that decides to expand its product line or to diversify suddenly faces new and generally unfamiliar problems and may not be able to cope.

Other potential problems predicated on both personality and the capabilities of management further cloud the issue. When economic conditions are good and sales are coming easily, and the company is adequately financed and there are no production problems, a management team can be perfectly capable of showing profits. But how can an analyst judge how that same management will function when money becomes tight, when competitors start hitting the market, when a strike hits the plant, when there is a material shortage, when there is a takeover attempt by another company, when there are price controls, or when—as in the case of the transistor problem—the market becomes saturated with its product?

When a company has the only water hole in the desert for 200 miles around, a manager doesn't need a degree from the Harvard Business School to know how to sell water. But most companies function in a competitive economy. The history of American business is laden with managers of major companies who made the wrong decision. When Mr. Campeau bought the department store chains, he did it with the best financial advice available at the time. Yet, he paid too much, borrowed too much to pay for it, and although the individual stores were successful (as they had always been), he could not raise the cash to pay the debt he had incurred. And so all the economic wisdom in the world was unable to keep him from making the mistake that brought him into Chapter 11 bankruptcy.

Credibility

It is absolutely imperative, for success in the capital markets, for an executive to build a record of consistent openness and truthfulness. Any misrepresentation will not only be readily found out, but will reverberate throughout the financial community like a lion's roar. Furthermore, the number of eyes on a public company are many. A public company is under constant scrutiny. It took only one disgruntled employee and one astute analyst to topple the fraud-ridden Equity Funding empire. Any corporate executive who thinks he or she can deal with the investing public by misrepresenting facts or by refusing to disclose pertinent material necessary for judging his or her company will not long succeed in the capital markets.

It's in the area of management analysis, particularly where credibility is involved, that the investor relations professional functions best as an advocate. Numbers can say a great deal in themselves, although they don't always say the same things to different people. The judgment of management, on the other hand, is subjective, and responds well to strong investor relations guidance and support.

How, then, is credibility generated? One can hardly stand before an audience and say, "This is what I want you to think about me." Company presidents can hardly stand in front of an audience of security analysts and boast of their abilities.

It's good form, on the other hand, for them to describe, in speaking and writing, their management team as being excellent, forward-looking, and skilled. But why should they be believed? It's true that some corporate leaders are clean-cut, strong-jawed, and clear-eyed—obviously exciting and believable people—at least at the moment they are talking. Other extraordinarily competent corporate leaders are shy, reticent, introspective, and poor public speakers. Some of the most striking photos of chief executive officers appearing in annual reports show men and women of vision and forcefulness, obviously the kind of people in whom widows and orphans should invest their faith and savings. Training corporate executives in public speaking, dress, and television presence is now a big business.

In fact, credibility is a function of three things—corporate performance, consistent truth, and a willingness to deal forthrightly with the public and those who analyze securities in behalf of the public.

Projecting Management as Credible

The most tangible gauge of management is still track record. How successfully has management performed? What has it achieved in the growth of the company? How has it survived and dealt with problems? What opportunities has it seized upon and how did it capitalize on them? How has management restructured itself to meet changes in its corporation and its environment?

These and other elements of management capability are projected in real ways. The history of the company, however brief, can be told in terms of management decisions. "When we realized that the next decade would see a population growth in the number of women between the ages of twenty-eight and thirty-five, we decided to design a special line of sportswear and merchandise it to that group."

"When we recognized that we were just a few years away from market saturation for our product, we began to explore feasible areas of diversification into products, the design and production of which were within our experience and existing capabilities to exploit."

"As our company reached the hundred-million-dollar mark, we recognized the need for broadening the management base, expanding middle management, and changing the nature of our management reporting systems."

"As we recognized that the average age of our management team was approaching fifty, we began a recruiting and training program to develop the people who would ultimately be our successors."

Projecting the Facts

Yet another way in which management can project itself is to clearly and authoritatively present facts about its company. Consider the erudite company president, surrounded by the executive vice-president and vice-president of finance, who clearly recites facts and figures about the company's operation, clearly delineates its present financial structure and its plans for future growth, and obviously has a grasp of his or her industry and the economy at large. He or she is much more likely to inspire confidence and credibility than the company president who merely recites, either by rote or from the printed page, material that has already appeared in the annual report.

Company presidents who demonstrate the ways in which they have constantly broadened the management base to meet the growing needs of their companies, and are constantly divesting themselves of responsibilities by delegating them to other able people, inspire infinitely more faith than the president of a company who is obviously a one-man band and keeps everything to himself or herself, regardless of the number of underlings hired to do his or her bidding. The future of a one-person company is no greater than the length of the president's arm, and every analyst knows it.

Analyzing Plans

Yet another intangible in which corporate evaluation must be made is the company's own plans. Any analyst with twelve minutes' experience has learned to make a distinction between plans and dreams, even though dreams occasionally come true. There are, after all, businessmen named Jobs, Canion, Kapor, Iaccoca, and Steinberg.

Fortunately, the experiences of the past decade have sharply diminished the number of corporate presidents who attempt to fool sophisticated analysts by passing their dreams off as valid projections or plans. It should be recognized by both management and investor relations professionals that the acoustics of Wall Street are magnificent, particularly as it pertains to bad news or direct misrepresentations. Certainly, it behooves the investor relations professional to lead management to the path of clarity, cogency, and credibility.

What is specifically of the essence here are the legitimate and carefully formulated plans and projections of a company that express more than just its wishes for the future, but are rather the blueprint and road map of company policy for continued profitability, expansion, and growth. The future is, after all, what analysts are concerned with. They know what the present is and what the past was. They may find the management of a company to be charming, sincere, bright, intelligent, highly motivated, ambitious, and trustworthy. But as analysts they must make an assessment of how these virtues are going to be applied to appreciate the invested dollar.

What Plans Mean

The president of a company with $1 million in sales may have dreams of heading a billion-dollar multinational corporation but may not have the foggiest idea of how to increase sales to $2 million. On the other hand, a company president who recognizes the potential in certain aspects of home furnishings, is planning to expand existing marketing and production capabilities to meet that potential, who hopes to supplement that capability with an acquisition or two, and who recognizes the limitations of his or her ability to finance those plans, should clearly delineate his or her corporate ideas. The president should recognize publicly the dimensions of the potential market, the need to divest certain unprofitable operations, however painful and without emotional consideration, the ways he or she intends to finance the growth and how much it's expected to cost, the kind of management changes he or she is going to have to make, the kind of economic climate in which he or she expects to function, and the downside risks.

In some cases the plans available for the analysts to consider are relatively simple and unsophisticated. "We are planning to grow through a program of acquisitions and our experience in the past has demonstrated that we can do this. This is the kind of acquisition we are planning to make, this is how we are going to buy the companies, this is the size company we are looking at." And so on and so on. Most of the factors, management is saying, are there for the analysis.

Or so it would seem. There are still many judgments to be made as to the validity of the program. One company in the office-cleaning services business had a very simple concept and seemed to have the capabilities to fulfill that concept. It was in an industry made up of predominately smaller privately held companies. The company simply went around the country combining the smaller companies into the larger one. Cash flow was good up to a point. It was an industry that management knew and understood well and seemed capable of managing. The stock was selling at a reasonable multiple, and there was enough outstanding to allow a considerable amount of it to be used as currency for making the acquisitions, and the banks and the institutions were in a mood to be generous. It worked very well for a while, and every analyst following the company could visualize the successful configuration of both tangibles and intangibles. But then the acquisition momentum outpaced both the ability to manage the rapidly growing company and to finance the continued growth. The company fell on its face. It had to sell off some of its properties in order to revitalize its balance sheet and make payments on its debt, and finally went bankrupt.

The Downside of Corporate Planning

Corporate planning is itself a very complex business. At best, even supported by sophisticated thinking and computer models, it's precarious. Necessary, but still precarious. To distinguish the dream from the plan requires as much luck as skill. The larger companies—IBM, General Motors, General Electric, and Exxon—have a far greater (but not absolute) capability to control their economic environment, and do plan more effectively than does the smaller company. IBM, after all, controls a lion's share of its market, has the wherewithal to finance any reasonable plan, has the scope and diversity to offset and survive most economic swings, and has the marketing capability to expand and develop new markets. As significant factors in their industries, companies like IBM receive little surprise from labor. Moreover, they have vast sources of input of economic information, not only domestically but worldwide. They have full staffs of economists to both gather and interpret material, and they have relationships in every corner of the world.

In other words, when IBM, or any company of comparable size, develops a one-year or a five-year or a ten-year plan for its growth, it does it with infinitely more certainty than one applies to planning next Sunday's picnic.

And yet when Compaq entered the market, and attacked IBM on its own ground, IBM was all but overthrown as ruler of the personal computer business. Compaq, an upstart that went from inception to Fortune 500 in just a very few years, led IBM on technology and on reading the market. It addressed its market with a very different philosophy than IBM's, and was so right that IBM began to lose share of market to the newer company, and then, for the first time in memory, began to fail to meet profit projections. IBM is still a giant, and still has economic power, but has clearly shown limits to its ability to control its own destiny. No one, it seems, can take the marketplace for granted.

The Smaller Company

If a vast and sophisticated corporate machine like General Motors could fail in its corporate planning, or an IBM, in the face of burgeoning computer technology, can be rocked back on its heels by newer and smaller companies, what can an analyst expect of a company a fraction of its size? A small company can blueprint, to a certain degree, its market opportunities and its plans to seize those opportunities, its capital expansion and the means for financing it, the normal growth patterns, and so on. Some of these plans may be perfectly valid, but not in an unforeseeable economic climate. Other plans may be reasonable, but perhaps not for the management as it is presently constituted. The projections may be unrealistic in terms of potential shortages of raw materials or foreseeable problems in distribution patterns and so on. The smaller company may at best have a fine grasp of its own operation and its industry, but its input in terms of the larger economic context or facilities for capitalization down the line are sharply limited, and the company is, of course, more likely to be buffeted in a rough economic sea than is the large corporation. This is the very element that gives a greater appearance of stability to the giant company—the so-called blue chip stock. The same elements that portend stability and reliability for long-term performance for the larger company are the elements that make it easier for the larger company to plan for the longer range.

There is among analysts a skepticism that was ingrained following the glorious years of the 1960s, the glorious late seventies, and for those following the energy industry, the glorious 1980–1981. Too many presidents saw the world as a boundless cornucopia and were free in their declarations of a utopian future for their companies. They had, after all, achieved marvelous records so far. The names of a very large number of these men still come to the mind of too many analysts for them to believe any projection of glory that is not specifically documented in terms of how those plans are to be accomplished, predicated upon a record of achievement and comparable activities. Today, some analysts even want to see contingency plans as well.

It is precisely these elements that the analyst must assess as part of his or her job to determine the ability of the company to generate a profit on the invested dollar in the near-, medium-, and long-range future.

Modern Portfolio Theory

No view of contemporary analysis can be complete without at least a passing acquaintance with Modern Portfolio Theory—MPT.

While there is very little a company can do, beyond dealing with analytic fundamentals, to influence portfolio analysis using Modern Portfolio Theory, the increasing use of MPT warrants at least a minimal understanding of it.

Essentially, Modern Portfolio Theory is predicated on a concept that the degree of investment risk should be measured in terms of potential reward for that risk. But it also takes as its premise the concept that the greater the range of uncertainty about a stock, the greater the risk.

Portfolio diversification is not a new concept, nor is any form of spreading risk. The aim here, though, is not merely to diversify, but to do so with a balance of stocks with varying degrees of risk, and therefore varying likelihood of performance, so that the average uncertainty of the total portfolio—and therefore the average of the portfolio's risk—is diminished in relation to potential return.

For example, in a two-stock portfolio, if both stocks perform in the same way in response to the market itself, there is no real diversification. If, however, each responds differently to market forces, then you do have diversification. But not necessarily the best diversification, unless the potential performance of one effectively hedges, or acts opposite to, the potential performance of the other.

Measuring potential performance, and thereby potential risk-return, is done with a series of complex mathematical functions, but the basis is still a judgment of fundamental analysis of the elements of a company's potential. Beyond that, however, portfolio analysis becomes complex.

The aim is to build an "efficient" portfolio, one in which the balance of potential performance of all the stocks in the portfolio is one of minimum uncertainty. Taken into account are two major elements of risk—the risk in the individual stock and the risk inherent in the market itself, keeping in mind that not all stocks react or perform in the same way in response to the market at any given moment. Using the Standard & Poor's 500-Stock Price Index as a basis, price fluctuations—the measure of risk used—is broken down into the two risk elements (market and individual stock). The statistical technique, regression analysis, is used to measure the potential risk. A complex mathematical technique, it measures functional relationships between two or more variables, particularly where a variable (such as a P/E) is measured against another variable (such as a market index).

Put simply, the term *beta* is used to indicate the measure of a stock's volatility, relative to the volatility of the market during the same period. The higher the beta, the higher the volatility; the lower the beta the more stable. A beta of one means that the stock performs exactly as the market does.

The term *alpha* is used to indicate the measure of average rate of return, in the same period, independent of the market return.

A portfolio that matches the alpha and beta of the S&P 500 should—and generally does—perform about the same as the S&P Index, and indeed many *index funds* have been started based on the concept. However, there is a serious question in the minds of many professional investors, particularly institutional investors, whether indexed return, rather than one that outperforms the market, is sufficient.

In the several years since the theory was developed by the statistician Dr. Harry M. Markowitz, it has grown in popularity among analysts. But even its strongest advocates warn that it is a theory with a great deal yet to be developed and proven, and more significantly, that it is only one tool of many that should be used by analysts. It does not portend, in the foreseeable future, replacing all analysts with computers.

Analysis for Credit

The analysis of a company for equity investment differs sharply from the analysis of a company for credit. The equities investor is concerned with the ability of the company to give him a profit on his invested dollar. The creditor is concerned with the ability of the company to repay the loan within the prescribed period.

While the approaches to analysis in each case are significantly different, there are many overlapping factors. Essential to both is a judgment of the viability of the company.

The fact that many debt issues are rated for quality by Moody's Investors Service, Standard & Poor's, or others doesn't mean automatic acceptance or rejection by individual bond or commercial paper buyers, banks, or other institutions. The competition for capital via debt is no less keen. And certainly few banks automatically lend to any company, no matter how apparently sound, that applies for it. Investors in debt issues have choices to make, even between two bonds rated AAA.

At the beginning of this decade, the total value of publicly traded debt issues, both corporate and government, is about $2.5 trillion. Most of it is traded institutionally, both by brokerage houses and individual investors.

There are about 800 analysts covering the bond market. They tend to specialize by type, industry, or quality.

It is somewhat more difficult to know who bondholders are, as one does with shareholders, because there are no mandatory bond ownership reports. Most bonds are held in Street name, as well, which makes identification for investor relations purposes doubly difficult. This causes further problems in that bondholders, who can accumulate sizable positions without being identified, are participating more than ever in corporate management and other corporate activities, using their strength as major debt holders to force management positions favorable to debt holders.

With its own special investment parameters, bond analysis can be rather sophisticated, and therefore require a more concerted effort to impart information to analysts and investors. Obviously, cash flow is important, because the strength of a bond lies in the ability of its issuer to make payments as required. In an article in the March 1990 issue of *Update,* the publication of the National Investor Relations Institute (NIRI), editor William F. Mahoney suggests that other concerns of debt analysts are:

- Historical trends in ratios and spreads
- Basis points of the issue compared with U.S. Treasury yield curve
- Terms of the indenture, and where the company stands now in relationship with each term
- How the proceeds will be used
- Cash to be generated by the asset
- Breakout of reportable segments

- Overhead costs
- Depreciation schedule

At the same time, it should be remembered that corporate debt is not isolated from equity; telling the story to fixed income investors and analysts requires telling the equity story as well.

Thus the effort to reach debt investors must be as intensive as for equity investors. Virtually every element about a company that is of interest to an equities analyst is of interest to a debt issue analyst (with perhaps different points of emphasis), whether it is an individual, a bank lending officer, an analyst at a bond house, an institution, or a rating service. The company story must be just as carefully formulated, and as energetically presented, as for an equity issue. This holds true, incidentally, for a municipal bond as well as for an industrial or utility bond.

The rating services themselves are not infallible. They function predominantly from set formulas, but also consider subjective factors of judgment, which can be just as valid a measure of a company's potential to repay debt as are objective factors. What this means, realistically, is that ratings can sometimes be upgraded by an intelligent presentation of facts to rating service analysts.

The Mechanics of Dealing with the Financial Community

Given the substance of what is to be communicated there remains only the mechanics of communicating it.

The strategy of selecting the specific techniques and structures to be used, the people to be dealt with, and the timing, is discussed in Chapter 12. The investor relations structure of dealing with the financial community consists essentially of the following:

- Financial community contact, including research and screening and follow-up
- Setting up security analyst meetings
- Meeting with or talking to individual analysts and establishing relationships with them
- Meeting with stockbrokers and establishing relationships
- Setting up brokerage meetings and follow-up
- Setting up money manager meetings and establishing relationships
- Establishing portfolio manager relationships, including understanding the analytic techniques of each of them

- Setting up trader and specialist meetings and follow-up
- Issuing a background report and corporate profile
- Preparing and distributing printed material, including annual and quarterly reports, to the financial community and shareholders
- Regular and periodic mailing of information about the company to the financial community, including copies of news releases
- Issuing news releases and getting features in the financial press
- Preparing corporate advertising and other promotional devices
- Handling unsolicited inquiries

Analyst and Broker Meetings

Setting up an analyst or broker meeting is like good tightrope walking. It looks easier than it is.

It would seem that the simplest way to hold an analyst meeting is to select the names of fifteen or twenty likely analysts from the directory of the Financial Analysts Federation, arrange for an appropriate dining room and catered luncheon, and invite them. Would that it were that simple.

Selecting the right analysts is a process described later on in this book in the chapter on strategy (Chapter 9). There are some basic considerations that should be dealt with here, however.

The number of attendees should be kept manageable. Sometimes, if the meeting is to be held in a large city rarely visited by the management group, as many as 20 or 25 attendees are appropriate—and on rare occasions, 50. Otherwise, 15 is a large number, certainly in terms of the ability of everyone present to ask intelligent questions and to allow time for questions to be answered. Any luncheon attended by more than 25 or 30 people can cause such problems as not allowing an analyst to get the important information that brought the analyst to the meeting. Moreover, most of the better investment professionals won't attend a very large meeting.

A luncheon meeting, which is the most common way of doing it, should be held in a private place, preferably a luncheon club or restaurant with private rooms. The club or restaurant should have some measure of experience in dealing with meetings of this type or else food service will extend well past the time to adjourn the meeting.

Timing is important. While most analysts are delighted to attend a luncheon, particularly if it's a company in which they are or might be especially interested, or even if they know it will be attended by other good analysts with whom they will have the opportunity to talk shop, they are still away from their desks during the time that the market is functioning. The rule is very simple. Luncheon meetings, in most cities, should be called for either 11:45 or noon. Cocktails should be served until virtually all of the invited guests have arrived, and certainly no later than 12:15 or 12:20. The presentation should begin a few minutes after the main course has begun, at about 12:25.

This may seem to be moving rather quickly, and putting pressure on the speakers, but it's how the professional investors now prefer it. They want to be in and out in an hour to an hour and a quarter. The days of the leisurely meeting are over.

Lunch and the presentation should be over by 12:50, allowing those who must leave to do so, although management stays to answer questions from the floor until 1:15, and afterwards for any individuals who choose to stay. Anyone who has the time beyond that point will stay around to chat with management, but that should be a personal option.

The current trend away from lunchtime drinking allows for an alternative formula in which there is no prelunch cocktail service. Everyone is seated by 12:10 and wine, beer, and soft drinks are served with the meal. That allows food service to start earlier, at about 12:15, and the presentation to start sooner, by 12:20.

An attempt should be made to determine whether any other meetings are scheduled for companies that would draw investment professionals who might find themselves in a conflicting situation. This is done by phoning one or two investment professionals you plan to invite and asking them if they know of any other company or any analysts' society group that's planning to have a meeting on that date and at the same time. Once the list of invitees is determined and the date selected, simple invitations to attend the meeting should be mailed out. (There are always some analysts, brokers, and money managers who will be invited by telephone.) Inviting is done three to four weeks before the meeting. Two weeks after the invitations are mailed out, there should be a phone follow-up to develop a preliminary list of those who plan to attend. Those who have accepted the invitation should then be sent a kit of printed materials on the company. This should include the latest annual report, subsequent interim reports, the Form 10-K and 10-Q (for analysts— brokers usually don't care about the 10-K or 10-Q), releases issued since the annual report, reprints of material about the company that have appeared in the financial press or the trade press (or even articles from the consumer press if they demonstrate the company's claim to product superiority or widespread promotion), reprints of an important and significant trade or consumer advertising campaign, business biographies of top management, and, if pertinent, product material. Include a pad, or at least a few sheets of paper on which attendees can take notes. If there is to be a graphic presentation, it might be useful to include copies of the material on key slides. In some cases, product samples can be effective. While it's rare that every one of the analysts attends, the phone follow-up gives the first basic idea of what attendance is likely to be. There is usually a 10 to 20 percent drop-off of actual attendees from the list of those who accepted the day before.

The afternoon before and the morning of the meeting, every analyst who has accepted the invitation should be phoned to remind him or her of the meeting. Convention-style badges should be made for everyone who is to attend, including management. While it would seem that these badges have a gala aura about them, there is rarely any objection. They allow the company officers to be readily identified and to be able to address analysts by name. They allow the analysts to identify one another and to build the valuable acquaintanceships among themselves, which are of great importance to them in an industry in which interchange of information is extremely important. By noting which badges are used and not used, the mechanics of taking attendance is reduced to a simple matter. All that is necessary is that a representative of the company be on hand to write out badges for the substitutes and uninvited guests that show up. Uninvited guests can be refused admission if there's a good reason for it, but that should be done cautiously.

Including the press at professional investors' meetings is generally not preferred, although opinion varies. Unless the meeting is going to be used to impart important new information, the two should be kept separate. Societies and splinter groups should be specifically queried, particularly since some have strict rules about press attendance.

These are the mechanics of the meeting. Preparation for it poses an entirely different set of considerations.

Premeeting Preparation

Whether a prepared speech or an outline is used is the personal choice of the executive who is to make the presentation. Of the two, the outline is preferred, if for no other reason than it demonstrates more readily the executive's grasp of his or her company. It's too easy to assume that a speech was written by someone else. Some speakers use the slides as an outline.

The organization of the presentation is extremely important. A typical outline can be found in Appendix 7.

Styles have changed in presentation. Until recently, presentations were rather formal, beginning with a very brief history of the company. Today's investment professional prefers not to waste time on preliminaries, but rather to get quickly to the heart of the matter.

The presentation should begin, then, with a brief statement of what management believes to be the most important factors about the company, including its strengths and competitive advantages. If appropriate, it can delineate those problems that the company has had or that the industry has faced. This is followed by an explanation of the company's long-range strategies—its plans to grow internally or by acquisition or by developing new markets, its new product strategy, and so forth. It then briefly describes the company as it's presently constituted—what it is, what it makes, how it distributes, the size of its markets, why it is in those markets. It then discusses the company's financial structure in terms described earlier in this chapter. This can be followed by the management structure and then the plans for the company in the short term—the current quarter and the balance of the year. The meeting is then opened for questions.

An important part of the presentation should be to focus on the core idea that epitomizes why the company is an especially good investment—the *Unique Investment Premise.* If no other point is made but that, then the presentation must be deemed a success.

It is absolutely essential that no company executive attend an investors' meeting without having anticipated as many questions as possible that might be asked by the investment professionals, and having prepared a thoughtful and considered answer. Preparing the questions and briefing management is a crucial role of the investor relations professional. For questions for which there's no immediate answer, there should be a prepared response, such as, "Give me your name and we'll get back to you with an answer by this afternoon (or tomorrow)." The most impressive presentation can be destroyed in a moment by one important question that's badly or hesitantly answered.

The Presentation

The tone of the presentation should be honest, forthright, and positive. Negative factors should be expressed clearly and in no way avoided; however, they need not be dwelt upon inordinately and out of proportion to their importance to the overall picture. Hostile questions should be handled patiently and forthrightly and, even if the answer is negative in terms of the total presentation, should be ended on a positive note. If the speaker doesn't know the answer to a question, he or she may refer it to another executive.

It should be recognized that despite all care taken in developing the invitation list, a certain number of investors will invariably show up who really don't care about the company, even if they discover it during the course of the presentation. They will seem uninterested or ask cursory questions. It should also be recognized that not everyone present will see the company in the same way, nor with the same degree of sophistication. In any meeting of ten or more investors, there will almost invariably be three or four unimportant or irrelevant questions—questions asked because some analysts feel they must say something to make their presence known, or because they frankly don't understand something. These questions must be handled with the same patience as the more serious and delving ones.

The investor relations consultant or officer has a definite role, in the course of a meeting, to keep the meeting on track and to the point. That means shielding management from irrelevant questions by intercepting them before management answers; helping to avoid confrontations by interceding as a mediator; gently interrupting to avert duplicate answers or misunderstandings or direct attacks, and so forth. While the consultant or officer should not be obvious in a meeting, he or she should be an active participant, when it's appropriate.

Using Visuals

A great many company stories are well told by visual presentations—a short film or slide presentation. This can be useful and effective if it's carefully done. If it's pertinent and tight, it's useful in visualizing product and service, as well as in graphically presenting complex financial material.

The visual presentation, however, should never preclude a personal presentation by the chief executive officer. It should merely visualize that which is best visualized—the star performer should always be the corporate spokesperson. How else can those factors about management's capabilities be demonstrated than by a CEO's or other executive's own physical presence and participation?

Despite the fact that each person invited has been sent a kit of materials about the company, a duplicate kit should be placed on each seat before the luncheon. Many investors will have forgotten their kits, or there will have been substitutes to whom no kit was ever sent. Extra kits are usually welcomed. A fatal mistake, incidentally, is to include a copy of the executive's presentation in the kit. There is nothing more distressing to a speaker than to look up and find 10 or 15 people following his words on the printed page, or reading ahead of him. It's good practice, on the other hand, to record the presentation and transcribe it for distribution to interested investors who didn't attend the meeting for one reason or another, or to pass it out after the meeting.

Analyst Society Meetings

In major cities, local analysts' societies hold regular meetings to which companies are invited to make presentations. The question almost invariably arises as to the value of the company's requesting an appearance before a city's entire society.

The problem with meetings of most analysts' societies is that attendance includes several analysts who don't follow any but a selected number of very large companies. This means that, except for the largest corporations, the overwhelming percentage of the audience is attending only out of curiosity. For the smaller OTC, NASDAQ, AMEX, or NYSE company, most of the value in a meeting before New York, Chicago, Los Angeles, or most other societies is the prestige and the usefulness of the reprint of the presentation. In most cases, those analysts who can best serve the company are readily identifiable, can be singled out, and can be better dealt with in other ways.

Splinter groups—segments of an analysts' society that specialize in covering a specific industry such as real estate, apparel, insurance, and so on—are increasing in number. For the medium or smaller company, appearance before the splinter group makes infinitely more sense, because there's a greater likelihood of interest in the industry. For the larger company, its value is obvious.

Growing in importance are brokerage groups that exist in a number of cities. They hold luncheon meetings, paid for by the company and not the brokers, at which presentations similar to those given before other groups are made. Some of these groups are sound and useful, and well worth the money. The problem is that, unlike other investor meetings, at some it's a free lunch for many more brokers than can help a company. These should be considered with caution. Particularly beware those groups run by promoters for a profit, and not by the brokers themselves. As has been noted, brokers tend to be less detail oriented in analyzing a company than are analysts, a point to be remembered when meeting with their groups.

The Postmarket-Close Meeting

Not all analyst, broker, or money manager meetings need to be luncheons. For companies with an especially interesting story to tell, a postmarket-close meeting can be useful. Investors are selected and invited in the same way as for a luncheon meeting, but the meeting is held at 4:15 P.M. EST, after the market closes, as either a cocktail party or, if convenient, at the offices of the company itself. Most investors will want to leave by 5 P.M. or a little before, although a few may stay on and chat for a half hour or so.

A variation is the single-firm sales meeting. Frequently, the sales manager or research director of a brokerage house can be persuaded to invite corporate management to the brokerage house's office after the close of the market, or during lunch, to make a presentation to the staff of registered representatives. The rules of the presentation are the same as for the analyst meetings, except that it should be anticipated that the questions are likely to be somewhat less detail-oriented than those from the analysts, and will dwell more heavily on such market factors as the recent movement and volume of the stock, which is, after all, the broker's prime concern. Presentations are a little shorter, with 20 minutes most useful, and 30 minutes at most.

In some cities, there is an increasing tendency to hold both analyst and broker meetings at breakfast. Except for the tighter time constraints, this can be useful and effective.

Earnings Projections

In speaking of meetings with analysts and investors, it's impossible not to address the problem of earnings projections. Whether spoken or not, earnings projections are very much in the thoughts of every investor—almost as an end product of analysis. There are many schools of thought about earnings projections.

An earnings projection by management that can be given any substance or validity is an analyst's dream. It gives him or her something on which to focus. The assumption is that any well-managed company can make at least a short-term projection of how it's going to perform, give or take a few percentage points. Certainly, every company is likely to have a short term budget.

On the other hand, earnings projections may have several inherent dangers. They may be viewed as an implied promise of performance that may well preclude factors beyond the company's control. They may place the company's credibility precariously on the line and are frequently misjudged. A projection of $1.30 that comes out as $1.23 can cause the market to overreact. A projection of $1.30 that comes out to $1.40 can cause the market to overreact on the upside, or to not react because management apparently doesn't have proper feedback programs.

An earnings projection also places an additional psychological burden on the management team by causing it to focus its energies on operations toward meeting that projection, which is not management's job.

Of course, properly handled, these concerns can evaporate. For the management willing to come forward and correct previous estimates as new data become available, projections can be a no-lose game.

What almost invariably happens, on the other hand, is that the analysts themselves will make a projection in the form of a question. If management chooses not to make a projection of its own, it can simply ratify the analysts' projection as "being in the ball park" or otherwise too high or too low. If management has decided to make no projection, it should in no way be bullied into it. There are sufficiently sound reasons to explain the refusal to do so if the remainder of the presentation has been forthright.

There is one important point regarding all investor meetings, and in fact, any form of financial communication. Although it will be dealt with in greater detail in Chapter 4, the rules of disclosure of the SEC very clearly apply here. Any statement made in an analyst meeting, whether it be before one or many analysts, that is significant in judging the company, that may affect the trading or price of the stock, and that has never been made before, must be publicly and widely released as quickly as possible, according to rather stringent guidelines. If management intends to make such statements at a meeting, whether it be an earnings projection or a major diversification plan, a release should be prepared well beforehand for appropriate legal public disclosure at the time of the meeting. This is extremely important.

Meeting with Individual Professional Investors

In addition to meeting with investors in groups, it's frequently more valuable to meet with them individually. A series of individual meetings may be more time consuming than group meetings to reach a large number of people, but the potential value to an investor relations program may be worth it.

Individual meetings should be limited to investors representing significant interest and funds. This includes analysts and investment professionals for retail houses, funds, or investment advisory services. The major criteria are the buying power and decision-making authority of the individual, and not the size of the institution.

There are distinct advantages for both the investors and management. Obviously, it represents a greater commitment for the investor giving time to the meeting, and because of the preparation that normally goes into such a meeting, the willingness to meet usually means greater than average interest in the company. In return, the investor usually gets a clearer and more intensive view of management. The questions tend to be more searching and the executive will be more challenged, since his or her answers are likely to be more detailed than they would be in response to questions from the floor of a larger meeting. Here, too, the company must be prepared to release publicly any information of consequence that had not theretofore been public knowledge. A record of the meeting—even on tape—should be kept so that it can be shown that no inside information was given, should it prove necessary to do so.

The meeting can be held at breakfast or lunch, or in the office of the chief executive, or in the office of the investment professional. Here the presentation, while almost as complete as for the larger investor meetings, and as well prepared, can be somewhat less formal, more direct and limited to key points. It's a discussion, rather than a speech.

Investor Inquiries

Frequently a company (and especially those that for one reason or another prefer to remain obscure) will capture the eye of an individual analyst without any effort on the company's part. The analyst then calls the president and asks searching questions. Sometimes an individual investor will feel lonely and concerned and will take it upon himself to call the company president. Nothing inappropriate about it, but sometimes a surprise.

These inquiries should be anticipated by the management of every public company, and prepared for in much the same way as is the presentation for a full-scale analyst meeting. An individual analyst who surprises a company president and gets the wrong answers can do considerable damage to a company's stock, no matter how well the company is doing. There is no need for it.

All inquiries should be treated courteously and in detail. The company should follow up the inquiry by mailing the same material that it distributes at meetings. If the caller is an analyst who represents an important enough faction of the investment community, it's certainly appropriate to invite him to come in for a personal visit and a plant tour.

It's extremely important, in anticipating inquiries and preparing the presentation, that the company story be uniformly understood and told by any member of the management team who is likely to get such an inquiry. In some cases it's appropriate for the chief executive officer to insist that all such calls be passed on to him or her, to the vice-president of finance, or to the investor relations officer. This may seem like a put-off, which in itself is an attack on credibility. It then behooves the chief executive officer to be sure that everyone who might receive such an inquiry is fully informed of the company's point of view, method of presentation, and proper answers to questions.

When the company is some distance away from a major city, when there is a story of particular interest to tell, and when a tour of the company's operations can contribute to the analysts' knowledge, one or several analysts may be invited to visit with management at the company's plant. This is frequently done at the company's expense, although a large number of analysts' firms prefer that they pay their own way. Analysts also make field trips on their own, touring a particular area and the companies within that area.

Follow-up

Apart from these formalized investor meetings, a properly run financial relations program, whether performed internally or with the aid of a financial relations consultant, must include a concerted effort to build and service a following of investment professionals.

Merely to address a meeting of investment professionals is not, as will be seen in Chapter 7 on strategy, to solve a financial relations problem, or to develop a marketing oriented investor relations program. The corporation is, after all, competing against hundreds and thousands of other companies, not only for capital, but for the investors' attention as well. This competition is a continuous effort. Simply because an analyst has met with management and heard its story once, and even if he or she is impressed, there is no reason to believe that interest will be sustained or that the analyst will not be distracted by six other companies that command his or her attention. This interest is sustained by putting every analyst and investment professional who attends a meeting—or expresses any sort of interest—on an active mailing list.

He or she must then be contacted periodically, updated on material, reminded of recent information that has been released, and have his or her questions answered. It's an ongoing process that, to be effective, must be consistent with marketing principles in both structure and attention.

Research Reports

A constant aim, in dealing with analysts, is to generate research reports by brokerage houses or research services. These are reports, issued periodically, for use by both brokers and investors. They may be either brief discussions of the company or intensive, detailed research studies. They almost invariably conclude with a purchase recommendation, or a recommendation to hold the stock for the longer term. A favorable recommendation by a major firm can be a virtual guarantee of increased buying, and frequently, a higher stock price.

A successful investor relations effort includes constantly developing new interest for a company in the financial community. A knowledgeable consultant will be aware, by virtue of his or her consistent efforts in the field, of many analysts and the companies that they're following, many of the changes among analysts and their affiliations, and the current basis for viewing companies. He or she will spend a considerable number of hours every month talking to analysts and other investment professionals to determine those who are likely targets to hear the company's story. Earlier contacts will be followed up to keep them updated and to help maintain their interest. The consultant will develop a constantly expanding following for a company and eliminate those investment professionals no longer interested or no longer available to be interested. This also leads to developing sponsorship for a stock, as well as new market makers.

In many cases, and only with the permission of the issuing firm, a favorable report may be reprinted and distributed to the shareholders and others in the financial community. Good judgment suggests, however, that an analyst from one firm might be skeptical about a report from another, while some will welcome the input. Don't guess—inquire.

Feedback

Feedback of market reaction to the company and its presentation is as much an element of the communication effort as is imparting information. By frequently speaking to investment professionals who follow the company, as well as to those who decide not to follow it, the consultant or investor relations officer supplies an extraordinarily valuable view of how Wall Street sees the company. The investor relations professional will identify the problems to be anticipated in telling the company's story, and will be invaluable in determining strategy for meeting objections and for developing sustained interest. Although the general function of the investor relations consultant and investor relations officer is dealt with in another chapter, it should be noted here that the more effective consultants are not only those who are specialists in the techniques of dealing with the Street, but also those whose communication and marketing expertise dovetails with intensive involvement with the largest number of investment professionals and investment companies to give them the basis for a constant two-way flow of information and intelligence.

The effective consultant will also supply the company, on a regular basis, with reports of each significant Street contact made in the company's behalf. This includes a report of follow-up discussions with each of the investment professionals who attended any meeting. The report covers the date of the contact, the person who was contacted and his affiliation and position, what was said by the contact—including negatives—and the consultant's impression of the discussion. This kind of report gives the company an effective and continuous feedback of financial community reaction to both the company and its presentation.

The Background Report or Financial Fact Book

Another effective device for reaching the financial community is the company or consultant-prepared background report. These are succinct overviews and summaries of the financial information needed by analysts to understand and evaluate a company. The background report and the financial fact book are discussed in greater detail in the following chapter.

Printed Material

Printed material—including the annual and interim reports, reprints of significant press articles, reprints of speeches and information folders on significant new products—is a useful tool for keeping investment professionals informed of a company's progress. This material is not only distributed directly to investors at meetings or in person, but should be mailed to them at regular intervals.

Also to be mailed regularly to investors—faxed or messengered if they're important and the investor is important—are copies of any financial news releases as soon as possible after they are issued by the company. It should not be assumed that any analyst has seen or retained material about the company that has appeared in abbreviated form on the Dow Jones, Reuters, or any other news service. In many cases the analyst will not have seen it at all on the wire. In other cases he or she will have seen it only fleetingly, when his or her mind was on something else. In some of the larger houses there may be several people interested in the company, but only one copy of the Dow Jones or Reuters tape may be readily available. By mailing the analyst or broker a copy of the actual release, he or she can focus on it, retain it for his or her own files, or share it with other investors.

The company and the capital markets in which it functions are lively and dynamic. Not only are there constant changes, but, each to the other, the relationships between them are constantly changing.

The nature of the stock market, as with any auction markets, is at least elusive. For both the professional and the casual investor, it's a will-o'-the-wisp. No surprise, then, that the best brains of the business and financial world devote themselves to fathoming it; to dissecting it as if it were a part of the brain thought to hold the seat of the soul. The result is not always light or wisdom, but the process reveals new and arcane systems, each more convoluted than the last.

Against this attempt to grasp the music of the universe is the corporation seeking capital. To bring the two worlds together—the corporation and the capital markets—requires a flow of information that includes not only facts, but the essence of the company. That's the role of investor relations.

4

Corporate
Communications

Reaching the professional investing community on a sustaining basis is also accomplished with a range of corporate communications that goes much beyond such standard and traditional shareholder devices as annual and quarterly reports.

If investor relations is a dynamic process, and one of advocacy, then there must be a consistent flow of information to the analytic community and to shareholders. Face-to-face meetings with analysts and investors is crucial; but so is the sustained relationship that comes from the flow of printed and other forms of communication.

It's all part of the marketing campaign; of focusing attention, and flowing information, to sustain an awareness, a concern and a consideration for the company and its stock. It's support, as well, for management in its operations.

While there are traditional forms of corporate communications, ranging from the financial corporate profile to the annual and interim reports to the press release, there are really only two limiting factors to what can be done—the law and imagination. True, there are certain formats prescribed by tradition and trade custom, such as the form of the press release (which must function within the context of media). But corporate communications devices are susceptible to whatever can be imagined that still accomplishes the objectives. An annual report, for example, can be on videotape. You can, if you think it will work, wrap bonbons in financial statements and send them to brokers. This is, after all, a marketing context.

The basic documents inherent in virtually every investor relations program are the annual and interim reports to shareholders, which are also basic documents for analysts and other investment professionals; the financial corporate profile, a supplementary document designed to be useful primarily to investment professionals; and press releases. There are, of course, other printed documents that can be used (such as reprints and product literature), and there are other forms of corporate communication to the financial community (such as letters and videotape reports).

The Annual Report

There is probably no subject in the area of financial or investor relations that's commanded more discussion than the annual report. Since every public company issues an annual report in one form or another, it's the one universal device in investor relations even for those companies that do nothing else in the field. Millions of dollars are spent (and sometimes wasted) every year in the production of these documents. Millions more are spent in their distribution, and the dollar value of executive time is incalculable.

Today, a great deal is written on the core issue of an annual report— what it really is and should be, and how it is to be used. An overwhelming number of annual reports are merely imitations of reports that have gone before, with the basic reasoning for the predecessor long since forgotten. A great many reports are issued that seem to be designed solely to fulfill an SEC or stock exchange requirement, and so lose the many great advantages of a thoughtful, well-planned and well-executed document.

Even the basic audience for annual reports is a subject of much discussion, most of it based on irrelevant issues. One school of thought believes that the annual report should be written so that it can be understood by the least sophisticated shareholder. At the other extreme there is the feeling that the annual report should be simply the company's Form 10-K—or at least as austere. Others think of the annual report in terms of a peculiar concept called the *corporate image*—a predetermined view of the company to be engendered and projected to the investing or general public, almost with total disregard for facts or realities. Even the elaborate regulations of the SEC, viewing the annual report and Form 10-K as a package, serve as a minimum document, in view of the potential value of the annual report.

There are two basic points that should be remembered in planning an annual report:

- An annual report is basically a financial document and a financial relations tool. It is not a graphics device. It is not primarily an advertising medium. It is the basic tool used by every segment of the investment community—the shareholder, the security analyst, the broker, the money manager, the bank, the institutional investor, the institutional lender, and so on—to help make the basic evaluation of the company as an investment or lending vehicle. Furthermore, it has an active life of at least one year—until the next annual report is issued. During that period it serves as the primary handbook for evaluating the company, regardless of what other documents or information are used to supplement the information in it.

- Each annual report should be approached virtually as if it were the first time in corporate history that any annual report has ever been written. The legal requirements of an annual report under SEC and exchange rules, that it report certain prescribed facts about the company, can be met with a word processor and a photocopying machine. Therefore any decision to go beyond the bare bones must not only be predicated upon the needs of the company, but, as well, may take virtually any form, in any format, that serves to present a clear picture of the company without distorting the truth. Successful and communicative reports have been in the form of national business magazines, movie scripts, analyst meeting reports, children's picture books, and even videotapes.

Thus, the greatest effort in developing an annual report should take place in the planning stage. A number of clear-cut questions should be raised early, and examined very carefully in all aspects, before any work is done on the report. It's frequently useful to put these questions, and their answers, in writing, as a form of prospectus for the report. The prospectus may even be longer than the report itself. The result of the effort, however, makes it well worthwhile. It becomes a clear document and statement of policy for everyone who will have to work on the report. It cuts down the almost inevitable rewriting, and it eliminates time-consuming discussions over drafts that must ultimately be discarded because not everyone involved understood the same things about the directions in which the report was to go.

The prospectus should include the following:

- Outline of issues and unusual circumstances, and outstanding elements that form a context for this particular annual report. This should evolve into a single central theme for the report.
- The objectives of this report—what we want people to know, think and feel after they've read it.
- The target audiences—Shareholders? Analysts and brokers? Suppliers? If all, then which are priorities?
- The format.

- Special features.
- Graphics.

Objectives

At the time each company prepares its annual report, it faces a specific set of circumstances and opportunities in regard to both its own operations and the capital markets that are pertinent at that moment. These circumstances and opportunities may be peculiar to the company, the economy, or the industry. They may pertain to changes within the company, its corporate structure, its products, the markets it serves, its people, or changes in financial structure. The company may be undergoing some unusual and highly visible litigation. The economy may have certain elements in it which particularly color a view of the company, such as the energy crisis, inflation, or devaluation. The industry may be undergoing significant changes or material shortages. The company may be appreciably outperforming its industry. This kind of situation may be short term, but it is the annual report that serves as the prime vehicle for management to address itself to the company's position relative to these factors. Or the situation may be long-range, such as a change in the direction of the company's operations or growth plans.

The point is that these factors pose the context against which the company's story is to be told in its annual report. All planning for the report must keep this context, and the company's investor relations needs of the moment, very much in the forefront. Those needs should never be opposed to the company's long-term interests.

This same planning context also forms the basis for developing the objectives of the report. Obviously its primary objective is to inform and, ultimately, to sell stock. But beyond that, each report each year not only faces a different set of corporate situations, but a different set of objectives as well. The objectives are determined as the answers to the question. "What is it we want our readers to know and think about our company after they have read this report?" Certain of the objectives are basic. For example:

- To define the essential nature of the company and its business within the context that augers well for the future.
- To demonstrate that management has a firm grasp on all aspects of the company's business; that it not only understands but controls all aspects of the business. This includes a full understanding of the company's markets and market potential, both currently and in the foreseeable future.

- To demonstrate that the company is internally sound and strong—both fiscally and in depth of management—or is aware of those areas in which this is not the case, and is taking steps to overcome these deficiencies as a foundation to engender further strength and growth.
- To demonstrate that the avenues of the future of the company are to a large degree clearly identifiable; that the company understands them and is attempting to build the kind of flexibility that allows it to move readily into them.

Beyond these general objectives, the company must develop additional goals predicated on specific opportunities it faces at the time the report is to be prepared. This may include clarification of industry, economic, or specific corporate activities, or specific corporate opportunities peculiar to the company. This might include the opportunity to increase market share, or to move into new markets with new products, or to take advantage of the company's favorable relations with the capital markets by increasing debt or equity, and using the money to expand globally.

The stated objectives should be clearly developed for the annual report, and should not be a broader statement of corporate philosophy or corporate objectives.

Target Audiences

The target audiences for an annual report must be clearly delineated. Without a firm understanding of who is to read the report, it's virtually impossible to determine intelligently how it's to be prepared. Each company must decide for itself the prime targets and their order of importance. For any public company there is no specific audience to the exclusion of the others. Nor are the audience priorities the same from one company to the other. Ultimately, the target audience for any annual report is that which is most important to the company at the time the annual report is written. And this can, of course, change from year to year.

The audience segments are distinctive, and can include . . .

- *The financial community.* This means the analysts, brokers, money managers, and other institutional investors whose knowledge of the company must be maintained in as great detail as possible, and whose support the company must foster over both the short and long range if the company is to compete successfully in the capital markets. Included are banks, insurance companies, and other lending institutions. Not to be ignored, in considering the financial community, are the ancillary activities, such as merger and acquisition, and competitor intelligence (for which Wall Street is a prime source).

This target is particularly vital for the smaller company, whose access to other means of communications is limited. For it, the annual report takes on an even greater value as a source of information about the company. It is the annual report that is frequently the first point of contact between the financial community and the company—the first opportunity the prospective investor has to become acquainted with it. There is no question that for the annual report of most companies, the financial community is the primary target.

- *Shareholders.* The basic legal purpose of the annual report is to report the company's position to shareholders. Therefore, while they might not be deemed a primary investor relations target in some circumstances, they are still an essential target. The objective in reaching shareholders, beyond the normal reporting requirements, is to demonstrate to them that their company is well managed, sound, and has growth potential.

- *The broader business community.* For many companies the report can be an annual demonstration to the business community at large of their structure, strength, and capability. Companies do business with one another. It demonstrates the soundness of the company to suppliers, customers, potential merger partners, and others with whom a relationship of one kind or another is valuable.

- *Prospective customers.* While an annual report is not a sales brochure, a certain amount of display of capability makes it useful as a sales tool by demonstrating not only the range of service, but the substance of the company behind it. In the case of consumer companies, the report has a measure of advertising value, in that shareholders and prospective investors are also consumers.

- *Internal staff.* For some companies there is a value in considering internal staff or prospective employees as a target audience. The report offers an opportunity to enhance morale and engender pride. Not to be overlooked is the fact that employees are sometimes potential investors as well, or through their ESOP, actual investors.

- *Unions.* There occasionally arises a question of the place of the annual report in labor relations. Some companies feel that there is a danger in displaying profitability in ways that might incite trade unions to demand a greater portion of it. This is an unfortunate and negative view. It's unlikely that any labor union of consequence is not already keenly aware of the company's performance, virtually in as great detail as is the management. To consider labor relations as a reason for not fully reporting performance is not only a delusion, but uses a smaller negative factor to override a larger advantage. (The same is true in considering explanations for high margins to the business community to be dangerous, in that customers might look askance at prices in relation to profit margins, or that potential competitors might be attracted by highly profitable market opportunities.)

- *Civic and public interest groups.* Today's corporate audience, closely watching the operations of companies, includes local and national civic groups, and those with such special interests as the environment, international issues (e.g., South African segregation), and political action.

- *Special government agencies.* More companies do business with the government today, not only in defense, but in labor, commerce, and treasury. Included here are ERISA agencies.

There are partisans for every point of view on the subject of audiences for annual reports. There are proponents for every target group, ranging from the unsophisticated holder of a hundred shares to the highly sophisticated analyst for a major institution. While no single statement can be expected to resolve that question once and for all, there are some basic considerations.

For example, if an annual report is designed to achieve a number of complex objectives for one or more financially sophisticated audiences, the report will obviously address many more issues, with a clear delineation of all aspects of the company's financial and other operations, than it would if the audience were just casual shareholders. But a report addressing complex issues shouldn't be more difficult to read and understand, however.

Furthermore, the report should be planned in a context of how investment decisions are made. The manager of a large fund makes his decision based not only on the contents of the annual report, but upon extensive analysis of other factors, such as actuarial projections, as well. The individual investor rarely makes an investment decision on his or her own. He or she may read the annual report, or any other document, and draw a conclusion. The number of such investors who will make investment decisions based on that conclusion, and without further consultation, is so small that this kind of investor must be excluded from any serious consideration as a target audience for an annual report. When the widow who inherited a few hundred shares of stock reads a report and makes an investment decision, she is most likely going to consult her broker. The broker will then presumably contribute his or her knowledge and sophistication, backed by appropriate research reports, to enforce or amend that decision. Thus, as a practical matter, the primary target audience is rarely the smaller individual investor.

This is not to say that the individual investor doesn't constitute an important part of the audience for an annual report. The report is ostensibly a report to shareholders. Nor should this be construed to mean that any report should be obscure for the average investor. The point is that the target audiences are determined by more than a responsibility to keep shareholders informed. As the company's annual statement, it's a document that clarifies the company to a much broader financial and business community.

Theme

Given a successful and well-conceived company, or a company with a firm grip on where it's going and how to get there, delineating a theme for an annual report readily enhances the ability to communicate the essence of the company to its target audiences.

In the context of investor relations, the theme is often the platform to project the company's *Unique Investment Premise,* that key structure that distinguishes the company's potential to appreciate an investment (see Chapter 9).

Projecting the essence of a company's performance and substance is almost invariably enhanced by a unifying theme, which can also be carried forth from the annual report to the year's quarterly reports. There are several tangible advantages to a theme:

- It helps to focus the essence of the company, both visually and in copy.
- It helps the designer visualize the company in the report, and the writer to write the text. The text and the design are then consistent.
- It serves as a benchmark against which to measure every element of the report.
- It provides quicker, simpler understanding of the essence of the company to the target audiences.
- It greatly increases what the reader absorbs from the annual report, adding impact to the report's messages.

A very large, but not nationally known, midwestern S&L holding company had a marvelous record of having avoided the classic industry problems, and of having made innovations in a number of areas. For its annual report, a few years ago, it chose (at its investor relations counselor's suggestion) as its theme, *selective growth.* In the cover, the text and the artwork, it carried out this theme to demonstrate its innovativeness, its avoidance of industry problems, and its conscious choice to compete on its strengths.

The theme said to the audience that management's ability to assess the company's strengths and weaknesses, and to choose where to compete, was an essential reason for the company's success.

This theme was carried out so effectively, and communicated its message to its audiences so well, that it won a *Financial World Magazine* award as the outstanding annual report for financial institutions with $1 to 10 billion in assets. The award cited "the power of its theme," and the effective use of the theme, as a major reason for the award.

Format

The format of an annual report is a function of objectives and target audiences. The financials aside, certain traditional practices have sprung up for the front of the report, which pervade an overwhelming number of reports. In some cases these formats are followed simply because they are traditional, and not because they bear any relation to the particular needs of a company. There is usually the president's letter, followed by some text, and illustrative material describing the company and its products (by division lines, if relevant) in glowing terms. The standard president's letter starts out with either a statement of how good the year has been or an apologetic note for the company's poor performance. Or it might begin with the trite and overused phrase, "We are pleased to report . . ." or some similar cliché. This opening is followed by several paragraphs recapping sales and earnings, and some brief cosmetic explanation of why earnings were not up to par, or a description of the several factors that resulted in superior performance. If the readers continue, they will find a few paragraphs describing some of the year's outstanding events, followed by a paragraph or two projecting the problems or opportunities that lie ahead, and a statement that the company intends to face the problems squarely or seize the opportunities effectively. The letter ends on an optimistic note for the future, with a bow of thanks to the loyal officers and employees without whom the company's success would not be possible.

The descriptive text, including pictures of the company's plant—which looks like every other plant—describes the company's products, processes, or services. Some reports discuss operations by divisional lines.

This format and approach to an annual report virtually guarantees that the report will not be read, nor will it be understood, nor will it be appreciated. Even if the company is performing magnificently and has great potential for the future, this performance or potential will be submerged and hidden in a deluge of dull words and clichés. The chances are that anybody in the investment community who reads one report will read many. It all begins to dissolve into one shapeless blur.

This need not be. Aside from reporting basic required information, the option of format lies entirely with the company. Hearken back to a point noted earlier—each report can and should be written as if it were the first time in corporate history that an annual report has ever been written. The number of legitimate and exciting variations is limited only by the imagination of the company or investor relations consultant who prepares the report. For two prime examples of excellent shareholder letters see Warren Buffet's Hathaway or Ralph Wanger's Acorn Fund reports.

Variations

For one annual report, a company's chief executive officer was put in a room with half a dozen leading security analysts and the interview recorded. The interview was then edited for style only, and printed in lieu of a traditional president's letter. Creative Management Associates, a publicly held theatrical talent agency, printed its report one year in the form of the publication, *Daily Variety*. All of the pertinent financial information was included, and the company's activities were reported as news or feature stories.

State Farm, the insurance company, used a *Reader's Digest* format to tell its story in one annual report.

A company that's consistently been a pioneer in health care information technology had a chief executive officer who is considered a visionary in the field. He had been virtually inventing an industry, and was seen as so far ahead of his industry that it was unseemly to have him do a standard report for his successful company. It was determined, then, that his letter should be a projection of the industry, its opportunities, and where it was going. Much of the traditional letter was written, instead, by the company's new president and chief operating officer. A third letter on financial results, usually included in the CEO's letter, was written and signed by the company's chief financial officer. The report, instead of having one traditional letter, had three separate letters, each uniquely appropriate to its subject.

In its first report as a public company, Jones and Vining, a manufacturer of shoe lasts, recognized that few of the people it wanted to reach would understand the shoe last industry, and devoted a full page to a discussion of the shoe last and its role in shoe manufacturing. It also recognized that the company could be judged properly only in the context of the total shoe industry, and devoted another full page to a discussion of the economics of the industry, its structure, and its current status.

Another company recognized that a description of its services in behalf of its leasing customers could be considered routine and mundane to those outside the industry. Its investor relations counsel suggested that these services be reported pictorially in the style used by *Life* magazine. The report pictorially followed a branch manager through a day of his activities—a fresh and effective approach to describing services that would otherwise have been of no interest to readers.

Some larger companies have included articles discussing international economics written by prominent economists outside the company. Others, functioning in several countries, have printed their reports in several languages.

Many companies include a discussion of end users of their products, and the benefits of their products to consumers. A discussion of all the company's appliances used by consumers in a typical American community could tell more about the company than any other description of it.

In other words, the effectiveness of the report can be enhanced by shifting wherever possible from traditional approaches. No corporate annual report can or should be an imitation of any other corporate annual report, since no two corporations are the same.

How Reports Are Read

From many surveys and interviews it's been determined that professionals who read annual reports tend to follow the same procedure. This is necessary because they read so many of them in the course of a year and must determine very quickly whether the company offers any basis for further interest.

Most analysts and investment professionals turn to the first page for a quick look at the summary of revenues and earnings. They then turn to the back of the book to review the financials, beginning with the auditors' names and opinions, and then the income statement, balance sheet, cash flow analysis, management summary, and so forth. If they are still interested after having read thus far, they turn to the president's letter in the hope of finding an intelligent explanation of the financial condition of the company, its operating results, and key aspects of its strategy. If they are still interested, they will go on to read the text describing the company's operations or industry.

No investment professional is ever overly impressed by the physical format of a report, although it seems unlikely that an attractive, and even an expensive-looking, report won't have at least a subliminal impact. Certainly, an attractively designed document is more inviting to read than one that's dull and mundane. At the same time, many investment professionals indicate a negative reaction to an expensive four-color report for any company that's not fairly large and doesn't show a significant earnings level. One of the most exquisite reports ever produced some years ago was for a multinational company. The graphics were extraordinary. The photography could have won prizes. It was obviously an expensive production. It reported an $8 million loss for the company for that year. The reaction of shareholders upon receiving so expensive a booklet when the company lost $8 million was explosive.

While expensive graphics seem designed for the shareholder, and not the professional, then, it's foolish to assume that professionals are inured to attractive packaging. Not to the point of being persuaded by well-packaged poor performance, perhaps, but certainly, an attractive document is more likely to get read seriously than an unattractive one. In fact, the objective of good design is to enhance readership, and to focus the eye on key elements of the document.

The purpose of an annual report is to impart information, and its format should be designed to do just that. Moreover, as noted in Chapter 6, the SEC and the Exchanges are insisting upon the disclosure of a greater number of factors, as well as more interpretation of those facts. But for the company competing for capital, the minimum requirements are rarely enough.

The Chief Executive Officer's Message

The CEO's message should be as complete and detailed a report as he or she might give in summary to his or her own board of directors. When one has read a chairman's or president's letter, one should have a clear picture of not only where the company has been and is now, but where it's going. There should be a good view, as well, of the kind of person who is leading it.

Experienced and knowledgeable readers of annual reports look to the CEO's message for a rounded picture of the company's performance and outlook. This doesn't mean a rehash of information delineated more succinctly in other parts of the report. Regardless of the format used, the chief executive's message should be simple, concise, free from clichés, and loaded with fresh information. It should not merely state financial data reported elsewhere. It should explain. It should point to significant changes in performance or financial factors and give sound reasons as to why those changes took place and what they mean. It should take note of critical variables—those elements in that particular business that are crucial to success or failure. It should dwell heavily on balance sheet factors, such as changes in inventory, accounts receivable, important ratios, return on investment, and so forth. It should deal realistically with inflation, as well as other economic concerns of the day.

It should outline the framework in which the business functions in terms of both the general economy and the industry, and should note any important trends, and should delineate a backup plan in case of recession.

It should describe the major changes in financial structure that have taken place in the prior year, not merely in keeping with the formal requirements outlined in Chapter 6, but in a concerted effort to communicate

The SEC has specifically indicated that annual reports be readable by nonprofessionals as well as professionals, and that annual report text not be in the same legal language as the 10-K. Other required information includes changes in accounting principles, dividend history, product mix, relative profitability of lines of business, advertising, research and development plans and expenditures, acquisition, or disposition of material assets, assumptions underlying deferred costs and plans for amortization of such costs, closing facilities, business interruption, and significant customers and new contracts. At one time, the SEC staff defined a material change as one in which any item of receivables or expenses changed by 10 percent and/or affects net income by more than 2 percent at any time during the prior three years. Now, however, they are much more realistic, and recognize that it's not just the numbers that count, it's the quality of the change as well. The numbers alone are no longer the sole focal point; the context, on the other hand, is considered very carefully.

This doesn't mean that the key financial factors shouldn't be spotlighted, as before. If a company's tax rate changes by more than 1 percent from one period to the next, separate disclosure should be seriously considered.

The SEC is quite clear that substantive material changes be included in the text, even though these items may be covered in notes to the financial statement. If a projection of the coming year's performance is to be made, it need not contain specific earnings projections, but it should certainly clarify specific reasons for optimism. It should clarify the debt picture as well as forthcoming plans for capital expenditures and how they are expected to contribute to the company's growth and future profitability. Potential returns in the light of the true cost of capital should be discussed. The SEC prefers that management comment not only on the year-end financial picture, but also on the company's current competitive position within its field.

It should clarify uncertainties that may affect future earnings. For example, will the ratio of retained earnings being reinvested in the business to earnings held in reserve change? It should clarify special problems such as international operations affected by foreign currency fluctuations, and special situations, such as an unusual tax structure.

There is an increasing tendency to discuss various aspects of corporate responsibility in reports. In some cases, such as environmental control, this is an essential part of a company's business, and would naturally be included. However, some companies, as a matter of corporate philosophy, recognize a larger role of the corporation in the total society. Some companies, such as IBM and Mobil, have gone to great lengths to define what they see as an obligation to society, and devote a good deal of their corporate effort toward that end. The move toward recognizing corporate responsibility in society is, in many cases, a function of the individual consciousness of corporate officers. In other cases, companies are responding to criticism from consumer groups, including activists in civil rights, equal rights for women, doing business in South Africa, and environmental considerations. On the one hand, it's argued that this kind of corporate activity is irrelevant to the corporation's profit-making function. On the other hand, it's argued that not only does this activity increase a company's favorable visibility, but it contributes to profitability in the long run, since by helping to guarantee quality of life in the future of the nation, a corporation also guarantees its profitability. Certainly in those companies with a position or with activity in this area, reports of the activities are valid and preferred in the annual report, or a companion piece. Moreover, there is an immediately tangible aspect in view of the costs and their effect upon earnings.

Many social issues directly affect the corporation to an increasing degree, and when appropriate, should be covered in the report. Issues such as maternity leave for employees, child care, the drug problem in the workplace, alcoholism, and so forth are very much a part of today's corporate responsibility, and are by no means ephemeral.

A word of caution . . .

While the social needs of the world are profound and legitimate, caution is the byword in corporate responsibility. Corporate responsibility certainly isn't a substitute for corporate performance. At the same time, there are fads and fashions in the area to which even the most dedicated and concerned citizen can fall prey. The problem with corporations taking up causes that are well on the way to being resolved in noncorporate areas is that it can redound negatively to an assessment of management judgment.

There is also a growing movement toward the corporate social audit, in which attempts are made to quantify the actual costs, commitments, and values of all facets of corporate responsibility, from environmental controls to minority-training programs. For the company involved in this kind of activity, exploration into techniques of reporting it on an economic basis should certainly be explored.

Management's Discussion and Analysis

Now a mandatory part of the annual report to shareholders, the MD&A— *Management's Discussion and Analysis of Financial Condition and Results of Operations*—is defined by SEC regulation. Those most comprehensive discussions of these regulations, issued by the SEC in 1989, clearly define what information should be included.

The purpose of the MD&A is to give dimension to the facts and ⌐____ to be found elsewhere in the report. It's intended, according to an earlier SEC release, ". . . [to] give the investor an opportunity to look at the company through the eyes of management by providing both a short- and long-term analysis of the business of the company. The item asks management to discuss the dynamics of the business and to analyze the financials."

In other words, to tell the shareholder what should have been told all along in at least the president's letter. This includes any information of a forward-looking nature that might materially affect the future of the company's operations or financial status, an analysis of cash flows, material changes, segment analysis, and so forth.

It's the SEC's continued drive for exposure to shareholders of all information that may contribute to making an investment decision.

A summary of the 1989 release is included in Appendix 2.

Financial Information

Elsewhere in the report, the largest possible number of financial factors should be clearly given, in addition to appropriate financial information. This includes:

- Sales, earnings, and performance by product line and division, where possible, as well as foreign activity. The product line information has been a subject of considerable contention. It has long been felt that reporting this information gives away competitive information. The fact remains that much of this information is available to competitors in other SEC-required filings, as well as from the marketplace. It's inconceivable that any competitor interested in the information will not have availed himself of it—or at least enough to make intelligent guesses. On the other hand, reporting by line gives a clearer picture of the company. And as with all financial disclosure, the greater the amount of information disclosed, the greater the credibility awarded to nonfinancial statements made by corporate executives.

- Financial statistics for eleven years or more. The SEC now requires at least a five-year summary of certain financial information (see Chapter 6), but ten years, when feasible, gives a better picture. (Keep in mind that you need eleven years of data to make a ten-year comparison, and six years of data to make a five-year comparison.) This is in addition to the two- and three-year summary given on the first page of the report (although smaller reports can use the five-year summary up front). The summarized information should cover as many factors as are relevant, including percentage changes and ratios. Granted that historical information contributes only partially to predicting the future growth of the company; it gives a rounded picture of progress over a reasonable period of time. It also demonstrates the effectiveness of management in moving the company through several financial periods and company business cycles. At least the following factors broken down by 10-K lines of business, where applicable, identical to the 10-K, should be included in the summary, with percentage increases over the prior year for each figure:

- Revenues, broken down by lines
- Costs and expenses, including cost of services, cost of raw materials, cost of sales
- Gross margins, in both dollars and percentages
- Income before provision for income taxes
- Interest income and expense
- Provisions for income taxes, both current and deferred
- Net income
- Net income per common share (pre- and postdilution)
- Number of shares outstanding, primary and fully diluted
- Total assets
- Stockholders' equity, including per share
- Return on revenues
- Return on assets
- Return on stockholders' equity
- Shareholder's equity as a percentage of total assets
- Dividend history
- Sales per employee
- Key ratios, including current ratio, debt to equity, etc.
- Plowback ratio (percent of net income paid out in dividends, and percentage plowed back into company each year)
- Working capital amounts
- Annual cash flow comparison
- Long-term debt
- Effects of inflation
- Research and development expenditures
- Marketing, sales, and advertising expenses, if relevant
- Frequency and amount of dividends during past two years and present and future dividend restrictions

- Inventory profits
- Compensating bank balances
- Effective tax rates
- Sales and earnings from foreign operations
- Breakdown of order backlogs
- New order amounts and rates
- Data on employee pension obligations
- Information on the exchange or market where the stock is traded, including market price ranges and dividends paid—for at least the most recent two years
- Unusual items, such as collecting on insurance policy from executive

The purpose of the special section for management discussion and analysis is to give a management interpretation of general performance and financial condition.

The SEC pays particular attention to this section, and has said that it will be quick to cite any company whose annual report is deficient in the discussion and analysis. It's indicated its clear intention to be tougher in this area in the nineties than before. The section must include discussion of at least the following:

- *Liquidity,* including factors that will have a materially favorable or unfavorable impact on it. Discuss, also, internal and external sources of liquidity and unused sources of liquid assets. The SEC says that if you see the beginning of a trend that would affect your liquidity, or any meaningful signs of potential change, you must comment on it.
- *Capital resources,* including material commitments for capital expenditures as of fiscal year end. Discuss material trends in capital resources and changes between equity, debt and off-balance sheet financing arrangements.
- *Results of operations,* including
  - Unusual events impacting income. These should be quantified if appropriate.
  - Other significant components of revenue necessary to understand results.
  - A narrative discussion of the extent to which sales and revenue increase are attributable to increases in prices, volume increases, or new products or services.

– Impact of inflation on sales and revenues from continuing operations. Some companies are specifically required to do this by accounting regulation, but those not so required should consider
doing so as well for clarity of results.

An increasing number of companies are reporting this kind of information in detail, and are going beyond the SEC's and the exchanges' mandatory disclosure requirements. In addition, the SEC now requires brief
biographical information about all officers and directors, including their
outside affiliations.

Board of directors' committees are also being recognized to an increasing
degree by many companies, and these committees are frequently described
in reports.

As more managers get the SEC's point that more disclosure must be
forthcoming in the future—that the goal is to have an investor truly
understand what is important to measure a business—then the more will
the competitive ante be raised for all companies. The information explosion begets additional information explosion, in order for a company to
compete effectively.

In other words, in reporting financial information the rule should be
greater rather than lesser exposure. The goal is to increase understanding.
For any company competing in the capital markets, the need for full and
prompt disclosure is overwhelming. Even for the company performing less
than magnificently, the value of full and fast disclosure far exceeds the
potential harm.

Descriptive Text

The primary purpose of descriptive material in an annual report is not
merely to demonstrate the company's business or products, but to do so
in a way that demonstrates the viability and potential of the company's
business, as well as its competitive advantages. The objective here is to
show where the company's money comes from—what generates the revenues and how it redounds to profits.

It must support representations made by the chief executive officer of
the company's potential for success. Thus it becomes important to describe
the company's business, people, plants, equipment, products or services,
customers, in the context of potential profitability. Simply to describe the
company's product is insufficient. It must be done in terms of the product's
value to the public and industry, as well as its competition and market
potential. It must be shown how that product or service contributes to
overall corporate profitability. It becomes too simple a matter for a company to take pride in its capital holdings—its magnificent new 500,000-

square-foot plant, or its new process or equipment that produces four times as many widgets with half as many people. But while this pride is justifiable within the corporate family, if it is not clear why the new plant will cut costs and improve product quality and productivity, facilitate distribution, and increase the ability to meet growing market needs, the report becomes a hollow exercise in self-aggrandizement.

The technique used to describe a company's operations is irrelevant, if it isn't dictated by the overall format and theme of the report. The report can be broken down by divisions or product line, segmentation of subsidiary companies, markets, service, or user segmentation. Explaining operations can be a separate section or part of a long narrative included in the president's letter. The decision as to the way to go is a function of better communication and clarity. Whichever technique works best to communicate clearly, in keeping with the objectives of the report, is the technique to use.

In describing the company's operations, a careful and objective view should be taken to avoid reporting the commonplace as if it were unique. Every manufacturing company has plants and machines. It's expected that every annual report for every manufacturing company will report that its plants are the most efficient, its machinery more modern and productive, its service superior, and its employees the best trained, the most clean-cut and clear-eyed. But if no way can be found to demonstrate these things in terms of their competitive advantages; their genuine uniqueness and superiority, then there's a virtual guarantee that the space will be wasted and the report will be unread outside the industry. In describing a company's operations, every effort must be made to demonstrate uniqueness and clear-cut superiority. If any statement in the description of a company's operations doesn't clearly demonstrate a contribution to cost cutting or profitability, it probably serves no purpose and probably should be left out.

Special Features

Every effort should be made to determine special features that might be included to enhance the value of the report. Certainly, basic to every report should be a brief description of the company's operations on the very first page, or inside the front cover. It should be unnecessary for anyone to have to thumb through 16 or 24 pages to find out what business a company is in. It's also an opportunity to sum up and clarify a description and perspective of a company as it sees itself and wants to be seen by others. This simple description is sometimes harder to do than it would appear at first glance, particularly if the company is a multiproduct operation or functions in some tangential area of an industry. This description, incidentally, must be consistent with Item 1 of the Form 10-K. But it should expand on it, as long as it doesn't contradict it.

Special opportunities or problems should be dealt with in special sections. A company that's complex in its operation should not hesitate to devote a section of the book, whether it's a few paragraphs boxed off or a full page, to describe itself. It shouldn't be necessary to read an entire report to fathom what the company is about. A company with special tax considerations should take a separate section of the book to describe its tax picture. A company that's ancillary to an industry and dependent upon it should take a section or page to describe the economics of the industry it serves. If your industry is one not generally understood, a special section to enhance understanding of that industry and how your company fits into it is clearly helpful to readers. Other special sections might deal with unusual aspects of competition or share of market. In some industries, glossaries can be helpful to understand the company better. An unusual educational program or retirement plan or public service program may also be useful in a special section. Research and development, marketing information, or user information may all be relevant and useful.

In fact, a context for any unusual aspect of the company should be included, and, where feasible, set apart from the body of the text.

A table of contents is sometimes warranted if the book is more than 20 pages and has sections. It certainly isn't necessary for a brief and concise report.

Graphics

The question of graphics shouldn't be confused by a conflict between reporting needs and aesthetics. As long as a report is complete, neat, and readable, its graphic presentation need not be elaborate. It should, however, contribute to making the report attractive and readable. There are several factors to consider:

- *Graphs.* The purpose of graphs is to give a quick view of the direction in which a company is moving in several of its operational or financial functions. Graphs are helpful if they are well done. They are confusing if they are irrelevant and designed only for looks. The decision whether to use a bar graph of one form or another, a pie chart, or a line graph is a function of the information to be reported, not the aesthetics. The decision is predicated on the form that best demonstrates the information. The kind of material that should be graphed includes:
  - Revenues, net earnings and net earnings per share. If you are going to use graphs you must graph all three—or use no graphs at all.

 – Any other significant factor that shows historical progress or puts
the company's situation in perspective, such as return on equity;
divisional sales and earnings as a proportion of total sales and earnings (This is frequently useful to demonstrate the growth of one
division or product line as an increasing portion of total revenues
and earnings.); sources of revenue; stockholders' equity; revenues
from acquisitions made in the past ten years; and so on.

 The location of graphs in a book should be determined by where
they are most pertinent. Sometimes it's useful to put the graphs on
the same page as the ten-year summary. Sometimes it's even more
useful to intersperse them with the president's letter, or in proxim-
ity to paragraphs describing the graphed information, such as the
two- or three-year highlights up front.

* *Illustrations.* There is frequently a battle between ego and value to the
report in determining whose pictures are to be included in the book.
It's very difficult to include the picture of one vice-president and not
another. If the members of the executive team are attractive, clear-
eyed, and exude charm and intelligence, by all means include their
pictures. On the other hand, if it's known that there is a general
feeling that the management team is considered too old and that there
is no middle management being primed for succession, it seems rather
foolhardy to lace the report with pictures of the management team.
Often, a compromise must be found between reality and accommoda-
tion to personal executive wishes.

Obviously, the CEO's picture belongs in the report. People want to see
the individual who has primary responsibility for the success of the investment. It should be a tasteful picture, and preferably an action photo and
not just a two-dimensional portrait. Nor should it appear three or more
times throughout the report, because that makes the company look like a
one-man show. The directors' pictures should also be used, if there's space
and if it's not inappropriate.

There is nothing duller than looking at pictures of people doing nothing,
unless it's machinery doing nothing. If the executives are to be pictured
in the report they should be shown working, and not just behind a desk.
The vice-president of manufacturing should be shown in a plant. The
vice-president of finance should be shown preparing his budget. Straightforward head shots, or posed pictures of people sitting at desks or talking
on telephones, belong in college yearbooks—not in annual reports designed to demonstrate the excellence of a company's performance.

Product illustrations that support the text are useful, but they must be
adequately captioned. Pictures of plants and machines that look like other
plants and machines are not helpful. Sometimes innovative ways can be

found to illustrate a particular point. For example, one truck leasing company has a service that computerizes a broad spectrum of state and local fuel taxes to give the customer a single printed report, where in the past he had to deal with many individual reports for each locality in which he operated. The company wanted to demonstrate the wide variety of information that went into the single report. The photograph used to illustrate it showed 35 people, each holding a form, a phone, and a computer tape—all standing in a triangle at the apex of which was one person holding the single completed form. The caption—all pictures should be captioned—read, "Behind the single piece of paper, on which is reduced an entire spectrum of details and services on fuel costs and state taxations, is FAST's large staff of experts."

The basic question of design of the report should be predicated on the contents of the report itself. First of all, the design of annual reports is a specialty that differs from the design of brochures or any other printed material. The designer should have at least a modicum of understanding of the financial nature of the report.

Second, an annual report is a financial marketing tool—it's not a graphics device. Too often the designer is asked to design the report well before any other aspect is addressed, and that, of course, is a serious mistake. The designer should be made part of the planning team, but should not dominate it. And certainly, the designer should be made privy to the objectives and all other aspects of the report's prospectus.

This is not to say that the designer's contribution should be minimized—design is an integral part of the report. Moreover, the designer is an expert in his or her field, and should best understand how to translate concepts into graphic terms. As a professional, his or her ideas should carry more weight than the personal tastes or vague feelings of a nonprofessional in design. But still, the report is a financial and financial marketing tool first, and a graphics device second.

The decision as to whether the report should be in one, two, or four colors, or simply black and white, also depends upon the objectives of the report, rather than on abstract design factors. It should be reiterated that no investment decision is ever made on the basis of color or graphic beauty, and, in fact, if the performance reported is not equal to the apparent cost of the report, the effect may be adverse.

There are times when color is clearly prescribed by the nature of the product or services illustrated (ladies' retail hair products, for example). There are times when crisp black and white is clearly dictated in order to give a dignified impression of the company. To use color merely because it's colorful is wasteful if its use doesn't enhance the content and improve the clarity of presentation. A mediocre color photograph may be more attractive than a mediocre black and white picture, but a fine black and white photo looks better than a mediocre color shot.

An increasing number of companies are separating the financial section from the text of the annual report and printing the financials as a separate supplement. This is a useful technique in larger companies where the financial and statistical information is extensive. Another use of the separate textual and statistical sections is the flexibility it allows in giving the report additional uses. The textual section, for example, separated from the financial section, can be the basis for a valuable sales brochure.

The SEC regulations require that all financial statements and notes to financial statements be printed in a modern, legible type face. This means that no smaller than ten-point or equivalent type may be used for body text, with one-seventh of an inch, minimum, between lines. Eight-point type (14 points equal one inch) or equivalent, two-point leaded, is acceptable in tables.

Some companies simply put a cover and very brief additional information on their Form 10-Ks, and use that as an annual report. Certainly this is an extreme recognition of the annual report as a financial document. But at the same time, it's really a message to investors that the company has had a bad year, or else doesn't much care about its shareholders and communicating to them. If there is no valid reason to supply the reader information beyond that which appears in the 10-K, which is rare, this is, at least technically, the ultimate fulfillment of every requirement of an annual report. To some management groups, it may seem to say to shareholders that the company is being run tight and spare. What it really says is that the company doesn't want to communicate, which, to investors and shareholders, is saying more than any management wants to say. And the truth, here, doesn't matter, even if by some remote chance there's a valid reason to do it. The perception does.

In the capital markets, this perception can be an expensive reaction to the company.

Timetable

The timetable for an annual report is a matter of serious consideration. The timing of the annual report is predominantly dictated by its juxtaposition to the annual meeting, because it's often mailed to shareholders with the proxy statement for the annual meeting. That brings it under the SEC proxy rules. Because brokerage firms require 30 days to mail to holders in Street name, time must also be allowed for them.

And a good schedule, incidentally, can save money in production and distribution.

The SEC requires that the Form 10-K, which is the legal annual report to that agency, be filed no later than 90 days from the closing of the fiscal year. The annual report to shareholders must be mailed no later than fifteen days prior to the annual meeting. On the other hand, with the annual reports being mailed with the proxy material, the stockbrokers now say that if they don't receive your annual report at least 30 days before the annual meeting, they won't guarantee to get it out to holders in Street name in time for the meeting. At the same time, proxy material can't go out more than 45 days before the meeting.

The NYSE requires that the report go out no more than 120 days after year end.

The best approach is to have the annual report deadline 32 to 40 days before the annual meeting. Sometimes, it's easier and cheaper to have the board vote to move the annual meeting, rather than to push through an unrealistic annual report schedule.

The problem is that there is almost invariably a tight squeeze because the auditors require a certain amount of time to do their work, and their report is an essential part of the annual report. Only when the annual meeting is set well ahead—and there is rarely an unalterable reason why the annual meeting can't be set with a consideration of the timetable for the annual report in mind—can an annual report be completed at a leisurely pace, without frantic last-minute rushes and expensive overtime charges at the printers. It's here, by the way, that investor relations professionals and annual report specialists make some of the greatest contributions.

The best time to begin planning an annual report is three to six months before the end of the fiscal year, depending upon the size of the company and the scope of the report. The very largest companies begin planning their annual reports a month or two after the prior one is completed, and it's frequently a full-time function for those responsible for it. The report is planned in much the same way as described earlier, and individuals within the corporation or the investor relations firm are assigned specific responsibilities. Considerable time must be allowed for researching the various elements of the report, and for photography and writing. Since most annual reports are carefully scrutinized by several officers of a company as well as attorneys and accountants, the best plan is for the first draft of every aspect of the report except the financials—the text, the photography, and the layout—to be completed by the end of the fiscal year. The next 45 to 60 days will be consumed with the tremendous pressure of editing the text, including the president's letter, to coincide with the anticipated financial figures, as well as supervising the production of those sections of the book that can be moved forward, such as the cover.

Production schedules should be carefully and realistically developed and adhered to. A timetable should be prepared—on paper—with a copy to every individual who has anything to do with the report. It should begin with deadline dates for research, photography, layout, and first draft. Approval dates for each aspect of the report should be scheduled. Deadlines should be set for initial planning and theme sessions, and for delivering the text to the art director, as well as delivering layouts, final mechanicals, printing, binding, and mailing. Arrangements should be made well beforehand with the transfer agent and others who are responsible for mailing.

It should be remembered that in the production of an annual report, if anything can go wrong it will. An attorney or an accountant will object to a statement on the grounds that it is potentially misleading. An attorney, accountant, or corporate officer will not be available on a crucial approval day. An operation will be altered, or a company will sell a division, after the text describing the operation is completed. There is a change in key officers or directors. A photograph will turn out to be inadequate. The first choice of paper may not be available in time at a reasonable cost. A failure to coordinate on annual report and mailing envelopes will cause a problem.

One potential danger is that when there is an unavoidable delay at the last minute, such as a printer running into high humidity and a drying or bindery problem, the delay will conflict with the date of the proxy. Obviously, a delay in mailing a dated proxy is illegal (although 24 hours may be acceptable). The only solution, other than reprinting the proxy, is to ask the attorney to hold off dating the proxy until the last possible minute, and to deliver it two days before the date that will be put on it. It may help.

Defining the various typesetting stages, often a mystery to an uninitiated management, sometimes helps to buy understanding that this inscrutable process does, perhaps, need a few more days. In the later stages, a tactful "this change of a word or two will cost $50 at this stage" sometimes helps prevent unnecessary changes.

The best answer to contingencies is to anticipate as many variables as possible, to plan as carefully as possible, and to try to include at least two extra days as a cushion for each part of the schedule.

Interim Reports

Unlike annual reports, interim reports to shareholders are not a legal requirement of the SEC, although both the New York Stock Exchange and the American Stock Exchange prefer them for their listed companies. Some companies now promise them to shareholders in prospectuses when they go public. There is no question, however, of their value in keeping the financial community informed of a company's operations and performance on a regular basis. In fact, there is momentum in the direction of expanding the interim report to include more information, and to relate it, for comparative purposes, more closely to the annual report. It's clearly entrenched as a key element in corporate communications and investor relations.

The problem with all financial reporting is that it freezes an ongoing process as of the moment of the report; it seizes only one moment of an operation that is in vigorous motion. It's like a still picture taken at high noon of a crowded downtown square in a busy city. It's a photo of the instant. Minutes after the picture has been taken everyone in it has gone off in different directions, and the scene has entirely changed. So it is with annual reporting. The interim report, usually issued quarterly, updates the picture.

The interim report serves several purposes:

- It indicates the company's progress and financial performance since the end of the last reported quarter, and since the end of the last fiscal year.

- It compares the performance of the current interim period with that of the comparable periods in the prior year. This is valuable since very few businesses are level in their performance throughout a single year. Some quarters are traditionally stronger or weaker than others, and a comparison on a quarter-by-quarter basis with the same quarter in the prior year gives a valuable measure of a company's performance. For most companies it's a more valid measure of performance than comparison with the immediately prior quarter.

- Textually, it reports significant corporate activities since the annual report.

- It indicates the degree to which projections made or implied in the annual report are being fulfilled.

- It reports short-term changes in the company's direction.

For the company attempting to compete in the capital markets, the notion of not issuing interim reports is unthinkable. In at least one respect, the interim report is even more important than the annual report, because it shows a commitment to keep information flowing. In the competition for attention, success is a function of an ongoing effort. As in any form of marketing, competing in the capital markets is successful only as a cumulative effort.

In fact, so significant is the interim report that it has been suggested that instead of an annual report and three quarterly reports, there should be four equal reports during the course of the year, with only the year-end report audited. General Electric did it once several years ago. CPT Corporation appears to be moving in that direction. Each of the four reports can be expected to continue to move toward equality in presenting the company in all its aspects. The SEC, moreover, favors an auditor's review of the quarterly, even though the report itself is not audited. Management can cite the auditor's review without making it appear to be an audit.

As in the case of some annual reports, many interim reports have fallen prey to a kind of mindless repetition of everything that's gone before, without any consideration of whether the principles behind doing them in the first place still apply. And yet the interim report offers the opportunity for some of the most creative work to be done in financial relations.

In its least complex (and least useful) form, the interim report can be merely little more than a copy of a release reporting the quarterly results. It can even be a reproduction of the SEC Form 10-Q. At the other extreme, it can be in an elaborate newspaper or magazine style, with interpretive articles covering virtually every aspect of the company's business, as well as the basic financial data and substantial financial analysis. The variety of formats between the two extremes seems endless.

As with the annual report, the format for the interim report is dictated by objectives (including marketing objectives). The shape and format of the report are determined in precisely the same way as for the annual report. The same questions about objectives and target audiences are asked, and, except where there is a significant change in the circumstances under which the company functions, the answers should be essentially the same as those for the annual report. Naturally, in any fast-moving company these objectives will alter slightly from report to report as different problems arise. Nevertheless, there should be some measure of consistency springing from the last annual report, in both content and graphic look.

Considering the fact that for most corporations the interim report represents one of the few opportunities during the year to demonstrate the company's condition in print, and to reach shareholders and prospective shareholders with current information, it seems sensible to include as much as is feasible. The report should include at least the following:

- The unaudited quarterly results. This includes not only sales and net earnings (broken out by lines of business), and net earnings per share, but any other financial information that is available at that point. This may include changes in cash position, changes in inventory, cost of sales, income before taxes, average number of shares outstanding—in fact, any pertinent financial information. Figures should be given both for the current quarter and the comparable quarter for the prior year. Percentage differences should be shown.

- Sales and earnings, broken down by line, or division, where applicable, consistent with the 10-K breakdown. Many companies show results by group, using a bar graph. Many also report backlog by group for the quarter.

- A cash flow statement and a sources and applications statement.

- Second- and third-quarter reports with both the current quarter and the six- and nine-month totals, both current and previous year.

- An abbreviated—but not a sparse—unaudited balance sheet.

- The balance sheet as of the close of the quarter, shown against the balance sheet for the fiscal year end.

- Because it's proving to be of such great value in analysis, and is also valuable to give a better picture of the company as dynamic, rather than static, an increasing number of companies are reporting, in addition to quarterly figures, figures for the trailing twelve months—the last four full quarters ending with the current quarter. This serves to put operations in proper and preferred perspective, instead of freezing the view of the company as just its last quarter of the current year. Many companies also include the figures for the last full fiscal year.

- The president's message should be as well thought out and almost as inclusive as it was in the annual report. In an active company, the events of any three-month period should be extensive and worthy of full reporting, including any update of goals and measures of performance against previously stated goals.

  It should also be remembered that the quarterly report should represent a full view of the company, without the necessity of having to refer back to the annual report, except for greater detail. The interim report will, for many of its readers, be the first document seen on the company. It should be sufficiently detailed and interesting to encourage readers to want to investigate further.

- If the use of graphs is appropriate for the annual report, it is just as appropriate for the interim report.

- The interim report is a useful vehicle for focusing on a single aspect of the company's operations with the kind of detail not normally found in the annual report. Some companies devote each issue to a biography of each of the key officers and operating divisional heads, with a description of his or her responsibilities, and a report on his or her performance since assuming the position. Some companies use each issue of the interim report to describe a product, its markets, its performance, and its potential.

In addition to favoring an auditor's review of the quarterly report, the SEC is pressing for more information, which may ultimately be mandatory. While the SEC's immediate concern is with the quarterly Form 10-Q, it seems reasonable to go beyond that to include the same information in the report to shareholders. They are also proposing that the annual 10-K and the quarterly 10-Qs reconcile significant differences between performance reported quarterly and annually. The trend seems to be to make the quarterly requirements much like those for the annual.

Typical of the problems these proposals seek to avoid is seen in the case of CNA Financial Corp. CNA reported, one year, that its first six months' earnings were the second highest in its history. It then showed a loss in the third quarter. At year end, it showed a twelve month loss of $79 million. It seems that in the first half of the year they had neglected to report to shareholders that a subsidiary was in deep trouble.

While the elements described seem to be profuse, the most germane of them can be included in a well-planned interim report without its becoming elaborate and expensive. Physically, it should be designed to fit in a standard letter-sized No. 10 envelope, unless it's an increasingly popular self-mailer. Unusual shapes and formats are not only expensive to produce, but require specially designed and expensive envelopes.

Some reports include summaries of presentations before security analysts groups. Others include a summary of the presentation before the annual shareholders meeting, with significant questions and answers.

Some companies, to maintain consistency with the annual report, use the same cover photograph from the annual report—or at least, the same graphic family feel—for each of that year's interim reports. Some companies also change the color of each quarterly, to help distinguish one from the other quickly. This clearly adds to the marketing aspects of the report.

One other interesting use of an interim report, particularly one filled with facts and reporting excellent results, is as a prospecting piece to broaden the base of interest in a company within the financial community. The interim report, which is infinitely less expensive than the annual report, can be mailed, with a self-addressed return postcard, to a larger, carefully selected list of analysts, brokers, money managers, and so on, than are normally included on the company's mailing list. This group can be all the analysts in a geographical area, or all the analysts covering a particular industry, or covering companies of a specific size, or other common financial specifications. The postcard indicates that the report is being mailed to them for their information, and the card should be returned if the recipient has any interest in receiving further material about the company. This invariably develops pockets of interest not formerly identified.

Corporate Advertising

Corporate advertising is a controversial subject. It takes many forms, ranging from a full-page ad in *The Wall Street Journal* extolling the virtues of the company, to participation in special editions of newspapers or magazines to advertise the availability of the annual report. Very large companies sometimes use television and radio as a corporate advertising medium.

Advertising, thoughtfully done, can be effective, although there are as many negatives as positives for it.

Corporate advertising is expensive, and should be viewed very carefully in terms of effectiveness. In 1989, corporate advertising expenditures exceeded $1 billion. The overall effectiveness of any kind of advertising is not the question here, except that there are very few publications in which everyone who sees the ad is a prospective customer. In corporate advertising the same problem exists, particularly institutional advertising—"Our company does great things." If the purpose of corporate advertising is to engender a favorable attitude on the part of the shareholders or potential investors, a very narrow view of that purpose must prevail.

In advertising to the financial community, it must be recognized that, first of all, there is a kind of inherent cynicism with which the company is viewed, predicated on some tangible facts about the company's performance. No company that's performing poorly is going to be loved by shareholders no matter how adorable is the advertising program. In fact, there is likely to be a contrary effect, since shareholders can calculate how much advertising costs.

While it's true that the overall psychological effect of large-scale advertising will still serve to focus attention on the company, a judgment must be made as to whether the contribution the advertising makes is sufficient to warrant the cost. In some cases the answer is favorable. It's difficult to imagine, though, that a small or medium-sized company with stock that's not performing well, even if it is undervalued, will accomplish a great deal in proportion to the cost of advertising. The same amount of money put into other aspects of financial relations will be infinitely more effective.

As is the case in all advertising, it's difficult to measure the contribution made by corporate advertising, particularly in relationship to its price. Certainly there is one basic factor that may be overlooked in any advertising. Success is a function of repetition and a total marketing program. Rarely does any single ad make sufficient impact to stand alone without the support of additional advertising or other promotional efforts. It's one thing for a major corporation such as Mobil or General Electric to take a full-page ad in *The Wall Street Journal* to sing of its corporate virtues or to announce its latest financial results. These companies are already well known and are supported by a consistent program that keeps their visibility high. It's yet another thing for a small company with no consumer brand-name franchise, such as Total Assets Protection, to buy an ad one time. It will be overlooked and forgotten.

Furthermore, the use of advertising by a small company to sing the praises of its latest financial results is an expensive buckshot load. With few exceptions, the number of people in the financial community who are concerned about a company to the point of doing anything effective about it is limited. Very few advertising media focus that intensively on an audience (although that number is growing), and so even in the smaller financial publications the likelihood is that the ad will be seen by many more people than can possibly be interested. When the ad is priced on a dollar per reader basis, it turns out to be very expensive indeed.

It can be argued that this kind of advertising reaches individual investors. However, there is a serious question as to the sources of information for judgment by individual investors. Will a person with $5000 to invest in the stock market read an ad reporting the financial results of a company or extolling the virtues of capitalism and then, without considerable consultation with his or her broker, invest money in that stock?

There have been studies, in recent years, that claim to prove that corporate advertising has a measurable effect on stock prices. It's a dubious assumption that's at best self-serving to the advertising industry.

This is not to say that some advertising can't be effective. Sometimes, local-response advertising is useful in getting leads to interested brokers.

Advertising can be useful in a total marketing context in which it's one of several elements designed to reach an investing public. Some ads are better than others, particularly those that are intelligently thought out, that have clear objectives, that genuinely distinguish a company. Professional advertising people do know things that make one ad better than another. For example, an ad campaign that addresses a specific theme consistently will eventually portray an impression about the company. An ad that offers something, such as an annual report, and asks for a response, seems to make a better impression than one that doesn't.

The same kind of judgment must be applied to annual report advertising. Sometimes it's useful for a larger company to summarize a favorable annual report in an ad. But again, the judgment must be made on the basis of cost versus results. Unfortunately, corporate advertising seems to be an easy way to tell the company's story. This is deceptive, because very little corporate advertising is effective on a one-time basis. Certainly no small or medium-sized company should expect miracles from a one-time ad without either a specific offer or repetition.

Advertising the availability of an annual report, either alone or as part of a large cooperative arrangement in a special section of a publication, is sometimes useful in developing broader interest—if care is taken in selecting the medium. But there is a hidden cost in this kind of advertising, which advertising space salesmen frequently neglect to mention. That's the cost of the reports themselves in the quantity usually necessary for distribution in response to ads. Annual reports can cost as much as $3 to $5 per copy or more, plus mailing. A successful ad in a major business publication can produce requests for thousands of annual reports. And if the people who make these requests are added to the mailing list, this can become tremendously expensive, since each name on a mailing list can cost the company as much as $25 a year in material, labor, and postage. Certainly, any report mailed out in response to an advertising request should include a self-addressed return postcard that attempts to ascertain the continuing interest of the inquirer.

Unfortunately, cooperative ads make it remarkably easy for the reader to request reports for a company in which one has only a casual interest.

Another word of caution. Under New York Stock Exchange regulations, listed companies are required to give sufficient copies to firms with holders in Street names to distribute to those holders. Some firms charge for that service. Caution is advised here. Scams have been uncovered in which payment was made, but reports weren't delivered. While not usually a problem when established firms are involved, payment shouldn't be made for a service regarding annual reports without very careful checking.

Advertising news releases, which some publications include in both full and summary form, can be an effective adjunct to an investor relations program. An element of their success resides in the prestige of the publications in which they appear. In highly specialized publications, such as *Barron's,* the readership is much more clearly identifiable than it is for the general business publications, and requests for information or reports are more likely to come from serious and qualified prospective investors. It's also useful, at times, for companies whose service is sold to other businesses. In this case, the release or annual report is being read not only by prospective investors but by prospective customers as well.

If it were possible to analyze the names of those who request information in response to an ad against transfer sheets, to determine the number of inquirers who ultimately become shareholders, the likelihood is that the company will conclude that the cost is not equal to the result. And since so many shareholders make their purchase in Street name, this kind of research is virtually impossible to do accurately.

Only clearly identified investment pros should be kept on the list, if possible. The list should be culled periodically to eliminate nonpotential investors, such as investment bankers, librarians, suppliers, and so forth. On the other hand, keep individual investors and others you judge to be of direct value to the company. Today's computerized mailing lists make it easier to track individuals, and the technology continues to improve. More and more companies are going directly to end users—the individual stock buyers. After two years, if these individuals turn out not to have converted to shareholders, they can be removed from the list.

But the true value of corporate advertising as an investor relations tool, except for the larger company that backs the advertising with a great many other activities, remains murky. There are times when a good local ad in the financial section of a newspaper, or in a financial journal, will develop leads from brokers and analysts, and that alone may warrant using advertising sparingly. But unfortunately there are many more opinions and myths about the validity of corporate advertising to the investment community than there are facts to sustain arguments in favor of it.

Advertising doesn't have a large place in investor relations at this time, although that may change. The rule, then, in corporate advertising, is not to do it unless there is a clear and realistic picture of potential return on the advertising dollar; make it pay its way.

The Financial Corporate Profile

An effective device for reaching the financial community is the company-prepared financial profile—a succinct summary of the pertinent operating, environmental and financial information needed by analysts and other professional investors to understand and evaluate a company. While in many respects the background report is similar in form to the research report prepared by analysts, it is by no means the same thing, nor should it purport to be. It should be clearly identified on the front cover as having been prepared by or for the company. It should not render an opinion that might be construed as part of an offer to sell stock. This would be illegal.

The purpose of this report is to summarize and focus, in professional form, most of that essential data that analysts and investors must search out before they can judge a company. It differs from the annual report in that its format is much more succinct and objective, and is much more in the form preferred by investment professionals themselves. The annual report is a more elaborate document, and puts forth the company's subjective view of itself and its programs. The financial profile is a more balanced document, in that it presents, objectively, those aspects of the company that are specifically meaningful to prospective investors. It is cast to help the company better compete for the investor's dollar. It costs considerably less to produce than does the annual report, and can be more widely distributed. Size is not of the essence; content is. It can be as much as 24 to 28 pages (most are 12 to 16 pages), so long as it sustains interest and enthusiasm for the company and its future. Smaller brokerage houses find it particularly useful, because it cuts costs in research reports by reducing analysts' research time.

The genesis of the modern, dynamic financial profile is virtually the history of investor relations. In its earliest forms, it was a tentative (and even considered presumptuous, by some) attempt to present basic financial data to analysts. It eventually became the financial fact book—a dry compendium of facts and figures, mostly financial, about the company. It emerged in its current form as a competitive marketing tool, in large measure because smaller companies didn't have the breadth of impressive financial data to produce an elaborate fact book. It also became apparent that numbers don't speak for themselves to the contemporary analyst or professional investor, and so the smaller narrative form was developed to lend perspective to the numbers. Its value and success led to more elaborate and, ultimately, more useful documents. It is now, for many, the mainstay of the investor relations marketing effort, because when it's well done, it's the most intimate look at the company and its management.

Primarily, in addition to the basic financial data, the report contains a brief summary of the company's position in its industry, a description of its business, a statement of management goals, an account of its recent performance in the market, a description of recent significant events, a description of some of the problems the company has faced and over-come—or is facing and how it is overcoming them—a discussion of compe-tition, a list of market makers and available brokerage house research reports, and a brief description of management.

It attempts to focus on the Unique Investment Premise. And signifi-cantly, it's a dynamic document, presenting the essence of the company as a live, moving, growing, and competitive entity.

Typically, a Profile might note that "management's goal is to reach a 19 percent return on equity," and report that "return on equity has risen from 12 percent to 16 percent during the past three years," and that using an analyst's formulas, "the company plans to go from 16 percent to 19 percent in the next year or two by a combination of increasing sales, increasing gross margins, reduced expenses, and a little leveraging, while maintaining the same plow-back ratio on earnings." The Profile might then use finan-cial formulas to illustrate management's expectations about how these numbers might fit together in the future to produce the 19 percent. It would be noted that this statement is a hypothetical financial exercise illustrating how management might meet its target, and not a projection or a promise. It's an active profile because it's written in active language about operations in motion, and it involves both the investor and manage-ment in actively communicating through a dynamic discussion.

For the reader of the document to feel that the company is one that's clearly understood, and certainly well worth investing in, management must speak to investors about not only the company's current position (including the following year), but its longer-range future as well. What are the strategic plans for the next three to five years? What programs are in place to attain that goal? What are the contingency plans to deal with radical changes in the economy, or industry, or competition? How does management view its markets for products or services, both domestically and globally? How does management see—and relate to—the capital mar-kets—both domestic and global? How does management interpret its own numbers? What are its financial targets, both near and long term?

At the same time, the raw facts—the numbers and other company and industry information—must be presented in a format consistent with current needs of investment professionals.

The Profile is used as part of the kit of materials given to investment professionals who attend meetings, or is mailed to investment professionals, both those who follow the company and those who can be persuaded to follow and invest in it. Because of its terse presentation of facts and management opinions, many investment professionals find it more useful than the annual report, not only as a research document and supplement to the annual report, but, in the case of those who have not been hitherto exposed to the company, as a primary tool in determining the degree to which they might ultimately become interested.

The Profile, as well as the classic fact books, are frequently printed as a supplement to the annual report, although they can be issued separately. In fact, the Profile usually updates the annual report by including data and financial information developed since the annual report was published.

The danger inherent in a fact book (as compared to a Profile) is the potential for overkill—for producing a booklet that's more elaborate than is warranted, and one that tells the reader more than he or she wants to know. The Profile is a marketing document in the form of a reference tool, and like the fact book, must not be so elaborate or obtuse that it's difficult to get to the facts.

Printed Material

Printed materials including the annual and interim reports, reprints of significant press articles, reprints of speeches and information folders on significant new products, are useful tools in keeping investment professionals informed of a company's progress. This material is not only distributed directly to analysts and brokers at meetings or in person, but most of it should be mailed to them at regular intervals.

Also to be mailed or faxed regularly to key investment professionals are copies of any financial news releases as soon as possible after they are issued by the company. Analysts frequently ask that releases be sent to them as soon as possible, either by fax or a commercial wire service. It shouldn't be assumed that any investment professional has seen or retained material about the company that's appeared on the Dow Jones, Reuters, or any other news service. In many cases the analyst will not have seen it at all on the wire. In other cases he or she will have seen it only fleetingly, when his or her mind was on something else. In some of the larger houses there may be several people interested in the company and only one easily available copy of the Dow Jones or Reuters tape. By mailing the investment professional a copy of the actual release, he or she can focus on it and retain it for his or her own files.

Television and Other Media

There's a growing use of videotape, closed circuit television meetings, and cable television business news programs. Annual meetings, annual reports, and discussions for investors particularly lend themselves to this kind of treatment, and have the advantage of giving dimensions to presentations. They are not inexpensive, however, and should be viewed in terms of the benefits, against cost, including duplication and distribution.

A growing number of companies are building in-house video capabilities, which they use for training and other purposes, including investor relations. If a company uses the facilities often enough, it can easily offset the initial cost.

Mailing Lists

As marketing concepts become more firmly entrenched in investor relations, the classic mailing list becomes a *database.* The difference is that the mailing list is a collection of names and addresses. The database contains considerably more information, such as ranges of size of companies an investor follows, investment interest, personal information, response record, and so forth. Moreover, the database can be accessed in many different ways—sorted by name or location or interest. This makes it possible to pinpoint a particular target group, narrowed down to surprisingly focused parameters. This makes it possible, using the computer, to bring niche or segmented marketing to investor relations. More and more companies are doing that now. Some are into database marketing, in which the database is used for market segmentation. As these techniques are refined, market segmentation should increase in popularity.

Nevertheless, the classic mailing list is still at the core of the database. And considering the amount of material that a corporation sends to each person on a mailing list in the course of a year—the annual report, quarterly reports, releases, and so on—the cost can easily mount drastically. For companies that accumulate names on mailing lists without ever reviewing the list, the cost can become exorbitant. It's essential that mailing lists be reviewed at least annually, and certainly every six months is better. Changes must be made immediately as information comes in, such as in returned mail. Returned mail, incidentally, carries important notations that can help you update your list. Check the post office for translations. Unfortunately, not all undeliverable mail is returned.

Lists are built in several ways. The basic press list is easily derived from several directories (see Appendix 12), from experience, and from discussions with management. Financial community lists can be put together from directories, such as Nelson's and the membership list of the Financial Analysts Federation, from institutional fact books developed internally for the company, from analysts and brokers who have phoned or written in to inquire about the company, and from lists of people who have attended meetings. Other names are added as a result of random inquiries and requests for information about the company from shareholders and prospective investors. In some cases the company has advertised the availability of its annual report or run its news releases as paid advertising, and has added the names of those responding to the list.

Every major financial relations firm and every major financial mailing house maintains general lists of the financial press and the financial community, usually with the financial community categorized by specialty of industry interest (apparel, energy, auto, construction, high technology, etc.). Computers speed the process, but computers must be fed correct information by people. There are a number of services specializing in selling this information to investor relations professionals.

There are serious concerns with mailing lists which, in view of the frequency of changes and the high cost of mailing, require considerable attention. Mailing lists are the nuisance of the investor relations industry. They are a basic tool that must be kept honed, and yet they require attention far out of proportion to the total role they play in a financial relations program. Some of the significant problems of mailing lists are:

- The turnover in the financial community is horrendous. A comparison between the Financial Analyst Federation Directories from any one year to the next would show a startlingly high turnover of names and addresses. Analysts and brokers leave the business and change jobs with great frequency, and rarely a day passes without at least half a dozen changes.

- The turnover in the financial press, though not as frequent, still exists to a very large degree. Press people change jobs, leave or enter industry, or change assignment at a very high rate.

- In the past several years the number of brokerage houses that have merged or gone out of business completely is, as has been noted, startlingly high.

- Professional investors' interests change. An analyst who has been following electronics may switch to diversified companies. A broker may no longer be interested in following a particular company for any number of reasons, ranging from the size of the company, to its listing, to his or her own impression that the company's performance no longer warrants his or her interest, and so on.

- Many individuals inquire about a company on a random basis or out of curiosity, and once their curiosity is satisfied they are no longer interested.

- Shareholders who are sufficiently interested in following a company closely will ask to be put on the mailing list for news releases not ordinarily sent to shareholders, and then sometimes sell their holdings and cease to be interested in the company.

The point is that it's very easy to add a name to a list and very difficult to find a basis for removing it. Computers help, but still need human input.

The standard practice in the industry, in periodically weeding out lists, is to take three steps:

- Amend the list upon any indication of change, such as a returned envelope or a news announcement about an individual's reassignment.

- Review the list frequently to eliminate those individuals known to be no longer interested or those firms known to have merged or gone out of business.

- Periodically include in a mailing a stamped self-addressed return postcard. The return of these postcards is never more than ten percent. Failure to return the card with any indication one way or the other, then, cannot be construed as a reason to remove a name from a list. Of those postcards returned, a small percentage will indicate that they are no longer interested in receiving material on the company. These names should be removed from the list, although they should be reviewed to determine whether any of the individuals are sufficiently important to the company to warrant a follow-up phone call to determine the reasons for the lack of interest, or to try to convince him or her to remain on the list. Another portion of the cards will indicate changes of address. And the largest portion of cards will simply reaffirm interest.

A question arises as to whether firms should be included on the list if there is no specific name. A sensible solution might be that if you believe that the firm you're mailing to is small enough so that the material will be seen by someone valuable to you, then by all means send it. Or you might call and ask. In larger companies, mailing to the company without a specific name is a waste. Considering the high cost of mailing, it pays to be selective. For example, should research departments or libraries of brokerage firms be included on lists? In most cases the answer is yes, since these files are central reference points for individual research people. On the other hand, should business school libraries be included on the list? Here the question of purpose comes into play. If there is any notion that the interest on the part of the school is for its own investment portfolio, then obviously the answer is yes. If the school librarian appears to be just building files for the sake of files, the answer is no.

There is a scam you should be aware of. There are charlatans who request large quantities of materials, ostensibly for mailing to shareholders or other interested (but unspecified) investors. You then receive a bill for this re-delivery service, which probably never took place. These firms, usually just a mail drop, are careful to bill less than $100, the amount at which most corporations don't bother to check invoices. One warning sign is the invoice with no phone number. The Society of Corporate Secretaries has lists of known fakers, as do some investor relations professionals.

The Financial Press

The financial press, which is dealt with in detail in the next chapter, is a significant means of communication with all segments of the financial community. It serves three purposes. The first is to impart up-to-date information. The second is to afford an independent editorial view of the company. The third and, in a way, most significant value of the financial press is that it's a powerful weapon in the competition for attention. Obviously a company that's written about in public print with some measure of frequency is better known, and an object of greater attention, than one which is not. Where appropriate, financial publicity should be sought in the most expert and assiduous way possible.

While many of the devices used to communicate to the professional investment community parallel those used to communicate to shareholders, the approach is generally more technical for the investment professional. Still, no marketing program to investment professionals is complete without a constant flow of printed information to those in a position to help a company compete in the capital markets.

5

The Financial and Business Press

The financial and business press is the major conduit of news about companies. No view of the press and its role in investor relations can begin without an attempt to understand, first, what news is, and second, how news really affects the capital markets.

What Is News?

All news is relative. Every day the editor of even the smallest newspaper must review all reported events of that day and make a subjective judgment as to which of them will concern or interest his readers sufficiently to warrant the allocation of rare and precious space. On any given day the news of the bankruptcy of a company of, say, the proportions of an Eastern Airlines will garner more editorial interest than will the news of a very large privately held company selling shares of its stock to the public. This in turn will preempt in importance the decision of a company to build a $10 million plant. And this in turn will preempt the news of record earnings for a $25 million company (unless the company is the major industry of a small town in which its success or failure affects a great many local jobs). Lower down on the list is the appointment of a new vice-president. *Yet sometimes, if not very much has happened in town that day, the news of a joint venture between two relatively small companies may be the most exciting thing the newspaper has to report as business news.*

Even feature material—background or general interest stories about a company or its individuals, and material that's not as time-sensitive as a press release—has its editorial stringencies. For all but the least consequential of the business publications, even the feature story must have its news hook—a fresh basis for writing it.

News and Target Audiences

Moreover, every segment of the press, financial and nonfinancial, has its own target audiences and therefore its own point of view—its own definition of news. For example, *Fortune* magazine's audience is managers. It considers itself a service book for managers, telling them how trends in the economy and society will influence their businesses. Its goal, say its editors, is to deliver the stories that count to constructively influence the strategies and actions of its readers.

Business Week, on the other hand, is a news-oriented publication, although as a weekly it has the time to go beneath the news to get at the heart of the story, and to put it into context with both industry and the economy.

Barron's prefers to update current knowledge and thinking about entire industries, new schools of thought about finance and the stock market based upon recent information or theories, or, in its occasional looks at individual companies, how the company relates to an industry and where the industry is going. Because of its stock market orientation (as opposed to *Business Week*'s industrial and commercial news orientation), *Barron's* prefers to have a research report on any company it does an article about.

Both *The New York Times* and *The Wall Street Journal* report general business news. But *The New York Times,* even with its expanded business news coverage, must necessarily deal primarily with major economic news or very important stories about companies. This doesn't entirely preclude coverage of smaller companies, if space (or the nature of the story) permits on any given day. While *The New York Times* is considered to be the newspaper of record, it is not necessarily the newspaper of business record, since its limited coverage cannot possibly cover as much as *The Wall Street Journal.* In recent years, it has substantially increased its coverage of business, and it is now undoubtedly the best in the country among daily newspapers.

The Wall Street Journal, on the other hand, covers reports of individual companies much more extensively. It, too, has limited space, and neither *The New York Times* nor *The Wall Street Journal* will run any but the most earthshaking stories on any domestic company whose stock is not quoted regularly in their stock tables. The *Journal,* like the *Times,* effectively covers broad economic news that it thinks will serve as a background for understanding the total economic picture at any given moment. The *Journal* occasionally reports material of a tangential nature to business that touches the economic news in ways that are somewhat mystical, but interesting. It also covers general news very briefly, and predominantly as its editors feel it serves as a background for understanding the economy. Its relatively new three-section breakdown allows it to broaden coverage, and to increase features, including more financial information.

The business news that makes the nonbusiness sections of the press is news of either a magnitude that affects the economy at large, such as the Exxon-Valdez, Alaska oil spill, or scandal and crime, such as the recent insider-trading scandals. Another example is the Ford Motor Company's acquisition of Jaguar, which made the front pages both for the size and importance of the transaction. Foreign acquisition of American companies and property, such as the Japanese acquisition of Rockefeller Center and the Canadian ownership of large American retail chains, are very much on the front pages of newspapers today.

Part of the problem in reporting business news lies in the fact that most business reporters—both good and bad—have very little business training. With exceptions, they come to business journalism from the general news side of the press, rather than from business. The increasing business coverage seems to be changing that to some extent, and more reporters with MBAs are being hired by major papers, such as *The New York Times*. While there are many good and astute business news reporters, and they are increasing in number, there are still a great many whose understanding of business and finance is shallow and superficial. There are, for example, very few really good investigative reporters, although there is a trend toward increasing their number. Those who do exist function for just a few major newspapers and business and financial publications and cable companies. Generally, the state of reporting business news in the press— including radio and television—is improving, although it's still far from ideal. There are now dedicated national and local business programs on cable and the networks, and both print and broadcast media are bolstering their news staffs with good business journalists.

Considering all factors, then, a review of the total spectrum of all business publications would make it very difficult indeed to produce a definition of news that would be applicable across the board—that meets the criteria of all publications.

How News Affects the Stock Market

A second and perhaps more significant aspect of news is the way in which it affects the capital markets. The news that United Airlines employees failed to raise enough capital to buy the airline was enough to trigger a major drop in the market in one day. Every time the prime rate hits a new high, or drops a fraction, the market reacts. And the market seems to react to every election, regardless of which party wins.

One thing is certain. The market the stock market as well as all other money markets—does respond to news.

In their excellent book on the subject, *News and the Market,* Frederick C. Klein and John A. Prestbo, two *Wall Street Journal* reporters, explored that relationship in great detail. They say, "It certainly makes sense to believe that the stock market responds to the news. Movements of the market as a whole and of the stocks that make it up spring from the decisions of thousands of investors. These people, be they steely-eyed fund managers on Wall Street or little old ladies in Dubuque—read the newspapers, watch television and so on, and presumably are affected by what they see and hear. If the United States economy seems to be functioning smoothly, it stands to reason that they will feel well disposed towards sharing in the bounty. If the opposite conditions obtain, a bank account or hole in the ground might seem more secure."

And *The Wall Street Journal* found itself having to recognize the effect of publicity on the market when it had to qualify the results of its popular feature, *The Investment Dartboard,* when it found that results were skewed by publicity in its own column for the stocks picked by the experts. On publication days for the column, they found, stocks featured in the *Investment Dartboard* column rose an average of nearly 3.5 percentage points relative to the Big Board index. On the following days, the *Journal* reported, there was an after-effect as those stocks continued to rise slightly.

In his popular book, *A Random Walk on Wall Street,* Princeton Professor Burton Malkiel covers many theories of stock market analysis and relates virtually all significant stock movement to news. Both books deal with time lag—the time between the reporting of news and the reaction to it in the stock market—an extremely important factor. The company issues a quarterly release that shows earnings lower than those of the same period for the prior year. The stock shows no motion or perhaps even advances a little. This frequently means that the market has anticipated the reduced earnings and sold off in proportion to them, or that the reduction is smaller than had been anticipated and that other events, or a new outlook, warrant stock purchase. The important thing is that all segments of the capital markets, from the individual investor to the manager of a major fund or trust department to the lending officer of a bank, are responsive to news.

Malkiel dealt with the "efficient market" theory, a basis of which is that the entire market is privy to the same information and so reacts accordingly as one. Critics point out, however, that the market isn't universally privy to the same news, particularly in smaller companies (which is why we frequently have a two-tier market), and not everybody interprets the same news in the same way.

How News Is Received by the
Financial Community

What is harder to fathom is the way in which any news—and all news—will be received by the financial community.

First, it should be recognized that since news itself is relative, most news is viewed in a total context. Nothing is absolute. A report of an FTC decree to divest a division is bad news if the division is profitable, and not such bad news if the division isn't. (It can be argued that no order to divest is absolutely good news; if it takes an FTC decree to get a company to unload an unprofitable division, then certainly a closer look at the company's total operations is warranted.)

Second, it must be recognized that the nature of the capital markets is such that because of mass psychology, there is never a reaction to news (particularly if it's not anticipated)—there is only an overreaction. Again, the market is *people,* and the reaction is a human, not a mechanical, one. The market almost invariably recoils at bad news in anticipation of the worst possible consequences. It's just as likely to overreact, in a burst of optimism, in the other direction at the announcement of good news. The problem is that the overreaction is immediate, and the adjustment to reality, if it comes, is slower, sometimes barely perceptible in the short range, and frequently spread over time.

Beyond that, the reaction depends as much upon the type of news as the news itself. Some events, for example, are anticipated and then discounted by the market. While it can be tremendously frustrating to a company president to announce record earnings for a quarter or a year only to see virtually no reaction in his stock—or perhaps a reaction on the down side—the fact is that his earnings have probably been anticipated by those who follow the company. Then the announcement itself is not news at all, but merely an affirmation of what had been anticipated. This, incidentally, is part of the problem with projecting earnings. If analysts anticipate earnings of $1.50, they predicate their recommendations on that. When earnings of $1.50 are announced, the effect of the earnings on the price of the stock has already been taken into consideration, and, in effect, the good news is no news at all. If the analysts have anticipated and projected earnings of $1.50 and the actual figure comes out to be $1.45, this can be a disappointment, with an adverse effect on the stock price, even though the $1.45 may be a record. Nobody ever said the market was rational.

Even this is an oversimplification. Since the news of record earnings can be qualified by other factors, such as an understanding that the earnings are derived from inventory profits and not improved operations, analysts know that the high earnings are not an accurate reflection of the company's performance.

Spin Control

News, then, is never quite pure and simple. It's always qualified by other factors. This, too, is a basic reason why news cannot and should not be manipulated by slanting, distorting, or withholding information—the infamous *spin control*. There tends to be further analysis and adjustment within a day or two, the truth emerges, and there is a loss of credibility that adversely touches all company announcements for a considerable time to come. Credibility cannot be overemphasized as a major factor in all relations with the financial community.

The straightforward announcement of even the most favorable news, then, doesn't of itself always offer a clean-cut cause and effect in terms of the capital markets.

It must be recognized that, except for very large companies, or companies of any size that for one reason or another are constantly in the news, no single news announcement is going to make much of a dent on the financial community, other than with those individuals who are already interested in the company. While it's always possible that a single startling announcement about a company that's not widely known will attract someone's eye and engender an interest, it's merely the beginning of a process of investigation for this person. It's not likely that an investor of consequence will read a salutary piece of news about a company that he or she knows little of and make an investment decision on the basis of that announcement—even if it reports a cure for the common cold. It may cause the investor to investigate further. But between the announcement of the news and the investment decision, there is a considerable amount of investigation.

This is not the case with the better known company, to which each news announcement adds one more fact to what's already understood. And being better known and understood by investors and investment professionals is, of course, a major value of disseminating news about a company.

Categories of News

Seeing news and its relationship to the capital markets in this context is absolutely essential in formulating an approach to the news media. News generally breaks down as follows:

- *General news.* This may appear on the surface to have no relationship to buying and selling 100 shares of the stock of a small over-the-counter company, or of a bank's lending a small company $200,000 to buy a new machine, and yet it clearly sets a context for judging the ultimate economic reaction to that news. It's not difficult to see the signing of a peace treaty in the Middle East in terms of its meaning in international oil affairs. Obviously, the attempted assassination of a president or a prime minister has economic implications.

- *General economic news.* This more readily poses the background for judging general economic performance. Raging inflation or deflation. An increase or decrease in interest rates. The devaluation or appreciation of the dollar. Or even more specifically, news of changes in the financial markets themselves, such as the attacks on program trading, or changes in banking regulations that permit banks greater latitude in selling securities. Or certainly, the activities in the control of supply of money by the Federal Reserve Bank.

    But these are news events over which few business people have control. Affected as anyone might be by the nature of events that make this kind of news, few business people as individuals are in a position to influence vast sweeping activities, the results of which affect the overall course of commerce. There are exceptions, of course. A business person in a lawsuit, for example, may obtain a decision that has consequences reaching farther than his or her own company. And it's also true that it's usually just a few individuals that are behind events of such magnitude as insider trading, or the Canadian inroads into American retailing. But there are rare occasions when an individual corporation or executive can affect such events by design.

- *Specific business news.* This is news that pertains to the activities of a company or industry. It concerns the reader as a business person and investor, and interests the nonbusiness reader as background to generally understanding the economy.

News-making Activities

There are a large number of newsmaking activities that come within the purview of the individual corporation:

- *The front-page news story.* When the savings and loan problem became a federal bailout, involving taxpayers' money, the consequences were of such magnitude as to warrant its being extensively reported in all media on other than just the business pages. Individual S&Ls were singled out, and the stories brought the S&Ls to the forefront as examples of both the best and the worst of an industry. This is news by any definition. A merger of such giants as Time, Inc. and Warner is consequential news. If a major company decides to close down a very large plant, this can be considered to have consequences that could affect a larger portion of the economic community than just the company or the plant's community. General Motors' search for a community in which to locate its plant for its new Saturn car held the front pages for an extended period of time. And this kind of news need not be generated by large companies alone. A smaller company announcing that it plans to compete with a larger and more established company in a particular field is sometimes of consequence. And certainly when a relatively small software company sued the giant Microsoft for patent infringement, it was front-page news.

- *Major corporate news.* This includes important business news regarding a company or an industry. The company can be of any size. The magnitude of the event is measured in terms of the effect upon the general financial community. An unusual merger, an exceptionally high record earnings report, the appointment of a well-known public figure, from government or otherwise, as head of a company. Zenith selling off a major part of its business. The crumbling of the Trump empire. McDonnell-Douglas getting out of the parts of the computer business in which it was so powerful, or General Electric selling off its small appliance business, are cases in point.

- *Routine financial news.* The rules of disclosure, which dictate the kinds of information that must be disseminated, and the timing, under the regulations of the SEC and the exchanges will be dealt with in another chapter. Essentially the basic news that's of consequence is financial data—reports on latest financial results—and news of any activity or trends the results of which could possibly be construed as affecting the economic future of a company. While this category of news is vital to investors, and is almost invariably reported on the Dow Jones and Reuters news tickers (for at least those companies whose stocks are quoted on the main tables of *The Wall Street Journal*), its importance to the media and its coverage is dictated first by the size of the company and ultimately by media space considerations. Nevertheless, under the rules of disclosure the news must be released whether it is printed or not.

- *Lesser company news.* This is a category of news that tends to be more important to the company, the trade, a local community, or an industry than it is to the business editors of most major media. Fewer and fewer executive appointments are announced in the financial pages.

The New York Times has virtually eliminated such announcements of any officer lower than president unless the company is a giant or the individual is notable in some other capacity. This is not to say that these announcements—along with similar reports of new products, new plant, discontinued operations, backlogs, order rates, and so on—should not be reported. They have interest in areas other than the major news media. But the decision of a $25 million company to open a $1-million plant in the Midwest is not going to throw the financial editor of *The New York Times* into paroxysms of excitement. Yet, when Wells-Gardner, a $40 million Amex-listed Chicago-based electronics company, named a new president who was noteworthy in its industry, it earned a two-column story in the *Times.* Extra effort sometimes breaks molds.

- *Feature material.* This is the descriptive article about the company, its management, and its activities that appears in the range of business and financial journals that go from *Fortune* magazine—read by industry leaders—to the *Equities,* whose concentration on small over-the-counter companies tends to make it a favorite of investors in smaller companies. It ranges from a broad-based, well-researched, and elaborately detailed company profile to a few simple paragraphs describing the company's recent performance, and perhaps quoting authoritative sources, inside or outside the company, on the directions in which the company is moving. It ranges from the brief, perceptive, and frequently skeptical searching of the short article in *Forbes* to the succinct page or page and a half review of a company's newsworthy activity in *Business Week,* to a company profile in *Financial World,* to a terse half-column in *Time* or *Newsweek* reporting on a startling company event.

It should be noted, though, that as the business press becomes more experienced and knowledgeable, it falls prey less often to the old-fashioned puff piece—the shallow handout that does a cosmetic job. Today, the feature story must not only be related in some way to a recent or current event—the news hook—but it must deal as well with some unique aspect of corporate strategy that offers information and guidance to the business world. Today's business editor is coming to realize, too, that most often the company story is really the story of management. "More and more," said one *Fortune* editor, "we find that a General Motors story is really a Roger Smith story, and a Microsoft company story is really about Bill Gates." An example is a *Forbes* story about Patrick Petroleum, a small energy company, that discusses CEO Pat Patrick in the context of his company, rather than the other way around. The result was an excellent story about not just Patrick, but the company—and its survival and revival—as well.

The Salutary Effects of News

It's very easy to see that imparting news about any company can have several immediate salutary effects, even if the news is adverse.

- The news itself adds further information for the investment decision.
- News that openly discusses the company adds credibility to all company reports.
- The appearance of the news keeps the company name prominent in the minds of those who make investment or lending decisions—certainly important in an arena in which the competition is keen not only for capital, but for attention. This is perhaps the most significant point, since in the competition for capital those companies that are best known and understood are those likeliest to succeed.

The Audiences for News

There are actually two audiences for news. The first consists of those who already know the subject company, either as investors or potential investors, or as analysts or brokers following it for one reason or another. The second is the larger segment of the financial community. For this group, ordinary news falls on disinterested ears unless it's startling, or itself gives reason to warrant further investigation.

The feature material that appears in the wide range of business publications from *Fortune* magazine to the business section of the Sunday *New York Times* offers a distinctive point of view of a company. There's no question that frequent coverage makes a vast difference. With some 18,000 plus companies traded, obviously those that are better known get the greatest attention from the investment community. When two companies are performing equally well, the difference between the higher stock price or price/earnings ratio of one company as compared to another is a function of its being better known and understood by a broader segment of the investment community. For the better known company, the simplest positive news announcement will have beneficial results.

The broader reputation engendered by feature material can stem either from press recognition of the sheer brilliance or uniqueness of a company's performance, or it can just as validly be the result of an organized and carefully executed financial publicity program. In fact, the likelihood of the press discovering a superior company on its own, without the help of an investor relations or public relations professional, is negligible. No press staff, in any medium, is large enough, nor are that many reporters experienced enough, to discover companies serendipitously.

In any event, the result of press recognition is to draw attention to a company repeatedly. Repetition is absolutely essential. While a single press appearance of an announcement about a company may gladden the heart of its president, if it's isolated and the company has never been heard of before and is not heard of again, its effect on any segment of the financial community that's not directly involved with the company is fleeting.

There is another major distinction between the news announcement, such as the earnings report or the report of a merger, and the feature article in *Fortune, Forbes,* or *Business Week.* The news announcement may be required by the rules of disclosure of the SEC. As long as the company is large enough to be included in the stock tables of *The Wall Street Journal,* the likelihood is that the announcement will at least be carried over the Dow Jones and Reuters wire services and in the agate line listings in *The Wall Street Journal* and *The New York Times.* This should also be supplemented by fax, direct mail, and computer distribution from the company to investors, analysts, and prospective investors—not everybody you want to reach may be reading the paper that day—or by purchase arrangements for news releases to be published in the corporate reports sections of the several publications that carry them, such as *Barron's, Fortune, Investor's Daily, The Wall Street Transcript,* or the *OTC Review.*

In the case of publicity material, the fact of editorial judgment comes into play—and this remains the purview of the editor, not the subject of the news. The company may only beseech the editor. There is no effective external power beyond that, and the judgment of the editor who must serve the needs of his or her readers is paramount. We propose, but others dispose.

Aims of Financial Publicity

Nevertheless, the value of visibility through feature material is high and warrants the specific effort that must go into achieving it. Its ultimate aims are

- To achieve and sustain visibility for the company, its products or brands, and its activities
- To project the company's capabilities in ways that demonstrate its ultimate ability to appreciate the invested dollar
- To demonstrate specific capabilities about the company—its abilities to earn, the capabilities of its management, its research and de-

velopment, its future plans, its grasp of its industry and markets, its ability to control costs and ultimately increase its margin, and so forth

- To demonstrate the consistency of the company's performance, as well as the credibility of its management in the veracity of all its representations of the company in the past

It's rare that a company, by virtue of its positive performance alone, will generate sufficient interest to warrant ongoing and continuous appearances in the financial press. A company in trouble, if the trouble is flagrant and the effect of the trouble is significant enough to a large segment of the financial community, has no problem in getting itself broadly covered by the financial press. Witness Exxon and Eastern Airlines. Since few companies purposely generate this kind of interest, professional efforts must be used to discern those elements about the company and its operation that are consistently newsworthy and valuable to these publications. This material must be presented to the publications in rather specific ways. Financial publicity on a consistent basis is at least a hard sell, best performed by experts, with full knowledge of not only the techniques of dealing with the press, but the individual requirements of each publication. There should also be a basis of experience that warrants credibility with the press for the financial relations practitioner, as well as for the company he or she represents.

Working with the Press

Dealing with the financial press breaks down into the following specific segments:

- News released under the rules of disclosure of the SEC and the Exchanges
- Major news events beyond routine financial announcements
- Feature material
- Inquiries from, and stories originated by, the press

Disseminating Basic News

The general rules of disseminating basic material required to be disclosed are essentially simple and mechanical, yet if a professional approach is ignored, the effect will be sharply diminished.

Rules for Working with the Financial Press

In dealing with the financial press—or any press for that matter—some simple rules apply universally:

- The ultimate judgment of news value by the press is made by its editors. Even in those publications that cross the line that delineates news from advertising, the publisher knows that if his editorial content does not consistently interest readers, the number of readers will diminish, as well as credibility of his publication. This is invariably followed by a cutback in advertising revenue, which is inevitably followed by bankruptcy. A primary factor in any publication, then, is its editorial judgment.

- Each publication is predicated on a different editorial format—for example, *Fortune* magazine does not print routine earnings reports, *Barron's* rarely does personality pieces on corporate heads, and so on. The editorial point of view of every publication must be discerned and understood before any approach is made to it.

- Competition for news space is extraordinarily keen. Even though business news coverage is increasing in many newspapers, editors receive five and ten times as much news as they can possibly print. Therefore, the form of presentation of news to a publication is extremely important. It must attract attention for its essential news value in the shortest possible time. It must be in a format traditionally acceptable to publications. Wherever possible, it must be written in a journalistic style acceptable to most editors.

The rules of disclosure dictate that certain material shall be released as rapidly as is mechanically feasible. Information most frequently considered in this category is operating results, or any news about activities that may materially affect stock prices. This may include merger announcements, dividends, consequential changes in a company's business, divestiture, an important change in management, a new director, change in accountants or accounting principles, the discovery of a new mine or oil well, and so forth. The rules of disclosure are considered satisfied when this information is released, as soon as possible after it is known to management, to both the Dow Jones News Service and Reuters, plus the other major wires (AP and UPI), the company's major local newspapers, *The New York Times,* and the company's exchange or NASD and NASDAQ. What is essential is that the news is released through the broadest possible media spectrum reaching the largest number of investors or potential investors.

This is best achieved by the following procedure:

- *Simultaneous release,* by a PR wire service, computer, fax, telephone, or hand, to both Dow Jones and Reuters news services, as well as other required outlets. This is necessary because the two wire services are highly competitive and each is as important as the other. Neither likes to lose the advantage of time to the other and each is quick to say so. Simultaneous release is the simplest and fairest way, although in most instances Reuters will disseminate the news faster, because Dow Jones generally calls back to confirm the release.

- *Distribution via PR Newswire or Business Newswire.* PR Newswire Associates, Inc. is a private organization owned by Western Union with direct wires into every major financial publication in the United States, as well as the general wire services, general publications, and major brokerage houses. Business Newswire is the same kind of service, focusing primarily on business publications and brokerage firms. Both cover more than 2,000 brokerage houses and similar firms. There are also regional private wire services. Most wire services interface with others around the country. It's the fastest and most efficient way to disseminate news. Distribution to Dow Jones and Reuters, as well as to all other appropriate publications, is covered by PR Newswire and Business Newswire. The release may be sent to the commercial wires by fax, phone, or computer, or hand delivered. It takes them about an hour to service the material and move it out on their wires. You may want to follow up with Dow Jones and Reuters, if the news is particularly sensitive, to explain any nuances or background. The commercial newswires will service local bureaus first. They usually service the Dow Jones and Reuters New York headquarters too, if you specify any New York distribution—which is important to know because it may conflict with your own primary distribution to those services.

- *Hand delivery.* Depending upon the nature of the news, it's frequently a good idea to *hand deliver a copy of the release* to the business editor of the local newspaper. Notify the local editor that there's a Dow Jones or Reuters story or feature on your company. While he or she will ultimately receive the news from one of the wires, it's a courtesy editors appreciate.

  An example of how that works in practice may be seen in Wells-Gardner Corporation's investor relations consultant's following up a wire announcement by calling William Barnhart, assistant financial editor of the *Chicago Tribune,* and discussing the release with him (the stock had risen 33 percent that day). The result of the follow-up was a major feature that included a color photo. The Associated Press saw the feature and followed it with a major feature of its own.

  It's essential that news be distributed *early enough in the day* to warrant its being received by editors in the early morning for deadlines for the afternoon paper. The same is true of wire service distribution. Late releases may not make it through all the necessary distribution steps before market closing or by 5 P.M., after which readership drops off considerably.

- *Advance notice by phone.* In some cases, if you're known to the local editor, and you have more than run-of-the-mill news, it's not a bad idea to *call by phone* and alert him or her to the fact that the news is coming by wire or by hand. Considering the amount of news the editor must deal with on any given day, this call focuses attention on your news and can sometimes make the difference between its being printed or not. Issuing unfavorable earnings reports very late in the day or managing not to be prepared to release them until Friday (for Saturday's paper) is bad practice. In the first place, it's illegal to hold any news of that nature for one minute longer than is absolutely necessary for the broadest possible dissemination. Secondly, it fools no one. Bad news reverberates as urgently and as loudly as a firecracker in St. Patrick's Cathedral at high mass. And there are, of course, editors who will happily give a story that arrives in those circumstances more play than it would normally receive. For companies in trouble there is no place to hide.

Beyond meeting the needs of disclosure, there are now myriad ways of reaching the financial community beyond the wire services. Business Wire and others now serve the vast array of computer-accessed databases—CompuServe, DowPhone, NEXIS, Standard & Poor's, and more. PR Newswire serves Bloomberg Financial Markets, which covers more than 5,000 brokerage firm terminals. A service called *First Call* is doing an excellent job of maintaining an active database (material stays active for 90 days) of information for brokerage firms, including analysts' reports. Many fax services will take your release or report to brokerage houses and distribute your one copy to hundreds of outlets at one time. See Appendix 9 for a more complete list and description of these services. Electronic mail is fine—if the person you want to reach subscribes to the same service, and checks the electronic mailbox regularly.

A word of caution about electronic distribution, particularly through computer or fax. The information in a computer-accessed database is useful only if it's accessed by a user, which is why information that must be in the hands of a particular publication or individual should be backed up by phone or hand delivery. Fax poses a problem, in that many publications either don't make their fax number available, or change it every few weeks to avoid being inundated. Uninvited faxes are not always welcome—inquire before you send one to the press.

An earnings estimate or some other news of urgency can sometimes be given in an exclusive interview to one of Dow Jones's reporters, such as for use as a *Dow-Joneser*—an in-depth interview that appears on the wire and usually in the paper—or in *The Wall Street Journal* column "Heard on the Street." The decision to do this is based upon circumstances. The "Heard on the Street" column, for example, usually uses the material immediately and is very widely read. Frequently its news results in an almost immediate stock reaction. Not quite so immediate is a *Dow-Joneser*, where the lead time can be three or four days before the confirming release of the quarter's final figures, although ten days is preferred. Dow Jones usually prints these interviews within 24 to 48 hours, although it has taken as long as four days, which means that it must be done more than that far ahead of the figures (or other news) being ready for public distribution. While this does not strictly follow the procedure for broadest possible dissemination, it is considered sufficient disclosure by the SEC.

Following the dissemination of the news to the wires and other appropriate media, the release should then be mailed to analysts, brokers, the trade press, shareholders (if appropriate), and any other interested parties. It's extremely important to distribute the release—by fax or hand for daily press and key market makers and investors, and by mail to others—even to those segments of the financial press and the financial community that might have received it over the Dow Jones or Reuters wires. First of all, it's unlikely that Dow Jones or Reuters will have carried the release in its entirety, even though the commercial newswires will have done so. Second, there is no way to guarantee that the individual at either the publication or the Wall Street house you are interested in reaching will have seen it on the wire or have it on a terminal. Third, it gives a file copy to those individuals in both the financial community and in the press who are following the company. And fourth, it is one more opportunity to make the company name visible.

News Release Form

The form of news releases is deceptively simple. Properly done, it looks easy. Nevertheless, it requires a substantial measure of expertise and experience.

The form should be that which is accepted and traditional in most newspaper city newsrooms. It should be remembered that most city newsrooms receive hundreds—sometimes thousands—of releases every day. The editors charged with poring over these releases grumble over the volume they receive, and invariably most of the releases end up in the wastebasket. They appreciate, however, those that are professionally prepared and which make their arduous job simpler. There are some basic rules:

The Printed News Release Letterhead

The subject of the printed release head versus the plain blank sheet is a matter of more debate in some quarters than one would find at an economists' convention. Obviously, there is an element of silliness in the printed head that has the big words "NEWS FROM XYZ COMPANY," and then reports that John Jones has been appointed assistant foreman of the third shift. "NEWS FROM IBM" or "NEWS FROM EXXON," on the other hand, is likely to warrant the editor's attention. The letterhead of a well-known investor relations firm that uses the words "NEWS RELEASE" is more likely to receive attention, since if it's a creditable firm, the editor knows that the release will at least have been professionally prepared. In the best formats (see Appendix 3), the name, address, and telephone number (including the home number) of the company contact appear in a conspicuous place right at the top, with the name, address, and phone number (including home phone) of the account person in the investor relations firm who is the point of contact. The name of the company contact is essential because Dow Jones frequently insists upon verifying most financial information with an officer of the company, regardless of the credibility of the financial relations firm. In other cases, an editor or an analyst might want some clarification or additional information. Having both names gives the recipient of the release an option. If the distributing investor relations firm has several offices, it should list them, so that in appropriate cities a follow-up call is a local call. Each of those offices should, obviously, be advised of the release and appropriate backup information.

It's also useful to put the stock exchange or NASDAQ symbol conspicuously in the news release heading and lead paragraph. This allows the recipient to quickly check the current stock price.

The Headline

Newspapers write their own headlines. Furthermore, the headline is never written—except perhaps in the smallest newspapers—by the man who writes the story. Some of the commercial newswires eliminate the release's headline and replace it with their own. The purpose of the headline in a news release is to summarize the meat of the story and focus on the crucial point, so that the editor can quickly determine whether the story warrants his or her further attention. It should consist of no more than two lines stating briefly and succinctly what the release is about—for example, "THIRD QUARTER SALES, EARNINGS, UP SHARPLY AT TRANSMATION." It should be centered, all in caps, at the head of the release. If the story warrants it, and sound judgment dictates it, a subhead in lower case with initial caps describing a second important aspect of the story can be useful, particularly if it has additional news value, and can be intriguing. For example, *Higher Sales and Earnings Achieved Despite Slowing of Major Contracts.*

Dateline

Following the format used by virtually all daily newspapers, the first words of the release should be the dateline. This means the city of origin of the story and the date it's issued: "Jackson, MI, July 10 ——— "

The Text

All releases should be double-spaced, with paragraphs indented. This makes it easier for the editor to read, to mark up, and to indicate notes in the margin. Newspapers have long since gotten away from the five W's— who, what, when, where, and why—as mandatory elements for the lead of the story.

Successful Release Writing

Successful release writing—writing a release that gets published—is a function of capturing the exciting essence of the story in the very first line of the lead. After all, a release competes for the editor's attention against hundreds of others. If that first line doesn't clutch the editor, the rest of the release may describe the cure for the common cold, but the editor may not read that far, and it will still wind up in the wastebasket. The best education in release writing may be had by carefully reading a good newspaper, such as *The New York Times.* The lead tells the most salient facts—the essence—and tells it in a way that defies you not to read on. Subsequent paragraphs develop the story point by point, the most cogent first.

Editorial wastebaskets are filled daily with journalistic mythology, such as the five W's, and the notion that editors still edit from the bottom up. Editors usually edit the entire story to meet their own journalistic and space requirements, which is done more easily now because of computers. Indeed, the last paragraph is frequently best used for a fuller description and identification of the company.

A typical company description for the last paragraph of a press release would be the following, used by the Rochester-based Transmation, Inc.:

Transmation develops, manufactures and distributes instrumentation used in monitoring industrial processes. Its products include analog instrumentation, portable test and calibration equipment, and computerized systems for supervisory control and data acquisition. Transcat, its distribution subsidiary, sells both Transmation products and those of approximately 200 additional manufacturers through catalogs produced by the company.

The primary audience for a release, remember, is really the editor, not the public. Obviously, if the story doesn't appeal to the editor then the public never sees it. It may make the management feel better to send out a release that reads, "John P. Jones, president of XYZ Company, announced today that. . . ." but unless Mr. Jones is a nationally known figure, that release goes straight to the round file.

On the other hand, "The first computer system that can speak was announced today by John P. Jones, president of XYZ Company (OTC) . . ." will be dismissed by only the most disaffected editor.

The first mention of the company's name, by the way, should be followed in parentheses by the company's listing and symbol—(AMEX:Ady), (OTC:Xdxy), (NYSE:Ge). This immediately tells the editor whether the company is listed or not, and on what exchange.

The text itself should be succinct and to the point. It should be written in simple English, grammatically correct, in the active—not passive—voice, and shouldn't read like a legal contract. There's no merit in dullness, nor in imitating every other release of its kind. It should focus on the unique, not the ordinary—on the original, not the mundane. Its job is to impart news, not merely to fulfill a legal commitment.

While the release should be written interestingly, it shouldn't be confused with a feature, or a proposal to an editor for a feature.

The text should not editorialize in any way. Adjectives should be kept to an absolute minimum. Opinions, projections, and other subjective points of view should not be reported as facts. They should either be put in quotes or attributed as indirect quotes to an officer of the company by name.

It's a good idea, if the release runs more than one page, to write *MORE* at the bottom of each page, and the company name and page number at the top of successive pages. In a busy newsroom, pages of a multipage release can get lost.

The release is then ended with the traditional ending marks . . . # # #. The old telegrapher's ending mark—30—is quaint but has long since gone out of style.

Releases should be written by people who are experienced in release writing, or who otherwise have journalistic skill. Unfortunately, since most financial releases are issued under the rules of disclosure, they are too often written by lawyers. Lawyers—even the most literate—should not be allowed to write final drafts of releases. With rare exceptions, they tend to confuse releases with contracts, out of fear of being misinterpreted, misconstrued, or any of the other things lawyers worry about.

This is not to say that lawyers shouldn't assist in writing releases, or that they shouldn't be cleared by lawyers when appropriate. Financial releases can have legal consequences, and it is this potential for trouble that should be reviewed by a lawyer. But the lawyer's purview is not literary style. It is fact and law, and the possibility of misinterpretation of facts as stated.

And which is not to say that a good lawyer can't be helpful in writing a release, if he or she understands the investor relations and press process, and will cooperate rather than attempt to dominate the release-writing process.

Releases sent to the financial press should usually be addressed to a specific editor by name only in those cases where it is known that the editor or reporter to whom the release is addressed is in fact the appropriate person to receive the release, is still employed at that publication in that capacity, and is in residence and at his or her desk the day the release will be received. A release specifically addressed to a reporter who is out that day sits on the desk until he or she shows up. If it is important that an earnings release get into the hands of a specific editor at, say, *The Los Angeles Times,* the release should not be mailed; it should be sent by messenger and followed up with a phone call to make sure that it's not stalled at the financial department's reception desk. Otherwise, the release should be addressed to the Financial Editor or to the City Desk.

If a release isn't printed, it may still not be a wasted effort, according to some editors. They feel that some releases give them a sense of trends, or perspective, and alert them to future events. Small consolation to the CEO and his or her representatives, but consolation nevertheless.

Except under extreme circumstances, it's bad form to call a newspaper to find out why your release was not printed. The chances are that it wasn't run because the editor didn't think it was important enough to print in the paper's limited space, in relation to other information received that day. No newspaper is legally required to print any news, no matter how important it is to the company, and pestering an editor will only incur animosity and risk that subsequent releases will find their way directly to the wastebasket. If you do have something special, it is, however, appropriate to phone ahead, talk to the particular editor, advise him or her that the release is on the way, and that it addresses some noteworthy points. In view of the large number of releases received every day, if the news is important enough, the editor will appreciate it and watch for it. It will not guarantee that he will print it. There are times when it seems obvious that a release should have been printed and wasn't. It would be surprising, for example, if the earnings report of a major company in the apparel industry were not published by *Women's Wear Daily*. Under these circumstances, it's appropriate to phone the editor—not to ask why the release wasn't printed—but merely to confirm that the release was received. This is a subtle difference and frequently the publication will appreciate it if the editor has reason to believe that news he or she should have received never reached him or her.

In this context, it should be noted that the press sometimes makes mistakes. Releases do get lost. A paper will print the wrong number, or the broadcaster will get a fact wrong. Corrections become a problem, particularly if the error is minor (and certainly if it's the fault of the issuer, and not the press).

When your story is one of hundreds received or dozens printed that day, it's not likely to be of great concern to the publication unless it's a consequential story. It's a serious mistake, and you might be wasting your time—and risking the animus of the press—to make a fuss about its not being printed. If it's a consequential mistake, you're likely to get a rational response to a quiet (but not angry) presentation of the facts. The wire services particularly dislike taking up wire time with corrections, and Dow Jones can be made very happy by being told, "Look . . . don't worry about the wire, but get it straight in the paper." That's terrific—the record is in the paper, and the mail you send out to the data services will cover those records. But everybody's human, and everybody makes honest mistakes, and everybody does his or her best to correct them. Both Reuters and Dow Jones will correct mistakes if they think the correction is important, but the sooner after publication that the mistake is noted, the easier to get a correction.

Radio and Television

Radio and television shouldn't be overlooked. Many stations carry some business news, although considerably less than most newspapers. This is changing, to a degree, as economic concerns generate more public interest in business news, and as cable networks demonstrate success in reporting it. The measure is the importance of the news to the largest number of viewers or listeners. The newspaper reader disinterested in business can turn the page; the listener cannot. This is why radio and television editors choose only major or the most interesting business items for their newscasts. In most cases, it is pointless to send routine releases to radio or television stations, unless you know that they have expanded business news coverage. If there is reason to believe that something is particularly newsworthy, the station's news editor should be dealt with in exactly the same way as the newspaper editor. It should be noted that most broadcast media newsrooms receive Dow Jones, Reuters, and PR Newswire reports.

Major News Coverage

Major news can sometimes be treated somewhat differently than routine releases. If the news is of sufficient consequence to warrant greater attention than just routine dissemination, there are other techniques that can be used.

The News Conference

News people are too busy to spend several hours away from their desks to attend a news conference. They get particularly disturbed—and appropriately so—if they are invited to a news conference and are led to believe that they will be given news of greater importance than it actually is. The fact that they are wined and dined is not of the essence. There is no law that says that a newspaperman who accepts your hospitality has to print your story. Press people are further annoyed by being invited to a news conference to be given news that can just as easily be covered by a news release or even a telephone interview.

A news conference should be called only when:

- The news is monumental.
- There is some clear reason, such as a demonstration of a new product or the need for an elaborate explanation, why the news cannot be covered in a press release.
- Full understanding of the news requires questioning and elaborate answers.

If a news conference is warranted, there are some basic procedures to be followed.

The Invitation

The invitation should be sent out several weeks in advance of the event, if possible. It should state the purpose of the conference (focusing on the news value to the public), the time, the place, and the speakers. If there are specific visual aspects to the story, this should be indicated and a separate invitation should be sent to the photo desk of the publication if there is one. Broadcast people should be apprised of facilities and limitations, both radio and television. They should be told of arrangements for engineers, lighting outlets, etc. If the news is important and urgent enough, invitations can be sent out by telegram or fax, but certainly not a week before the event. The urgency of the news as implied by the telegram is defeated by the time lag. It is a good idea to telephone the invitees soon after the invitations have gone out to verify interest or to determine whether others in their organizations are interested, and on the afternoon before or the morning of the conference, to remind them and to verify their attendance.

The Place

The site should be appropriate for the event, and should be convenient to the press (particularly the broadcast media, which may have heavy equipment to transport). If it is convenient, the best place is always the office of the chief executive. Next best is a private room at a restaurant, hotel, or club. Consideration should be given to having wide aisles for television cameras. Obviously a public table in a restaurant is an inappropriate place to hold a press conference. The room should be large enough to hold everybody comfortably, but not so large that the crowd seems dwarfed and the room seems empty. It should be set up and prepared well beforehand to assure that all speakers are visible, can be clearly heard, and that all graphic material is easily presented.

The Time

The time for a news conference is determined by press deadlines. The best time for a news conference is late morning, lunch, or very early afternoon. A 10:00 A.M. news conference will make both the afternoon and the morning newspapers. If it's a major story, the afternoon newspapers (which are getting to be scarce commodities and are not as widely read as the morning newspapers) will preempt the story, which will not please the morning papers. On the other hand, it is better if a major story makes the financial wires while the market is still open. This means that time should be allowed for everybody not only to hear the news but to write it. News people still go back to their offices and pound typewriters—or rather, word processors. Only in the movies do they rush to the phones to call the city room.

Preparation

A complete press kit should be prepared for every news person attending. This should consist of a basic release, a background sheet on the company, any financial background material such as an annual or quarterly report, biographical material and photos of executives, and product data sheets. If product or plant photos are appropriate, they should be included. While the press kit should be as complete as possible, care should be taken not to overload it with so much material that a reporter can't find the facts for all the paper.

The Format

If cocktails or coffee are to be served, the length of time allocated should be just sufficient for everybody to arrive. Service should last no longer than 20 or 30 minutes. The press conference can begin while people are still drinking. Reporters' time, remember, is valuable. If a lunch seems in order, it should be treated essentially the same way as an analysts' luncheon—20 minutes for cocktails, a rapidly served lunch, and the conference to begin over dessert or as the main course is cleared.

The presentation itself should be short, simple, and to the point. While there is a great temptation to dramatize, few newspeople are impressed by this. The drama should come from the material. The material should be direct, and graphically illustrated. It should take no longer than thirty minutes to present. Time should be allowed for questioning. Immediately following the press conference, the officers of the company should be prepared to spend a few minutes to answer questions of any reporters that may linger behind the others. The chief executive officer should also be available in his or her office for the remainder of the day to answer any questions that may occur to a reporter back at his or her desk writing the story.

The Electronic Conference

Increasingly feasible and cost effective is the video conference, in which the main conference is televised and sent to other cities by closed circuit television. This allows you to have interactive conferences in many cities at once, because the setup allows questioners from the audience in any city to talk directly to the main transmission point, as if everybody were in one place.

You can hook up with local press or trades, analysts and brokers, or anybody else you want to participate.

The Individual Interview

There are times when the most effective way to break a major story is to give it to a single reporter in an exclusive interview. The strategy for this approach can be very subtle, such as an implied trade of major coverage in exchange for the exclusive, or when the reporter is important in his or her own right, as a columnist or well-known broadcaster might be. It's sometimes valuable, as well, when the story is somewhat technical, and requires a knowledgeable and concerned reporter for accurate coverage.

This may be effective, but it has an inherent danger. If there is any information imparted that comes under the rules of disclosure, that reporter's lead time and exclusivity may be lost, since the rules may require that the story be distributed to the general public within a reasonable period of time—and certainly the same day—as it is released to an individual. This is a matter to be discussed with the company's attorney. An exception is a *Wall Street Journal* or Reuters interview which, as has been stated before, is accepted by the SEC as having broad enough coverage to be considered adequate under the rules of disclosure.

Basic Interview Guidelines

Here, too, the general guidelines for the interview are the same as for the press conference—careful preparation, no nonsense, to the point, and frank discussion.

In both the individual interview and the press conference there are two basic cautions to consider:

- *Be prepared for full disclosure.* Beware any question on a material matter a reporter might ask that you can't answer. If you can't answer because you don't know, say so—but be prepared to explain why you don't know. Promise to get the information and forward it on a timely basis. If a reporter feels you have anything to hide, his or her story based on the interview may nullify much or all of the positive effect that the story might otherwise have. Certainly, as in an analyst meeting, all possible questions should be anticipated and the answers prepared beforehand. Obviously, it's impossible to anticipate every question, and if an unanticipated question is asked, don't answer hastily, without considering how your words will look in type. And material questions should be anticipated. There should be no surprises, if they can be avoided.

  At the same time, no matter how open you're willing to be, there may be questions that you shouldn't answer, for competitive or strategic reasons. Decline to answer those questions, but again, state the reasons. Again, these are questions that should be anticipated, and for which responses should be rehearsed.

- *Absolutely nothing should be stated off the record,* unless its pertinence to the story is for background only. An off-the-record statement places an unwarranted burden on a reporter. His or her job is to print information—not to be a repository of facts. It is a burden that reporters rarely appreciate. Furthermore, it almost invariably leads to the impression that something else is being hidden. If you don't want a reporter to report something, don't tell him or her—on or off the record. On the other hand, don't confuse *off the record* with *not for attribution,* which means that he or she can use the material, but please, shouldn't quote you on it. Know the difference, and follow the rules.

Feature Material

The approach to developing feature material in business and financial publications, as well as the general press, is considerably different than it is for the straight news announcement. The attempt, in developing features, is to project a somewhat detailed and rounded picture of the company or some aspect of it, and to do so in a favorable way. The value of feature articles about a company lies not only in the general exposure of the company to the publication's readers, but in explaining the company with some measure of depth; to engender the impression that it's functioning well; and to increase the understanding of the company.

An article about Pat Patrick, the president of Patrick Petroleum, included his involvement in auto racing as a car owner, which told a great deal about the manager as an individual and personality. Articles about Compaq Computer frequently talk of Chairman Rod Canion's designing the first Compaq on a napkin in a diner. The feature article, then, may deal with the personality or idiosyncrasies of its managers, or the work of its research department, or its unique approach to using raw materials. It doesn't matter which approach is used—it tells more about the company than do the numbers.

Guidelines for Feature Articles

In approaching this kind of press coverage there are several basic rules and guidelines that are imperative. These rules apply whether the story is generated internally by the company or by the investor relations or public relations consultant.

- *The target publication must be clearly understood.* Several issues of the publication should be studied to determine the kind of material it seeks, its point of view, its style, its editorial viewpoint, and its apparent taboos. Any attempt to try to convince a publication to print a story that is not in keeping with its general editorial policy, or that is similar to one recently printed, is not only a waste of time, but could lead to adverse reaction by the editors to the company or the investor relations consultant.

- *Even a feature article must have a newsworthy point of view.* Sometimes this is a hook—an event or activity that serves as a focal point for the story; an indication that the timing for the story is appropriate. Or it can be an angle that is at least unusual and perhaps unique, such as a company's new approach to financing or a new production or distribution technique that should result in significantly altering the direction of the company. Or the reorganization of a management team to take into account the changing economic conditions under which the company must function.

- The story should delineate, in one aspect or another, a *significant change in the company's operation.* It is only under the rarest circumstances that a publication will publish a story about a company in which absolutely nothing significant has happened, or in which the company is shown to be no different than any other company in its field. An exception might be when lack of change is significant and salutary in itself, such as when every other company in the industry has made significant changes with unfavorable results and the subject company, by changing nothing, has outperformed the industry.

Developing Feature Material Angles

Developing feature material for publication usually requires a measure of skill, if not artfulness. Some time ago, as part of its investor relations program, it was deemed valuable to develop a feature article about a medium-sized insurance company. Basic investigation indicated that the company's operations seemed no different than comparable companies in its industry. Furthermore, an additional obstacle existed in that newspapers infrequently find most stories of insurance companies of sufficient consequence to print. Every aspect of the company's business was carefully explored in the attempt to fathom some point that was unusual and newsworthy. There came to light the fact that the company's return on its investment portfolio was higher than most other insurance companies', including some of the giants. Further investigation showed that this was a function of the investment department's imagination and daring. It was company policy to seek out unusual situations, perhaps with somewhat more risk, and to be considerably more venturesome than is traditionally expected of the insurance industry. The company, for example, was one of the first to invest in the cable television industry.

This extraordinary success in portfolio management became the focal point of a proposal to *The New York Times,* which resulted in a large feature story on page one of the Sunday *New York Times* business section.

When a man murders his wife it takes no public relations skill to get his name in the paper. The skill is in fathoming the unusual but accurate in an otherwise usual story, and projecting it as the basis for a feature article.

Approaching a Publication

Approaching the publication requires some relatively simple procedures.

- Once a *target publication* has been selected and its editorial policies analyzed, develop the story specifically for that publication. The same general story may function for several different publications, but each approach must still be tailored.

- *The proper reporter or editor* is determined either by reading the masthead, reading the publication, or by calling the publication and inquiring. In most major business publications, reporters can initiate stories, without assignment from an editor. In some publications, such as *Business Week* or *Fortune,* there are specific areas of specialty. In a smaller publication, the ranking editor on the masthead is the first point of contact. In larger magazines, such as *Fortune,* several people are given the specific responsibility for reviewing all story ideas. If there is a local bureau of the publication in or near your city, you will probably be better off working with it, rather than with the publication's national staff. (See Appendix 13 for appropriate directories.) This is particularly true of *Business Week* and *The Wall Street Journal.* (However, being turned down by a local bureau doesn't preclude going to the head office of a publication, if you're sure that's the right publication for the story, and the local bureau is informed of what you're doing.) In some cases, if you know a staff reporter but want to pitch to an editor, you can call the reporter for advice about who to send the story to—but don't abuse this privilege.

- Write a letter to the editor or reporter describing the story. In some cases the letter may be preceded by a phone call or even a meeting with the editor. Experience will tell you who prefers letters and who will take phone calls first. Almost invariably, and with very few exceptions, the story will ultimately have to be presented to the publication in written form. Sometimes the letter can be prepared before the first contact. Sometimes, if a discussion with the editor beforehand is feasible, the letter should be written only after the meeting, and should be patterned on the guidelines set forth by the editor. If the phone call came first, the letter should follow within one day.

  The letter should be concise and to the point. The editor is busy and businesslike, and even the fact that he has been bought a sumptuous lunch at an expensive restaurant is not going to preclude the necessity he faces to maintain the level of his publication. The essence of the story should be stated in the first paragraph, with emphasis on the reasons why this story is newsworthy and warrants his consideration. The remainder of the brief letter should include facts to support the basic premise. It should indicate the availability of the people involved, and of graphic and visual material, if appropriate, that is available or can be made available to supplement the story.

If you feel that the story is too long and complicated to cover in one page, consider using an outline, as long as you can still make it sound interesting. The letter should rarely be more than two pages long.

The letter should not begin with the sentence, "John Jones, president of XYZ Corporation, is going to be in New York City at two o'clock next Wednesday afternoon and is available for an interview." If this is the case, then Mr. Jones's visit to New York should be stated further along in the letter—after the story idea has been clearly delineated.

Follow-up Strategies

A few days after the letter has been sent it is appropriate to follow up with a phone call to determine the editor's interest, to answer questions he might have, and to make arrangements for whatever interviews or further discussions are necessary. Because press people are so busy, it's a good idea to be sure not to call at deadline time (usually late afternoon, for morning papers), to say immediately who's calling (name and firm) and in regards to what, and to ask, "Do you have a minute?" If the answer is no, ask when you should call again. If the answer is yes, inquire, and tell your story quickly.

- The course of all interviews should take precisely the same form as interviews for major news events, and should follow the same rules described earlier in this chapter. The executives involved should be prepared to be frank and open. Nothing should be off the record except material that is necessary for background, but not necessarily newsworthy in itself. Questions should be anticipated and careful preparation made for each answer.

  Sometimes (but not always), an interviewee can control an interview to some extent. First, you should have a clear idea of what you want the results to be, in terms of tone and information imparted. Then, with careful rehearsal, you can assure that the information comes out by being responsive to questions, and then going beyond the answer. For example . . .

Q. Do you think you'll make more acquisitions?

A. It's not in our immediate plans. However, we didn't plan to make the last acquisition, but the opportunity came up and we took it, because we always look at every opportunity in terms of our long-range needs. That, to us, is as much a part of our planning as a dedicated acquisition program, because the aim is growth and diversification—not acquisition. We do, however, have the financial resources to take advantage of such opportunities.

In the case of smaller newspapers, or papers in other than the ten largest cities in the United States, the letter may ultimately turn out to be unnecessary. Arrangements can be made by phone. If an executive is planning to be in Birmingham, Alabama, next Thursday and there is reason to believe that there is a newsworthy aspect to either his presence in that city or to his company, it is perfectly appropriate to phone the financial editor of the *Birmingham News* a few days ahead, to indicate the fact that the executive will be in Birmingham next Thursday and to go on to delineate the basic points of the story in exactly the same way as is done in the letter. Be sure to point out a local angle to the company that might interest readers. Arrangements for the interview are then made by phone. Because unanticipated assignments may change plans, last-minute confirmation is prudent. Obviously, more lead time than a few days affords a better chance for success, but that shouldn't preclude at least a try on a few days' notice when that's all you've got.

In some cases an executive may be appearing in a city for purposes other than strictly company business. For example, the company president may be appearing in town to make a speech before a local organization. The procedure is to phone ahead to the editor and inform him of that fact. If the editor is not short-staffed and can afford time for coverage of the event, arrangements should be made. If possible, prepared material should be made available to the editor at the time of the interview. If the story is still considered newsworthy, but the editor is unable to assign a reporter to cover it, it is worth the effort to prepare a news release covering the event and to hand deliver or fax it to the editor on that morning.

Other Press Opportunities

Other press opportunities offer interesting possibilities.

An increasing number of publications, including *Barron's* and *Fortune, Investor's Daily, Equities,* and *The Security Trader's Handbook,* reprint press releases in a special section for a small fee. This is particularly useful for the smaller company that is not likely to get wide press coverage for its routine news. While this kind of service might well be construed as advertising, it can be useful in hitting a well-defined target audience.

The *Wall Street Transcript* reprints the research reports of brokerage houses, and speeches given before analysts' groups, and also interviews with CEOs.

Cable television has become a major outlet of business news. Aside from excellent business news coverage on such shows as Myron Kandel's business news program on the National Cable Network, a number of local cable outlets offer special business and financial news shows. In some cities, such shows already exist on ultrahigh-frequency stations. In Chicago, for example, Ben Larson's program on Channel 26 is particularly popular. In some cities, these programs charge a small fee for a 15- or 20-minute interview, although most, like Larson's show, are free. Financial News Network, on cable, also sells time for interviews. There seems no question that the growth of cable television will bring with it increased opportunities for disseminating business news.

Not to be overlooked is the trade press. Articles and interviews, as well as press releases with financial information, frequently find hospitality in the industry trade press for a company. Analysts read the trade papers of industries or companies they follow. People in an industry are investors as well as readers of the daily press, and there are good marketing reasons for a company to be seen in its industry's press. The rules for dealing with the trade press, incidentally, are no different than they are for dealing with the financial press.

Increasing in popularity are new computer networks and forums serving brokers, analysts, money managers, and individual investors, to which companies can subscribe. One such outstanding forum is Telescan, in Houston. For a fee, a company enters its information into the computer forum. Investors who subscribe can then enter questions for the company, which the company can answer by computer. A relatively new approach to information dissemination, it seems to be effectively reaching a growing number of participants.

Listing in Stock Tables

Extremely valuable to any company is its listing in the stock tables of newspapers. For the exchange-listed company, there's no problem in any paper that carries the complete listing. For over-the-counter companies the listing is supplied by the National Association of Securities Dealers (NASD). NASDAQ—the *National Association of Securities Dealers Automated Quotation* system—is emerging as a major market, on a par with the AMEX and

NYSE. Its criteria for listing in the tables in newspapers changes as its growth warrants, based upon such rigid criteria as company size, stock price, shareholder equity, and trading activity. About 2600 securities are carried daily in most major newspapers, as well as *The Wall Street Journal.* Supplemental lists are carried in some papers, daily or weekly.

NASD does supply the wire services with the quotations and volume on substantially all of the more than 3000 issues in the system. Local newspapers frequently print the bid and asked quotations of over-the-counter companies located in their area, supplied by the wire services under special arrangement with each paper. It's important to recognize, though, that the companies listed are determined by NASD criteria, and not, for the most part, by the newspapers, except for those local papers for whom the wire services prepare the lists. The NASD is most cooperative in supplying listing criteria.

Occasionally a company may feel it is eligible to be included in the newspaper listings by virtue of changed circumstances, such as an increase in price or an increase in the number of shareholders. The company can make direct application to the NASD and ask to be included on the list by virtue of the changed circumstances.

There are two aspects of news coverage that are extremely important to business people, even as they pose potential danger. The first is the story developed by the publication for reasons that might appear to be unfavorable to the company. The second is the routine press inquiry.

The Unfavorable Story

Forbes magazine is noted for ferreting out unfavorable stories about companies—or so it would appear. *Forbes* prides itself in anticipating danger points in industry or the economy, or potential disasters in companies. Their reporters are thoroughly professional and well trained. *Forbes,* in dealing with a story on a company in trouble or potentially in trouble, has often been accused of doing a hatchet job. It isn't always the case.

A *Forbes* editor may hear of a potentially negative story about a company. In the course of investigation one of the first things the editor will do is call the company's chief executive officer. The chief executive officer, aware of *Forbes*'s straightforward and irreverent attitude, becomes defensive. He tries to hide facts or to sugarcoat them. He sometimes makes himself or his executives unavailable. To the *Forbes* editor this is a red flag. It indicates that something is being hidden—that there is more to the story than meets the eye. The article will then be developed on the basis of *Forbes*'s own research, without benefit of the company's side of the story. The result is a negative report written in *Forbes*'s breezy style.

Unless the company truly has something to hide, the first reaction to an inquiry from an editor of *Forbes*—or any other publication—should be complete openness. If the company does indeed have something to be wary about, initial remarks should be restricted. For example, they called at the wrong time, or you don't have all the facts at your fingertips. In other words, without being defensive, buy the time to consult with your lawyer or investor relations professional. Rarely does a reporter call when he doesn't have fifteen minutes or more to wait for an answer. Experience with any major responsible publication, including *Forbes,* indicates that a publication is responsive to an open presentation of the facts—both positive and negative—by the company. No responsible publication ever refuses to hear the company's side of the story. This is not to say that the negative facts will not be printed. Very few publications will be deterred from printing pertinent facts, negative or positive. But at least the negative side of the story can be cushioned by the company's point of view.

It should be recognized that for the public company there is no place to hide—that's one of the things that being public is about. It is the most destructive form of self-deception to believe that there is any way in which a negative story, once it has been discovered by a publication, will not come out in its worst aspects. It should also be recognized that no company ever takes a consistently straight line to success. Not all decisions are correct, nor is any chief executive perfect. What's more important is that if the total story is told and told honestly, the resultant article may not read like a puff piece, but at least the company will come out ahead, with its credibility preserved, and possibly enhanced.

Does this always work? Of course not. Sometimes, despite all of the investor relations professionalism, and despite all the cooperation with the press, the story comes out badly.

The picture you so carefully and accurately painted is distorted, the wrong people are quoted and the right people are not, the facts are warped and bent beyond recognition, and the whole piece reads as if it were written by your most malicious competitor.

Assessing the Damage

Beyond the first scream of outrage, what can you do?

The most useful course is to do nothing until you've recovered from your anger. Even doing the right thing in the wrong frame of mind can perpetuate, not cure, the damage. So . . .

- Don't act precipitously. Think of every action in terms of possible reaction. What seems like a good idea at the moment may be a backfire next week.

- After you've gotten over the emotional impact and the anger, don't think vindictively. You may have to live with that publication again someday, and vindictiveness in any event is not profitable.
- Assess real—not assumed or presumed—damage. That's where you've got to focus your attention. Much assumed damage at first light disappears when the sun comes up. What's left is damage you can deal with.

It's this last point that's crucial to successfully limiting the damage of bad press. *Too often, the defense is predicated on imagined damage, in which case the reaction is an overreaction, and causes more damage than the original article.*

Experts rarely concern themselves with *why* it happened. Unless libel is involved, or it's part of a bear raid, it doesn't really matter. The reporter could have functioned out of ignorance or laziness. Reporters are people, and are not immune to such foibles as preconceived notions that can subvert the professionalism of even the most experienced journalist. The reason for an adverse story is rarely an element that can be dealt with in damage control.

There are some specific questions to be addressed:

- What does the article *really* say? Is it bad because it's wrong—or because it's right?
- Is the article distorted because the facts are wrong, or because they are put in a wrong context that distorts the facts?
- What is the real damage? Is it libelous? Misleading enough to cause real business damage? Or just embarrassing?
- Consider the publication. Is it widely read, or will people you care about never see it? (Consider that under certain circumstances, your competitor may want to make a point by sending a reprint of the article, along with a favorable one about himself or herself from the same publication). What's the publication's reputation for credibility?
- Is the potential damage internal as well as external? Sometimes an unfavorable article can hurt internal morale more than it affects an external perception of the firm.

Staying power is an important consideration. How long after publication will the story, or at least it's negative aura, linger? Depending upon the publication and the nature of the story, considerably less time than you think. As one experienced marketer put it, the impact fades quickly, but the impression can linger.

Assessing the damage accurately allows you to choose the appropriate response. There are, in fact, a number of inappropriate responses. You can:

- Sue, but only if there is real libel and real—and demonstrable—damage. There rarely is.
- Get on the phone and scream at the editor. Good for your spleen, lousy for your future with at least that segment of the press. And you'll never win.
- Write a nasty letter to the publisher. Only slightly better than screaming, but with the same results.

Rallying a Response

On the other hand, there are some positive things that can be done:

- Avoid defensiveness. Plan positively.
- Warn people. If you know an article is going to appear that might be unfavorable, alert your own people, so that it doesn't come as a surprise.
- Have a plan and a policy, preferably before you need it. This should cover how to deal with the press, who does it and who doesn't, how to deal with customer reactions, how to deal with internal reactions. It should cover how calls are handled, who responds and who routes calls to whom, what to say to customers and who says it, and so forth.
- A letter to the editor is important, if only to go on record. But it should be positive, nonvitriolic, and deal only with the facts. It should not sound petulant or defensive.
- Deal with the real damage. If the real damage is in specific markets, mount a positive public relations campaign, and even an advertising program, aimed specifically at those markets. If the damage is internal, try to assess the root causes for the negative reaction. It would take a powerful article in a powerful journal to demoralize a firm that's otherwise sound and comfortable with itself.

No story is so bad that it should warrant extreme reaction. No publication that's still publishing is so devoid of credibility that some readers won't accept what they read. The role of the professional, trained, and experienced marketer is to maintain perspective, to assess the damage appropriately, and to see that the response is equal to—but does not exceed—the damage.

If bad press meant nothing, then neither would good press, and we know that consistently good press means a great deal. But one story— good or bad—rarely has sufficient impact to seriously aid or damage a company (although a negative story is more titillating than a positive one). Most positive public relations is a consistent series of positive articles, interviews, and news stories. If a negative press consists of more than one story, then the problem is usually not the press—it's the subject of the stories.

The perspective of the bad story, then, requires dealing with it as an anomaly. This means dealing with it as a calm and rational business decision. And no business decision, in any context, is ever a sound one if it isn't arrived at rationally and professionally.

It would be naive not to recognize the fact that not all reporters, editors, or even publications are honest. There are individual reporters on the take. There are hatchet jobs. There are publications that are unethical. There are publications that tie their editorial columns to their advertising sides. This is unfortunate and frequently illegal, particularly for a financial publication that purports to present honest investment advice. It's just as bad to tie advertising to favorable news without in some way making clear to the reader that the editorial material is not objective or that it has been paid for in some way.

There is nothing that can be done about unscrupulous publications except to assiduously resist all blandishments to tie advertising or any other revenue—including reprints, gifts, and junkets (free press trips)—to editorial material. For the company in trouble, it is a short-term solution to a deeper problem. Since, on Wall Street, bad news reverberates loudly, there is no such thing—regardless of popular lore—as cosmetic public relations, particularly in business news. Other than protesting vigorously, which is usually a waste of time, the only recourse a company has to an unscrupulous publication that prints an unfavorable story is to deal more intensively with the honest publications in the attempt to disseminate the truth. Yes, it takes twice as much truth to counteract falsehood. But it's worth the effort.

Incidentally, the notion that news people can be bought is nonsense, despite the individual anomaly. It's true that a newsperson who has friendly relations with either the company or the company's investor relations firm can in some way extend a minute measure of editorial favor to the company. This usually means listening to a story more patiently. But in the final analysis, the publication is almost invariably bigger than any of its editors or any story. In order to survive, the publication must be editorially consistent. True, there are exceptions. And occasionally, favor can be curried with a reporter or an editor resulting in a favorable story that might otherwise not have appeared. But no public relations program can ever be built, or sustained, on such a structure. In other words, don't depend upon it.

The Unexpected Inquiry

A reporter may hear a rumor, or have an intuitive thought, or otherwise draw a conclusion about a company—and call the CEO to follow it up. Whether the call is hostile or friendly, it's frequently unexpected.

The unexpected inquiry should also be dealt with in a straightforward manner. Remember, an officer of a public company has a fiduciary position. This means that public comment may have legal implications. This should be kept in mind in every aspect of dealing with the press, including the electronic media.

In responding to an inquiry, no attempt should be made to hide or dissemble—it will only make matters worse. The company president who is called by a reporter or an editor and asked to comment on an unfavorable rumor should react calmly and rationally. If the facts are clearly at hand, he should state them simply and straightforwardly, with no obvious attempt to influence the editorial stance. If he doesn't know the answer he should say so, take the reporter's name and phone number, get the information as soon as possible, and return the call with the facts. If warranted, he should invite the reporter to discuss the question in detail, and here too the same rules apply as for any other interview. It's absolutely imperative that every company have a basic news policy. Specific executives should be designated as spokespeople for the company. The corps of spokespeople can be broad, consisting of specialists in each field, but they should not be arbitrarily selected, and each should be capable of dealing with the press calmly and intelligently.

There should be a clear and simple directive from the chief executive officer to all executives and employees that spokespersons have been designated and that all inquiries should be referred to the appropriate spokesperson. Under no circumstances should an unauthorized person be allowed to supply vital information to the press, and this should be made clear not in terms of authority alone, but rather for the simple reason that only the spokespeople have all pertinent facts and policy at hand. It should be made clear that it is as unfair to an unauthorized person to allow him or her to supply information as it is to the company, since it puts the unauthorized person in an untenable position. Unauthorized personnel should be advised to deal with all inquiries politely, to indicate that they are not sufficiently armed with the facts to answer the question, and then to indicate the name and phone number of the designated spokesperson.

Designated spokespeople should be kept abreast at all times of company news policy and procedures. They should be briefed as well as possible on all potential inquiries and the appropriate answers. They should know company policy and the limits of the information they are authorized to divulge. They should be made to understand clearly the basic procedures for answering inquiries in terms of dealing with reporters politely, rationally, unemotionally, and openly. When a question exceeds the limits of a spokesperson's authority, he or she should politely say so and refer the reporter to the proper executive to handle that inquiry. All inquiries and the answers given should be made known—preferably in writing—as soon as possible to the chief executive officer.

When to Say No

But are there ever times to tell the press to bug off, and leave you alone? Maybe.

If you're dealing with a hostile reporter or publication, and believe you're in a no-win situation, you may have more to gain than to lose by refusing to cooperate.

If you're dealing with a publication whose editor thinks it's more important than it really is, and you know you're not going to get a fair shake anyway, why waste your time?

If you're asked to comment about a competitor, or about a situation in your industry to which you're ancillary, and there's a good chance that your comment may be misinterpreted or even misreported, "no comment" is a great response.

If you know that you're going to take a beating no matter what you say or do, or if you know that the reporter is unlettered or unknowledgeable in the subject and is only passing through the beat, or if you know that commenting is going to get you involved in something that may turn out to be unprofitable to you, then tell the press, politely, that you choose not to participate.

If you know that a reporter is misrepresenting to you what he's writing, in order to get your participation in a story that you might otherwise be reticent about, or if that reporter has done that to you in the past, you're perfectly right to decline.

In fact, participating in a roundup story should be done cautiously anyway, with you asking the reporter as many questions as he or she asks you. And if you do consider participating, take notes of what you're being told about the nature of the story. You may want to complain later.

The press has an inalienable right to pursue. They don't have an inalienable right to catch. There's a difference between being firm in declining and being rude. Rudeness is somebody else's game. Declining firmly and politely may very well be the way for you to win your game.

Except in terms of their training, and the motivation of individuals to do their jobs as well as possible, newspaper reporters are no different from

anybody else. The range of the capabilities, understanding, and limitations
is about on a par with the total population. There are competent reporters
and there are incompetent reporters. There are a great many of them in the
financial press who seem remarkably ignorant of business and finance.
There are a greater number who are remarkably well versed in the field.
Editors and newspaper reporters are no more exempt from hostilities, bad
days, fights with their spouses, and toothaches than anybody else. Nevertheless, if they are dealt with professionally they will normally function
professionally.

The editor and the newsperson usually have no ax to grind. The realities
of the world are that they react as humanly to a confrontation as does
anyone else. Few newspersons, however, will react unfavorably to an
honest, simple, and straightforward presentation and to an unflinching
response to even the most cutting questions.

The proper function of an investor relations consultant in dealing with
the press is not to act as a spokesperson for the company—unless he or she
has been properly trained and specifically designated in this capacity by
the chief executive officer—but to act as an intermediary, smoothing the
way for direct relations between the company and the press. Nor should
the investor relations consultant ever be used as a buffer—as a shield
behind which the company can hide. The press resents this and rightfully
so. Yet the major source of company news is still the investor relations
consultant or officer.

And it's clearly acceptable to the press that the investor relations professional can be an advocate for the company he or she represents. A senior
Fortune editor has said that she understands that a public relations or
investor relations professional is fulfilling an advocacy function when
talking about a client or employer. A *Wall Street Journal* reporter who sometimes writes the "Heard on the Street" column sees it from a different
angle, saying, "I assume that everyone who gives me a positive story idea
is long in the stock, and that everyone who gives me a negative idea is
short." At least some reporters are aware of the sometimes unscrupulous
use of the press by shorts.

Still, if there were no investor relations industry, every editorial body
in the United States would have to treble its staff to ferret out the massive
amount of news that is now brought to the attention of the press. Most
reporters recognize this. Some newspeople, however, given reason to feel
that the investor relations consultant is inserting himself or herself between the company and the press, will rightfully and vocally resent it.

The press and electronic media, when properly dealt with, is an important conduit to the financial community and the investing public. It's
worth the effort of every corporate executive to learn to work with the
media properly and effectively.

6

Rules of Disclosure—The SEC and the Markets

At the core of all investor relations is disclosure—who tells what to whom, and when. In the securities markets, the rules of disclosure are promulgated by both governmental bodies—the SEC and, in some cases, state authorities—and for those companies whose securities are traded on exchanges or NASDAQ, the governing bodies of those organizations.

But more significantly, the driving force for disclosure goes beyond regulation. In investor relations, telling more usually means getting more. Disclosing is not only legal, it's good investor relations.

There is a keen difference, in fact, between the requirements of disclosure under the regulations of the SEC and the exchanges and the need for disclosure for a public company seeking acceptance in the capital markets. The rules of disclosure are requirements, not electives. The needs for disclosure are dictated by the attempts of a public company to keep itself visible to the financial community, and at all times clearly understood. One does not preclude the other, and in fact, the values of disclosure far exceed the limitations of the rules of disclosure.

The SEC

All securities, of both publicly and privately held companies, are regulated by the United States Securities and Exchange Commission, a federal regulatory body established by Congress under the Securities Exchange Act of 1934. Its chairman and board members are appointed by the president of the United States. It has a very large and enthusiastic

155

staff, with offices in major cities throughout the United States, as well as in Washington, D.C. Its major assignment is to regulate and monitor the offer to sell, the sale, and the trading of securities for virtually all public and private companies, stock exchanges, and securities dealers in the country. It does its job well and takes it seriously.

While the commission tends to take on the character of the administration it serves and the commission's chairman in its emphasis on any particular aspect of securities regulation, it never strays from its basic purpose. Under the Reagan administration, for example, the drive to deregulate made it easier for some companies to go public, but didn't deregulate or ease enforcement. Under the Bush administration, deregulation seems to be deemphasized, while response to public reaction to insider trading, takeovers, the incursion of foreign capital, and concern for penny stock trading may change the commission's regulatory focus. The assessment of the Bush administration is that it wants fewer rules, but wants those rules stringently enforced. But regardless of who heads it, protecting the investor is still the SEC's primary role.

Each state also has its body of securities laws and regulations, most of which are enforced by the state attorney general. These laws are known as "Blue Sky Laws," since they were originally designed, many of them prior to the establishment of the SEC, to prevent unscrupulous securities dealers from promising and selling investors everything but the blue sky.

All companies selling securities to the public must conform to the laws and regulations of both the SEC and every state in which those securities are sold. A stock must be registered in every state—"Blue-skyed"—in which it is sold. Some states allow *manual exemption*—except that automatic clearance is given to stocks listed on national exchanges or on the NASDAQ National Market List.

All exchanges have rules and regulations governing disclosure practices of companies whose stock is listed on—traded through—those exchanges. Naturally, these regulations are often developed to parallel, comply with, or function to complement, SEC and state regulation. The exchanges, however, frequently define or expand the regulations for listed companies. Securities of companies not listed on exchanges, or listed on the NASDAQ system, are affected by virtue of the regulation by the National Association of Securities Dealers member firms who trade on NASDAQ or otherwise in the over-the-counter market.

The vast body of regulations covers every aspect of security practices, including company practices relating to information about itself that affects the value of that company's stock in the public market. The regulatory concern here is principally with the legal aspects of the dissemination of that information—the rules of disclosure.

While the subject of securities regulation is complex, particularly as it pertains to corporate relations with the financial community and the general public, there are two basic points that are foremost. All of the rules of disclosure, whether formulated by the SEC, the Exchanges, or the National Association of Securities Dealers, are designed to cover two major points—material information and inside information.

Material Information

All material information necessary to evaluate a company and its suitability as an investment vehicle must be made public and available to all interested parties on a timely basis.

Inside Information

When material information about a company or its operations that could affect the evaluation of a company or its suitability as an investment vehicle, or that might influence the sale or purchase of its stock, is known by only a limited number of people, they may not trade on that information, or misuse it for personal gain. To protect against insider trading problems, all such information must be made available to as many segments of the financial community as possible, including the investing public. This must be done by those means most likely to broadcast it to the widest possible degree. It must be disseminated to the public before any insider trades on it. Timeliness is of the essence in specific cases, and is prescribed in specific cases, such as the Board's firing the CEO. While some information may be withheld for valid business reasons, so long as no insider trades on it, information is sometimes not containable—in which case it must be fully disseminated immediately. In the case of earnings statements, it's the better part of wisdom to disclose as soon as possible, and certainly within 24 hours.

In any segment of securities regulation or public corporate activity (such as changing a board or an officer), these two basic points apply universally and without exception.

The myriad cases of insider trading promulgated in the last part of the 1980s continued to raise the nagging question about the apparent lack of definition of the term—and crime—*insider trading*. Perhaps legal definitions of it may not be as precise as for, say, murder. But the definitions are not so imprecise and subjective as they are for, say, pornography. Of a practical, philosophical definition of pornography it may be said that "I know what it is, and you know what it is. But I can't tell you, and you can't tell me." In fact, an understanding of insider trading is quite clear for those in a position to do it (at least, the most obvious kind), and nobody seems ever to have been convicted for doing it inadvertently.

Compliance with Securities Law

Primarily, the burden of compliance to securities law remains within the purview of the attorney. Unfortunately, securities regulation is not only complex, it's not always completely clear. There are areas in which judgment must be exercised, as for example, the moment at which prospective mergers become likely and must be disclosed. Since these judgments are invariably made within the framework of regulation, and are interpreted by a wide variety of regulatory and judicial decisions in different jurisdictions that sometimes disagree with one another, they need the professional assistance of a competent securities attorney.

The primary burden for compliance with disclosure regulation, however, remains with the corporation's management, with the assistance of its attorneys (not the other way around), and in the area of communication, its investor relations counsel.

It may be valuable to note here the difference in viewpoints that frequently arises between attorneys and investor relations consultants. The attorney, charged primarily with being able to defend his or her client to the point of walking into court "with clean hands," frequently takes positions that are extremely defensive. The investor relations consultant, on the other hand, is charged with keeping the client viable in the marketplace, which means outreach. The points of view frequently conflict. It's well worth the effort, though, for management, its securities counsel and the investor relations professional to work together. Each has a distinct point of view and experience to offer.

Disclosure Philosophy

Because the body of regulation is so elaborate and so much of it is a question of judgment, much of the direction necessary to make those judgments is not codified. Those covered by securities law have sometimes felt that in some cases, such as the classic *Pig 'n Whistle,* the SEC seems to be saying, in effect, "Do it first, and then we'll tell you whether you should have done it or not."

While the ultimate judgment may depend heavily on attorneys' advice, the corporation and its financial relations counsel should nevertheless adopt a basic philosophy that should pervade its disclosure program. This philosophy should include two basic points.

Full Disclosure

The company should be prepared to disclose any and all information that could conceivably affect a judgment of the company as an investment vehicle. If there is any question—disclose. Certainly, this includes any activity that warrants filing a Form 8-K with the SEC. The Form 8-K is used in between formal reporting periods to report significant changes in corporate activity, policy, or practice.

Disclosure Timing

Pertinent or disclosable material, such as earnings statements and dividends, should be processed for release no more than a few hours from the time the information is known by any officer of the corporation. The machinery for disclosure should be well established beforehand, whether it's done by the company itself or through the auspices of the investor relations counsel. It should then be a routine matter to prepare and disseminate any information.

For many corporations, this kind of policy may seem harsh and arduous. But the balance must be sought between the basic responsibility to investors and potential investors on the one hand, and the value of competing in the capital markets by disseminating every element of information that materially assists in the judgment of a company on the other. And while these two parallel goals may occasionally conflict, and there may be a temptation to hedge on the rules, it should be clearly understood that administration of the rules of disclosure can be rigid and assiduous. The SEC and the exchanges, it should be perfectly clear, mean exactly what they say. Furthermore, as understaffed as the SEC or any other regulatory body may be at any given moment, the agency is rarely lax in the enforcement of securities regulation.

And let us dispense immediately with any question of secrecy on the basis of competitive advantage. While the SEC has frequently said that it has no intention of putting any company at a competitive disadvantage, and will allow competitive disadvantage as a defense in some cases, it still considers the dissemination of material information more important under the rules of disclosure. This can sometimes raise thorny points for a corporation asked to break down its performance by product line or by division, or for the corporation that feels that premature disclosure of merger negotiations might adversely affect those negotiations. Here, competent legal counsel is essential. But counsel not withstanding, the SEC is quite clear. Disclose.

Furthermore, to the extent that individual and presumably unsophisticated investors are in the market, the SEC is increasingly concerned with protecting those investors. Purely and simply, the SEC wants no investor or prospective investor ever put in the position of buying, holding, or selling stock on the basis of incomplete or inaccurate information. The drive is toward greater and greater disclosure, however painful this may appear to be to corporations, or however time consuming this may be to corporate officers.

The SEC and Investor Relations Consultants

Significantly, the SEC doesn't automatically exempt from its regulations agents of the corporation. For many years it was the practice of companies to use investor relations consultants and public relations firms as mere conduits of information. Traditionally, corporate presidents relied on investor relations consultants to simply take the information supplied to them by the company, cast it into its appropriate release form, and disseminate it. Investor relations consultants, since they are seldom accountants or lawyers, are without the means or facility to judge the validity of information supplied to them. They once relied on their clients to supply them with complete and accurate information. Unfortunately, they were frequently fooled. For many years this rankled the SEC, and quite appropriately. The particular anxiety was that investor relations counsels were unwittingly being used to *condition the market*. In 1969, the SEC decided to include investor relations consultants in its regulation of disclosure.

Now, if appropriate systems and procedures to verify information are duly established and followed, and properly documented in the agency's own files, an investor relations consultancy has fulfilled its public reponsibility and is not compelled to insure the total validity of the information.

The SEC takes into consideration the fact that investor relations consultants are not in the same position to verify information as are auditors and attorneys. However, the investor relations consultant is entitled, and should be encouraged, to ask for documentation on any information supplied by the client. Steps can be taken to assure, within the limits of any investor relations firm, the most feasible precautions against dissemination of misleading or inaccurate information. They may vary from company to company, but essentially they rely upon documentation of instructions from client to counsel, with approval in writing for all releases.

A compliance procedure for practices by investor relations consultants in issuing information should be standard, and appropriate parts disseminated to all clients. It protects both the company and the consultant, as well as the investing public. It assures that all issued information is carefully reviewed (and if necessary, questioned), and that all sources are clearly identified. And certainly, the consultant, for his or her own protection, should review carefully all available financial and corporate data and background on each prospective client, to assure representation of only reputable companies.

A primary factor in compliance procedures for an investor relations consultant is to know his or her client. In a proper relationship, the consultant works closely with the chief executive and financial officers, and should come to know a great deal about them and the company. He or she is well informed about the company's financial and corporate structures, as well as its day-to-day operations. This basic knowledge provides a framework in which to judge new financial and operational information, and should assure the consultant that he or she is not complicitous in disseminating false information. At the same time, the well-informed consultant may be considered an insider, in that he has access to inside information. The consultant must function accordingly. (The concept of *insider*, incidentally, is not simple, as you will see in the following pages.)

Proper compliance procedures require that all issued material must be accompanied by an appropriate form, retained with a copy of the material by the consultant, indicating the source of information, the time it was given for release, the time it is to be released, whether the copy has been or is to be amended, and by whom. Additional comments might indicate who prepared the original material, recommendations made by the consultant but not accepted or followed by the client, and how the information was transmitted for preparation for release. If additional approval is required, or was given by attorneys, accountants, or others, it is indicated. The form is then signed by the company officer responsible, as well as by the consultant responsible. In the case of a release approved by telephone, or supplied by mail or fax, a variation of the form, designed for that purpose, is used, and signed by the consultant who received it.

Many consulting firms designate a senior firm member as compliance officer. His or her job is to oversee all procedures for compliance with SEC, exchange, NASD, Blue Sky regulations, and the firm's own policies, and should include a periodic review of all material and the ability to confer directly with the firm's securities attorney.

For the corporation intent upon disseminating false or misleading information, very little can be done by anybody to prevent it. Nevertheless, as has been noted before, the acoustics of Wall Street are magnificent. The value to any corporation of issuing false information is remarkably short-lived, and the penalty, in terms of at least investor reaction, if not the law as well, is swift and intense.

Prior to the Securities Acts of 1933 and 1934, corporate disclosure was minimal. In 1926 all corporations whose stocks were listed on the New York Stock Exchange published balance sheets showing current assets and current liabilities. In these statements only 71 percent showed depreciation, 45 percent showed the cost of goods sold, and 55 percent showed sales. Today, it would be unthinkable for any published report of a public corporation not to include this and a great deal of other pertinent information. And even so, it's only within the past few years, with the growth of conglomerates and diversified companies, that corporate annual reports break down performance by lines of business, whether by division or product line or other business segmentation. Until the SEC made it mandatory to do so some years ago, there were still relatively few companies that included in their annual reports information that covers the range of material demanded by law in the Corporate Annual Report Form 10-K—despite the fact that the Form 10-K of any public corporation is available to the public.

To the company that recognizes that it must compete for capital over the long run, the problem of disclosure should be viewed not only as one of regulation, but as the opportunity to display every aspect of the company that can contribute to a rounded picture for the prospective investor or lender.

Insider Information

Nor should the danger inherent in insider information be overlooked. This should be abundantly clear, in view of the events of the 1980s, which saw some of the most widely publicized insider-trading scandals in American business history.

An *insider* is generally defined as anyone who has material information about a company that has not been publicly disclosed. It is assumed that any insider who trades on material information in buying or selling stock to his own advantage thereby functions to the disadvantage of other investors. Recent cases on both insider information and other categories of misuse of nonpublic material information have resulted in many a Savile Row suit exchanged for prison garb.

In 1964, the problem of inside information dramatically came to the public's attention with the classic Texas Gulf Sulphur case. Several engineers working for Texas Gulf Sulphur came upon a rich mineral body. This discovery was kept within a small group inside the company. Several members of that group, taking advantage of their inside information and with full knowledge that the value of the company stock would be greatly enhanced when that information was generally known, purchased Texas

Gulf Sulphur stock for their own accounts. This resulted in civil charges against the offenders. The court said that you must **either disclose** the information, or abstain from trading on it until it is available to all investors. It also strengthened and clarified the law regarding inside information.

Shortly thereafter, several Merrill Lynch, Pierce, Fenner & Smith staff members were given reason to believe that a forthcoming financial statement for the McDonnell Douglas Company would show a sharp decline in earnings. Before this information was made generally public, advice to sell their stock was given to selected institutional clients, at the same time that other Merrill Lynch customers were being given a buy recommendation. When the information was ultimately made public, the price of the stock declined sharply. The SEC took a dim view of the fact that there had been specific benefit from inside information to a selected few, and once again penalties were imposed.

Perhaps the major new category of misuse of information has arisen as a result of a 1980 Supreme Court decision dealing with a printer who, in 1977 and 1978, traded stock on information he got from a confidential financial document his company was printing.

The Justice Department case was that the printer (whose name was Chiarella), who had been entrusted by his employers to print confidential documents regarding a prospective takeover, had defrauded the shareholders of the target company (who weren't aware of a proposed tender offer) by trading on that information. The Supreme Court exonerated Chiarella, saying that he didn't have a duty to those shareholders, and that if you don't owe a duty, you can't breach that duty.

However, in a dissenting opinion, Chief Justice Burger said that what Chiarella had done was to misappropriate—Burger used the word *stole*—the information from his boss, the printing company. Thus arose what is now known as the *misappropriation* theory. As subsequent events showed, had the government been able to apply that concept, the printer's conviction might have been sustained.

In 1982, in a case in which several investment bankers had traded on inside information obtained from their employer, Morgan Stanley, the government indicted on the *misappropriation* theory that had arisen from Burger's dissent. The investment bankers were convicted, and their conviction was upheld on appeal.

It was on the *misappropriation* theory that some of the most famous insider-trading indictments were developed, including Winans, Levine, Boesky, and Milken.

Subsequently, other cases substantially emphasized the SEC's willingness to prosecute under insider-trading statutes. In one case, Foster Winans, who wrote the important "Heard on the Street" column for *The Wall*

Street Journal, was found to have fed information to selected brokers about material prior to its appearing in the column. Because "Heard on the Street" is the most popular column in the paper, and because many people trade on that information when the column appears, knowing what's to be in the column before it appears offers a great trading advantage. The court ruled that the information in the column, and the column itself, was proprietary—that it belonged to *The Wall Street Journal.* Winans was convicted for misappropriating the property of *The Wall Street Journal.*

In the most famous case of the decade, arbitrageur Ivan Boesky, highly regarded for his success in selecting companies about to be taken over in leveraged buyouts and other acquisition deals, was found to have been trading on inside information. Boesky and many of his associates, including some of the most respected names on Wall Street, were brought down by the revelation, and many were successfully indicted.

Probably nothing is so seductive to the investor as the idea of being privy to—and trading on—inside information. It seems so safe. But it's amazing how sophisticated are the regulatory agencies in seeking out and finding wrongdoing in trading practices. The jails are full of those who discovered too late the skills and enthusiasm of the SEC in dealing with insider trading.

The Rules of Disclosure

As the economy has become more complex, SEC regulation has demanded more and more in terms of disclosure. Finally, in 1980, the SEC attempted to recodify and simplify some of its rules of disclosure. While the basic concepts remain the same, there have been significant changes in the mechanics.

Perhaps the primary change is based on a new understanding of the uses of the Form 10-K and the annual report to shareholders. Under the new regulations, the SEC attempts to unify the two in a new comprehensive reporting system.

In the past, the SEC tended to see the two as separate documents, and added disclosure requirements to each independently of the other. Now, it sees the two as integrated. The current rules attempt to achieve a standardized reporting package that will make it possible to use the annual shareholders' report information in the Form 10-K and several other forms. In interim periods, the annual reporting financial package need only be updated by the condensed financial information in the quarterly Form 10-Q.

The required information is essentially in management's discussion and analysis of performance, and in audited uniform financial statements.

Two other forms about which the SEC is deeply concerned are Form 3, which discloses when an insider (either an officer, director or 10 percent shareholder) takes a position in a stock; and Form 4, which discloses when an insider buys or sells company stock. *Deeply concerned* means that the SEC monitors these situations, and may impose large fines for each day of noncompliance.

Accounting Rules and Disclosure

In recent years, the increasing complexity of both domestic and international business, and the effects of the economy, have generated a number of issues that seriously affect disclosure. Problems of inflation, reporting the effects of foreign currency translation in an era of fluctuating currency valuation, extraordinary interest rates, the growth of pension fund assets and their treatment on the balance sheet—all these and more have taken what was a simple reporting matter in other times and generated today a morass that requires legions of accountants and attorneys to penetrate. One result is that the SEC and the Financial Accounting Standards Board— the accounting profession's rule-making body—work more closely than ever in developing acceptable accounting principles designed to generate valid and useful information for investors, shareholders, lenders, and management itself.

Thus, regulations in financial reporting are constantly being developed, much of them concerning information never before required, to keep abreast of changing economic conditions and business practices. Most recently, this has included:

- FAS 52, which deals with techniques of reporting the effects of fluctuating values of foreign currency translation. While issued in the early part of the 1980s, the growing internationalization of business brings new importance to this ruling.

- FAS 87, which deals with the treatment of pension fund assets and liabilities on the balance sheet and expansive footnote disclosure. This ruling, while controversial, addresses the growing importance of pension funds in corporate financial structures.

- FAS 94, issued in 1987, generally requires consolidation of all of a company's majority-owned subsidiaries. No longer exempt are non-homogeneous but majority-owned operations. Under this ruling companies are required to provide summarized information about the assets, liabilities, and results of operations of previously unconsolidated majority-owned subsidiaries. The FASB continues to develop rulings, forthcoming in the near future, that will address other consolidation issues.

- FAS 95, also promulgated in 1986, requires that after July 15, 1988, all annual financial reports must include a statement of cash flows, and must include specified information about noncash investing and financing transactions.

- FAS 96, issued in 1987 and subsequently amended, mandates a liability (balance sheet) approach for computing deferred income taxes, rather than the deferred (income matching) method. It allows some choice in selecting timing and methods of adoption and mandates others, such as adoption of calendar year by 1992. The focus on the balance sheet for income taxes, rather than the income statement, is essentially the new and distinctive characteristic of FAS 96.

- Continuing interpretive guidance in the requirements for the section in reports to shareholders known as *Management's Discussion and Analysis of Financial Condition and Results of Operation (MD&A)* are aimed at bringing operational perspective to the president's letter and financial reports. The aim is to include information that gives dimension to the business, such as trends, demands, commitments, events, and uncertainties facing management; liquidity and capital resources; material changes; commentary on changes in operating results and financial condition; segment analysis; preliminary merger negotiations, if appropriate; participation in high-yield financings or highly leveraged transactions; and the effects of federal financial assistance, if appropriate. Here too, it's expected that changes and amendments will be continuous, reflecting both the degree to which the reports effectively inform investors and shareholders, and changing business and economic conditions.

- The changing nature of retirement policies, including both pension funds and other postretirement benefits (OPEB), continue to concern both the SEC and the accounting profession. While specific rules regarding reporting of OPEB have not yet been promulgated, it has become clear that the FASB concludes that OPEB represent a form of deferred compensation that should be recognized on an accrual basis.

International Accounting Standards

Such is the nature of accounting that the accounting standards of one country are rarely the same as those for another. Thus, the financial statements of, say, a French company would tell an entirely different story to an Italian than they would to a Frenchman.

So long as most investment stayed within national borders, these differences were merely an academic problem. But the globalization of business, soon to be followed by the 1992 consolidation of the European

Economic Community, makes the promulgation of uniform international accounting standards somewhat more urgent than before.

Thus, a number of bodies, including the autonomous International Accounting Standards Committee (IASC), have been addressing the problem. IASC has more than 100 organizational members from 70 countries, for example. The U.S. representative to IASC is the American Institute of Certified Public Accountants (AICPA), and FASB monitors IASC activities and is a member of its consultive group.

Changing Role of the Auditor

In the past decade or so, there has been a radical change in the role of the auditor. At one time, the auditor had been limited to financial statements. Now, under pressure from both the SEC and the FASB, as well as other auditing and accounting bodies, the auditor is given other and nontraditional responsibilities, such as reviewing the president's letter in the annual report and other supplementary material outside of financial statements. Congress makes periodic sorties into the question of the auditor's role, usually following news of corporate fraud that a congressman or two thinks the auditor should have caught. There has long been a clear trend toward expanding the auditor's role, which portends, many believe, a substantial danger of bringing the auditor into areas beyond his or her training and expertise, and possibly, his or her authority.

Current Reporting Requirements

It's in the attempt to address dynamic realities in business that new views of disclosure emerge. These disclosure regulations include both SEC and FASB requirements. Looking, then, at the basics of current reporting requirements we see mandated:

Audited Financial Statements. The balance sheet must cover both the current and prior year, and statements of income and cash flows must cover both the current and the prior two years. Under the regulations, minimum elements of disclosure, conforming to generally accepted accounting principles, must be included in all public documents. In addition, SEC Regulation S-X requires incremental discussion, including:

- Analysis of common stock and other shareholders' equity must be included in either a footnote or a separate statement.
- The balance sheet must disclose the amount of preference on involuntary liquidation of preferred stock, and a separate balance sheet pre-

sentation of the preferred stock to subject to mandatory redemption provisions.

- Separate disclosure of current and deferred, and federal, state, and foreign, income tax expense; an analysis of the effects of income tax timing differences; and a reconciliation between the effective and statutory income tax rates. This will change as FAS 96 evolves, and additional disclosure may be required.
- Significant amounts of material related party transactions and balances must be presented on the face of financial statements, rather than in footnotes.
- Significant restrictions on cash dividend payments by a subsidiary to a parent must now be disclosed.
- The excess of replacement or current cost over LIFO value of inventories.
- Details of receivables and inventories under long-term contracts.
- Disclosure of components of various balance sheet items, such as disaggregation of other current assets when an individual component exceeds 5 percent of all current assets (prepaid insurance, for example).

Selected Financial Data. A fluid summary that must include at least the following:

- Net sales or operating revenues
- Income from continuing operations
- Earnings per share from continuing operations
- Dividends per share
- Total assets
- Long-term obligations and redeemable preferred stock

Companies are expected to include, in this summary, any other material information of significance in understanding its operations, its trends, and so forth.

Management's Discussion and Analysis. Some years ago, the SEC mandated that annual reports include a discussion of operations, and this has become standard in annual reports to shareholders and the SEC. As indicated, the SEC constantly fine-tunes the requirements for this section.

Essentially, the SEC requires management to present, in one section of the report, a coherent analysis of the company's financial condition, including information in the following areas:

- *Liquidity.* Full disclosure would require a lucid discussion of those elements that indicate the company's ability to generate cash as it's needed. This information would include trends and events that might affect liquidity; the structure of plans to meet liquidity requirements; internal and external sources of liquidity; unused potential sources of liquid assets; and, of course, the outlook for future needs, including cash for taxes that exceed current tax expense.

- *Capital resources.* The aim here is to give a clear picture of the company's capital needs and resources. This would include commitments in the near and long term; sources and potential sources; relative costs of sources; and changes in debt, equity, and off-balance sheet financing arrangements. Here, too, the SEC is particularly paying attention.

- *Results of operations.* Unusual or infrequent events that may have a significant impact; uncertainties that may affect the validity of information about potential results; the extent to which sales increases are attributable to price increases, volume increases, and the introduction of new products or services; and the effects of inflation and changing prices on revenues and income. And of course, under FAS 94, reporting that includes results of majority-owned subsidiaries are consolidated.

In addition, the SEC encourages management discussion that reveals a sense of where the company is going when such concepts can be reasonably drawn and are based upon sound information. In other words, as full a picture as is possible that would allow the reader to understand the company, its financial structure, its performance, and its capabilities.

Market data. As noted, the annual report to shareholders should contain pertinent information about the market performance of the company's stock. This must include the principal markets for the stock; the high and low quarterly price for two years; the number of shareholders of record; a two-year dividend history; and a brief description of dividend policy and restrictions.

Form 10-K

The Form 10-K is in four distinct parts:

Part I. Disclosures pertaining to the company's business properties, legal proceedings, and management ownership of company securities. The industry segment information required covers only three years, rather than five.

Part II.   Information required in annual reports to shareholders, particularly financial and operational material.

Part III.   Information about management and officers, including proxy material.

Part IV.   Significant supplementary financial information such as components and changes in certain balance sheet items, and, where appropriate, the separate financial statements of a parent company or unconsolidated subsidiaries.

The 10-K must be signed by the principal executive officer, the principal financial officer, the principal accounting officer, and a majority of the board of directors.

Form 10-Q

Form 10-Q information should be distributed to shareholders. Included should be condensed balance sheets at both the quarter end and the preceding year end; income statements for the most recent quarter, the corresponding quarter in the preceding year, and the year-to-date periods for both years; statements of cash flows for the year-to-date periods of the current and prior year; and management's discussion and analysis of financial condition and results of operations. While an audit of quarterly results is not required, a company may have a review, and may include the auditor's report on its review of the figures if it chooses.

The significant factor in quarterly reports, as in annual reports, remains open, frank, and accurate disclosure of information that enhances the understanding of a company and its performance.

Exchanges and Disclosure

The exchanges, while they control only listed companies, have been no less lax or intensive in their own drives for disclosure regulation. The New York Stock Exchange, recognizing the value of credibility in obtaining investor confidence, has a number of guidelines to increase corporate financial disclosure that parallel those promulgated by the SEC. The American Stock Exchange and NASDAQ have their own comparable disclosure regulations as well. In other words, every regulatory body concerned with the publicly held company is not only deadly earnest about fully disclosing information that's required to be disclosed, but is accelerating its drive to accomplish it and to increase those aspects of a company's operation to be disclosed.

Information Vehicles

The primary vehicles for disclosure and dissemination of information to shareholders and others are basically these:

- The prospectus
- The proxy statement
- The Form 8-K (significant changes and events)
- The annual and quarterly reports
- Personal presentations to investors
- The news release
- The direct letter to shareholders
- The corporation's own profile
- The annual meeting
- Speech and article reprints
- The *Dow-Joneser* or Reuters interview

The Prospectus

The prospectus, issued when stock or a public debt offering is sold, is basically a legal document. It's almost invariably written by attorneys, to legal prescription, and is written in legalistic terms. Therein lies the problem. In the attempt to fulfill every legal requirement of disclosure, prospectuses are meticulously prepared, and therefore read like contracts. Unfortunately, it's virtually impossible for any but the most sophisticated nonlawyer to be expected to have the patience to read all of the information contained in a prospectus, much less to understand it. The SEC has recognized this in recent years, and as a result, it's encouraging companies to be somewhat more readable and graphic in prospectuses. The change is coming slowly, but it's coming, and increasingly, investor relations professionals are bringing to bear communications skills. The SEC wants a prospectus to be understood by the average prospective investor.

The general belief is that a prospectus can be concise without being obtuse. Furthermore, the SEC believes that while a prospectus should not be a marketing brochure, and should be objective, there is no reason why a prospectus cannot be illustrated, especially if the illustrations increase the understanding of the company. Little by little, this feeling is having its effect, and more and more prospectuses now include illustrations, color, and a more narrative style. While the subject of prospectuses is primarily the province of attorneys, there is no reason why a company president should not recognize that the prospectus is the basic document for reaching into the public segment of the capital market, and therefore should be understandable and readable.

The Proxy Statement

The proxy statement is the legal document sent prior to an annual meeting to shareholders, who must understand and vote on the business to be presented at that meeting. While proxy statements contain the basic and routine agenda of items upon which the shareholders must vote, such as the election of the board of directors, the election of auditors, the approval of pension plans, and so forth, here, too, there is no reason why a proxy should not be readable and understandable.

More than just a simple basic document, in many cases the proxy is a crucial means of communication for a company involved in an out-of-the-ordinary situation. In the case of mergers requiring shareholder approval, for example, it must contain considerable detail, sufficient to allow the shareholder to understand every aspect of the merger—not only the financial arrangements, but the reasons for it, a description of the other company, the structure of the company after the merger, and so on.

In proxy fights, it is a major document that must present management's point of view to shareholders whom management is trying to win to its side. By law, in some states, it must also report any proposal by a predetermined percentage of shareholders.

In other words, there are times when the proxy is much more than a routine document. And, as in the case of prospectuses, new formats are emerging for clarity, including illustration and pictures of officers and directors. Clarity and readability need not subvert disclosure.

The Annual and Quarterly Reports

The annual report is the basic document in which the company attempts to tell its story to shareholders, the financial community, and the investing public. The annual report must be mailed to shareholders with or preceding the proxy statement.

An annual report is a financial document and not a graphics device. Historically, it was once used by an overwhelming number of companies as a cosmetic vehicle to show the company's good side, to make the company appear to be in better shape than it was. In recent years it's improved, and become a more balanced document. Each year, the SEC and the exchanges increase their demands for greater and greater disclosure in reports. While this has put an increasing burden on companies for more elaborate disclosure and inclusion of a greater number of facts, the ultimate result has been salutary. No company, even one performing badly at any given moment, has ever suffered as mightily from full disclosure in an annual report as it has from the confusion and uncertainty that arises from inadequate disclosure.

Letters to Shareholders

Letters to shareholders are sometimes a useful device to advise shareholders of major events that affect the company between reporting periods. They are prescribed in those circumstances where special action must be taken, such as a merger that will ultimately require the approval of shareholders, and for which a proxy for a special meeting is forthcoming. They are also useful to amplify a news report, to clarify a serious rumor, or to share news of special import.

The News Release

The news release to the financial press and broadcast media, which was treated in the last chapter, is the basic tool of disclosure. Not only are news releases prescribed for routine reporting, such as earnings, but they are essential for announcing any event that might affect the evaluation of the company, whether it be a major contract, the development of a new product, the resignation or promotion of a senior officer, or a potential merger or acquisition. News releases may also be used as prospecting tools, to attract potential investors.

The Annual Meeting

The annual meeting is the official gathering of all shareholders to conduct the company's corporate business, and is the appropriate time to report on the past year's activities. It's also the time at which the annual "state-of-the-company" address is given, and the year to come is examined. As will be discussed in Chapter 7, it must be realistically recognized that the annual meeting is rarely attended by any but the smallest portion of shareholders. It cannot be assumed that any announcement made solely at the annual meeting is proper dissemination of information. Any such announcement should be followed immediately by a news release.

Investor and Analysts Meetings

Frequently, material information about a company is disclosed at meetings of analysts, brokers, or other investors. Sometimes this is by design, but sometimes it happens inadvertently.

Should this happen, it's mandatory to issue a news release about the information as soon as possible, even by telephone from the meeting to the wire services.

There are, then, two areas of information that are the province of disclosure—detailed financial data and news of significant company activity.

Generally speaking, detailed financial data should include any information that can be construed as useful in understanding the performance of a company. In the first instance, this includes balance sheet and operational information. In appropriate vehicles such as the prospectus, the annual report, or the corporate profile, this material goes much beyond basic operational information to include material that gives both historical perspective to the information and, increasingly, consideration of the market value of the company's stock. The basic intent is to make every effort to give the fullest possible picture of a company's financial structure, and to include every bit of information that will reasonably contribute to that picture.

Informing the Exchanges and NASDAQ

It's important that copies of all material—releases, proxies, and so on—be filed with any exchange, including the market surveillance section of NASD, on which the company is listed as soon as possible after they are issued. This includes both the company's listing representative on the exchange and its specialist. At the same time, it's important that while he or she be kept up to date on the company's business and trading activities, the specialist never be made privy to any material information about the company before it's made public. His or her posture must always be one of objectivity, and he or she could be seriously compromised by any inside information. Only in extremely sensitive cases, where an announcement might have significant effect on the market and on trading, will the exchanges and the NASD want the material before it's released.

Conflicts Between Attorneys and Investor Relations Consultants

A basic element of disclosure seems to be the conflict that frequently arises between attorneys and investor relations consultants, and others involved with disclosure. This is a conflict that's legitimate in its foundations and difficult to resolve. The investor relations consultant is concerned with the dissemination of as much information as possible. The attorney, inherently cautious, is charged not only with seeing that his or her client complies with the law, but also with anticipating prospective legal problems. The lawyer feels that anything said in print may ultimately be held against his or her client. The concerns of both parties are legitimate, but each must recognize that only the lawyer has the experience and training to support the point of view that the company must be protected against future attack. At the same time, the attorney must recognize that the company must compete in the capital markets, must compete for the attention of the financial community, and must compete for the attention of the financial media. If each party recognizes the other's needs, these conflicts can be resolved. The attorney must protect and the investor relations consultant must communicate. Both purposes serve the company.

Disclosure by News Release

The subject of disclosure by news release is somewhat complex, simply because what material information really is defies easy definition. This is where judgment plays so great a part. It's also difficult because events that in hindsight might be deemed material may not seem so as they unfold.

The SEC uses, as its definition of *material,* the Supreme Court decision in the 1976 case of *TSC Industries, Inc.* v. *Northway Industries, Inc.* That decision said, "An omitted fact is material if there is a substantial likelihood that a reasonable investor would consider it important in making his or her investment decisions. Put another way, there must be a substantial likelihood that the disclosure of the omitted fact would have been viewed by the reasonable investor as having significantly altered the 'total mix' of information made available."

This definition may best be seen in a consent decree some time ago against Investors Diversified Service, Inc., containing this language:

"Material inside information is any information about a company, or the market for the company's securities, which has come directly or indirectly from the company, and which has not been disclosed generally to the marketplace, the dissemination of which is likely to affect the market price of any of the company's securities or is likely to be considered important by reasonable investors, including reasonable speculative investors, in determining whether to trade in such securities."

Any material information by that definition must be disclosed immediately, using the procedures described in the last chapter. While the kind of information that comes under that heading is impossible to list to the fullest extent, there are certainly some obvious activities that should always be reported:

- Financial results for a period.
- Changes in corporate structure of any magnitude.
- Mergers or acquisitions. Here, as in other areas of negotiation, timing becomes sensitive, since premature disclosure can sometimes adversely affect such negotiations. It is now generally accepted, however, that such negotiations should be announced at any point at which there is any feeling by both parties that the negotiations will reach a successful conclusion. This can be a verbal agreement or a letter of intent. The Supreme Court has recently thrown out the *bright line* test of the letter of intent as the right time to disclose. Certainly, failure to disclose the negotiations at the time a letter of intent is signed is potentially dangerous. But the time to disclose prior to the letter of intent is still an educated guess.
- Earnings forecasts or estimates.
- Exchange offer or tender offer.
- Stock split or stock dividend, or any other significant change in capitalization.
- Decision to make a public offering.
- A substantial loan or changes in terms of loans.
- Listing on an exchange.
- Changes in accounting.
- Management change.
- Major new product introduction.
- Opening or closing a plant of considerable size.
- Amendment of corporate charter or bylaws.
- Any information that legally requires special filing with the SEC. In this context, include any consequential information filed in the 8-K report filed with the SEC.
- Significant environmental or civil rights matters.
- Decisions of regulatory bodies other than the SEC, such as the Interstate Commerce Commission or the Federal Trade Commission.

- Litigation.
- Significant board changes.
- Rumors that may be either damaging or too helpful.

The list goes on and on, guided only by one's definition of material information for a particular company or industry.

Registration for a Public Issue

One area of disclosure that's been perhaps the most difficult to understand is the regulations that govern a company that has a public issue in registration. A company in registration is severely limited and prohibited from any activity that might be construed as offering, selling, or assisting in the sale of stock. One conflict arises in that a public company with a secondary offering is required to conform to other rules of disclosure, even while in registration, in order to support earlier issues for both current shareholders and the financial community.

The basis for this regulation is the Securities Act of 1933, which prohibits the offering or sale of a security unless a registration statement has been filed with the SEC, or selling a security unless the registration statement has become effective. There are three periods of registration. There is the time before the registration statement has been filed. There is the period during which the registration statement is on file, but not yet effective. And there is the period after the registration statement has become effective. It's during the second period—when the company is in active registration review—that it's illegal to issue any material relating to the security, other than through the statutory prospectus. This is particularly true for an initial public offering. That second period is then clearly defined by the SEC as being "at least from the time an issuer reaches an understanding with a broker-dealer," and it ends with the completion of the dealer's prospectus delivery obligations. While the registration period is normally defined as 90 days for an initial public offering and 25 days for a secondary, completion may be considered by the SEC to be when the issue is completely sold by the underwriter, even if its been only a few days, so long as the SEC has approved the issue. This situation is interpreted differently by various attorneys, and there is no consensus. Not included are the initial discussions or negotiations between the company and the underwriter. It's only when there is some form of commitment by the underwriter that the period actually begins in which the company is considered to be "in registration."

With an *initial public offering*, it's during this registration period that the corporation may take no action, nor issue any publicity, that can be construed as an effort to sell the stock or enhance the ultimate sale of the stock. And here, in view of other aspects of disclosure regulation, lies the paradox between what can and cannot be publicized. However, if approval of the prospectus is delayed, and an earnings statement is ready, it can and must be released. If the prospectus is already approved and the issue is selling, the earnings are released and the prospectus is *stickered* by adding the information to the prospectus. Other forms of information that might affect the company and be construed as selling the stock, however, remain questionable regarding release.

Acceptable Dissemination of Information

The SEC recognizes the problem, and further accepts the fact that it's impossible to define in absolute detail those activities that a company may or may not pursue. Each set of circumstances must rest on its own facts. Nevertheless, the SEC has issued seven categories of information that it deems not only acceptable during an initial public offering, but which it in fact encourages. They are:

- Continued advertising of products
- Continued distribution of customary reports to stockholders
- Continued publication of proxy statements
- Continued announcements to the press of "factual business and financial developments"
- Answering unsolicited inquiries from shareholders, the press, and others (if the answers are responsive to the questions and prudently do not go beyond the bounds previously described)
- Answering unsolicited inquiries from the financial community
- Continuing to hold stockholders' meetings and answering stockholders' inquiries at such meetings, without breaking new ground, unless information is disclosed in acceptable ways and added to the prospectus if necessary

Obviously, the information disseminated under these seven categories should not include predictions, projections, forecasts, or opinions with respect to value. Nor should it include any attempt to describe the company in ways that might be considered promotional and supportive of a securities sales effort. And so once again we come to the question of judgment. And once again we come into a potential conflict between attorneys and investor relations consultants. Here, too, attorneys and investor relations consultants must consider one another's positions in light of the company's needs and responsibilities.

Without attempting to skirt or stretch the seven categories of information approved by the SEC, it should be recognized that not only is there tremendous latitude in the amount and kind of information that can be disseminated by a company in registration, but that both the need for, and the value of, such continued dissemination does not diminish.

The rules are perhaps more lenient during a secondary offering. Current shareholders must be kept informed, as in nonregistration periods, and the company's stock must be supported in the marketplace. Subject to advice of legal counsel, it may be assumed that the same seven categories of dissemination apply, plus normal dissemination procedures. As with initial public offerings, projections of any kind that might be construed as selling the stock of the new issue must be avoided. This is a murky field, best navigated in conjunction with experienced securities lawyers.

There is also substantial value in an investor relations communications program begun well before the company goes into registration, in that such a preregistration program sets the tone for what may be deemed permissible while the company is actually in registration. On the other hand, there may be a problem if a company that has never communicated to the financial community suddenly begins such a program the minute it gets into registration. It's in this area that the experience of the investor relations consultant can be of exceptional value.

In the third stage, when the company is out of registration, all bounds are off for a financial communications program that's otherwise legal under any SEC regulations or sound business requirements.

In conforming to the disclosure regulations of the Securities and Exchange Commission and the exchanges, it's important to be thoughtful and considered. Premature and untutored disclosure may be even more harmful than no disclosure. You can't disclose piecemeal.

To avoid piecemeal or inadequate disclosure, consider whether you have all the facts needed to make disclosure, and then, if you don't have all the facts, you must ask whether disclosure will have a worse effect on the company than nondisclosure. The concern should be not only with the timing, but with the content of what's disclosed.

7

Going Public

Good health care, the medical profession tells us, begins before the patient becomes ill. Good investor relations, in the same way, begins before the company goes public.

For the company choosing to go public, there is a vast area of concern in terms of relations with the financial community. Investor relations activities begin well before the public stock offering, and continue well afterwards.

In addition to helping develop the process of introducing the company to investors, developing investor relations objectives, and helping to position the company for the investment community, investor relations enters into the selection of the underwriter, includes structuring and dispersing information about the company to the financial community, follows through the period of registration, and enters yet another phase with the sale of the issue and the after-market (the period following the initial sale of the issue). In view of SEC regulations regarding dissemination of information while a stock is in registration, an investor relations pattern must be established that cannot be construed as having been developed solely for the purpose of selling stock.

The Background

The process of going public is much more than a device for raising capital. It's a ritual that feeds on the dynamics of the stock market, and that has a mystique of its own. The initial public offering of a company—the IPO—is fraught with an excitement that, to investors, seems to know no equal; that transcends rational investment principles. Perhaps more than

any other aspect of investor relations, then, it's important to understand
something of the context and background of going public.

There have been times in American economic history when the simplest—if not necessarily the best—means of acquiring capital for a corporation was to go public. The late 1960s and a part of 1971 and 1972, for
example, were periods of extraordinary economic growth in America,
manifested by a flood of IPOs. In 1972, a record 568 companies went
public. Corporate profits for most companies were high and the economic
boom showed no signs of abating. The mid- and late 1980s were another
such period, in which the economic boom bred an overwhelming number
of IPOs. In 1980, 237 companies went public, and by mid-1981 that number had already been surpassed. In 1989, in a very different market climate,
there were 241 IPOs. By mid-1990, there were about 130, just as the notion
of an economic downturn began to be perceived.

In the 1980s, however, there was a quality to the IPOs that was different
from IPOs of earlier periods. First, this was the decade of the new technology. Companies such as Compaq and Lotus went from start-up to Fortune
500 in the blink of an eye. Genetic companies, such as Genentech, went
from start-up and obscurity to lords of the stock market faster than it takes
a home-run king to circle the bases.

Second, the 1980s was a decade of rapid economic growth, new millionaires, precarious leveraging and other financial shenanigans the likes of
which the nation hadn't seen since the turn of the century. It was the age,
also, of leveraged buyouts, insider trading, and the glorification of greed—
literally. Witness the success of the motion picture *Wall Street*. Even though
the villainous takeover specialist got his comeuppance, he was still the
hero of the piece.

It all came apart on a black Monday in October, 1987, when for complex
reasons that go beyond the usual reaction to economic conditions, the
stock market took its worst bath since the 1930s. That the market recovered within two years, and even brought back the market for IPOs, is one
of the anomalies of economics.

The Psychology of the IPO

During periods that are so fertile for the newly public company, the psychology that fuels the stock market seems to be predicated on confident
anticipation of consistent and sustained growth, which could only mean
to the investor a consistent and sustained increase in dividends and the
price of stocks. Price/earnings ratios for some stocks reached astronomical
multiples of 20, 30, and even 60 during the 1960s and early 1970s. The
price/earnings ratio of the Dow Jones stocks reached an average as high
as 17.3 (the more rational general average is about 13). Heaven only knows

what the market and investors were anticipating in the way of corporate profits in the ensuing years to justify those multiples.

The recession of 1973–1974 put a quick halt to that period's breathless growth, as did the 1987 crash in its time. In both cases, the market quickly fell, brokerage firms (and particularly the quickie underwriters) disappeared by the score, and the individual investor returned to cultivating his and her own gardens. It would seem, in each case, that the Go-Go years were over.

But nothing is forever, not even good lessons learned. The ultimate return of the economy strengthens, as it should, the stock market, and the needs for capital see a steady growth in companies going public primarily because they needed equity capital. In the 1980s, this was enhanced by companies with new technology. The darlings of the 1990s have yet to emerge, although it may be anticipated that the institutions, and not the individual investor, will predominate. Which is not to say that individuals are not still part of an underlying strength in the stock market; are not important investor relations targets. Indeed they are, even if they are not the market's newsmakers.

Choosing an Underwriter

The choice of an underwriter is an investor relations concern because the underwriter will serve as a significant conduit to the financial community. Choosing the wrong underwriter can be an investor relations disaster—one for which no investor relations program can offer quick relief.

An underwriter is an individual or a firm that acts as an agent for developing and distributing a public issue of stock. Usually (but not always) an investment banker as well, the underwriter quite literally underwrites the issue—supplies the money from the sale of the stock issue. In the real world, the money doesn't come from the underwriter's pocket, but from the sale of the stock. The underwriter takes a predetermined percentage of the issue, in both cash and stock, as commission. When the lead underwriter guarantees the sale of the stock, it's called a *firm* underwriting. In some cases, however, the underwriter and the members of the syndicate merely indicate that they will sell what they can. This is known as a *best efforts* underwriting.

The underwriter sells stock both by distributing it to other brokerage firms and to its own customers. The other brokerage firms form a syndicate with the underwriter, in which each firm agrees to take a fixed amount of the stock for resale to its own customers.

The difference between an underwriter and an investment banker is really one of services performed, rather than a clearly defined professional distinction. The underwriter's primary responsibility is to underwrite and distribute a stock issue. The investment banker, on the other hand, has a broader role in guiding the company in its financial activities and in finding other sources of capital in addition to public sale of stock. (See Chapter 2.) An investment banker may also sell securities, but his or her job is primarily to understand the nature of all capital markets. The investment banker must help the client structure a company for the intelligent use of capital as well as to acquire it, to supply information on not only the capital markets and alternative sources of capital, but the total economic picture as well. In an underwriting, the investment banker must guide the company through its many tortuous steps before, during, and after the underwriting. This is very different from merely putting out a public issue that serves as merchandise for the stockbroker to peddle.

The Wrong Underwriter

Most companies choose the wrong underwriter for the wrong reason. Before the Wall Street debacles of 1973–1974, there was a great proliferation of underwriters. These were predominately brokerage houses that did underwriting—who helped companies go public, not to capitalize the companies so much as to supply product to be sold by the brokerage end of their firms. They were not investment bankers.

Back in the halcyon days, when virtually any company could go public, underwriters were wooing privately held companies not only to solicit their underwriting business, but to persuade them to go public even in cases where it wasn't warranted. Smaller unstable companies, eager to go public and take advantage of the rising stock market, frequently accepted the first offer to do an underwriting that came along, often with disastrous results. Frequently, an underwriter was selected simply because somebody knew somebody. Many smaller underwriters calculated that if only a small percentage of their underwritings succeeded, the profits would offset the many that didn't make it. Playing these kinds of odds, the trick was to do as many underwritings as possible, regardless of the quality of the companies being taken public. Another device, particularly with speculative ventures, was for the underwriter to take exceptionally large blocks of stock options as a kind of auxiliary fee for doing the underwriting. Here, too, the odds game was being played. If just a portion of the issues succeeded and the stock price went high enough, the underwriter made enough money to cover those issues that did not succeed. Forgotten in this whole procedure was the company—and certainly the shareholder. This wreaked particular havoc on the better companies that survived and thrived only to find themselves saddled with a poorly devised equities program that hurt the company in the long run. There are now hundreds of companies originally taken public by underwriting firms that are no longer in existence, or for which there is no longer a market at any price for their stock. The poor structure of the original issue left the company inadequately capitalized for its growth, which forced early demands of other sources of capital, such as banks. Many of these companies found themselves in the position of being unable to split their stock because the price was too low, unable to issue new stock because they gave away too large a percentage of the company in the original underwriting, and too highly leveraged because they had to go to banks to finance growth that should have been paid for by a proper equity issue.

Fortunately, most of the old-style and questionable underwriters are now gone from the scene. Those companies that survive are predominately investment bankers who predicate their own operations on long-range financial structures that serve companies in so many ways that they are able to withstand the assault of sustained bear markets.

Preparing to Go Public

Properly done, the company that feels it should consider going public must begin by doing a great deal of homework. This should include taking a realistic view of its long-term capital needs, and assessing alternate sources of capital. A complete financial analysis should be done including proforma operating statements and balance sheets for at least five years ahead. This program should be done with the assistance of the company's own internal financial staff and with the help of its accounting firm and attorneys.

The willingness of an underwriter to take a company public does not, of itself, mean that the company is doing the right thing in going public.

The company should review its decision to go public not only in the light of opportunities, but obstacles as well. The costs of going public are tremendous. Legal fees are astronomical. Printing costs for prospectuses are high. Most underwriters insist that a company going public use one of the larger accounting firms—one of the so-called Big Six—and this almost invariably means an increase in accounting fees. Furthermore, most company presidents don't discover until it's too late that when they go public they are suddenly in two full-time businesses—their own and the public corporation business. There is a tremendous difference between running one's own business and running a public corporation. There is a whole raft of new regulations and reporting requirements to conform to. Suddenly there are shareholders to deal with, annual meetings, annual reports, and so forth. These are all factors that somehow don't get calculated until it's too late.

Choosing an Investment Banker

In choosing an investment banker, there is always a subjective element in the judgment of intelligence, personality, and the evaluation of skills as they will be applied to the wide range of corporate problems.

The company should select and approach no more than three or four investment banking firms. With the aid of the accountant and the attorney, the firms can be readily identified on the basis of:

- The strength of reputation
- Limitations of size of companies they will accept as clients
- The number of comparable client companies they have in terms of size, industry, and capitalization
- The history of the issues they have taken public

Even more significantly, the investment banking firms selected should be precisely that—investment banking firms. They should:

- Be at least reasonably large and well-established
- Offer a full range of services that include departments for acquisitions and mergers, fixed-income securities, syndication, research, financial consulting, and all other aspects of the financial spectrum

The size of the retail operation is of lesser importance than would appear at first glance. Some of the most successful underwritings are achieved not by the firm's own retail operations, but by the ability to syndicate. The firms normally included in an investment banking syndicate are more important in the distribution of stock than the number of retail branches the underwriter has. The size and quality of its research department are better gauges of the investment banker's operation than is the number of registered representatives in the company's roster. The investment banker's trading operation is more important to the aftermarket than is the length of the list of underwritings it has done.

In other words, the measure of the investment banker's capabilities lies not in its obvious first capability to do an underwriting so much as in its ability to help the company over the long range.

Evaluating the Investment Banker

When the company has gone as far as it can go in identifying at least three good investment banking firms, it should then invite representatives of each of them to meet separately with its executives for discussions of a potential relationship. The evaluation should be based not on some ancillary issue, such as the pricing of the stock—that's a problem to be faced further down the line—but on the ability of the investment banking firm to serve the company's total financial and financial service needs. In fact, the investment banker doesn't price the stock—the market does. The banker simply assesses the price that the current market will accept.

Another value of these interviews is to further review the company's total capital needs, including its decision to go public. On the strength of these interviews the investment banker should be selected.

Basic Considerations

Within the context of these criteria, there are a few basic points that should also be considered:

- Get the best quality available. The smaller company need not feel it must settle for second best. Very few investment banking firms will refuse to discuss a relationship with any company of any size that can demonstrate real growth potential. Don't be put off by awe for the name of a Donaldson, Lufkin & Jenrette, a Goldman, Sachs, a Lazard, or a Morgan Stanley. An investment banker is interested in the future as well as the past or present. But don't be unduly flattered, either, by being approached by a name firm.

- On the other hand, don't be overimpressed by reputation. A lot of history has gone into building that reputation, but it may be just history. Or the reputation may have been built on elements irrelevant to a corporation's particular needs. A firm's present investment banking skills may not be sufficiently broad and innovative to deal effectively with today's capital markets and corporate needs.

- How important is your firm to the investment banker? If you're going to be a small fish in a large firm, you may have a problem getting the attention you need. On the other hand, don't assume that because you're small you won't be important to the firm. Apple computer was just beyond being a gleam in its founders' eyes when Morgan Stanley, who wanted to be strong in the computer field, took them public.

- Who in the firm will handle your account? Will it be a junior person— in which case, decline and walk rapidly? Or will it be one of the more experienced and seasoned people? Your company need not serve as the training ground for the investment banker.

- Where is the lead banker located? An underwriting requires a lot of hand-holding. If the lead banker is 2,000 miles away, either a lot of hand-holding won't get done or a lot of expensive and exhaustive traveling will. If there are co-managers, the lead banker does most of the work, and should be accessible on a consistent basis.

- Don't overlook the regional firms. There are some very good ones.
- The really superb firms will dazzle you not with their history or reputations or private dining rooms, but with their people. At the point of day-to-day contact, it is an individual with whom management must work, and not a firm's history. Nor are one or two superstars an indication of depth of capability and service.
- In this context, some newer and smaller firms have more capability to offer than do many of the older giants. Size and age are sparse measures of investment banking skill.
- The number and size of deals a firm has done are less a measure of capability than the *kinds* of deals they have put together, and the imagination with which they have been formulated in times when a more traditional approach to financing has not been possible. Aggregate amounts of private placements they have done will not help a corporation if it needs $2 million in a tight market, and the investment banker can only boast of $25 million placements for blue-chip companies. The reverse is true as well.
- Ask questions. Lots of them. Simple and broad questions are the best, the better to gauge the investment banker's ability to grasp and understand a company, its industry, companies of comparable size, and the company's specific problems. See how thoughtful are the answers—or how glib and evasive.
- Ask to speak to their clients, especially those in comparable positions. Was performance as promised? Did the investment banker understand at all times the dimension and difficulties of all the problems? Was the range of service broad and intensive? Was the strategy functioning as planned? Did initiative come consistently from the investment banker, or was prodding necessary?
- Don't go to an investment banker for the wrong reasons. Don't hire an investment banker because he promises to support your ailing stock price with research reports you might not otherwise get from the Street, and certainly don't retain one that promises shallow short-term solutions when you have long-range problems.

Some Caveats

And one more thing—don't be romanced by an investment banker. That's how so many companies got taken public in the 1960s—companies that are now either out of business, or undercapitalized or looking to go private again.

The best due diligence in choosing an investment banker, according to the noted venture capitalist Benjamin Rosen, of Sevin Rosen, is to interview five or ten institutional investors who are likely to buy into the deal. In today's institutional market, they are the ones who are best able to define for you the best investment bankers who do the best deals, and with whom they most prefer to work. If you can't depend upon reaching the market you most want because of your potential investment banker, you've got the wrong banker.

It's most important to remember, in choosing an investment banker, that times and the economy have changed. This is now the time of full service, the time for the broadest possible understanding of the full range of corporate needs and how to serve them, and the time for greater sophistication than ever before. The investment banking hero of the vast debt placement for the giant company is not necessarily the person capable of the hybrid deal so important today for the smaller or medium-sized company—nor is that individual always right to serve the full range of corporate needs for the emerging company. The investment banker of the past is clearly not the investment banker of the future.

A thorny point. Many companies have on their boards a representative of the underwriter who first did the public offering. Too often, this board member sees the investment banking function subjectively, in terms of the limitations of his or her own firm. The investment banker's presence on the board should not preclude objectivity in the search for sound investment banking relationships.

More significantly, there's an inherent danger in having on your board any service people, such as bankers or lawyers, when you may have to go outside for that service. The potential for conflict of interest is overwhelming. RCA had just such a problem, with its investment bankers on its board advising about acquisitions. The result was to load up with acquisitions of clients of their own board members. The ultimate divestiture of some of those acquisitions was expensive. In fact, you don't need anybody on your board whose objective advice you can buy when you need it.

The Syndicate

In any underwriting syndicate, as seen in the *tombstone* ad placed in a newspaper to announce the new issue, the firms in the listing are not in alphabetical order. They are in pecking order—the order of importance.

At the head of the list, standing apart, is the managing firm—or underwriting partners and co-managers if there are more than one. Next come

the major firms, listed in order of the size of the portion of the issue each
has agreed to market. This is followed by the secondary firms smaller
national firms taking a smaller portion of the issue. Last come the regional
houses and smallest firms.

While the tombstone ad is ostensibly for the company and its new issue,
it's also an ad for the brokerage firms. This is why the tier in which a firm
appears is important to that firm. And this is why the order of listing is
a pecking order. The firms on the lower tiers are considered by Wall Street
to be the lesser firms.

Regional Firms

In most major cities, there are investment banking and brokerage firms
whose operations are generally limited to serving the geographic areas in
which they are centered. Many of these regional firms are excellent, both
in marketing securities in their areas and in serving investment banking
needs for smaller companies in their territories. Properly structured and
staffed, a regional firm can frequently offer the smaller company better
service than can a major national banker. They are more likely to give
attention to a small company in their area than will a New York-based
national firm. A good regional firm that is generally included in a good
syndicate also has access to that syndicate, which means that a regionally
generated underwriting can be distributed as broadly as can a national
underwriting.

There is a growing trend away from the traditional investment banking
fee predicated on a portion of an underwriting, and toward the straight fee
structure for investment bankers. A good relationship with an investment
banker is extremely important for a growing company, and particularly a
public one. To expect any kind of service from an investment banker
whose total source of income from a company is the underwriting fee is
a peculiar form of self-deception that almost invariably costs the company
more in the long run.

The Nonpublic or Prepublic Company

It's generally believed that the financial community will not concern itself
with information about a privately held company. In an overwhelming
number of cases, fortunately, this is not true—assuming that the program
is properly handled. In skilled hands, a certain amount of premarket preparation can be done. An effective program has two advantages—it serves to
notify and inform the financial community, as well as the general public,

of the facts about a company and its industry, and it establishes a pattern of public relations activities which, if they don't flagrantly function to sell stock, serve as a pattern and precedent for an allowable level of public relations while a company is in registration.

Under skillful examination, any company can be found to have aspects about it that should be of interest to the general business press, even though the company is not public. It can be an unusual facet of the company, it can be an unusual relationship to its industry, or it can be an unusual approach to routine problems in an industry. Following the procedures outlined in the chapter discussing press relations (Chapter 5), a nonpublic company can expect a measure of publicity in the financial and business press. Granted that it takes considerably more skill to develop newsworthy material for a nonpublic company than for a public company, but a review of the business press will show that it's done with regularity.

In many cases, and in selected industries, a nonpublic company can be a valuable source of general information about that industry to the financial community. Analysts specializing in any industry are always eager to receive fresh and pertinent information from any valid source. There's no reason why a nonpublic company can't take the initiative to supply the information to the very analysts they will ultimately be dealing with when they go public.

Certain kinds of product or service publicity in the nonfinancial press can also be useful to the financial community in contributing to its knowledge of a particular industry. There is nothing untoward in sending reprints of such publicity to selected analysts specializing in that industry.

The objective, of course, is to precede any public offering, much before registration, with a public relations program that engenders recognition of the company name and understanding of the company's activities and position in the field, even while it enhances the view of the industry in which the company serves.

The Prepublic Pattern

As for establishing a pattern of public communications that will be acceptable while in registration, the basic rules of disclosure apply (see Chapter 6). Nothing is acceptable that can be construed as offering to sell stock or conditioning the market for the sale of stock. Nevertheless, the SEC says that, barring those specific exceptions, the company may continue its normal pattern of publicity. The point is to establish a normal pattern of publicity.

Prior to registration, and as part of putting the company's story together for presentation to prospective underwriters, the company should orient its material. This should not be done in the legalistic terms of a prospectus, but in ways that are acceptable to the financial community in general. One approach used with some measure of success is the financial annual report for the nonpublic company. The report need not be expensive or elaborate, but it can follow the same general procedure as used for an annual report for a public company. This kind of report can also be used for customers, employees, suppliers, and, of course, the financial community, as part of a program to acquaint them with the company and its position in the industry. It can include full financials.

It may also be worth considering the preparation of a background report similar to that recommended for distribution to the financial community by a public company.

At all costs, in any prepublic publicity, or representations by a prepublic company to the financial community, all SEC regulations pertaining to a company in registration should be kept clearly in mind. Nothing will defeat an ultimate public issue so much as misrepresentation of the facts about a company even before it has gone public. And certainly, if the program is to succeed, it must be done in such a way that the prepublic material will be remembered well after the company has gone public. Any significant discrepancies in the information given in the two periods will seriously and adversely affect the financial community's view of the ultimate issue.

Registration

When a company is in registration for a public stock offering it enters a period of silence. That is, it may do nothing in the way of disseminating information about itself that can under any circumstances be construed as marketing the stock, promoting it, or conditioning the market for the sale of the stock.

This doesn't mean that the company must go into hiding from the public or the financial community.

First of all, the SEC requires that the normal rules of disclosure for a public company be maintained even for a company in registration. Any basic information about activities that alter the nature of the company, such as a merger, an acquisition, or a major contract, must be disclosed. The basic rule remains, however, that no activity should be undertaken, nor new public relations effort initiated, which can in any way be construed as selling stock or conditioning the market. This particularly includes any form of projections, any subjective material that implies growth potential for either the company or the industry, or any material that interprets any information being disseminated. The exception, perhaps, is product information, which is consistent with an historical pattern of marketing established well before registration.

The New Issue

Once the company is out of registration it can begin to pursue the normal investor relations activities described throughout this book. The first step is a press release that simply announces the new issue, made available by prospectus. It should include the underwriter, the size and details of the issue, and a brief description of the company's business. This release and the tombstone ad in the financial press is usually taken care of by the underwriter in conjunction with attorneys.

The Due Diligence Meeting

Immediately prior to the effective date of the registration, the underwriter holds a meeting for representatives of all the underwriting firms that might participate in the syndicate to distribute the stock. Legally, the purpose of the meeting is to demonstrate that due diligence has been exercised in the preparation of the issue and in the presentation and updating of facts about the company, and so it is referred to as the "due diligence meeting." The more realistic purpose of this meeting is to assure that all participants understand the nature of the issue, to develop some enthusiasm on their part about the company, and to persuade some of the firms to sell the stock. Another purpose, however, is to assure the participants in the syndicate that they haven't made a mistake in their participation. There may be several such meetings in different cities.

Due diligence meetings used to be cut-and-dried affairs, attended reluctantly by people who have already decided to help sell the issue. But times change, and the marketing opportunities at a due diligence meeting are now better realized. For this reason, it's now the better part of wisdom to put on a thoroughly professional performance in explaining the company in order to engender the kind of enthusiasm necessary to make the issue a success.

The presentation should be carefully prepared so that the material is presented in an orderly fashion, and that it is succinct, precise, and to the point. The objective of the meeting is to have each participant understand the company's current financial structure and, in the case of analysts, to demonstrate the company's ability to appreciate the invested dollar. And, as with analyst meetings, questions should be anticipated and the answers rehearsed. Management should appear confident, open, and willing to answer all questions.

In planning the investor relations activities, the syndicate is a key to developing the geographic aspect of the program. Since the location of the syndicate members is basis for the geographic distribution of the stock, there is a first inkling of those cities that might be targets for analyst meetings and press attention. Moreover, a representative of a syndicate member can usually be depended upon to assist in identifying the key people in the local financial community.

The Aftermarket

The aftermarket is what happens to the stock after the public issue. In too many cases, a company is led to believe that the underwriter will take and maintain a proprietary interest in the stock issue after the company has gone public. This is rarely the case, even for companies that do well in the stock market following the original issue. There are several reasons for this.

Maintaining a sound aftermarket beyond the period legally required is arduous, time consuming, and sometimes expensive. It demands skills and facilities that are frequently beyond the capabilities of even the larger underwriters. In order for the price of a stock—and particularly a new and untested one—to reflect consistently the company's earnings and earnings potential, there must not only be market-makers, but quality sponsors. Presumably the underwriter will serve as both—but this is a presumption more often honored in the breach. Frequently, the underwriter will issue a research report, primarily to assist its own registered representatives in the sale of the stock, but the report is plainly qualified to indicate that the firm issuing the report maintains a position in the stock, or brought the stock public, and is therefore not entirely objective. Unfortunately, unless the company is growing at a consistent rate of 30 percent a year and expects to do so for the next five years, and its stock price reflects this growth, the underwriter has very little time to spend on any one stock— and that amount of time diminishes the farther away from the date of issue.

There is a realistic aspect to the problem, too, in that the underwriter has probably earned a fee from just the underwriting. Unless the stock really takes off and sharply increases in value, there is a limit to what the underwriter can profitably do.

He or she may continue to sponsor and make a market in a stock, but one sponsor and one market-maker are not sufficient for an issue that is not performing superbly on its own. He or she may call upon friends and associates in other firms to help, but there is a limit to the time he or she can profitably spend in pursuing this activity, and to the sustaining results he or she can achieve.

There is also the question of exposing a company to a broad spectrum of analysts and brokers. This, too, is beyond the capability of most underwriters, both in terms of time they can profitably spend and the overall perspective necessary for developing a strategy tailored to a particular company at any one time in the market's performance. Even the largest and soundest underwriting firm places a strict limit on what it can reasonably do in developing additional sponsors, market-makers, research reports, and exposure to the financial community at large. Underwriters are not geared to support an issue to any degree that might enhance its long-range acceptance by the financial community. This is essentially the purpose of a separate and professionally performed investor relations program.

The Employee Stock Ownership Trust (ESOT)

An increasingly popular way to raise capital, particularly for the private or closely held corporation, is the employee ownership plan and trust.

The company sells stock to a noncontributory trust fund it sets up for its employees. The trust uses the stock as collateral for a loan from a bank. The trust, in turn, gives the money to the company in payment for the stock. The company then pays an expensible maximum of 15 percent of its payroll annually to the trust. With ESOT, it is paid with pretax dollars. Furthermore, the plan is allowed to function with the margin requirements usually applicable in a stock pledge. Instead, the ban accepts the corporation's guarantee.

In a specific example, a company needs $1 million for five years. It has 300 employees with an annual gross payroll of $3 million and is in the 54 percent tax bracket. The ESOT borrows $1 million from the bank, which the company guarantees. The ESOT then pays the $1 million to the company in exchange for $1 million in company stock. The company pays $300,000—or 10 percent of its payroll—annually to the trust. The trust pays the bank $254,976—principal and interest—annually on the debt, leaving it $45,024 for its reserve account. As the loan is paid off, the stock is allocated to the employees' account and is usually vested over a period of ten years.

The plan has several advantages:

- For the nonpublic company not in a position to go into the equities market, it allows the company to go public, in a limited sense, without registration.

- Because pretax dollars are used to finance the debt, there is a substantial tax savings.
- Cash flow is increased substantially.
- Net worth is increased substantially.
- It creates liquidity at fair market value, comparable to that of a public company, without SEC registration or underwriting costs or time.
- It allows for capital gains sales by individual shareholders.
- The stockholder-employee accumulates values in the ESOT that are not subject to estate taxes.
- It establishes a definite valuation of shares for estate tax purposes of major shareholders.
- Buy/sell agreements for the stock of major shareholders may be funded by life insurance, with premiums deductible from pretax income by flowing it through the trust.
- For the employees, it builds unity and team spirit by allowing them to share in the capital growth of the company, to realize capital gains on income, and to accumulate values that are funded by employer contributions, with no dimunition of employee take-home pay.

The ESOT is also for the closely held company, or for the company already public but not in a position to issue additional shares due to existing stock market conditions. Recent experience has shown that the ESOT is not an unalloyed blessing and so should be considered with a great deal of independent advice from accountants, lawyers, and investment bankers.

The ESOT is sanctioned by the Internal Revenue Service. An ESOT is best established with the assistance of one of the several firms specializing in such programs.

Going Private

In the chastening cold light of changing economic conditions, an increasing number of companies sometimes come to feel that they are better off as private companies than as public companies. The procedures for going private are relatively—*relatively*—simple, so much so that the SEC tends to take a dim view of the process, as do many individual shareholders. When stock prices are very low and management feels the company is undervalued, and particularly when the stock price is considerably lower than book value, the decision to go private is very tempting. Unfortunately, the shareholder who bought stock at $20, now sees it at $3, and is being offered

$5 for it in a tender offer by a management that wants to go private and will obviously benefit from the transaction, is not likely to be overjoyed at the company's action. In some cases there have been stockholder suits, although considering the high cost to an individual for filing such a suit, these have not been overabundant.

Globe Security Systems, Inc., a subsidiary of Walter Kidde & Company, Inc., is a typical example of a public company going private. It had 335,450 shares of its common stock in the hands of the public. It tendered for that stock at a cash price that was 38 percent higher than the last sale price on the American Stock Exchange. Globe had once traded as high as 31 1/2, but at the time of the tender it was trading at 3 7/8. As a result of the tender offer, Kidde's holdings in Globe went from 81 percent to 95 percent. With fewer than 300 shareholders, Globe was exempted from SEC regulations and was delisted by the Exchange. It was, in effect, a private company. Those shareholders who did not tender their stock might just as well have done so, since there was virtually no further public market.

It doesn't always work that easily. Fuqua Industries tried it, and was slapped with 11 stockholder suits. For some time, the stock, at $14 a share, had been selling at a P/E of less than four, and had been consistently below a book value of $18.66 a share. It seemed to be a good idea. The firm tendered at $20 a share to acquire all outstanding stock. The offer failed, in large part because of shareholder objection to the plan.

Fuqua's response was interesting. While abandoning the plan to go private, it still decided to buy back a large number of its shares, at $20 a share. In recent years, corporate stock repurchases have become increasingly popular, as the market fails to reflect the value of a company. Some of the nation's largest companies have done it, including IBM, Sears, Roebuck, Ashland Oil, Texaco, PepsiCo, and many others. It is frequently a good corporate strategy that can at least represent a sound investment of the company's assets. Other advantages are to fine-tune the balance sheet, to make shares available for acquisitions or stock options (within the limits of SEC regulations), or to increase earnings per share by reducing the number of shares outstanding. A typical success story in repurchasing is Mary Kay Cosmetics. At one point, more than 40 percent of its stock was held by institutions. When the institutions decided, at one point, to get out of the stock, the market couldn't absorb all of the institutional holdings. Mary Kay tendered for 800,000 shares at $13.25, thereby reducing the number of shares outstanding by 30 percent. Within a year or so, reflecting the reduced number of shares, the stock was selling at $39, with a P/E of 12. The strategy clearly worked.

Among those techniques for going private, there are several that are more commonly used in addition to the tender offer.

One of the most popular methods is to offer a new nonconvertible debenture in exchange for the common stock. Another technique is a merger or liquidation, usually using a dummy corporation. Management establishes a dummy corporation into which it merges the original company. The public shareholders don't get shares in the new company, but are instead offered a price for their stock in the original company. The merger is then voted by the shareholders, but invariably the buyers have enough votes to carry their proposal. Another technique is a reverse split, which sharply reduces the number of shares outstanding and leaves each share at a price so high that trading is precluded. The variations on the technique are myriad.

Among the dangers of going private, which are many, is the very strong barrier of antifraud and antimanipulative provisions of the Securities Exchange Act of 1934. This becomes particularly cogent in a deal in which the public shareholder is obviously going to lose out. A great measure of care must be taken in presenting any such arrangement so that there is no misrepresentation and that there is full disclosure of every aspect of it. Naturally, a company in the process of buying its own stock under any procedure must pay strict attention to SEC regulations.

There is also a question, the answer to which is difficult to anticipate, as to the future of any company going private. Perhaps it should not have gone public in the first place and going private is a proper amendment of that mistake. On the other hand, at some distant future date, the public company going private may need equity money to expand to meet changing conditions. How then will the market view that company, if, in going private, it had not done right by its shareholders?

For the company planning to go public, it's certainly a good exercise to view the experience and reasons of companies that have gone private.

Going public to find a source of capital that is appropriate to a company is fraught with pitfalls and expenses that somehow don't get readily talked about in discussions prior to an underwriting. While it's unlikely that these activities should reach a proportion to preclude a public issue where one is otherwise indicated, it would be foolhardy for any corporate management to plan to go public without being aware of the problems and expenses inherent in doing it.

The point has been made that the securities industry is in the greatest state of flux it has seen in the financial history of our country. The facts are too commonly known to review here. However, one thing becomes crystal clear. In whatever form the industry ultimately evolves, it must be predicated on its primary purpose—to finance business, not merely to sell securities. No matter what else happens to alter the structure of the securities industry, that remains primary.

8

Shareholder Relations

It seems to be obvious that the essence of investor relations is to compete in the capital markets by getting more people to buy your stock; to invest in your company and its vigor and growth. Yet, there is an axiom of marketing that wisely notes that it's easier and cheaper to keep a customer than to get a new one. It's easier and cheaper to keep a shareholder, and perhaps to get him or her to increase holdings, than to get a new one.

The Rationale

Thus, there is sound rationale, aside from legal requirements, to painstakingly pursuing the loyalty of existing shareholders.

Presumably, an effective investor relations program will result in a warm feeling of loyalty to the company by its shareholders. But how many chief executive officers are now walking around with a glazed look in their eyes because, despite an intensive investor relations program, their loyal and intensively informed shareholders tendered their stock to the other side in a takeover attempt? How many loyal and informed shareholders, subjected to many years of a meticulous investor relations program, have sold their stock when it became apparent that the company was in for a rough year?

On the other hand, how do you gauge the degree to which shareholders held on to their stock when the company anticipated a bad year, because they fully understood that the company was inherently sound and would recover from any short-term problems? How many shareholders increased their holdings when it was made clear that the company was about to enter a particularly favorable period? A careful analysis of the stock transfer sheet offers some measurable evidence, quantitatively, of a sound shareholder relations program. But not all evidence of value can be quantified, and certainly not at reasonable cost.

There is also the paradox of liquidity. In a company with a relatively small float—the number of shares outstanding that are available for public trading—satisfied shareholders who do not sell their stock can, in a measure, be self-defeating, since if there is no stock available, there is no auction market. And if there's no auction market, the price of a stock tends to stay static or decline. At the same time, investors who might want the stock in any sizable amount leave quickly if they can get only small pieces of their orders.

And yet despite these questions, there is clear evidence that a carefully planned and effectively performed shareholder relations program is warranted. And the evidence is more than clear that a well-executed program makes a significant contribution to the company's capital goals. That evidence is in the success, in the stock market, of those companies with active shareholder relations programs.

Certainly, beyond legal obligations, there's an inherent responsibility to keep investors informed of not only current operating data, but of both the general performance and outlook for the company.

Theoretically and legally, management is employed by the shareholders, and therefore the shareholders are entitled to an account of the way their company is being managed. With exceptions, this is, of course, little more than theory. The control of most companies is held by either the management group or a relatively small group of investors close to the management. The theoretical concept of shareholder democracy is, again with exceptions, a pleasant myth. While it is true that minority shareholders, by dint of legal methods or highly visible and publicized activities that pressure the company, are able to effect policies counter to management's original plans, the fact is that companies are run by management. The exceptions are so few as to be notable. Even the efforts of highly visible minority shareholder leaders, such as the famous Gilbert brothers, are successful only by attrition, and then only over a very long time. It is to the credit of the Gilbert brothers that they have accomplished a great deal in the field of shareholder democracy, and to a large extent their efforts have been salutary. But these efforts have taken a very long time, many years, in fact. Even after several decades, they have barely made a dent in achieving their own stated objectives.

The Institutional Shareholder

Now a new element—institutional holdings—enters the picture. The vast and overwhelming growth of institutional holdings in even smaller companies poses a new problem in corporate governance, which means, as well, a new problem in shareholder relations. It is becoming increasingly evident that many of the institutional holders, such as pension funds, are moving from passivity to aggressiveness. The institutional holders had heretofore not voted their shares and had paid little attention to day-by-day management activities. Now, they are increasingly looking at the potential power they can wield from holdings of 5 percent or more of a company's stock. Suddenly, such issues as investment in South Africa, or pollution, have been awakened in the minds of fund managers and the people they represent.

Where once institutional shareholders could be reasonably ignored, or at least catered to no differently than the ordinary shareholder, now attention must be paid. They must be kept as informed as is legally possible, and they must be wooed by management as never before.

Shareholders as a Source of Capital

Shareholders must be viewed for what they are—a source of capital. And as such they must be as intensively cultivated as is any other group. The fact that they are already shareholders is a twofold advantage. They have already made a decision favorable to the company, and management usually knows who they are. This doesn't mean that the selling aspect of financial relations is in any way diminished—a shareholder can become an ex-shareholder with relative ease. It merely means that the job of reaching him or her is simpler. It also means that, as a legal owner of the company, he or she has a claim to management's ear. Dissatisfied shareholders have a right to make their opinions known to management, and they have many ways to do it. They can ask embarrassing questions at an annual meeting, and be highly visible while doing it. They can write letters to management. They can telephone or call on management in person. They can sue if they feel there's a basis for it. And then, of course, they have that ultimate weapon. They can become ex-shareholders.

If the shareholder is satisfied, he or she can use these weapons in management's behalf. The shareholder can get up at that same annual meeting and publicly praise management. He or she can write letters of praise. The shareholder can be an effective spokesperson for the company and its stock to friends and to brokers. And since shareholders are sometimes effective management people themselves, they can sometimes contribute useful ideas. As for the ultimate effective weapon, the shareholder can hold his or her stock during the company's trying periods, and buy more stock if the company's outlook is good, refuse to tender that stock to outsiders, and buy more stock in a secondary offering.

And so, on balance, an effective shareholder's program is warranted and has tremendous value, unquantifiable as the specific results of such a program might be.

It should be remembered, as well, that aside from keeping shareholders informed, the ultimate objective of an investor relations program is to engender understanding and a favorable attitude toward the company on the part of the investors.

Tools of Shareholder Relations

While the normal functions of an investor relations program will ultimately reach and serve shareholders as well as prospective investors, there are some quite specific devices used as tools in an investor relations program. These are:

- The annual report
- Interim reports
- The annual meeting
- Letters to shareholders, or a periodic newsletter
- Distribution of product literature or internal house organs
- Distribution of press reports
- Phone contact with shareholders
- 800-numbers to corporate headquarters
- Advertising and other promotional devices
- Speech reprints
- Dividend reinvestment plans

These are the tools—but the tools are not a program. Certainly, every public company issues an annual report and many companies issue interim reports. All public companies hold annual meetings. Many companies frequently write letters to shareholders to inform them of special events or activities, and may even write welcoming letters to new shareholders or query letters to selling shareholders. But not only must each of these devices be looked at separately and used artfully, it must also be recognized that each functions best when it's part of an overall plan or program. They must not only interrelate and reinforce one another, but they are all judged in terms of specific objectives.

Shareholder Relations Policy

For a shareholder relations program to be effective, there must first of all be a clear-cut decision by management that commits the company to such a program. Internally, a specific officer must be charged with shareholder relations responsibility. If the program is considered important enough to do in the first place, it should be considered a serious responsibility. Too often, left-handed recognition of the need for such a program results in a half-hearted attempt from which the chief executive divorces himself, assigning the responsibility to a low-ranking officer, and allotting the performance of the program either to inexperienced personnel or to an advertising manager clearly not qualified to deal with it. In order for a shareholder relations program to succeed, it should ultimately fall under the personal aegis of the chief executive officer, no matter who is assigned to perform or oversee the actual task. Of course, for the company with internal or external investor relations counsel, the professionalism of the program is enhanced. But here, too, the investor relations counsel is thwarted unless the chief executive officer is not only dedicated to the success of the program, but understands the necessity of keeping the investor relations counsel keenly attuned to all aspects of the company's operation, as well as to current corporate policy. While the day-by-day activities of such a program—or any investor relations program for that matter—may be supervised by a designated executive, there must be clear access to the chief executive officer.

The Program

The program itself must have clearly stated objectives. The ultimate objective is to keep shareholders informed, and to do so in ways that engender a favorable attitude toward the company. But aside from the basic rules and requirements of disclosure, how far does that go? The basic requirements of disclosure for even the largest company can be fulfilled with a mimeograph machine. The degree to which the company goes beyond the rules in the elaborateness of its disclosure, as well as the graphic devices used as a medium, must be predetermined. What is the basic attitude of the company toward its shareholders? Are they a cherished group to be assiduously wooed and won, or are they to be considered as transitory, with the obligation to them minimal and limited only to basic information? Are they to be accepted merely as a necessary evil attendant to a public corporation, or is each new shareholder to be greeted with a personal letter from the president welcoming him to the family?

Are they to be seen as a distant group to be dealt with only as the occasion arises, or shall the program include a careful and regular analysis of transfer sheets to keep informed of changes in shareholders of record? This, incidentally, is a basic and important device in any investor relations program. It not only indicates changes in shareholders, but changes in geographical distribution, the entry or exit of participation by brokerage houses, unusual purchasing or selling patterns that might indicate the necessity for specific action or alterations in the investor relations program,

or warn of prospective takeover attempts. Transfer sheets should be reviewed regularly, and each week a summary should be prepared for the
chief executive officer, indicating changes in shareholding of large blocks.
Specific patterns should be watched for such factors as regular purchases
of small or medium-sized lots by one buyer, or selling patterns in a particular geographic area.

CEDE

To some extent, the message of the transfer sheets must be seen in light
of the fact that an increasing number of trades—perhaps half or more—are
done in Street name now, and will be listed as being made through CEDE
(*The Depository Trust Company*). This doesn't diminish the value of tracking;
it simply qualifies it. The CEDE printouts should also be summarized
often, and compared to prior periods to spot trends.

Today, more sophisticated techniques are used to poll shareholders to
determine attitudes toward the company as an investment. Research is
replacing guessing. Good research tells the company what the investor
thinks about the company, and what's important and what isn't. But a
word of caution. Attitudes change, and if an investor relations program is
to be predicated on current investor attitudes, then these attitudes must be
fathomed frequently.

Only when the investor relations program is carefully planned can specific decisions be made on such questions as how elaborate should the
annual report be? Should interim reports be simple statements or extensively illustrated descriptions of company business? Should an audiovisual
or film presentation be developed for the annual meeting, or should it
consist solely of a president's message? Without a clear-cut overall policy
regarding investor relations, decisions and answers to these questions and
myriad others are arbitrary.

As with much of investor relations, the tools used for dealing with
shareholders are not as important as the ways in which they're used. Nor
are the tools of shareholder relations immune from being used imaginatively. As was demonstrated in Chapter 4, the devices of corporate communications—annual and interim reports, and so forth—although
prescribed by law, are still susceptible to imaginative treatment. And still,
there are other conduits to shareholders.

The Annual Meeting

The annual meeting of shareholders is a legal requirement rarely looked
upon by corporate executives with pleasant anticipation. Even if a com-

pany is performing beautifully, and management expects that the event will be a display of mutual pride, it requires a great deal of preparation that seems to most corporate officers to be irrelevant to the specific business of running a company. They may be right, but they cannot avoid the annual chore.

In smaller companies, meetings are rarely well attended unless the company is facing some specific problems. In even the largest companies, only the smallest portion of outstanding shares is represented in person, and most matters on the agenda have been predetermined by the mail proxy vote, combined with the votes of the shares held by management groups.

In companies with problems, the president anticipates being roasted by dissident shareholders who are more vocal and visible than usually seems warranted by the number of shares they represent. Some companies' meetings are sometimes besieged not only by legitimate representatives of minority shareholders, but by publicity seekers who seize the opportunity to be difficult in public; to use the meeting as a vehicle for their own personal publicity and aggrandizement.

The Meeting Date

The date of the meeting, usually prescribed by corporate charter but not difficult to change, further serves to put pressure on the production of the proxy material and (if it's to be mailed with the proxy) the annual report, which should be mailed 30 to 40 days prior to the meeting, and certainly no later than 10 days for unlisted companies.

And so it's not difficult to understand why few chief executive officers look forward to an annual meeting as anything but an unpleasant but necessary chore.

Yet, properly run, an annual meeting can go beyond its basic legal requirements to be a useful communications tool. It can be a focal point for presenting a company point of view not only to shareholders, but to the entire financial community. For listed or NASDQ companies, it can be publicized. It can serve as a sounding board to allow management to fathom the reactions of its shareholders to its activities. And there is no question that shareholders have frequently come up with useful suggestions at annual meetings.

The secret of success of an annual meeting is in its preparation. Its basic elements are prescribed by state corporate law. The meeting is generally run under Roberts' Rules of Order, follows the agenda prepared well beforehand by the attorneys, and covers specific items that have been outlined in the proxy statement. Predetermined motions and seconding are usually assigned to executives and directors who own stock, so that the meeting runs smoothly. These usually cover the motion to dispense with the reading of the minutes, motions to cover the business of the agenda, such as elections of the board of directors and auditors, and any other business that must be legally covered. Proxies are collected and officers are appointed to tally both proxies and votes made in person. This formal part of the meeting is usually scripted by the attorneys to assure that the format protects the company under legal requirements.

These activities are formalized and cut and dried. The potential problems come in three areas—the president's message, the questions and answers, and new business.

Every meeting, even those where minimal attendance is anticipated, should be prepared meticulously and with every detail covered. The president's message should be either written, with ultimate publication in mind, or outlined in great detail.

Anticipating Questions

Every question that might be asked should be anticipated in writing and, in a rehearsal, the appropriate answer carefully worked out. It is important for the success of an annual meeting that every likelihood be anticipated. There should be no surprises.

The President's Message

The key to the meeting, of course, is the president's or CEO's message. The annual meeting is the president's report to shareholders—to his or her ultimate employers. The CEO is expected to report on the condition of the company, its progress, and the directions in which it is going. It's easy to assume that the message will be essentially the same as the message in the annual report, which presumably all shareholders will have read. The fact is that most shareholders will not have read it, or if they have, will still appreciate hearing the report in person.

The message will also differ from the report in several ways. The company will have several months' progress to report since the time the annual report was written. In all probability the first quarter figures will be available, and if the timing is right, the annual meeting may be used as the medium to report the quarter's results. Some companies release preliminary numbers at the meeting, but this is generally frowned upon as "milking the news." Since the target audience is quite specifically the shareholders, the kinds of information and the format in which they are presented will be much more focused for them, even though it's anticipated that the speech will be either reported by the financial press or will subsequently be mailed to shareholders and the financial community in a postmeeting report.

Furthermore, if the speech is well prepared, and addresses the key points of the moment, it should tend to anticipate—and therefore forestall—some of the thornier questions that are likely to be raised in the question and answer period.

More and more companies, today, hold the president's message until after the formal meeting has been held and adjourned. The presentation, then, doesn't become part of the official minutes. This is particularly useful in today's litigious society. The speech is heard by those present, and copies of the speech, with answers to questions, can then be distributed to shareholders in an *edited* (but not distorted) version. Other companies, and shareholders, feel that they would rather have the speech on the record to protect and prove what was said.

Contents of the Message

The message should be as short and concise as possible and still cover the material to be presented in 10 or 15 minutes. It should contain the following elements:

- A summary of operating results, including, if appropriate, the first quarter's results, and general estimates for the coming year (but not necessarily the numbers).
- The operational condition of the company in terms of its products, services, markets, and finances.
- Special events during the course of the prior year that are significant to the company's past, present, and future activities.
- The economic climate in which the company is now operating, or expects to be operating during the coming year.
- The near-term corporate strategy, longer-term strategy, and a general prognosis for the future. Here, great care must be taken to be realistic and cautious. Better to err on the side of caution. External economic events can alter the best laid plans, and it's better to do better by 1 percent than to do worse by 1 percent. It's well to remember here, too, that any significant projections made for the first time must be reported immediately that day to the general public under the rules of disclosure. The process should be set up beforehand.

Questions and Answers

Following the president's message come the questions and answers. It's at this point that many meetings that might otherwise be successful turn into a shambles. The importance of anticipating questions cannot be overemphasized. And if the company is large enough for press coverage, it must be anticipated that questions and answers reported out of context can sometimes be distorted. Some years ago, the chairman of the board of a large company had anticipated announcing that since he was gradually withdrawing from active participation in the business, he was taking a reduction in salary. Prior to the meeting he was advised to include that statement in his presentation. He waited instead for what he deemed to be an appropriate moment during the question and answer period. As it turned out, questions were somewhat hostile. His announcement of a pay cut was reported in the context of the hostility, and appeared in the press to have been a decision forced by the attacks made during the course of the meeting. The report was wholly inaccurate, but arose naturally from a failure to anticipate the effect of bad timing upon the announcement.

The question of executive compensation is a classic example of the kind of problem the CEO must face from the podium—a problem that seems to absorb shareholders for generation after generation. During periods of economic downturn, and certainly in a company reporting lower earnings or slower earnings growth, it's almost certain to arise.

Nor does there seem to be any relevance to the actual size of the compensation. It happens as often in companies where the CEO earned less than $200,000 as in those where the CEO earned more than a million dollars. The question is most often raised in companies with $10 to 25 million in revenues, where the CEO makes about $500,000 annually. It happened, as might have been expected, to a CEO who earned $900,000 in a company with revenues of only $11 million.

It's here that the value of anticipation and preparation is best proven. Compensation questions can be anticipated by clearly understanding how the compensation package is arrived at. Interview the Board's compensation committee, if there is one. How was the package determined? Were comparisons to comparable salaries made within the industry? With companies of comparable size? With companies with comparable profitability? Was an outside compensation consultant used? What were the criteria that the consultant used?

What are the particular accomplishments of the CEO that justify the salary? Were there demands? Were there negotiations? Did the CEO get what he or she asked for? On what basis and with what terms?

Every possible question should be asked, and the facts marshaled to formulate a cogent, direct, and documented response.

The response should not, of course, come from the CEO, but rather from a responsible and credible spokesperson, such as the chairman of the board's compensation committee, or an independent board member. The answer should include not just the rationale and process for arriving at the package, but a strong presentation of the CEO's skills, virtues, and contributions to the company's past or future growth.

The ultimate message should be, "We need this person, and his or her compensation is fair."

Shareholder Resolutions

Under clearly defined circumstances, shareholders of a corporation are allowed, under the Securities Act of 1934 and subsequent SEC regulations, to submit resolutions to be voted upon at annual meetings.

To do so, a shareholder must have owned at least 1 percent (or $1,000 in market value) of the stock for one year, and must submit the proposal to the corporation at least 120 days before the proxy statement is sent to shareholders. Each qualified shareholder is allowed to submit only one proposal a year.

At the same time, management may veto these proposals if they are substantially the same as other proposals submitted in the past five years; if their acceptance would require the company to violate the law; if they are submitted with false or misleading arguments; if they relate to a personal claim or grievance against the company; if they seek to require the company to pay a specific dividend; or if they cannot be put into action by the company.

Should a proposal be made that fully qualifies, it must be dealt with on the floor as would a management proposal, although there is ample opportunity for management to prepare and present arguments should it be deemed valuable to do so.

Hostile Questions—The Dissident Shareholder

Aside from anticipating questions, the basic rule for every chief executive officer presiding over an annual meeting is to keep cool at all costs. Failure to do so, even in the face of the most hostile and irrelevant questions, tends to inflame shareholders and to evoke even more hostile questions. Any appearance of being evasive has the same effect. Patience is of the essence.

Even for a company in deep trouble, most questions are cursory and honest, reflecting the legitimate interest of shareholders in their company. Some questions, on the other hand, are flagrantly designed to attack and to antagonize management. Dissident shareholders, dissatisfied with anything from the stock's performance to the dividend policy to the company's environmental practices, come well prepared and armed with their own research data.

Lewis and John Gilbert run a nonprofit organization called Corporate

Democracy, Inc. In addition to the Gilberts, the organization consists of a large number of individuals located throughout the United States who are dedicated to increasing the voice of minority shareholders in corporate activities. The Gilberts themselves attend a great many meetings each year of corporations in which they hold shares of stock. They have devoted themselves to achieving quite specific aims in the name of corporate democracy. They strongly advocate such corporate practices as cumulative voting, locating meetings at places convenient to the majority of stockholders, distributing postmeeting reports, the use of more effective and informative annual reports, the presence of all directors at annual meetings, improved accounting procedures, audit committees, opposition to stagger systems in which only a portion of the board is subject to election each year, and executive compensation programs that are responsive to the company's losses as well as to profitability. While considered a thorn in the side of many executives, they have, through attrition and constant public exposure, achieved remarkable success over the years in moving corporations toward accepting their points of view. Rarely do the Gilberts succeed in any motion on the floor that's not expressly the wish of management. However, the publicity they've garnered has resulted in exposing management practices that they oppose. This has been an effective device in making them successful over a period of time because most shareholders were unaware of the issues involved until the Gilberts spotlighted them.

Other special interest groups have also become prevalent in recent years. These include environmental and women's rights groups, and groups opposed to investment or doing business in undemocratic or segregated countries. The participation of these groups, and others that will undoubtedly emerge, becomes increasingly forceful, and must be recognized as a fact of corporate life.

The executive who doesn't allow any such dissident shareholder his or her full measure of public voice will almost invariably find himself or herself in trouble, not only during the course of the meeting, but in the press. For the press, most annual meetings are dull and not particularly newsworthy. A dissident stockholder is the most exciting event, and therefore the most reportable event, at most meetings.

The dissident shareholder is best disarmed by being given the fullest and most polite audience possible. He or she must be recognized and his or her point of view given full consideration, even if the outcome is predetermined and the views are inconsistent with corporate realities. There is no better answer, in situations such as these, than, "I want to thank you for your suggestion. We will certainly take it under advisement."

There are times when the complaints of the Gilberts and others are particularly pertinent. For example, the Gilberts have always defended the rights of a successful corporation to make legitimate charitable contributions. However, some time ago, Eastern Airlines made a $500,000 five-year pledge to pay for a new production of a Wagnerian opera by the Metropolitan Opera Company. Particularly in view of the company's profit picture at the time, Mr. Gilbert's statement at the annual meeting was quoted in *The New York Times* as follows: " 'I defy anyone to prove one extra benefit to the company from that gift. It is for the social benefit of one man so he can sit at the opera,' said Mr. Gilbert." Whether Gilbert was right or wrong didn't matter quite so much as the fact that his highly damaging statement was widely broadcast in the public press.

The environmental and women's interest groups are functioning on a rising tide of favorable public sentiment. They both deal with issues of national concern that quite naturally focus on many aspects of a corporation. This is particularly true of any corporation that functions in areas that might in some way contribute to pollution, and in companies in which women are not represented as executives or members of the board of directors. Larger companies, such as AT&T, have been through some highly publicized and expensive problems in affording equal employment opportunities for women, and naturally the subject has been a matter of concern to shareholders.

Comparable action has come from consumer groups, a subject also very much in the realm of general public awareness. In fact, a most successful attack was made on General Motors in this area, with the annual meeting used as the focal point. Public interest groups even went beyond that to approach universities and other institutions that were holders of large blocks of General Motors stock, in an attempt to pressure them to vote their stock in behalf of specific measures proposed by the groups. Among the responses made by General Motors was agreement to include on the board of directors individuals who specifically represented public interest viewpoints.

For companies subject to shareholders' discussion on these topics, the questions can be anticipated by covering the subjects in the president's message.

Running the Meeting

In physically setting up a room for a shareholders' meeting, arrange seating for the convenience of shareholders and particularly for those who wish to ask questions. If the meeting is for a company large enough or sufficiently newsworthy to warrant television coverage, wide aisles to accommodate cameras are important. A sufficient number of microphones should be strategically placed in the aisles, or should be of the handheld type that can be passed to a shareholder at his or her seat.

If the meeting is orderly, as it should be if the chief executive officer is calm and patient, the question and answer period should be allowed to last as long as is necessary for all shareholders to have a fair chance to participate. Any attempt to rush a meeting, or to cut off the questions, will only serve to inflame the shareholders and turn the meeting into a fracas. Which is not to say that, in the interests of fairness, each speaker can't be limited to three or five minutes. Or a generous period of time—a half hour or so—can be specified beforehand.

The chief executive officer should not allow himself to be goaded into anger, or to allow the meeting to get out of hand. There are some shareholders who make a practice of disrupting meetings, apparently for publicity purposes. Their questions are antagonistic and irrelevant. A meeting should be run strictly under Roberts' Rules of Order, and in some cases it may be necessary to advise a questioner politely that his or her question is out of order or irrelevant. Some questions, particularly thorny ones, can sometimes be deferred by suggesting that the topic is not of interest to the entire group, but will gladly be discussed after the meeting. There are even times when shareholders become unnecessarily abusive and may have to be physically ejected. The judgment resides with the meeting's chairperson. A good rule of thumb, however, is to visualize tomorrow's headlines before taking any extreme action. In some cases in which the chair has had to physically eject obstreperous shareholders, it's been done so deftly as to garner sympathy for the chair rather than for the ejected party.

In answering questions, the chairperson of the meeting should call upon other executives to participate. The purpose is to demonstrate the depth of management—that the company is run by others besides the chief executive officer. Properly prepared, it can also be expected that the vice-president of finance will give a more detailed answer to financial questions, or that the vice-president of marketing will give a more specific explanation of marketing programs.

It's a good idea to decorate the meeting room with a display of the company's products and services. There are times when meetings are further enhanced by supplementing the president's message with either a film or a slide presentation. Care must be taken that the audiovisual devices are supplements, and not a substitute, for the president's report. If the room is to be darkened for presentations, care should be taken to keep the speaker lit.

In some larger companies, where meetings may be expected to take several hours, lunch is sometimes in order. For shorter meetings, refreshments should be served. This can consist of coffee and pastry, or perhaps a light snack.

Meetings held on a plant's premises can usually be enhanced by a postmeeting plant tour. This, too, should be carefully planned.

Press Coverage

Press coverage for a meeting, aside from the company's own desire for it, depends on the size of the company, the prospective newsworthiness of the information to be imparted, and the availability of a reporter to cover the meeting. Certainly, the press should be invited beforehand by letter and phone. It's pointless to believe that the press can be excluded from a meeting that might prove to be unfavorable to management. If the company is important enough, any attempt to exclude the press will not only fail, but will result in hostility and a negative or erroneous report.

The presence of any representative of the press will, of course, be known, since all shareholders and guests check in at the door. If a member of the press does come to the meeting, a representative of the company, and preferably the investor relations counsel, should spend a few minutes with the reporter before the meeting, and then sit with him or her to answer questions as they occur to the reporter during the course of the meeting. Prior to the meeting (assuming there is something newsworthy to say), a news release should be prepared for immediate distribution, either during its course or immediately following. Complete press kits, including the release, should be on hand for any member of the press who attends. The kit should contain not only the release but, if possible, a copy of the president's speech and material on the company including a background report, an annual report, product information, and any other printed material that may be available.

Analysts and Brokers

Frequently it's advisable to invite selected important analysts, brokers, money managers, and other representatives of the financial community. The meeting affords them a good opportunity to see management in action at first hand, as well as to gather more information about the company. Regardless of the number of this group who attend, each one will be qualified in terms of expressed interest. The same kind of material prepared for the press should be made available to any representative of the financial community who attends.

Immediately following the meeting, the officers of the company should make themselves available to meet shareholders, reporters, and analysts, and to accept or place phone calls to or from the press, especially major wire services. This should be done even if a directors' meeting must be kept waiting for a few minutes. Frequently some have questions that they prefer not to ask from the floor. These are usually questions that are most important to the questioner, and should be answered in the same responsive, forthright manner as were questions from the floor.

It's sometimes appropriate to use the occasion of the annual meeting to arrange for a specific interview by the press with the company's officers. This can be done beforehand, with an opportunity to sit down in a separate room or a quiet corner where the interview can proceed undisturbed. Dow Jones and Reuters readily accept telephone interviews, provided that they're called immediately following the meeting, and the information is newsworthy.

The Postmeeting Report

The postmeeting report is an extremely useful device to multiply the value of the annual meeting for the financial community at large, and particularly those shareholders who didn't attend the meeting. It can be a simple printed version of the president's message, including an edited selection of questions and answers from the floor. In a more elaborate report, photographs of the meeting can be included. This report is facilitated by taping the entire meeting, even though the president is speaking from a prepared text. Some companies include a summary of the meeting in their quarterly report, although this is not quite as effective as issuing a special postmeeting report. The postmeeting report is then mailed to both shareholders and segments of the financial community that have expressed interest in the company. It can be used as well for prospecting for new investors. The timing of the quarterly report may make combining the two feasible.

The report should include information about required actions resulting from the voting, new directors, new auditors, stock option plans, how many shares were eligible to vote, and how many did vote for each item, and so forth. If this information is not reported in print, it's not easily available later on when it's needed for other investor relations purposes.

Through careful planning, then, the annual meeting can be turned from a legal chore and unwanted responsibility into a favorable investor relations device.

Letters to Shareholders

There are times during the course of the year when special events warrant a letter to shareholders. For the company that issues interim reports, these occasions should arise infrequently. A letter is particularly useful in announcing an impending merger or a major change in business direction, or to dispel a serious rumor. Some companies use a letter to shareholders to introduce a new product by making it available as a sample or at a discount to shareholders.

A welcome letter to new shareholders is an effective investor relations marketing tool. It's a standard form, signed by the president, welcoming the new shareholder and describing the company, its products, and its aims in a few short paragraphs. Unfortunately, there seems to be little tangible research to provide evidence that the letter to new shareholders contributes to a sense of loyalty. It certainly won't overcome bad performance over the long term. There is no question that it contributes to the overall goodwill that's useful in shareholder relations. Whether the expense is warranted by the results is open to some question. As part of a large and full-scale investor relations program, it's certainly useful. As an isolated activity unsupported by other activities, it's questionable.

The use of the publicity reprint as part of regular or special shareholder mailings, as well as for other marketing activities, is especially effective. It focuses attention on favorable articles that the shareholder isn't likely to have seen. With a little covering note attached, it puts the article in its proper context. Since press coverage is presumably objective, a news or feature article adds a kind of editorial third-person endorsement to the company's story, which has an effect of giving added credibility. The reprint takes on the aura of the publication in which it appeared. Also included in this category are reprints of favorable research reports by brokerage houses.

One word of caution in the use of reprints of either articles or research reports. Such material is copyrighted and may not be reproduced without written permission of the publisher. This is usually easy to obtain, and there is no excuse for distribution of such material without prior permission.

Many companies publish internal house organs for employees or external house organs for customers. Shareholders, too, are interested in this information, unless the internal house organ is too completely taken with purely personal information such as bowling scores or engagement announcements. If the house organ contains useful information about the company, it should certainly be considered as part of a regular mailing to shareholders.

Inquiries from Shareholders

There is nothing more startling—although legitimate—than the unexpected phone call from a shareholder to the chief executive officer of the company. The shareholder may own 50 shares, but feels entitled to information, and that it should come directly from the president. When a chief executive officer does take the call, it should be dealt with in exactly the same way he or she would handle an inquiry from a security analyst or broker. No matter how busy or inopportune the call, the shareholder must be dealt with politely and given the information asked for, if possible. Perhaps the best way to handle these inquiries is to be simply responsive to the question and to volunteer no more information than is asked for. Going beyond that leads to more questions.

Naturally, a measure of judgment must be exercised. A shareholder with a block of 5000 shares will certainly want more intensive information than a generalization of the company's progress. In any event, patience, courtesy, and being solicitous wins the day. A written record of such communications should be kept to offset any questions about inside information.

Shareholders frequently write the chief executive either to complain or to inquire. These letters should be answered politely and promptly. The answers should be specifically responsive to the question and should be brief.

As part of a full-scale investor relations program, it's sometimes useful to plan plant tours and visits for shareholders. Plant tours, too, come under the category of shareholder activities that are meaningless as isolated practices. They work best only as part of a total program. Certainly it's out of the question if it means disrupting operations. A plant tour is also useful in dealing with environmental groups, to demonstrate at firsthand the measures the company is taking to deal effectively with any problem.

Special Situations

There are special situations that sometimes arise in shareholder relations that require specific attention. There is the situation, for example, of the company that is potentially subject to a takeover attempt because management holds too few shares of stock outstanding. This is discussed in Chapter 11. There is the problem of geographic distribution of stock where too many shares are concentrated in too few geographic areas. There is the concern of the company whose stock price is being buffeted by large block trading by institutions over which the company has no control. Sometimes deleterious rumors must be dealt with, using letters to shareholders, news releases, advertising, or press contact, as appropriate.

These situations must be dealt with thoughtfully, and with as much planning and foresight as possible. Most of these situations are dealt with throughout this book.

Dealing with shareholders is frequently a function of looking inward rather than outward, as one does in dealing with the financial community at large. But if experience is any measure, no CEO has ever gotten into too much trouble, under the worst of circumstances, by dealing frankly, honestly, and directly with the company's own shareholders.

Effective investor relations is a marketing function that relies on management and financial relations skill. Since it's so difficult to measure results on a day-to-day basis, the program must always be viewed with perspective, and constantly monitored. It rarely works if it's treated as an isolated jumble of irrelevant activities. It almost invariably works if it's planned, programmed, and executed by sensitive management and experienced investor relations counsel.

9

Strategy

The profound changes in the capital markets, during the last decade, substantially alter and redefine the strategy for investor relations during the coming decade.

At the same time, the increasing intensity of investor relations practice, during the last decade, has had a marked effect on the stock market. The constant and accelerated barrage of more competently prepared information from companies to investors, and the increasing sophistication of the information delivery systems, seem to have established a new relationship between the company and the investor; between the company and the investment professionals who make or influence buying decisions. Today's investor has the ability to know more about a prospective investment—and to know it faster—than ever before, a salutary consequence of the competition for capital. Clearly, the intensive practice of investor relations has altered the expectations of the Street regarding information—what it is, where it's coming from, and how to interpret and use it. Today, computers and computerized databases deliver the facts. The investor relations professional must now supply the background, context, information, judgment—and perhaps even the aura—that gives meaning to those facts; that demonstrates why a dollar invested in the client's company is likely to appreciate faster than a dollar invested in other companies.

Factors Dictating Strategy

It seems reasonable to assume, at the same time, that the thoughtful practice of investor relations has helped many companies think more clearly about their own management and direction. One can hardly focus

217

on external appearances without looking carefully at internal structures.

Strategy—the plan and configuration of specific activities, and their timing, to achieve investor relations objectives—becomes more important in this decade's marketplace than ever before. The increased number of public securities issues, the increased competition for the investor's dollar, the broadened and diversified sources of capital, and the internationalization of the economy all dictate the need for a plan—a strategy. The greater number of investor relations practitioners competing for the Street's attention, and the overload of information flowing to the financial community, all demand greater skills, more imaginatively applied, in order to get the attention of the professional investor. No longer will random sorties into the marketplace suffice, as they did for so long. And the strategies of the 1990s call for an investor relations professionalism of the kind that's emerged only relatively recently.

Several other factors affect investor relations strategy. For example, the current generation of investor relations professionals are not only more sophisticated in the practice of the craft, but are also much more skillful and enthusiastic advocates for the companies they represent. Where once the investor relations professional was merely a conduit to the Street for information, today's professional is knowledgeable in the skills and techniques of Wall Street and marketing, as well as those of investor relations. This means that the investor relations professional has the knowledge and skills to represent a company in the most persuasive way; to sell ideas, rather than merely to report facts that are available from other sources. This alone alters investor relations strategy.

But even more significant is that the investor relations function, once merely a vehicle to convey information, is now a full-fledged marketing function, in every sense of the word. As Laurence Udell of Bear, Stearns put it, "There is always a reason to sell a stock, but people have to be provided a reason to buy."

That means that strategy is dictated by marketing considerations, as well as by such traditional factors as the nature of the company and the nature of the market. The investor relations matrix, today and in the coming decade, is infinitely more complex than it's been in the past.

It's important to recognize, in this context, that strategy is dynamic; so many of its elements are in a state of flux that the strategy must be developed with an eye toward the changing relationships between many of those elements.

It must be designed just for each company. Some rather specific factors must be considered, catalyzed by a large dose of intelligence—perhaps wisdom—perspective, and foresight. It must be tempered, as well, by a substantial measure of imagination and initiative, simply because it's a competitive situation, and those are the factors that other competitors in the capital markets will try to bring to bear. There is no such thing as reaching into a drawer to pull out Plan A as a program to meet the needs of all companies. Each company has its own needs, its own problems, its own strong points to sell to the financial community, and its own weak points to overcome.

The Strategic Matrix

Unfortunately, investor relations is not a science, and it can hardly be called an art form. It's a skill and a perspective. Planning a program calls for a strong measure of understanding reality. To be insensitive to the structure of the market and to rely merely on mechanical techniques mindlessly performed, simply because that's the way they've always been performed, is foolish, wasteful, and expensive. It is also frustrating, since the results can be relied upon to be negative in relation to the effort.

The elements of this matrix are a function of:

- Marketing
- The nature of the capital markets
- The nature of the economy
- The tools of investor relations
- The nature of the company and its financial structure
- The nature of the company's industry
- The corporate objectives and growth plans
- The nature of the CEO

The Elements of Strategy

As each instrument in an orchestra—its definition, its range, its capabilities, its potential contribution to the whole—must be understood individually by a conductor before the orchestra can work together in concert, so must the elements of strategy be understood before they can be orchestrated.

Marketing

Marketing is not only the crucial glue that allows a company to compete successfully in today's capital markets, it's also a relatively new concept to investor relations. Investor relations has resided in the realm of pure corporate finance for so long that the emergence of marketing techniques has gone virtually unnoticed. And now, suddenly, they're here.

The Unique Investment Premise

For all the esoteric definitions of marketing, perhaps none is more relevant to investor relations than that it's the discipline that takes the essence of a company, in terms of its value as an investment, and presents that essence to the market for the company's securities—the investor and those who inform and persuade investors. In some cases, that essence may be the company itself; in others it may be derived as a *Unique Investment Premise*—a basic concept that best projects the unique investment values inherent in the company.

Elements of Marketing

Essentially, the elements of marketing break down into four major points:

- Identify the market
- Identify the product
- Identify the marketing tools
- Manage the marketing tools

While marketing can be generally construed to be an aggressive pursuit of activities to bring the essence of a product or service—in this case the advantages in investing in a particular company—to its target audiences, the structure for doing so successfully resides in these four points.

To *identify the market* means to understand the particular segments of the financial community that it's most advantageous for a particular company to reach—that's most likely to invest in its securities. Today, more than ever, identifying the market means more than intuition; it means research. The complexities of the market and the exigencies of the economy require a more intense understanding of who is interested in what; in attitudes toward (or against) a company; in fathoming investors' needs and desires. It means knowing who is following the company and who is not, and why. It means understanding the investor and the potential investor.

Research

Research should include an analysis of existing shareholders as well as potential investors. It's been noted that for every 100 shares of stock that's not for sale, a company has to find one less buyer for 100 shares. And in fact, most companies are too small to afford a program that includes both outreach to new shareholders and care of existing shareholders. Given a choice, it's probably cheaper to keep shareholders than to get new ones— assuming that there's some measure of understanding of who they are, and how they fit into the picture of the target markets.

Research in investor relations, today, goes well beyond generalities. Those companies, of any size, that best understand their shareholders and prospective shareholders, and the professional investors who influence buying, should succeed with higher stock prices, better price/earnings ratios, and increased trading activity. This means knowing, *sometimes to the individual name,* a great deal about the wants, desires, and investment preferences of each buying group. Where once investor relations practitioners were content to have only the broadest definitions of a prospective market, today's investor research may go as deeply into the market as does traditional product research.

Good research means going directly to the most important segments of a prospective market, which means, conversely, not wasting time or money on investors who are least likely to buy. Thus, good research is cost effective, by affording the opportunity to put the investor relations dollar to work where it's likely to do the most good.

Research is particularly important in situations in which the most effective way to reach investors is through segmentation, or *niche marketing.* Niche marketing, in which a very narrow strata of investors are defined as most likely to buy a stock, and then in which these investors are identified and targeted, is particularly useful for stocks that, for one reason or another, may have no broader appeal. A high-tech company, for example, may appeal to investors who follow high-tech companies. A company with yet unrealized growth potential may appeal to investors who specialize in speculative or growth stocks. While niche marketing isn't applicable to all companies, it can be particularly useful in marketing the securities of many companies of different size.

And because, today, carefully targeted direct mail is so significant a part of investor relations marketing, in which mailing lists are extremely important, research must be more meticulous than ever before.

Without research, there is wasted effort in reaching the wrong people with the wrong message, even given the boundaries of a company's performance and potential. And while the degree and depth of research may vary for each company, depending upon size and other considerations, knowledge of the market remains a crucial and powerful tool.

The Product

To *identify the product* means to truly understand those elements of the company that can be projected to give target audiences an accurate and understandable picture of the company's ability to appreciate and effectively use the invested dollar. No company today that seeks investor support is so shallow or singular in its ramifications—has so little to say—that its story cannot be focused to answer the needs—or to generate the needs—of target audiences. This doesn't mean, of course, misrepresentation. It does mean professional skill in communication, which begins with understanding what is to be communicated.

Here, the *Unique Investment Premise (UIP)* becomes increasingly important. In effect, it's a useful concept to help put a company in perspective as a way to most powerfully make its investment advantages known to the financial and investing community. It's a useful marketing tool in that it summarizes quickly and focuses on what the company has to offer investors, in terms of the potential to appreciate that investment. It may be a distinctive growth concept, or an unusual or leadership position in an industry, or a strong position in an emerging industry. It's the one most exciting view of a company, in terms of its investment potential.

There is a caution, however, to avoid being overwhelmed by the trappings of marketing. Sometimes the most exciting premise about a company is that it's consistently successful. Sometimes there is nothing distinctive about a company, in which case the UIP must spring from an amalgam of the company's features, such as its financial position or its dynamics. The point is that concepts such as UIP are useful shortcuts to successfully presenting the essence of a company; but sometimes shortcuts can cut too short.

The Marketing Tools

To *identify the marketing tools* is to examine the full arsenal of marketing tools available to achieve the marketing objectives, and to choose those that will work best for a specific company. As may be seen from discussions in this book, the array of investor relations marketing tools is extensive—from basic communications techniques to sophisticated financial devices. The options, then, are extensive. However, not all marketing tools, in the same configurations, will work for every company. Each company is different; so too are marketing plans.

The trend toward sophisticated marketing has resulted in increased use of such marketing tools as carefully targeted direct mail and niche (market-segmented) advertising. Where once direct mail to nonshareholders was unheard of, or at least primitive, today's research techniques identify individuals who are prospective shareholders with such perception and detail that direct mail can be done cost effectively.

Where once advertising was limited to institutional advertising by larger, well-known companies, and to advertising annual report availability, today's advertising is used more effectively by even smaller companies. Offerings of material for investors, for example, helps build mailing lists.

Sometimes these lists can be offered to local brokers, who use them to develop their own clientele, but within a context of selling the company stock. Advertising is used more thoughtfully today than ever before, and should find many newer uses during the coming decade.

In fact, there is no marketing tool in use today that won't ultimately serve investor relations to one degree or another. This includes billboards, bus cards, and radio and television ads. It includes newsletters, brochures, editorial advertising sections (sometimes called advertorials), and even premiums.

Managing the Tools

And to *manage the tools* is to use the skills of marketing and investor relations thoughtfully and effectively. This means tailoring the program to reach the target audiences most efficiently, running the program skillfully and imaginatively, adjusting and correcting and changing as circumstances alter, and monitoring the program carefully.

It means using each tool meticulously, and integrating the tools and the skills to reinforce one another—techniques sorely lacking in the 1980s. Each tool of marketing serves its own end and purpose. When used in concert, they reinforce one another, to make the whole greater than the sum of its parts. This is as true of the investor relations program for the smallest companies as well as for the largest.

In fact, there's always been an element of marketing in investor relations. When a CEO makes a speech before a group of analysts or brokers, for example, that's an element of marketing. But today, and in the foreseeable future, a company's marketing effort must be organized, and not random, if it's to compete successfully in the roiling capital markets.

The Capital Markets

A decade ago, it was felt that any Wall Street firm that survived the 1970s was going to be around for a long time. Today, more than half the firms that existed in 1980 are no longer around, or have merged with others. Firms with household names like Bache, Hutton, Blyth Eastman Dillon, and Lehman Brothers are now either gone or part of one side or another of hyphens. *Sic transit Gloria.*

The equity capital in the largest firms, in 1980, were measured in millions, with Merrill Lynch, at $784 million, perhaps six times larger than its nearest competitor. Today, firms are measured in the billions, with Merrill Lynch, at $3.55 billion (1989), *second* to Salomon's $3.63 billion.

In 1979, average daily volume on the New York Stock Exchange was 32 million shares. In 1989 it was 165 million.

Perhaps most significant is that, according to the Securities Industry

Association, while 50 percent of the revenues of brokerage firms came from commissions on the buying and selling of securities in 1979, today only 17 percent comes from commissions on securities. It's a different business today.

Wall Street is changing, is ever-changing, and will continue to change. The emerging markets worldwide—London, Luxembourg, Tokyo, Frankfurt, Madrid, and now Korea, Russia, and Hungary—are stunning. To understand investor relations strategy is to understand that it's played against this kaleidoscopic backdrop.

In that sense, there is no single financial community. Throughout this book we have talked of the financial community as a unified body. Realistically, it exists and is defined only in terms of a company's trying to establish a liaison with it. Obviously, the financial community for a petroleum company showing a fantastic increase in profits as a result of finding a new pool of petroleum reserves is very different from that of a capital-intensive public utility trying to find funds when it's already highly leveraged, the prime rate is climbing, and there is virtually no viable equities market. The financial community is different for a company with a float of 300,000 shares than it is for a company with a float of more than 10 million shares, and very different for a company with a float of 50 million shares. The company with a five-year annual growth rate of 27 percent, virtually no debt, and a strong market for its products deals with a very different financial community than a company, no matter how basically sound, that has just come through several very bad years and yet has a potential for ultimate success and growth.

Perhaps some day economists will develop the formula for tuning the economy so that it will be absolutely controllable. But it won't be this week. In the meantime, it can be said with some measure of certainty that if the market is up it will eventually go down, and if the market is down it will eventually go up. This is small consolation for the corporate president whose stock is selling at four times earnings while plans for a necessary expansion sit, unable to be financed, on his desk. But whatever the nature of the market, at any given moment, two things are clear. First, any public company must continue to function within the framework of that market. And second, no company can expect the market to react immediately to its efforts in the normal course of events.

And so the investor relations program must be an ongoing effort in bad times if it's to be successful in good times. When there is an upward market shift, the first companies to come back are those that are best known and understood by the financial community.

Another point. There is no such thing as a normal market. When the Dow Jones average is climbing in the face of dire predictions about the economy, there is a tendency to speak of the "current market" as if the roaring bull markets of the late 1960s, or even the 1980s, were the normal market. When the market hovers around 3000, is that the normal market? As the late investment banking genius, Richard Hexter, put it in discussing a bull market, "This is the once and future market."

When the market is on the rise, and there is a great deal of buying power, and the economy is strong, and the banks and institutions have lots of money to lend, the emphasis is on reaching as many professional investors as can be interested in the company. If the company is performing well, and the economy is sound, and there is a favorable future foreseen for the company's industry, the task is relatively simple. The focus is on analysts who specialize in the industry, and if the company's float is large enough, it's on the institutional analysts and money managers, and analysts and brokers at brokerage houses servicing institutional customers.

If, on the other hand, the market is down and interest rates are up and there are more stocks seeking fewer investment dollars, then the strategy must be more acute, and aimed more carefully at shrewdly selected targets.

In the 1980s, with the growth of pension fund assets, and the problems of managing them, the performance orientation became more precise. Analysts, in the observation of Hill & Knowlton vice chairman Richard Cheney, became amateur arbitrageurs, listening and looking for potential takeover candidates, even while they were looking for good stocks. And with interest rates at peak levels early in the decade, the capital market targets were as much the banks as they were the stock market. Later in the decade, when interest rates began to decline and inflation came under control, the configuration of the markets changed once again, emerging to produce the complex market we have going into the 1990s. This is a market of wide swings, vast institutional control, computer program trading, and, since the market crash of October 1987, a scarcity of small individual investors, except in mutual funds. The year 1989 ended with more than a trillion dollars invested in mutual funds. In that last year of the decade, monthly net sales of mutual funds averaged $2.5 billion.

Clearly, the capital markets are more international, and more complex in other ways. International capital flows, abetted by the computer and myriad new investment instruments, not only accelerate the stock market, but complicate it tremendously. The size and power of the pools of pension funds in the 1990s is awesome.

Even for the small local corporation, no less than for the larger one, investor relations requires more attention and skill than ever before. Once, the ordinary investor relations specialist was sufficient for most programs. Today, ordinary is not good enough.

But the point remains that while the nature of the market may change, there is still a market. It must be discerned and fathomed and the strategy directed accordingly.

The Nature of the Economy

In simpler times—whenever that was—there seemed to be a one-to-one relationship between the economy and the stock market. There may have been a lag, but when the stock market perceived a coming downturn in the economy, it acted accordingly, and turned down itself. Was it Samuelson who said that the stock market has anticipated 11 of the last 10 recessions?

Today's economy is far too complex for that, as are the current capital markets. The market, in 1990, seems to have a life of its own, although, certainly, the state of the economy affects the companies in any nation.

We enter the decade with one of the longest periods of prosperity in American history—eight years. There are signs, in 1990, of weaknesses (the peculiarly named "soft landing," which means the nonrecession recession). And yet the market's reaction to declining economic indicators seems to be to deem them irrelevant. The Dow Jones closed the decade at 2753, and then struck new records as it approached (and actually crossed) 3000 at mid-1990, which hardly seems to reflect the growing signs of economic decline, including rising unemployment, rising inflation, and a general prediction of only 2 percent growth in the year 1990. In a dynamic world, old rules, like old styles of clothing, tend not to apply in quite the same way. Only the mid-East crisis slowed the market.

There is also, of course, the uncertainty generated by the events in Eastern Europe of the last year of the decade, in which the gods of Marxism and Leninism ran out of steam. Construe these events as you might, the fact is that there are many countries in Eastern Europe that will spend the next decade groping towards capitalism. This will obviously affect the international economy, and especially the coming European Economic Community. But how? How will it affect international capital flows? How will it reflect in the bourses and exchanges of the world, and especially New York?

There is no science—or art—as maddeningly elusive as economics. Too bad. It plays a significant role in the tides of the stock market and the bond market. And so it is a crucial element in strategic planning in investor relations.

The Tools of Investor Relations

In the preceding chapters, the myriad tools of investor relations have been explored in detail. That each of them should be used artfully and imaginatively is clear. Corporate communications to both the financial community and shareholders should be professional, skillful, and intelligent.

In investor relations today, there is a proven body of knowledge that's been tested extensively during the past 25 years and more. We know a great deal about the financial press, and dealing with analysts and brokers, and communicating with shareholders.

Each tool, whether it's a news release or a meeting of brokers and analysts, should be examined to see if it's the right one, used in the right way, for the particular circumstances at hand—or whether it's a reflexive return to applying the familiar solution to the unfamiliar problem.

During a bull market, in earlier days, when merely the availability of stock in virtually any company may have been sufficient to warrant its rise in price, investor relations firms simply had to perform their mechanical routines and then pat themselves with self-satisfied glee as their clients' stock prices rose. Today, after a few severe bear markets and a couple of recessions, the market no longer responds so readily to just mechanics. It not only needs better and more sophisticated investor relations, it needs larger doses.

It may appear easier to measure the effects of investor relations activities in a bull market than in a static or bear market, and the measurements may even look better, but in any event, the effects of each of the investor relations tools, singly and collectively, are always abundantly clear if the tools are well and skillfully used, and time is put into researching the results.

Two things should be considered. One is that as the nature of the stock market and the other capital markets has changed, so has the degree of effectiveness of each of the devices used in financial and investor relations.

Second, as the financial community becomes increasingly insensitive to certain investor relations activities—if for no other reason than that the financial community is sharply altered—then it becomes clear that things must be done differently, and certainly more imaginatively.

This is not to say that the mechanics of an investor relations program are of themselves not sound. Every technique delineated in this book continues, in its own way, to be effective. What is significant, though, is that the strategy for using these devices changes as the structure of the financial community changes. That strategy is guided by priority, degree, and timing.

Priority is a function of the changing value of each technique relative to the others. There are times when an intensive program of security analyst or broker meetings has a greater potential for effectiveness, relatively, than a full-blown press relations program. There are times when it's the other way around. The one activity takes precedence in the program over the other.

The *degree* to which emphasis is placed on each activity is yet another function of the nature of both the market and the company. There is only so much time and so much budget available for any corporate program.

The allocation of effort depends upon the structure and receptivity of the various aspects of the financial community, the structure and performance of the company at any given moment, and the talents and judgment of the investor relations counsel. Here again, the choice should be made of the degree of outreach to prospective investors compared to serving existing shareholders.

Timing is that sensitive element that not only dictates the exact point at which something should be done, but whether a particular activity should be undertaken at all at any given moment, in terms of the structure of the financial community.

Despite some 25 years of experience in investor relations practice, it still hasn't peaked in innovation and skill. New things are tried and discovered every day, and so it should be. There is more to be learned in the future of investor relations than has been learned in the past.

The Nature of the Company

Strategy is also dictated by the nature of the company at any given moment. A growing company is a constantly changing company. It grows internally, and it grows externally to reach out to meet the changing needs of its markets and the nature of its sources of supply. As this happens, so does its relationship to the capital markets change.

It must also be recognized that the market is slow to accept a change in a corporation. When a company has been seen in one configuration, the job of changing the view of that company is enormous, unless there is some drastic and dramatic activity. It's almost as if the entire investor relations program must be started from the beginning, except that most companies change slowly and don't make a clear-cut transition. This change must be constantly monitored and communicated.

Shaping Strategy

There are many elements of a company that contribute to the shape of investor relations strategy. For example:

- *The nature of its business.* Finding and projecting a Unique Investment Premise in an American automobile company, in a period in which an overwhelming percentage of cars sold in the United States are made abroad, is very different from finding a UIP in a company making breakthroughs in genetic engineering.
- *Its strengths and weaknesses.* The strength of IBM, at the beginning of the decade, is its size and power. The strength of Compaq is its success in leading IBM at its own game of technical innovation and facile

management. The weakness of IBM, at the same time, is the erosion of its technical superiority over its competitors. The weakness of Compaq is that it's not IBM.

- *Its size.* Obviously, the investor relations strategy for a national company whose products are household names and whose management is highly visible to the general public is different from one for a small regional over-the-counter company.

- *The size of its float.* A company with many millions of shares outstanding has many more options in investor relations practice than has a company with fewer than a million shares outstanding. Obviously, a major fund, given to buying 25,000- or 50,000-share blocks of a stock, is not going to be interested in a company with a float of 250,000 shares. A purchase of 25,000 shares in a company with a float that size is 10 percent, and can of itself increase the price of the stock by a substantial percentage. But that purchase also adversely affects liquidity. Some smaller companies sometimes find themselves in positions where mutual funds, anticipating rapid growth and therefore a rapid increase in the price of the stock, buy large blocks, trading the price upward. A company with a market value of under $50 million dollars, then, will have a difficult time making headway with an investor relations program based on large institutional contact. At the first sign of trouble these blocks are unloaded, rapidly driving the price not only downward, but lower than it might be in relation to the companies' real growth potential. Focusing attention on the large funds, for the smaller company, then, has its dangers.

  On the other hand, for the smaller company buying by small institutions and money managers can be useful to develop a stability in the stock and increase the price. There are smaller pension funds, private funds, and some of the more solid but less glamorous mutual funds, or a small offshoot of a larger fund company. There are special situation funds and special industry funds, many of which deal in smaller companies as well as large, and are of a size that does not consume a small float in one bite.

- *Its particular problems or opportunities.* The strategy for a company in real estate development at a time when interest rates are high and new housing is down is very different than it is for a company with patents in a cure for a common and serious disease.

- *Special factors or activities.* Tandem Corporation makes computers with redundant components that back up parts that may break down. As a result, the Tandem computer at the New York Stock Exchange was one of the few that didn't break down during the record trading day of October 29, 1987, when the market crashed. Delta Airlines, because of its management and labor policies, continues to thrive when its competitors struggle. These factors contribute to shaping investor relations strategies for their respective companies.

- *Management.* When the CEO is a quiet, plodding, undramatic individual, the strategy doesn't pivot on his speeches before large groups. When the new CEO has a track record of successfully turning around failing companies and building great ones from smaller ones, then the strategy will hinge on the CEO's magnetism, or prior accomplishments in motivating a team.

The Nature of the Company's Industry

The nature of the industry in which a company functions frequently plays an unduly large role in how the financial community views the company. At a time when the apparel industry was depressed, industry analysts were sour on all apparel companies, including those that were substantially outperforming the industry. When the failure of several major toy companies made industry analysts wary, the well-managed company in that industry suffered the same low multiple as the rest of its industry. When Dayco, a fairly large midwestern company, had not effectively communicated the fact that only the smallest part of its profits came from the automotive industry rather than from plastic and other products, the company was awarded the same low multiples during and following a depressed period for automotive stocks as were the automotive companies. In each of these cases a shift in strategy was dictated. Ways had to be found to separate the company from its industry; to refocus attention on the company's performance as a company rather than as a segment of an industry.

Granted, this is difficult to do. When a company is outperforming its industry, either the management of that company is superior, or the managements of other companies in the industry are inferior, or there is something basically wrong with the industry. It can be argued that the best-managed company in the buggy whip industry had no great future when the automobile was invented. On the other hand, it can be argued that if management was really that good it would have anticipated the shift in its market and taken steps to alter the nature of its business. This is what good management is about, after all. A case in point is Philip Morris and RJR, two giant companies built on tobacco. As smoking began to decline dramatically, both companies began to acquire companies in nontobacco industries, such as food and beverages. By the time the smallest percentage of Americans smoked, the smallest percentage of their business was in tobacco.

In another case, Patrick Petroleum Company suffered in the market from the poor press given the entire energy industry from 1984 through 1989, despite Patrick's survival, comeback, and increasingly excellent condition. It was felt by the company's investor relations consultant that because the problem arose in good measure from poor press for its industry, good press might help solve the problem. But it had to be significant press coverage. A carefully developed in-depth presentation resulted in a full-page, completely favorable story in *Forbes*. *Forbes* has extremely high credibility, and with the favorable Patrick story, the financial community paid attention. The result was an immediate increase in interest in the company and in the stock price.

Early in 1990, Geodyne Resources' management felt the company was not receiving sufficient recognition from the financial community. Geodyne is a *program* company—an independent energy company that funds its operations by raising money from the public through limited partnership income programs. These programs are registered through the SEC for retail sales to investors.

The problem is that traditional methods of evaluating independent energy companies are based on the breakup value of assets, or multiples of cash flow, neither of which is useful in accurately measuring program companies. They frequently look worse, relative to their stock price, than do standard independent energy companies. Yet they might still be undervalued.

Geodyne's stock price was $2.50 a share, with a market value of about $42 million. Instinctively, Geodyne and its investor relations counsel believed the company was undervalued. The problem was how to prove it to an energy security analyst. Or more significantly, how could an energy security analyst prove it to investors?

The company's breakup value was estimated at $1.50 by some analysts, $2.00 by others. It was decided that the $1.50–$2.00 range should be a base value. But what value might be added to that?

PaineWebber owned 50 percent of the company and alone raised $100 million a year for its programs through its 4,300 brokers. Never before had so much money been raised by a brokerage house that owned such a large part of an energy company. The proposition that management and its investor relations counsel set forth was that the brokerage house ownership gave Geodyne a unique *franchise* for which it should receive some ongoing credit, essentially in the way a retail company is given some credit for the number of stores it has open, or is opening, to do business. As a going concern, that franchise is worth some intangible amount, and will produce some business regularly. For every $100 million raised, Geodyne got a little more than $8.5 million additional annual cash flow, independent of cash flow from its existing business, its oil and gas wells and interests, or reimbursed expenses from past programs.

The company began talking to the financial community about this franchise in April 1990. The premise was that with 50 percent ownership, PaineWebber was less likely to walk away from Geodyne than from other program company relationships with their broker-dealers. Therefore, the revenue stream was somewhat more dependable and worthy of consideration on a value-added basis. By July 1990, a respected energy analyst appeared to accept the idea and was using it internally to indicate a higher-than-market-price value for Geodyne's common stock, although no recommendation had yet been issued.

The Corporate Objectives

While any number of strategies may work for any one company, perhaps the guiding factor in devising an appropriate strategy for a company is its own corporate objectives. Where is the company going and what does it want to be? Or more particularly, in this context, what does it mean to accomplish in regard to the capital markets? Is it a matter of sustaining a stock price at a high P/E to help it with further capitalization? Does a sound view of the company to the financial community help with acquisitions, or in employee stock options, or ESOPs, or in dealing with suppliers?

A successful investor relations program can accomplish many things. But the choice of what management wants to accomplish isn't arbitrary; it must spring from corporate objectives, and be consistent with them.

The end of the 1980s has seen some extraordinary corporate activity in many industries. A decade ago, the concern of the investment community was the conglomerate. In the late 1980s, it was acquisition via leveraged buyouts, and the acquisition, as well, by the foreign company, as capital moves across borders like a heat-seeking missile. Today, it's the loss of the technology battle that adversely affects even the best of American companies trying to succeed in an affected industry, and productivity, and international competition, and access to new international markets.

This is the context in which the investor relations professional must function. Success in investor relations strategy, then, depends upon the skill and originality with which it's practiced in the context of the corporation's objectives.

The Strategic Concept

Essentially, the strategic concept is the plan that uses all of the elements of strategy to meet the corporate goals. This is the plan that takes the structure of the company, and especially its Unique Investment Premise, and using the tools of marketing and investor relations, persuades investors—and those professionals who influence them—of the value of investing in the company.

The Strategic Focus

As we move into the 1990s, the economic configurations that serve as a backdrop to any investor relations program are very different than they had been in the past. The power now lies in both the institutions and the pension funds. The body of individual investors is much smaller. Internationalization is growing rapidly, which means not only direct foreign investment in American business, but increasingly, the need to go abroad to sell securities to a growing European or Asian market.

Now more than ever, debt is a significant part of the financing pattern of most companies. Debt to equity ratios are at an all-time high for American companies, and show little sign of diminishing. Those who issue debt—banks and debt underwriters—and those who judge debt—the rating services—have become targets for the investor relations program.

While the traditional techniques of investor relations—communications to shareholders, brokers, and analysts, etc.—still apply, strategies to reach out have changed considerably.

For example, while individual investors seem to have diminished in number in the market, the outreach to the remaining individual investors is more important than ever before. And while they can still be reached on certain levels through the recommendations of influential brokers and analysts, more and more investor relations professionals are going after investors individually, using direct mail, telephone contact, publicity, advertising, and even seminars. As individual investors are identified, the prudent investor relations professionals are building dossiers on them, identifying as much information about their investment habits as possible. The result of this kind of activity is to make the outreach more cost effective; to narrow down the target market to the best buyers, to find the fastest and cheapest ways to reach them, and then to sell them stock in sound companies.

The corporation's place in its life cycle is extremely important in developing strategy. Is it a new company? Is it—or its industry—emerging, or declining? Is it a mature company seeking stability? All these and more are significant considerations in strategic planning.

Financial Publicity

If interest, attention, and maintaining the flow of information are essential, the answer to a diminished market of individual investors is frequently an increased financial publicity campaign. In such cases, greater emphasis must be placed on assiduously pursuing attention in the financial and business press. If visibility cannot be achieved to a satisfactory degree by direct contact with the financial community, then it must be done indirectly through the press. For the eligible company, the *Dow-Joneser*—the Dow Jones interview—and the Reuters interview must be sought as frequently as possible, twice or four times a year, as feasible. Every aspect of the company's operation must be scouted to determine those activities that may be deemed newsworthy, and those must be energetically projected. The emphasis must shift, and shift in force, to those aspects of a company that make it a more viable investment. Articles must be developed for the financial and business press and interviews must be arranged.

Marketing Communications

More attention must be paid, as well, to marketing techniques that sell the company to the shareholder and the investing community. Communication must be intensified, and it must be good—clear, well written, attractive, and compelling. Better-than-ever research must be done to know who the shareholders are and what they want and, to the extent that it's possible, what they want should be given to them in terms of information and presentation.

Too frequently, the research will show a body of shareholders to be disenchanted out of proportion to the facts. This happens when they are uninformed. The remedy for this, the investor relations program aimed at communicating to them, unfortunately doesn't succeed overnight. The flight uphill is longer and more arduous than it is downhill.

In 1988, Federal Signal, an NYSE company, had an excellent track record and had performed better than the DJIA over a period of years. For seemingly inexplicable reasons (beyond the fact that it had never had an investor relations program), its stock was selling at a price below the Dow Jones average, and with a price/earnings ratio of 10. Management strongly felt that the stock was underpriced.

Research showed that corporate communications to shareholders was effective, and that shareholders liked the company. The strategy for an investor relations program begun in 1988 focused, then, on the press and direct contact with the investment community.

A small story placed in *Fortune* was part of a basis for broadening interest with retail firms, rather than institutional investors. The retail following was built up with intensive contact of both national and regional firms in several cities. Research reports were generated early in the program from such houses as Josephthal (now Jesup Josephthal) in New York and then A. G. Edwards, which triggered other reports, such as two by a technical analyst at Shearson, who put out two buy recommendations, and subsequent reports by Dean Witter and Oppenheimer. Brokerage meetings were accelerated in cities throughout the United States, with emphasis on market support for the analysts' research reports developed by meetings with Federal Signal's management.

The retail program succeeded in raising the price/earnings ratio to 14 within a year, including a market-value increase for the stock from $180 million to $300 million during the period.

The Trader

There was once a time when OTC traders were totally ignored by most investor relations practitioners. The trader is a mysterious person who functions in the back office, executing buy and sell orders at the instructions of others, or perhaps for his or her firm. He is considered to be a mechanic (by some—a fighter pilot by others) with nerves of steel, the ability to make split-second decisions, to work under enormous pressure, and to negotiate shrewdly. With the exception of a few prominent people, such as the extraordinary Gus Levy, the late senior partner of Goldman, Sachs, traders were viewed in some dim, dark context that seemed only ancillary to the glamorous end of the brokerage business and corporate finance.

But as the bear market entered 1974 and the so-called two-tier market idea emerged, there began to be a subtle shift in the buying and selling activities of Wall Street. The two-tier market was a concept derived from the fact that most analysts viewed as safe only a select number of blue-chip stocks. This was the first tier. Everything else was ignored and placed in a second tier. The trouble with the concept was that, first of all, it fell apart when some of the larger companies in the first tier began to respond to the same economic ills that affected the total economy. Second, despite the concept's popularity, the two-tier market existed only on a relative level. It seemed to imply that no trading was being done in second-tier stocks, which of course was not the case. The market opened every day at 10:00 A.M. and closed every day at 3:30 P.M. And if volume was not what it had been a year or two earlier, trading was still being done.

It was at this point that the formerly uncourted trader began to emerge as a figure of importance, particularly for the smaller over-the-counter company, which constituted a third tier. Many of the traders were actually trading in 100- or 200-share lots of stocks not heavily traded. They were taking positions—buying for their own account for resale later at a profit. The over-the-counter market was—and still is—being made by traders, who set the prices minute-by-minute.

When this little-known fact was perceived, it was also discovered that the traders were dealing in stocks in which they frequently had only a minimal amount of information. Most stocks were simply "traded on the numbers"—the stock was simply a commodity that they traded on a supply and demand principle. In those firms that had research departments, there was some information about companies being traded, but not much. In large segments of the Street, where this kind of activity was taking place, information was sparse. A trader is required to know some basics about the company he trades, but these are just bare facts. Until several financial relations consultants discovered this phenomenon, most traders were simply ignored.

Broadening the Base

In early 1974, when volume was down, brokerage houses were falling like leaves from trees in October, and purchasing power was sharply diminished. But if fewer shares of stock were traded in any one financial center, if the buying power at any geographic point became sparse, then that volume had to be made up by going abroad geographically. If each apple tree is producing fewer apples, then you have to gather apples from more trees, and sometimes from trees further afield, in order to fill a bushel basket. To maintain or rebuild liquidity and volume in any stock whose volume has fallen off, more houses may have to become involved and the geographic base of trading must be expanded. And sometimes, with a thinly traded stock, just a few more traders may have to make a larger commitment.

Changing to meet shifting economic needs is not only a function of good management, but it is precisely what must be communicated. A company is, after all, more than just a structure for producing and marketing products. It is a vehicle for making a profit—for appreciating the invested dollar. The ability of a company to appreciate the invested dollar rests not merely in its production, marketing, or distribution capacities, but also in its management—and carrying a company successfully through a negative period is precisely the role of a good management. The question is, how is this very difficult fact to be projected?

Primary, of course, is the clear-cut orientation of the facts—the way the story is presented, supplemented by a good financial publicity program.

The Targets

Equally important is to identify those segments of the financial community that are willing to look at a company as a successful entity rather than solely as a representative of its industry. Strictly to be avoided, in this context, are the industry specialists. They know all the reasons why not. This is a time for the generalists and the special situations analysts, for the brokers, and the traders. They are interested in success and the reasons for it, and in the potential for future success. They tend to be generally more free of prejudices regarding a particular industry than are the industry specialists. This is the time for the pension fund, with its greater emphasis on long-range investment potential, and for the institution that invests for the long term and is the kind not dependent upon the exigencies of the tape. The decision makers for these groups must be identified and exposed to the company as forcefully and effectively as possible. This is not to say that the industry analysts are to be ignored in terms of the normal dissemination of information, but certainly they are not the prime target. At the same time, the concept of increasing the size of the total audience applies as well. By broadening the geographic base of coverage, more potential investors can be reached.

In the late 1980s, Total Assets Protection stock was .75 bid/$1.00 asked on the over-the-counter market—an all-time low for the company. The balance sheet was adequate, but earnings from operations were not consistent. A technological service leader that was ahead of its time, the company had several significant developments that dramatically changed its outlook for the better. But while these developments had been appropriately disclosed, the market hadn't put them together yet to affect the interest in the stock. Included was an agreement with IBM that had led to more than $7 million in contracts—which was almost double the company's revenues for the first half of 1989. This further enhanced the company's acceptance by its market for its services.

Although dealing with technology industry analysts seemed the obvious route to take, experience dictated that the company was too small for this group. The strategy chosen was to seek out active investment advisors among brokers and small institutions known to be interested in small companies, who were also known to make fast investment decisions. Because the story was complex, a two-hour personal meeting format was required of all prospects as a device to attract only those who might be sufficiently interested to make a commitment. The time was also needed to clarify the company's past problems and to explain how they had been overcome. This required a keen knowledge of the Street and the appropriate houses, analysts, and brokers.

The meetings were followed up with intensive telephone discussions to assure that everyone fully understood the advantages of the company.

These meetings resulted immediately in heavy purchases, including some blocks of 40,000 or more shares. The strategy produced sales of more than 435,000 shares in the six days between the first half of the group of meetings and the second half. The stock price rose to $1.50 bid/$1.75 asked in that six days, and two weeks later hit a high of $2.13. Toward year end it backed off with the tax-selling season in full stride.

Dividend Policy as Strategy

In recent years, a good deal of research has been done on the use of dividends as a strategy for attracting investors. Many companies boast of their long uninterrupted dividend record, and analysts are sometimes quick to advise a company to boost a sagging stock by declaring or increasing dividends.

But the answer is not so simple, particularly under changing economic conditions.

When General Motors, in one of its worst years in history, continued to pay dividends, it gives cause to look again at the concept of paying dividends at any cost. When 19 companies in the Fortune 500 increase their dividends regularly over a ten-year period and still show a decline in stock price over the same period, there is good reason to wonder about dividend policy as a device to improve stock prices.

There are some basic realities, the most significant of which is that when the cost of capital is high, and when retained earnings are the cheapest capital a company can get, to pay out that capital in dividends must make the wisdom of the company's management suspect. And this is apparently what happens in some cases.

With the tax rate on cash dividends and capital gains equal, as they are at this writing, investors appear to have moved toward a "pay-now" attitude. Demand for cash dividends is on the rise. Should management succumb or resist? Will shareholders award a higher stock price to the company that satisfies its shareholder dividend needs to lower its cost of capital to make up what it needs after the payouts?

For many years, there has been a tendency for many companies, particularly smaller ones, to try to woo shareholders and to increase stock price by declaring cash dividends. If it works, it works in the short term, and stock prices invariably go back to reflect the company's true value. And for companies with long-standing dividend policies, there is a tendency for management to begin to think of dividends as a kind of fixed cost, to be paid out as if there were not options.

True, cash dividends sometimes send a positive message to shareholders, and there are clear-cut cases where attempts to cut or eliminate dividends have had a deleterious effect on stock prices. When one utility tried it a few years ago, the outcry was horrendous, and the stock price dropped sharply. During regulatory hearings for AT&T in 1980, when its dividend policy was attacked for floating new equity and then paying out that equity in the form of dividends, AT&T produced some ten years of shareholder research to prove that dividends were what their shareholders wanted, and that to change that policy would cause severe dislocations in their market.

But herein lies a clue, perhaps. And the clue leads to the suggestion that there is no pat answer, but rather that each case requires its own policy.

For example, for the company whose stock is largely held by institutions, of what use is the dividend as a harbinger of a favorable view of the company (unless it's the price of admission to more institutions)?

On the other hand, for the company depending upon the smaller individual shareholder, and particularly the shareholder who invests for income rather than long-term appreciation, the dividend has another meaning. And the company needs to know if it has income or appreciation investors.

All of which hearkens back to the fact that investor research has become increasingly important.

For the company changing dividend policy, one way or the other, there is at least one caveat—communicate. When Brown-Foreman Distillers changed its payout ratio from the 30 to 35 percent range to 20 to 30 percent, the market didn't blink an anthropomorphic eye. But, according to a report in *Institutional Investor*, "The company was also careful to point out in its annual report that change 'in no way reflects reduced optimism' about future earnings and that the additional retained capital would fiance 'a number of investment alternatives, including acquisitions, new product developments and growth of existing brands.' "

Stock Splits

In this same general category are stock splits, in which each share owned is split into two or three or more shares. The effect is to appear to give the shareholder more stock, except that the value of each new share is exactly the same as before the split. The price is reduced arithmetically, so that a stock that sells for $10 is split into two shares selling for $5 each.

There appears to be only one valid reason for doing a split. When the price is so high that it's priced out of a market. But studies show that beyond that, it's a cosmetic device that has no real value in the marketplace. Interviewed on the subject in *The Wall Street Journal*, Leon Cooperman, a Goldman, Sachs partner, said, "A stock split unaccompanied by a cash dividend increase is like giving somebody five singles for a $5 bill. You've got a thicker billfold, but it has no economic significance whatever." Added James L. Cochrane, senior vice-president at the New York Stock Exchange, "We've done research on this, and it shows a split really doesn't seem to matter significantly."

Special Strategies

Special problems, or special factors or activities, frequently require a shift in strategy. They frequently need special explanation, and sometimes the nature of the company is altered. A company forced to divest itself of a large segment of its business by order of the Federal Trade Commission or, in an antitrust situation, by the Justice Department, or a company restructuring to enhance shareholder value, must reevaluate the kind of company it has now become, and shift its investor relations strategy accordingly. It may find itself having to deal with an entirely new group of analysts and very different segments of the financial community.

This, of course, also applies when there is a merger or acquisition.

A case in point is Maremont Corporation, a well-run Chicago-based supplier to the automotive aftermarket.

Some years ago, Maremont found itself under the shadow of an FTC order to divest itself of a segment of its business. Under the consent decree, it appeared that the company was to lose a substantial portion of a source of revenue, although, in fact, this was not the case. The division to be divested was comparatively new in its structure at the time, and was not yet the major contributor to profits that it might ultimately have become. As a result of the long-drawn-out FTC proceedings, the stock of the company was appreciably undervalued. At the time of the consent decree it was selling at around $10 a share.

The start of the program for Maremont was devoted to explaining and clarifying the exact effect of the decree on the company. This was done with a press release, which was also distributed to analysts, and through newspaper interviews and direct communications to shareholders.

Starting from a base of an undervalued stock, it was determined that the quickest way for the company to reach a price/earnings ratio appropriate to the market at the time was to focus on special situations analysts. These analysts, who concern themselves with companies that seem to be undervalued for one reason or another, were identified and a series of meetings were held with management. The story came across very effectively and the stock started to rise. As it went past $18, it became apparent that the stock would soon no longer be a special situation—that it would be appropriately priced. What was needed, it was determined, was some price stability. Groups of analysts representing or dealing with smaller and medium-sized institutions were then identified, and the emphasis of the program shifted to meetings with them. As institutional buying began, the price of the stock headed toward $30. All of this happened in the unusually short time of about one year.

With the advent of institutional buying, concern began to develop about possible liquidity problems, with large blocks of stock being held by institutions. And so the emphasis shifted once again, this time to the large retail houses such as Merrill Lynch and Bache. With the successful record in earnings to back the company, and with the sound support of institutional purchasing, the stock was readily accepted by the retail analysts, and the desired liquidity was developed. Within less than two years the stock had gone from $10 to $60, and volume was well up.

Investor Relations in a Down Market

Must investor elations be abandoned when the market is headed down? No, as was seen following the market crash of October 1987.

While many companies were overwhelmed by events, and some were frozen in the headlights, many investor relations officers and consultants served their clients by reinforcing information about their companies and clients. Communications with the Street were intensified, and fact books and other sources of data were updated. Contacts with analysts, brokers and major investors were increased. Research to more carefully identify stockholders was intensified. As one investor relations executive, Hospital Corporation of America's Victor Campbell, put it, "The key is to try to do the right thing, not to look at just the short term."

There is evidence that those companies that increased postcrash communications ultimately fared better than those that didn't.

Marketing Devices

As the practice of investor relations becomes more professionally marketing oriented, companies are turning to a number of unusual—and sometimes effective—devices to generate interest in their stock. Some of these devices are frank gimmicks of dubious value. But some are clever, particularly when used in conjunction with a full range of appropriately programmed activities. The trade press, and particularly *Institutional Investor,* report on these devices with great and gleeful regularity.

For example, a few years ago Dr. Pepper proposed a national sweepstakes in which its stock would be given as prizes. They were cautious enough, incidentally, to check with the SEC, which gave them a "no-action" letter (meaning that the SEC neither approved nor disapproved, but would take no action if the contest followed the submitted rules).

Many companies tie their product advertising in with promoting their stock, particularly in institutional campaigns. Nabisco claims to have done it successfully. Other companies offer shareholders discounts on products. Esmark included a discount coupon for its peanut butter in a quarterly report. Quaker Oats claims that sending coupons to shareholders in interim report mailings is a good way to save postage on couponing, even as it supports shareholder relations. Chrysler offered shareholders a special rebate on its cars. The list is very long, and ideas are limited only by the imagination of the investor relations staff.

There are some risks in these kinds of activities. While the SEC has no rules about minor shareholder bonuses, they should be checked if there is any question. On the other hand, there are cases on the books of closed corporations where individuals with large holdings choose to accept corporate planes or similar major gifts in lieu of taxable dividends. The IRS did not look kindly upon this. According to strict interpretation of this "constructive dividend" rule, anything given to shareholders at less than true market value might theoretically be taxable. There is a legal risk, albeit a small one.

There is an unusual amount of interest in finding new methods to market stock to various natural constituencies. For example, a recreation company tried to sell stock to members of a bowling league in a systematic and continuing program. While the SEC rejected the idea for technical reasons, it seems possible that other companies may be able to devise a similar program that would meet SEC approval.

Local Advertising

Many companies use local advertising to help local brokers. A firm advertises information about its performance, offering an annual report or informational brochure. The names of those who respond are then given to a local broker to use, for mutual advantage, to directly sell the company's stock even as it develops new customers for the broker.

Crisis Management

There are indeed times when the unexpected happens to a company or its products that can adversely affect a stock. A Tylenol poisoning case, or an Exxon oil spill.

This kind of crisis tends to be better handled on the product or public affairs side, when, as a reasonable period of time passes, the stock price usually returns to precrisis levels.

The serious investor relations crisis is one in which the financial side of the business is affected. This can be a major disaster, such as an embezzlement or fraud or a natural disaster, such as a major fire or earthquake, or it can stem from the product. When Lotus Development Corporation failed to deliver a new version of its key computer program, Lotus 1-2-3, for more than a year, the company found itself facing a crisis of credibility on Wall Street. By carefully communicating with the financial community on the progress of the product's development, and by stressing the success of other of its products, the stock faced disaster, but didn't succumb.

And therein lies the fact of the matter—the best crisis control is quick and complete communication with every segment of the financial community and with shareholders.

On the product side, a crisis can be anticipated and a plan developed. Certain aspects of that plan can apply to a financial crisis, such as agreeing upon a public position and designating spokespeople. But in investor relations, crises are best dealt with by careful and rapid communication of the facts in an ongoing program. An informed public is rarely as hostile as one that's uninformed, or has reason to doubt credibility.

Ethics

Ethics, in the context of Wall Street, is a strange word. It would seem to be almost a paradox, if Wall Street is viewed solely as a playing field for greedy games.

But fortunately, and despite highly visible lapses from time to time, ethical considerations do indeed prevail in the securities industry. There is no great moral basis for this; morals rarely enter into it.

What does drive ethical behavior, on the other hand, is the need for people to rely upon one another in a fast-moving, complex and fast-paced activity. If brokers and traders and others couldn't be relied upon to live up to their word and their promises, the market would quickly collapse. Indeed, the motto of traders has long been—and will long be—"My word is my bond." Like the trapeze artist, if I can't rely upon you to catch me today, who can you rely upon to catch you tomorrow?

No concept in Wall Street, and certainly in the practice of investor relations, is more crucial than *credibility*. Without credibility, there is no investor relations.

And so while there may be lapses, and foolishness, these lapses are such poor business that those who commit them rarely survive, cause damage though they may.

There is one overriding factor that is essential for the success of any investor relations program. This is credibility. The acoustics of Wall Street are magnificent. Misrepresentation, misdirection, inflated projections—all will ultimately come home to roost and tarnish, perhaps permanently, the reputation of even the most profitable corporate management.

No strategy is complete or effective if it lacks credibility.

All of this adds up to the fact that the effectiveness of an investor relations program is a function of not merely the performance of its mechanics, but the intelligent and imaginative use of these mechanics in different configurations to meet changing needs. What works for one company will not necessarily work for another. What works under one set of market conditions or in one economic structure will not necessarily work in another. What worked once will not necessarily work at a different time.

Strategy has its cautions, too. In a declining market, for example, it is very easy for the company to take defensive action to try to revitalize its stock. It might declare a larger dividend, or it might try to buy blocks of its own stock.

But actions like these not only have a short-term effect, they can sometimes subvert the company. Decisions to declare dividends or to repurchase stock must be viewed primarily in terms of the company's operational needs. Patience, in a down market, is sometimes a better solution than short-term action. Can that money be put to better use internally? Then the dividend or stock purchase is a poor investment. And what must be done to follow the act, to keep the stock at its new price, if the action should work? When the market goes up again, will that cash be easily reclaimed so that it could be put to better use? Short-term strategy is sometimes poor strategy.

One thing is certain, however. For any reasonably sound company, under any economic conditions in which there is still a viable stock market, no matter how diminished, a proper investor relations strategy will serve that company in its effort in the capital markets.

10

The Investor Relations Counsel

With all the changes in the competitive arena of the capital markets during the past 15 years, none has been more acute than has the role of the investor relations counsel.

Until about 1975, during the early days of this craft, investor relations was performed primarily by public relations people. The greatest skill required of them was to send out a dividend or earnings release, and perhaps to set up a meeting with security analysts. Gradually, former investment professionals were hired, and they became among the first people in the practice who knew how to read a balance sheet. The concept of investor relations as a discipline to help companies compete in the capital markets was so new, a decade ago, that many people had to make a broad leap to get the connection between the world of finance and the practices of communication.

Today, the investor relations counsel is either someone with a strong financial background, or with a profound understanding of both corporate finance and the capital markets. No longer the purview of public relations, today's investor relations professional tends to be a financial person with well-honed communications skills. One has merely to read the publications of the National Investor Relations Institute (NIRI), the association of investor relations professionals, and the technical nature of its content, to grasp the new sophistication of the practice.

Marketing and Investor Relations

Now there's yet another element—marketing.

As the competition in the capital markets continues to increase, and to become more intense, classic marketing skills must be adapted to telling (and selling) the corporate story to the financial community—to investors, shareholders, and those who advise them. And the more that marketing skills are applied to investor relations, the keener the competition becomes. And the keener the competition becomes . . .

Moreover, the arsenal of marketing skills, when aptly applied, frequently moves the investor relations practitioner into yet another nontraditional role—advocacy. Where the earlier practitioner was merely a messenger—a conduit of information from company to investor—today's competitive arena means that the investor relations professional must now sometimes advocate the company's position, earnestly and forcefully, to gain the attention and confidence of those in the marketplace responsible for buying or recommending that others buy the clients' stock.

And so today, and certainly in the coming decade, investor relations will be successfully practiced by those who are skilled in not only the financial aspects of the process, but in the marketing aspects as well.

Like most marketing and financial skills, the techniques and mechanics are the relatively easy part. It's the artful practice of these skills that matter. There is no certain body of knowledge that qualifies the practitioner, as in law or accounting, nor that can quantify the artfulness of it.

Many corporate executives have a natural talent and affinity for visibility, for example. Many companies are glamorous and deserve wide attention just by virtue of their own performance. After all, when a man murders his wife he doesn't need a public relations professional to get his name in the paper. When the cure for the common cold is found no news editor will have to be harangued by a public relations practitioner to report the event in detail.

But exposure for itself, without focus and adjustment for changing circumstances, can never be more than partially effective. The truly effective investor relations program is one that is well rounded, and includes at least several of the elements described in this book. Obviously it requires a measure of time and attention. The question is, who is to do it?

Sources of Investor Relations Expertise

Setting aside for the moment those facets of a company's operations that attract attention by virtue of their own performance—and even they must be focused to function effectively in investor relations—there are three possible sources of investor relations expertise and performance:

- The company's investment banker
- The internal investor relations executive
- The external investor relations counsel

Excluded from this discussion are those ancillary services that are sometimes called upon by virtue of their ability in one or another facets of communications, such as the nonfinancial public relations firm or the advertising agency. As will be seen further on in this discussion, unless there's a specifically experienced and qualified person in either of these structures, neither is in any way qualified to function effectively in investor relations. Investor relations is not, after all, merely public relations directed to the financial community. It's a separate and distinct practice, and is as different from public relations as it is from advertising. The two are not interchangeable.

The Investment Banker as Investor Relations Consultant

The investment banking firm would, on the face of it, seem to be a logical candidate to conduct an investor relations program, by virtue of its involvement with the financial community. Unfortunately, this rarely turns out to be true, for several reasons:

- The investment banker, through his or her own research and brokerage structure, is sometimes equipped to deal with only one dimension of the investor relations program—limited Street contact. Rarely does an investment banking or brokerage firm have the capability to deal professionally with the financial press or to prepare corporate shareholder literature, nor does it have the structure to direct an effective marketing-oriented investor relations program
- No investment banking or brokerage firm is financially structured to supply a full-scale service, either from a physical or an economic base. Most investment banking firms are paid a fee earned from performing specific investment banking services, such as underwriting, or financial structuring. To allocate time and personnel to such a nonremunerative activity as investor relations, even though it helps support their clients' stock, is uneconomical, and investment bankers are not likely to give it their greatest attention.
- It's unfortunate but true that the perspective of most brokerage houses and investment bankers is limited to the scope of their own activity. Their view of overall market conditions tends to be pervaded by conditions at the moment, which invariably means undue opti-

mism in an up market and undue pessimism in a down market. There is all too frequently lacking the perspective necessary to develop the kind of strategy, in its totality, described in the previous chapter.

- The pursuit of an investor relations program requires an up-to-the-minute understanding of changes in both attitude and personnel throughout the entire financial community. Investment banking firms are not geared to do this, as *au courant* as they may be with current conditions in the industry.

- The scope of the investment banker's contacts in the financial community is usually limited to his or her own circle of friends and business relationships. In some cases, this may be adequate to the needs of a program. In most cases it is not.

- There is a great potential for conflicts of interest.

- They simply don't understand the marketing function of investor relations. They're not in the business.

On the other hand, the good investment banker or broker does have a service to perform in behalf of his or her client, and can contribute in some measure to an effective total investor relations program.

The Investment Banker's Responsibility

There is certainly a responsibility to the client to support the aftermarket for a new issue, and indeed any issue the banker has been responsible for underwriting. This includes, when appropriate, issuing a research report (qualified by the fact that he or she is the underwriter), sponsoring and making a market in the stock, and introducing the company to those houses and institutions he knows. Certainly, no investor relations program, whether done internally or externally, should be performed without the complete cooperation and participation of the investment banker, since he or she is not only a beneficiary along with the company, but is also a valuable source of information.

Internal Investor Relations Capability

Internal capability, if the company is of a size to warrant it, can be tremendously useful, either alone or in conjunction with external counsel. If the task is assigned to a qualified person, there is a singular advantage in that the internal counsel has an ongoing feeling for the company and its activities, operations, objectives, and plans. If properly qualified, he or she can also function as a spokesperson for the company in ways that even the best qualified external counsel rarely can.

When there is external counsel, the internal person serves as a liaison and as coordinator. In many cases, the internal person performs most facets of the program, usually aided by a staff, as effectively as does the external counsel. Frequently, when there is good in-house capability, an external counsel is used only to supplement the staff people in designated areas. Sometimes, the staff person is highly qualified in one or several—but not all—functions of investor relations. He or she may be a former financial writer whose efforts in dealing with the financial press or in writing annual reports cannot be excelled. Or perhaps he or she is a former analyst who superbly understands the needs of analysts and brokers, or a former executive of an investor relations firm, in which case the knowledge of the total investor relations function is well rounded. In these cases, it's sometimes found that the outside counsel merely supplements efforts in those areas in which the internal practitioner's experience is not as strong as in others, or supplies additional manpower as needed, or supplies the broader perspective and expertise that should be expected of the external counsel.

Today, most staff investor relations executives are former analysts, financial or legal executives. This seems to be working remarkably well in many companies. Indeed, some of the best work now being done in the field is being done by internal people.

In some cases, the size of the company, the nature of the program itself, and the budget available for such a program, may dictate the feasibility of using internal counsel. His or her skills and capabilities may be all that are required to perform a program for a company at any given time (although as demonstrated in previous chapters, these circumstances frequently change rapidly).

In determining whether internal capability is feasible, there are only two hard and fast rules. The first is that the person be properly qualified. A public relations person with no financial background, or an advertising manager with a smattering of knowledge about public relations, is in no sense qualified to function effectively in investor relations for any company of consequence.

Second, it's next to useless to retain an internal investor relations counsel who doesn't have the ear, the respect, and direct access to the chief executive officer. Without this, the person, no matter how well qualified, is merely a clerk. If there is no respect within the company for the investor relations professional's value and capabilities, he or she will quickly cause the company to lose respect in the financial community and with the financial press. The financial world is very quick to discern the degree of authority a spokesperson has. To attempt to deal with the financial community through even the most highly qualified internal investor relations executive who doesn't have access to the inner councils is foolhardy and wasteful.

External Investor Relations Counsel

Properly qualified, the external investor relations counsel has several distinct advantages in serving the company competing in the capital markets. The external counsel is:

- A specialist. Not merely a public relations practitioner practicing only familiar aspects of investor relations, the professional's total concentration and effort are in the area of investor relations.

- With a firm that's mechanically structured to deal with all aspects of an investor relations program. The firm is equipped for the quick dissemination of releases, as well as for the direct contact with the financial community. It's geared to maintain up-to-the-minute mailing lists and lists of appropriate personnel in both the financial community and the financial press, which change constantly. In some firms, there is the capability and structure for financial community research, investor surveys, and proxy solicitation.

- In constant liaison with the financial community and the financial press, which should make him or her aware of shifts in attitudes and personnel, and which allows the professional to supply an extraordinarily valuable perspective of changing needs and changing attitudes in those areas.

- Able to bring to each investor relations program the breadth of experience in serving many companies with a wide variety of problems, and a broad experience in solutions.

- Objective. Any investor relations counsel must serve two roles—objectivity and advocacy. One is useless without the other. Advocacy that's not based on objectivity is weak, frequently irrelevant, and often borders dangerously close to creating problems of credibility.

- A marketing expert. Today, investor relations is as much a marketing function as a financial one. The skills, talent, and artistry of marketing are necessary to help companies compete successfully in the capital markets.

- A reliable source of information not directly related to investor relations, such as shifting sources of capital, as a result of ongoing relations with the financial community. In fact, for the company seeking new investment banking relationships, the experienced and qualified investor relations consultant is an excellent source of information about the capabilities of a wide variety of investment bankers

- Economically feasible. Whereas there are hidden overhead factors to be added to the cost of an internal counsel, the expense of an external counsel can be budgeted. The external counsel is accountable for fees and expenses. This is particularly pertinent for those consultants whose fee is based on an hourly rate, where each month's bill itemizes the amount of time spent by each executive in each of the several categories in which he or she is functioning for the company.

- Responsible and knowledgeable in the field of SEC and other regulation as it pertains to investor relations and disclosure. While the investor relations professional may be neither an attorney nor an accountant, qualifications must include knowledge of all SEC and exchange rules that pertain to an investor relations program.

- Head of a staff that includes the wide variety of skills—financial press, Street contact, writing, and so on—necessary for a well-rounded program.

While these advantages would seem to weigh the argument very heavily in favor of using external investor relations counsel, the judgment is made, in many respects, no differently than is the decision to retain house legal counsel or internal auditing staff. The use of one doesn't necessarily preclude the other, and frequently they supplement one another. At the same time, it must be recognized that the nature of a particular company or of a particular investor relations problem contains factors that make the internal staff sufficiently effective to defer consideration of external counsel. On the other hand, the size of a company or the nature of a specific investor relations consideration may make the external counsel more economically feasible.

Qualifications of an Investor Relations Practitioner

Selecting an investor relations consultant, either internal or external, is a matter of judging qualifications. Unfortunately, unlike the law or accounting, there are no certifiable qualifications that define or certify the financial relations counsel.

The problem with qualifications for investor relations is basic. It may be defined by noting that very few 15-year-olds plan to be investor relations consultants when they grow up. This means that the people in the industry are drawn from no single source that has prepared them educationally for the total investor relations counsel's role. Unlike the public relations person, the investor relations counsel can't subsist on merely an inventive mind, an outgoing personality, and the ability to express an idea on paper.

Qualifications for an Internal Investor Relations Officer

The qualifications for an investor relations counsel or officer, or the qualifications that should be inherent in the staff of an investor relations firm, are at least the following:

- A sound financial background. This is primary and essential. He or she should understand corporate finance, accounting, the investment banking function, and corporate structure. While not necessarily capable of professionally performing any of these tasks, he or she must be able to converse easily, authoritatively, and with understanding with the chief executive officer, the vice-president of finance, the attorney, and the accountant.

- An intimate knowledge of the workings of the capital markets. Not just Wall Street and the stock market, although that may be the primary area of activity, but with all the capital markets, including— and this becomes increasingly important—the foreign capital markets. He or she must understand both the mechanics and the élan of the market in all its subtleties.

- He or she must be experienced in dealing with the entire cast of characters to be found on Wall Street, from the registered representative to the security analyst to the money manager to the trader to the investment banker.

- The investor relations professional must have both communications and marketing skills, as well as a strong sense of advocacy.

    Many investor relations counsels are themselves former investment professionals. While this is basically good, there is a peculiar problem here. The fact that a person is a former investment professional doesn't of itself qualify him or her for investor relations. A really good security analyst can earn considerably more money practicing that craft than he or she can in most investor relations positions. These are the economics of both industries. It applies less, however, to the internal officer. Those investment professionals who have made the successful transition to investor relations are the ones who have done so because they feel that investor relations offers them a broader scope for their total personal needs, talents, and desires than does the investment world. Those who are successful are the ones who bring to investor relations a range of skills and interests that supplement their financial background. An analyst who fails in his career as an analyst does not automatically become a good investor relations counsel. On the other hand, many excellent investment professionals have joined the ranks of investor relations successfully because they've found that the wide variety of investor relations activities offers a better outlet for their more varied interests than does security analysis alone.

- The investor relations professional should be marketing-oriented. He or she should understand the tools and processes of marketing, and be able to apply them, within the context of an investor relations program, to meet the client's investor relations goals.

- He or she should have the breadth of experience of dealing with a great many firms, and facing a great many problems under all kinds of market conditions. It takes no great skill to function successfully for a growing and prospering company in a raging bull market. The question is whether that person can function just as effectively in a bear market.

- There should be an understanding of the full scope of corporate activity, including management, production, research and development, marketing and distribution, and finance.

- The investor relations professional should have a thorough experience and knowledge of the financial press, both in its mechanics and in its ever-changing structures.

- He or she should be a capable and facile writer of releases, annual and interim reports, and speeches. And this means not merely the ability to repeat the clichés of what has been done before, but to approach each problem with a fresh viewpoint. He or she should, in this context, be an effective communicator.

- An investor relations firm should have the mechanical structure and the manpower to deal effectively with all facets of the investor relations program. This includes the equipment to disseminate information at appropriate speed and with professional quality to the entire financial community and financial press. Manpower should be sufficient to allocate an appropriate amount of time to each client to effectively fulfill a program. An account executive with sole responsibility for twelve clients cannot possibly serve any one of those clients effectively.

- He or she should be familiar with the financial community nationally as well as locally in every major financial center of the United States. This means being knowledgeable about the various financial centers, and physically capable of dealing effectively with each of them.

- A firm's manager should be a sound business person running a sound business. While the individual practitioner is sometimes useful for his or her experience and wisdom, to serve solely as a consultant he or she should still function in as businesslike a way as does the largest investor relations firm.

- The investor relations firm's people who work on any account should each be intelligent, knowledgeable, and personable. The effective investor relations counsel, as an advocate, should be capable of speaking for the company and its executives in clearly defined circumstances. Rarely does any segment of the financial community write off an inept investor relations counsel and then accept as wise and capable the management he represents. The investor relations counsel is also exactly that, a counsel. He or she may have all the skills, mechanical capabilities, and experience in the world, but would still be useless to a company if his or her judgment cannot be respected and utilized with confidence.

- While there are several general-purpose public relations firms with excellent investor relations staffs, there is a danger in the smaller staff of a general firm in which the staff doesn't have full and autonomous capability.

    The situation would be comparable to using an auditor who is on the staff of a firm of attorneys. The chances are that his or her role is secondary to the company's primary business, leaving the auditor without facility and sometimes without portfolio. For the company seriously competing in the capital market, investor relations is primary—not an auxiliary. And so there is greater likelihood of finding more effectiveness in a specialized rather than a generalized firm. Moreover, as has been noted before, investor relations is not public relations to the financial community. It is a highly specialized financial function.

Selecting a Firm

Selecting an investor relations firm from among the several that specialize is in a sense no different from selecting an auditor or an attorney. Qualifications must be clearly established. Reputation is important. A Dun & Bradstreet rating is essential.

In choosing a firm, a preliminary interview should demonstrate not only qualifications, but also an understanding of the description of the company, its problems, and its opportunities. There is probably no better rule for judging a prospective investor relations counsel than to interview the individual as if he or she were being hired as an executive vice-president. Assuming the proper qualifications, you should be as personally impressed with his or her firm's representative as you would expect yourself to be with any candidate for a high managerial position. That is, after all, a function the investor relations professional serves.

Certainly references should be checked very carefully. These should include a broad spectrum drawn from clients, the financial press, and the financial community itself. A great deal of trust is placed in an investor relations counsel, and the responsibility in serving the company is great. No chief executive officer should retain any investor relations counsel with whom he or she is not totally impressed and upon whose judgment he feels he cannot rely.

Judging the Program

The results of an advertising campaign can be judged by sales. The results of a public relations campaign can be judged by favorable clippings, although ultimately the larger result is usually also sales. An investor relations program, although it should ultimately result in some rather specific objectives, such as an increase in stock price or price/earnings ratio or volume, is judged in terms of continuous effectiveness.

The nature of the capital markets, and particularly the stock market, is such that there are rarely immediate results visible in terms of stock price from even the most effective investor relations program. It should, however, bring a stock's price to a market valuation that's at least appropriate to the stock's actual value (in terms of the company behind it). A company undervalued by the market should gain in price and P/E ratio from an effective investor relations program sooner rather than later.

What an investor relations program *can't* do—at least for any sustained time—is get a stock price higher than the stock is substantially worth. This can be accomplished only by the kind of market manipulation that's probably not legal. Be cautious of any practitioner who promises that kind of instant result.

But there are other values as well. An investor relations program will be effective in fulfilling its objectives if it successfully communicates your story to a broad and appropriate financial community. Over a period of time, an infinitely larger segment of the financial community should know, know about, and understand your company in all its aspects. There should be a clear and discernible interest in your company as a result of the investor relations program. This is sometimes measurable by surveys, but only if two surveys taken over a period of time are compared.

There should be a marked increase in the company's following on the Street. More brokers, analysts, and other investment professionals should be following the stock, and recommending it to their clients.

The ultimate results of such an interest can be, over the long run, an improved price/earnings ratio, active sponsorship of your stock, an increased number of market makers (for an over-the-counter company), discernibly greater liquidity, and increased trading volume. However, there is unfortunately rarely a direct one-to-one relationship between any activity or group of activities in an investor relations program and any of these results. There are too many external factors affecting the market at any given moment to allow it to be immediately responsive to any activity in an investor relations program, other than the specific news of an event or activity of momentous nature.

This is one reason why, in order to be effective, a financial relations program must be assiduously pursued over a reasonable period of time before any judgment is made about its performance.

Ultimately, the best judgment of the investor relations program is the judgment of management that the various facets of the program are being intelligently and actively performed, and that the receptiveness of the financial community is evident.

There must also be consistency. Since the market, the economy, and the company are all in a constant state of flux, and since the competition for capital is exceptionally intense, the cumulative effects of a program stopped at midpoint are very quickly lost. There is remarkably little residual value. In order to be effective, the once discontinued program must start up again, sometimes virtually from scratch.

In the final analysis, investor relations is a function of people—their intelligence, their skills, their eagerness, and their dedication. The final judgment of the success of an investor relations program is a judgment of these elements and their application.

11

Corporate Restructuring and Takeovers

Mergers, acquisitions and takeovers serve to restructure corporations, which is like saying that atomic explosions alter the nature of the atom. What really happens is that old entities cease to exist, and the new entities pose more questions than there are immediate answers. The dislocations, both internal and for the financial community, can be awesome.

All of which means that in mergers, acquisitions and takeovers, the work of the investor relations practitioner explodes and expands and proliferates.

The exception, of course, is the investor relations consultant for the acquired company, who is now probably minus one client, or the investor relations executive who's out of a job.

Because of the subtleties in relating the meaning and effect of mergers and acquisitions to the financial community, it's important to examine some of the recent history and ramifications of these profound corporate restructurings.

Why Companies Merge

Once upon a time, companies merged because there was a community of interests. A steel company would buy a coal or an iron company, because coal and iron are commodities used in making steel, for example. Companies merge, classically and in textbooks, to expand capability, to enhance distribution, to broaden a product line, to assure a source of supply, for increased technology, for diversification to offset the cyclical nature of a business, and ultimately to improve the ability to appreciate the invested dollar.

Then, in the 1960s, ignoring textbooks, mergers and acquisitions became a game of acquiring assets for assets (and presumably earnings) alone.

In 1967, there were some 3000 mergers in the United States. By the end of that decade, merger fever had struck the corporate community like a plague. But by the early 1980s, an overwhelming number of acquisitions made in the 1960s and 1970s were on the block. The game, it seems, had changed.

Companies such as Colgate-Palmolive, which had acquired such disparate businesses as sporting goods, cosmetics, and ladies clothing, began to shed these businesses as frantically as they had once acquired them. Divisions were spun off from one conglomerate after another in virtually a 180-degree turn from the practices of just a few years earlier.

Some of the sales were made to correct earlier mistakes. Some were made for sound financial reasons, such as realizing that the dollar value of the asset, invested in the period's high-interest climate, was greater than the asset could return as an operating division. Sometimes the divestiture was simply to raise cash. Pan American, choking on losses from the acquisition of National Airlines and bleeding at every pore, sold off assets, such as its Park Avenue building, its profitable hotel chain, and even its aircraft, like a nineteenth-century steamboat throwing furniture and railings into the boiler to win the race. And some even sold, they claim, to simplify the company so that Wall Street would better understand it.

With the recession of the early 1970s, the merger fever ran its course. For several years, those mergers that subsequently took place had a sounder business rationale behind them.

But the economic tide changed again, and in the late 1970s and 1980s, a new strain of the merger virus took hold. While not quite as virulent as the earlier strain, mergers began to increase, impelled by economic factors that, once again in many cases, had nothing much to do with the textbook reasons for merger.

In the 1980s, the leveraged buyout—the LBO—rose to a high profile, in which a company would borrow money to buy or take over another company, and then repay the debt with the acquired company's own assets. In the 1980s, there were some 2,800 LBOs. In 1989, about 2,400 companies merged. Lost were such established names as RCA. And in the first half of 1990, there were about 1,200 mergers, despite turmoil in the marketplace.

And where did the money come from for the loans to make the purchase? From a financial instrument that became known as the *junk bond*. A junk bond is a high-interest, but high-risk, bond. Because bonds seldom fail to pay off in this country, the risk was masked by the potential profit, for both the seller and the buyer.

If the financial world is indeed measured by decades, then the 1980s was the decade of the LBO and junk bonds and profits that made more millionaires in a decade than had been made in entire centuries before. The 1990s also opened the new decade with many of the leading figures in the junk bond industry in jail, or on their way to it. It seems that they had traded on the inside information they acquired in the course of playing the game.

While the rationale for the mergers of the 1980s may be found in the economic conditions of the time, and the divestitures of divisions acquired earlier give force to the concept that too many mergers are made with short-term expedience, the current wave of mergers does reflect something different, something new.

It may be seen more clearly, perhaps, in the mergers on Wall Street. In the 1970s, brokerage firms merged to survive. But when, in the 1980s, an American Express merges with a Shearson, or a Prudential merges with a Bache, or, most significantly, a Sears, Roebuck merges with both a giant real estate company and a major brokerage firm, then the mergers are for reasons that go beyond the classical textbook. It is obviously a change in the structure of the economy. The merger partners are reacting to something new in an economy that is more complex, more competitive internationally, more involved and convoluted in its texture.

One answer may be seen in the growth of service industries, which is a reflection of changing technology. It's long been recognized that we went from an agricultural to an industrial society, and are now moving from an industrial to a service economy. Many of our industries have matured, particularly in the United States. General Motors and U.S. Steel no longer dominate our economy, and we have certainly given over vast segments of our markets to Japan and others. At the same time, technology has made many of our fixed assets obsolete, and these are being replaced by less labor-intensive operations. Peter Drucker has made the point, as have others, that we should stop investing our energies and capital in labor-intensive industries that are more effectively handled by nations with vast labor pools, and concentrate on high technology and service industries, in which we excel. That this is beginning to happen seems clear. Witness, for example, the concessions to technology made in the 1970s and 1980s by labor in the automotive industry and in printing, where the Linotype operator has been replaced by the computer and desktop publishing.

This change comes about not through a conscious decision based upon a philosophy—little in history does. But in the day-to-day mergers of expedience, it seems clear that it is this direction in which the economy is moving.

Mergers and the Capital Markets

Mergers, as we've seen, happen for many reasons—some sound, some foolish. But in the final analysis, long- or short-term, the most potentially successful merger is one that is seen ultimately as a solution to a capital problem, either to improve the capital position or to improve the company's overall capabilities in ways that will improve the company's capital position. Naturally, the improved capital position is expected to generate greater profits and return on the investment.

In a classic article entitled "How To Sell Your Company" in the *Harvard Business Review* in September 1968, the late Richard M. Hexter, then executive vice-president of Donaldson, Lufkin & Jenrette and later president of Ardshiel Associates, wrote:

> Not only is selling a company an investment decision, it is the *ultimate* investment decision. There are at least two reasons for this—no investment decision so totally commits the company's assets, and no investment decision is so irrevocable.
>
> A stockholder group selling its company for $20 million in stock to the PDQ Corporation is making the same decision as would a portfolio manger in considering a $20 million investment in PDQ stock. If a cash sale is planned, the seller is presuming he can reinvest the cash in another portfolio with equal or better prospects. In both cases the same question must be asked: Can an investment be made wisely so that the new holdings will grow faster than would equity ownership in the selling company? Unless viewed in this light any decision to sell must be considered somewhat arbitrary.

While this was written as a guide to the company as a potential seller, it also holds true for the potential buyer. It is an investment decision.

How the Financial Community Views a Merger

For the company considering merger, for whatever reasons, whether as a buyer or a seller, the financial community will view the transaction in just these investment terms. For the shareholder or the prospective investor, the merger will be looked upon in terms of its value in appreciating the investment. For other segments of the capital markets, and especially those called upon to help finance the merger, the question of how the action will enhance the company as an investment vehicle is no less pertinent.

Traditionally, Wall Street reflects its views of any such action in the stock market. If Wall Street sees the merger as salutary, the price of the stock will go up when the merger is announced. If the value of the merger or acquisition is not understood, the price of the stock will go down. Nor is this market activity solely the result of the activities of arbitrageurs—traders who specialize in taking advantage of differences in stock prices in different markets. It's invariably a genuine Wall Street reaction.

Therefore, the investor relations projection of a merger or acquisition must be expressed in terms that allow the financial community to see the merger as salutary, and to make clear the ways in which the merger will enhance the company's growth potential.

Attracting Candidates

For the company with a growth pattern that includes acquisition, or for the company that may ultimately want to merge, the process begins well before merger partners are identified. Most mergers are a result of a formalized search by the company, investment bankers, attorneys, accountants, and others, and so high visibility remains the key to attracting merger partners. This, of course, is a function of a well-executed investor relations program. Particularly important in the total investor relations picture here is the annual report. It becomes a kind of brochure—a selling piece for both merger partners. For the company that is merger-minded, certainly this fact should become one of the objectives in planning the annual report.

In a bull market, when high price/earnings ratio stocks are the commodity for purchasing a company, visibility in the financial community is essential to maintain high stock and volume. Price/earnings ratios are still an essential factor in a merger, even when cash or notes are used instead of stock. Thus the investor relations program becomes even more important in maintaining the P/E ratio at a reasonable level. Companies whose shares are undervalued have a considerably more difficult job in acquisitions and mergers, regardless of the stock price, than do companies whose stock prices more accurately reflect earnings and earnings potential. Companies whose asset values are not clear have a harder time selling. At the same time, as will be seen further in this chapter, companies with low P/Es may be targets for raiders.

Factors to Be Projected

In determining those factors that must be projected in an investor relations program designed to enhance merger possibilities, at least the following should be included:

- *The financial value of the company.* This should be projected as clearly as possible, and with a full understanding that hidden factors remain hidden only for the briefest period of time.
- *Management.* As in any form of investor relations, management's strengths must be clearly exposed and projected.

- *Marketing and production strengths.* Both the current structures and the anticipated needs and capabilities should be projected in the growth pattern.

- *Current and anticipated funding needs.* This is a point to be emphasized in the projection of plans.

- *R & D,* particularly in industries that lend themselves to technological growth.

- *Long-range management objectives.*

- *Attitudes of management toward growth.* How does management see merger in terms of both its own future and the future of the merger partners as well?

Essentially, then, these areas of concentration for displaying the acquisition-minded company differ from other investor relations practices only in emphasis, and in the fact that the investor relations program, while continuing to be concentrated on the financial community, must also include the general business community. Further emphasis must be placed on such factors as those directions of growth that delineate the kinds of mergers sought by the company, in terms of the company's needs. This includes growth for diversification, source of supply, management distribution, and so on.

Divestiture

It's inappropriate to talk about visibility for merger without considering, at the same time, divestiture. In many respects, they are opposite sides of the same coin. Frequently, a company will find itself with a segment or a division that no longer serves its corporate needs. It may arise from a market that the company no longer wishes to serve, or a division that's no longer profitable under the company's structure, or an operation that has not responded to the company's management. It could be a forced divestiture by order of a government regulatory body.

In the case of divestiture, there is the added problem of projecting the company's need to sell without diminishing the overall view of the company's abilities or of the unit's potential. There's frequently the problem, as well, of internal morale during the course of the divestiture program, in which the management wants to avoid a negative feeling on the part of those responsible for the operations of the unit to be divested. To the extent that operational efforts of the unit to be divested are diminished, this is not only an internal problem, it also tends to undermine the strength of the unit, and therefore makes it harder to sell.

The Divestiture Program

The program for divestiture, then, must be carefully formulated with these factors in mind. The positive aspects of the unit to be divested must be emphasized, as must the positive aspects of the reasons for divestiture. This is not to imply that any misrepresentation is warranted. The key word is *emphasis* in the course of disclosure. It must be recognized by even the most insensitive managements that not every kind of operation functions well or consistently in every management or corporate context. Clopay Corporation, a Cincinnati-based manufacturer of housewares and plastic products, purchased an office products operation at one point in its expansion program. At the time of the purchase, the move was reasonable, both as a diversification move and because the office products industry offered great potential. During the several ensuing years, however, both the nature of the office products industry and Clopay's corporate directions changed. Clopay's otherwise satisfactory earnings were, for a brief period, diminished by the negative results of the office products division, and divestiture seemed in order. Clopay management wisely recognized the fact that the problem was not the office products division so much as the mixture of the division's operations with the company's other operations. The office products industry was still promising, but not necessarily so under the Clopay corporate structure that had emerged over the years. Approaching the problem in this positive way, Clopay managed to divest itself of the division in a reasonable period of time. Furthermore, by properly anticipating the sale and setting up reserves, the divestiture was accomplished at a loss to Clopay that was not too serious. Once the divestiture was completed, the company moved on to increase its success in its remaining operations.

Divestiture is not always as uncomplicated as in the Clopay situation. When it's ordered by federal decree, a number of additional problems are posed. To the challenge of finding a buyer under pressure is added the problem of convincing shareholders and the investment community that the company, after the divestiture, is still a sound investment vehicle. When Work Wear, Inc., a manufacturer and renter of uniforms and working clothes, was ordered to divest its entire rental operation, the problem was further compounded by the extraordinary procedure the company used. First, there was the need to explain to shareholders that the company was still sound despite the fact that the units to be divested represented half the company's earnings. This was done in the annual report, which went to great lengths to analyze the potential market for the company's products, and demonstrated the company's strong position in its field.

Second, Work Wear divested its rental division by splitting it off under its own separate management, and then offering Work Wear shareholders the option of exchanging Work Wear stock for stock in the new company on a proportional basis. This, too, was explained in the annual report, as well as in the proxy statement.

But the annual report came out at about the same time that the split-off company went into registration for the new stock. This meant that the report had to be written so that descriptions of Work Wear's continuing potential did not interfere with the registration by appearing to condition stockholders who might opt to exchange their stock. This was handled by hewing closely to the language of the registration statement. The same approach was used at the annual meeting, which was held during the registration period.

When Maremont Corporation was forced to divest its warehousing division, the problem was quite different. The warehousing division was relatively new, and had not yet reached a point where it was a major contributor to corporate earnings. This was easy to explain in news releases, analyst meetings, and the annual and interim reports. But the division was most likely going to be sold to several buyers, piece by piece. The problem was to develop a divestiture program to sell the several pieces. A written presentation for each unit was prepared, outlining its history, its assets, its operations and performance, its market potential, and so forth. Prospective purchasers were identified and approached. Publicity in the trade press about the units to be divested developed other potential purchasers. Ultimately, and within the deadlines set by the divestiture order, all of the units were sold.

Announcing the Merger

A merger negotiation is a sensitive situation. Under the best of circumstances, many more mergers are seriously discussed than are consummated. There are many stages of discussion, ranging from the first query to the actual consummation of the merger, and at any one of the stages something can happen to upset it. Throughout the discussions secrecy is essential—not for any Machiavellian reason, but to avoid undue speculation, to protect employee morale, or to avoid a counter offer by companies that otherwise might not have known that one of the merger partners was available.

At the same time, there's a point in a merger negotiation at which a number of insiders are aware of the potential of the merger and are therefore in a very precarious position under the SEC rules of disclosure. At this point, the timing of the announcement of merger discussion becomes crucial.

First Press Release

Obviously, the safest time to announce a merger negotiation is at the first sign that it becomes clear to both parties that there is general agreement to merge. Ideally, the signal to disclose would be the signing of the letter of intent. Sometimes, however, the discussions have made considerable progress well before a letter of intent is drawn, or there may even be no letter of intent planned. In a 1988 case, the courts ruled that announcement is not mandatory until there is an agreed-upon price or merger structure. Beyond being driven by rumors, whether to wait for signed agreement or to announce the merger negotiation in the drafting stage is a question of judgment. The timing of the disclosure should be when it's felt that both sides are in general agreement, and that the weight of the inside information on those who hold it, or the number of people in either or both companies that are privy to the information, has reached a dangerous proportion in view of the general principles of the rules of disclosure.

At that time, a simple one-page release should be issued by either party or jointly, announcing that the merger negotiations are taking place. The announcement need not state the specific terms of the merger except generally—for stock, for cash, for notes, and so forth. The press will undoubtedly make further inquiries, but these should be politely put aside by the simple statement of truth that the negotiations have not yet been completed and that the terms have not been set.

The Canceled Merger

If, after the first announcement, the merger is called off for any reason, another announcement must be made immediately. If, on the other hand, negotiations continue for several weeks beyond the original announcement, a subsequent release should be issued merely to indicate that further progress has been made in the negotiation. The specific details in subsequent announcements should be limited to those facts that are needed to update the original announcement. The purpose of the second announcement is to maintain an orderly flow of information that precludes undue speculation as to the cause of the time lag since the first announcement, and to announce those regulatory hurdles that may have been overcome, such as antitrust or tax rulings.

Binding Agreement

As soon as the merger is reduced to binding agreement, the announcement must go out immediately. It should include all facts about the merger, including details of terms. There is no reason why the release can't be prepared beforehand, agreed to by both parties, for distribution within an hour or two after signing the agreement. Distribution of the release should follow the normal pattern for news distribution described in Chapter 3.

There are times when, following the announcement of the consummation of a merger, the two parties then decide to disagree. This can happen for any number of reasons, ranging from personality conflicts to the discovery that the facts weren't as represented. The simple announcement of change of agreement then poses some thorny problem, since the required explanation may be embarrassing to either party. But explanation there must be, since the speculation can be more damaging than the facts. And explanations will be demanded of both parties by shareholders, the press, the investment community, and perhaps even the SEC.

Shareholder Approval

In those mergers in which shareholder approval is necessary, the description of the merger in all its facets is given in a proxy statement. In some cases, the nature and timing of the merger require a special shareholders' meeting.

But the proxy is frequently written in formal, legal terms, which rarely show shareholders the advantages management sees in the merger. There are two ways to logically reduce the barrier between management and shareholders constructed by legal language. The first is to be sure to include shareholders on mailings of all releases relating to the merger. The second way is to send a personalized letter from the chief executive officer to each shareholder, describing the merger and its advantages in simplest terms.

This kind of consideration becomes even more necessary for the shareholders of the company being acquired. In many cases, it's the smaller of the two companies. Many of the acquired company's shareholders are often employees or former employees, or individuals who bought their stock in the company's earlier days.

They want to know that the deal they're getting as individuals is a good one and doesn't subvert the reasons for which they originally bought stock.

Many a merger has been delayed or scuttled by a suit instituted by a dissident shareholder of an acquired company who believes, however falsely, that only the company's management will benefit—that the shareholders will not. This kind of suit is frequently avoided by doing a good job of keeping all shareholders of both companies well informed at every step of the way.

Follow-up

Once the merger has been consummated, there remains the job of convincing the financial community that the merger is indeed salutary. There is also, frequently, the internal job of communicating to the executives and employees of both companies the nature of the merger and its potential effect on their future.

Community and Press Relations

Following the merger, an intensive financial community and press relations program should be undertaken. A new background report should be prepared, describing the newly structured company, and a vigorous program of meeting with analysts, brokers, money managers, and other professional investors should be started, with representatives of both companies involved, if feasible, to explain the reasons behind the merger and the ways in which it will help the new combined company to grow.

Press Relations

A press relations program should include interviews with executives, stories about the company in relation to its industry, and so forth. For the listed company or the OTC company whose quotations are carried by *The Wall Street Journal,* it is a marvelous opportunity for a *Dow-Joneser*—an in-depth interview about the company and its potential, which appears on the Dow Jones tape and frequently in *The Wall Street Journal* in abbreviated form. A similar interview with Reuters should also be arranged. Remember, the idea is to establish in the minds of the financial community, as quickly as possible, the favorable nature of the marriage, as well as to reaffirm the growth potential of the company.

Internal Communications

Employee morale problems arising out of uncertainty in a merger can be devastating to a company's operations during and immediately following a merger. Hill & Knowlton's vice-chairman, Richard E. Cheney, notes that mergers are like nineteenth-century marriages. "The lawyers and the parents dicker over the terms and the size of the dowry and then sign the contract," he says. "It's left to the children to make the marriage work. Too often, though, the newlyweds have no experience to guide them and no commitment to making the match a success beyond parental expectations."

What too frequently happens, then, is that the marriage produces fear, suspicion, and rebellion. Says Cheney, "Anarchy prevails in top management, capital is wasted, schedules for delivery are missed, markets are disrupted." By the time the uproar dies down, the key managers who gave real value to the target company have usually jumped ship.

The key to avoiding this kind of disaster is to plan the postmerger communications program well before the merger becomes effective.

At the earliest feasible moment, even before the consummation of the merger, a meeting should be held for executives and employees of both companies to clarify the nature of the merger and the probable effects it will have on employees of both companies. Frankness is essential, even if it means imparting bad news. Employees whose jobs may be in jeopardy must, of course, be treated diplomatically. Key employees shouldn't be lost through uncertainty, although it may take some time, subsequent to the merger, to determine who is to be kept and who is not.

A letter to all employees from the chief executive officer is very much in order. The idea is to encourage calm and to engender a sense of security—as best as possible—in an uncertain situation and in a period of transition. It's also an opportunity for the chief executive officer to convey the spirit of optimism in which the merger was consummated.

Corporate Identity Program

An integral part of a merger or acquisition is establishing the identification of the newly merged company as part of the parent or survivor. Unless carefully planned, this can be a painful and expensive problem.

Some years ago, an old and famous privately held company, Sossner Tap & Die Company, was absorbed by HeliCoil Corporation, along with a number of other small companies. Sossner was a well-established name in the field, and, in fact, was better known throughout the world than was HeliCoil. Merely to have changed the Sossner name to HeliCoil would have eliminated all the marketing goodwill that had been built up over the years. This, combined with the fact that HeliCoil had absorbed a number of other small companies within a short period of time, dictated the need for a new corporate identity program that would bring all the companies under one umbrella without losing the identity and goodwill of the individual companies.

Corporate Identity Programs and Corporate Image

Judging the value of corporate identity programs enters a gray area. They are frequently seriously oversold by zealous designers who seem to imply that by changing the corporate logo there would be a significant change in something called the *corporate image,* and that by changing the corporate image all kinds of miraculous good would accrue to the company. This, of course, is patent nonsense. First of all, the term *corporate image* has been flagrantly perverted since it was first used in a somewhat different context some years ago. The implication seems to be that people have an image of a company that, if favorable, carries with it a public attitude that will help it in all of its dealings with everyone, from the financial community to the consumer. If the corporate image of General Electric, the idea suggests, is that of a company that deals well with consumer suppliers, the financial community, employees, and society in general, then the public will buy its products regardless of quality, invest in it regardless of sound investment principles, and smile blithely if it pollutes its industrial environment. Moreover, the notion is fostered that this corporate image can be achieved by changing and modernizing the company's logo and graphic appearance, supported by cosmetic public relations. It seems to say that a perception of a company can be altered by manipulating symbols—that reality can be hidden by illusion. Unfortunately, this ludicrous idea is accepted by a great number of people.

There are times when a company's graphics should be modernized and, in the case of the absorption of another company through merger or acquisition, when its graphics can be used to identify the new subsidiaries as part of the parent company. But no corporate graphics program is going to change a public impression of a company by itself. Only the realities of a company's operational factors can do that. If you don't like the reality, change the company, not it's graphics.

A particularly successful corporate identity program was achieved by Eastern Airlines some years ago. It modernized its logo, its graphics, and the appearance of its outlets and personnel. After a short period of time there was no aspect of the public appearance of Eastern, from its advertising to its airplanes, that was not readily identifiable as being Eastern Airlines. This graphics program, however, did nothing to improve the quality of the airline's service. Its planes were still maintaining poor on-time schedules, its personnel didn't improve their efficiency, nor could all the graphics and advertising improve the quality of its operations. What resulted was an instant and consistent identification of an operation that was considered so generally inferior that its profits were below those of its competitors for many years, and ultimately contributed to its bankruptcy.

On the other hand, a corporate identity program is useful in unifying, in the minds of all with whom it must deal, the view of a company in its many elements and improving visual recognition—if certain safeguards are taken in the transition.

A Good Corporate Identity Program

A good corporate identity program begins with an analysis of the company and all its operations, including its subsidiaries, its divisions, and so on. More than just a view of graphics, the analysis must concern itself with the consistency of not only corporate literature, stationery, and logos, but titles and descriptions as well. For example, too often terms like *divisions* and *subsidiaries* are used interchangeably. These are precise terms in the corporate sense, and no corporate identity program can function without a clear understanding of the difference.

The Graphics Manual

A well-designed graphics program will include a manual that indicates the company's standards for the use of its logo in every aspect, including size, color, and terminology. It should be remembered that no corporate identity program succeeds overnight. It must be promoted and popularized. It takes time for it to sink in.

It is in cases such as a Sossner company that the problem arises.

Logically, the corporate identity program of HeliCoil dictated that the former Sossner company become simply the Tap and Die Division of HeliCoil. But when former Sossner salesmen began calling on their old customers as representatives of some strange new company, called the Tap and Die Division of HeliCoil, the salesmen were greeted with blank stares. This, despite a rather intensive advertising campaign in the trade press announcing the change in name. The solution was to print new double business cards with both names on them, to have the sales manager write letters of explanation to all former Sossner customers, and to be sure that salesmen clearly explained the change in each of their calls. There still remained the problem of new customers who had heard of Sossner but not of HeliCoil. Here, too, the double card was successful.

Promoting the New Corporate Identity

When the new corporate identity program is completed, it must be made known as quickly and as broadly as possible. The audiences for this campaign are:

- Customers
- Suppliers
- The general public
- Employees
- The financial community
- The plant community

A number of devices are used to reach these audiences. They include:

- *Publicity.* Press releases with illustrations of the new graphics and a description of how the company is incorporating its subsidiaries and divisions under the new graphics should be sent to every segment of the press that serves the target audiences. This includes the trade press, the business and financial press, local papers in which plants are located, employee publications, and the financial press.

  If feasible, public events should be instituted that are themselves publicizable, such as a sign-changing ceremony at a plant, or human interest pictures showing a sign painter facing fifty trucks on which he must paint the new logo. Under some circumstances, the change in logo can be a useful peg for a feature article on how the company has grown since it was first started 25 or 50 years ago.

- *Advertising.* An appropriate advertising campaign should be developed to announce the change. The obvious media are those publications serving the audiences to be reached.

- *Announcements by mail.* A letter, a brochure, or a reprint of the announcement advertisement should be sent to every company, customer, and supplier with which the company does business. If there is a case of potential confusion, such as the Sossner situation, a personal letter should go out to every customer served by the old company. This letter can be signed by the company president, by the sales manager, or by the salesman serving that customer—whichever is most appropriate.

The changeover cannot be so abrupt as to lose the values inherent in former names and earlier identifications. It takes time to establish a new identity, particularly if there is a corporate name change.

And, most importantly, it should be remembered that a new graphic identity will not enhance a company's image. Only superior service, product quality, and consistent good management can achieve that.

Because so many mergers in recent years have proven to be irrational, the financial community tends to be skeptical of mergers and acquisitions. This should be kept foremost in the minds of corporate executives who contemplate merger. The very fact of a merger alone, it should be recognized, will not be accepted with enthusiasm without considerable explanation and an intensive investor relations program to explain most clearly the reasons and hopes for it.

The Takeover

When a company is targeted for takeover, these days, the chances of its surviving as an independent entity are roughly about one in twenty. When the finger points at a company, as in a surrealistic movie, that company is in all likelihood gone. For good or ill, we have come to this.

There was a time when defenses against takeover were, under the law, more formidable. There was a time, even within the decade, when a company with any sense of vulnerability could anticipate a takeover by building defensible measures into its structure. But no more. In the 1980s, takeovers were enhanced by bankers willing to finance leveraged buyouts, by relaxed antitrust enforcement, and by the easy money of the junk bond. With luck the economic events of the past few years may have changed all that, or at least slowed it down. But still, for the dedicated raider, there is little to arbitrarily protect the target.

The Black Book

No more defensive devices, such as keeping a *black book* of defensive plans to pull out at the first sign of a tender offer. Now, for the targeted company, there remain only a few broad general defenses—the *poison pill* (amending company bylaws to allow a target company shareholder to buy stock in a surviving company at half-price if the predator wins, a cost which is too rich for a raider), and the *white knight* (finding a company that might be a more friendly merger partner and convincing it to compete against the hostile raider). Another increasingly used defense is the ESOP—the Employee Stock Option Plan—which puts large blocks of stock in the hands of the employees. Of these defenses, the poison pill has shown value not so much as a defense, but as a holding action—a frustration for the raider.

And there is, of course, the defense of not being vulnerable in the first place.

Economic philosophy aside for the moment, what happened is that in the 1980s, we entered a new economic era in which the sanctity of a company seems to reside not in the traditions of entrepreneurial ownership, but in the rights of the shareholders. You may have started the company from an idea you developed in your basement. You may have nurtured the company through many a sleepless night as one would an ailing, fragile child. You may have spent the best years of your life demeaning and prostrating yourself before bankers and investment bankers. But if yours is a public company, then the company belongs to the shareholders, and not to you.

In a takeover attempt, there may be all the reason in the world against the takeover, in terms of your company's role in the marketplace. The shareholders, and the acquiring company, may have only the vaguest notion of what your company makes. But if the shareholders can in any way be perceived to lose economic advantage in the near term through your antitakeover methods, then you lose. The economic advantages to the shareholders—even those who bought the stock yesterday (and, chances are, most did)—will prevail in any lawsuit.

And so goes the *black-book* approach. Any defensive measures structured before a takeover attempt may be construed by the courts as a preconception that ignores the potential good and welfare of the shareholders. How, the courts seem to be asking, can you predetermine that you will be functioning in the shareholders' best interests without looking at a specific offer?

In an article in the *New York Law Journal,* Richard E. Cheney, vice-chairman of the international public relations firm, Hill & Knowlton, and perhaps the country's leading takeover tactician, explored the black-book syndrome in the light of today's court findings.

"A typical black book would recommend setting up an antitrust situation by acquiring a company in the same business as the raider," he writes.

"Royal tried this (in its attempt to fend off a takeover by Monogram). The net result: the judge enjoined the acquisition."

Royal then tried another old standard stratagem—suggesting that their assets would be used by Monogram to finance the acquisition.

"The judge pointed out that Monogram didn't need Royal's assets to pay back the debt." Royal, it turns out, was much more heavily leveraged than Monogram, and Monogram had more net worth and cash, and fewer liabilities.

Royal then tried to get an investment banker to declare the offer inadequate. This, too, the judge denied, noting that the analysis was done virtually overnight, and without due deliberation.

Next in the black-book agenda was to claim that estimated earnings for Royal were going to rise, but the judge pointed out that they hadn't in the past, and there was no reason to expect them to do so in the future.

And on and on in the litany of classic defenses. Royal was thrown out of court.

The only valid defense, then, is a company that's so strong that their shareholders clearly won't benefit from the takeover.

Arbitrage

Complicating the problem is arbitrage. Classically, the professional arbitrageur anticipates the takeover and buys large blocks of stock in the potential target. He then sells at a profit when the attempt is made. But to the professional arbitrageur has been added a new breed of amateurs. All of those stockbrokers, and their customers, who so happily played the new issues game a few years ago are now busily involved in guessing takeover targets and buying stock in those companies. Between the professionals and the amateurs, the tender offer has become a stock market game that shoots stock prices up into unrealistic heights. This seriously distorts stock prices, and adds to the problem of the value of an offer to shareholders. Lost in the struggle is the company.

The Law

In recent years, takeover attempts have been considerably curbed by more than just economics. New laws and SEC regulations, as well as accounting changes, have restrained at least some of the excesses of the raiders of the 1960s.

In 1969, the Mills Act was passed into law. It limits the amount of debt that can be exchanged for equity in a takeover, while still permitting interest payments to qualify as a cost for tax purposes. Its purpose was to prevent convertible debentures from being used in a raid. Its effect was to produce an interest-bearing instrument known today as the junk bond.

The Williams Act requires that any individual or corporation making a tender offer must file a variety of facts with the SEC, if after the termination of the tender offer the tendering corporation would directly or indirectly be the beneficial owner of more than 5 percent of the class of stock for which it is tendering. But the intent of the Williams Act, notes Cheney, was not to give management job security, nor, for that matter, to further the interests of acquiring companies. Instead, it was intended to give shareholders a fair shake by providing them with all the information they need to make an informed judgment on whether or not to accept an offer. The result has been that the Williams Act has had virtually no defensive effect.

Another defense against takeovers is antitrust law. Since the Justice Department's and the Federal Trade Commission's positions on antitrust vary from one administration to the next, it's always a good idea, when defending against a takeover, to run to the FTC and the Justice Department, on the possibility that the attempt can be aborted. But antitrust is not an automatic solution. Judge Friendly of the Second Circuit Court of

Appeals, in a landmark decision, warned not to draw Excalibur (the anti-trust sword) against a hostile offer when it would doubtless remain sheathed in the face of a friendly offer. The courts have subsequently taken a narrow view of the antitrust defense, particularly when they feel that the shareholders are being deprived of the opportunity to get a premium on their stock.

Changes in accounting rules make many takeover attempts much less appetizing. Pooling of interests, where the combined earnings of two companies are reported as one, regardless of the length of time the two companies have been combined, is no longer acceptable in most cases. Goodwill must now be shown in the balance sheet and written off through annual charges against income over a maximum of 40 years.

The SEC

The SEC tends to be stringent in dealing with tender offers. It requires, for example, that a company must proceed with its offer within 5 days of initial public disclosure, and that the offer must stay open for 20 business days, with a 15-day withdrawal period. Furthermore, it requires that everyone who tenders stock within 10 days of the offer be treated alike, and must be given a similar proration opportunity if the price is increased. It ruled, also, that bidders have a right of access to shareholders.

There is an interesting problem in some aspects of SEC regulation, in that it frequently conflicts with state regulations. Many states, at the behest of their own domiciled industries, have passed laws regarding takeover offers. Some states, for example, require a waiting period of 20 days to the SEC's 5. But most of these state laws are being superseded by the SEC's regulation, and in an increasing number of cases, companies are filing suits against the states at the same time that they file the tender offer. More and more, federal courts are asked for restraining orders against state regulation.

State courts, on the other hand, have been an effective battlefield in some aspects of takeover, setting some interesting precedents. During the merger negotiations between Time Inc. and Warner Communications, Paramount made a hostile bid for Time. This was scotched in a Delaware court that ruled that directors, not shareholders, run a firm, thereby putting a crimp in the argument that a merger or takeover may be good for the shareholders.

Directors

The Time-Warner decision raises some interesting points about the responsibilities of directors in a hostile tender offer. On the one hand, if the directors vote to reject the offer, they may be guilty of depriving the shareholders of an increase in the value of their stock. On the other hand, if they accept the offer, they may be thought to be working against their own company.

Some comfort may be found, then, in the Delaware court decision.

Earlier court rulings emphasized that while the responsibilities of directors are to protect the company and the shareholders, the responsibility to the shareholders does not include concern for mere opportunism.

The very thorny question of the rights of the shareholders became a matter of focus when McGraw-Hill successfully rebuffed a takeover attempt by American Express. Some McGraw-Hill shareholders felt that the company had unfairly deprived them of the right to earn increased value on their stock. Their view did not prevail, but only because, in that particular case, the basis for takeover was indeed not in the shareholders' interest.

There is, then, some comfort in making sound defensive decisions. There is even some comfort in residing in legal and accounting devices. They do not, however, entirely preclude takeover attempts.

Takeover Defenses

If by the time a company knows of a takeover attempt it's so often too late, what does that leave in the way of defensive measures? If science can breed disease-resistant plants, can good management breed takeover-resistant companies?

There are, indeed, anticipatory steps that can be taken. They are all in the realm of sound management, and they all allow a company to come to court with clean hands in a lawsuit by another company in a hostile takeover. Among the steps that can be taken are:

- Maintain the best possible liaison with shareholders. It's still the best defense. The battle can be won or lost in the first 48 hours of a takeover attempt, solely on the ability to reach shareholders before they have a chance to take action simply on the basis of a small premium on their stock. And shareholders whose loyalty has been nurtured are more receptive than those who rarely hear from management.

- Know your shareholders, and what they are thinking. Frequent surveys, whether done by staff or outside consultants, are invaluable.

- Review bylaws defensively. Many companies change their bylaws to divide boards of directors into three groups, each of whose term of office expires in different years. Bylaws can also be changed to prevent removal of directors except for cause and, as an even stronger measure in some states that legally allow it, to require 80 percent shareholder approval of any merger. Many companies now write strong employment contracts for management that can discourage a raider.

- Strengthen the executive committee. Many companies, recognizing the necessity for fast action in preventing a takeover, have done so to build a stronger and faster-acting fighting body, and a few have even restructured their boards to include only members who live close enough to the company to get to a meeting on a moment's notice.

- Watch the arbitrageurs. In a tender offer, the enemy in the first instance is not the tendering company, but the arbitrageur. In a tender offer, a fast-acting arbitrageur can buy a tremendous amount of stock at trading price before the market is fully affected by the offer, and then resell it to the tendering company at the higher price of the offer. Since the arbitrageur deals in very large quantities of stock, he is willing to work for a very small spread in the stock price. This is one of the major reasons why it is essential to reach stockholders in the first 24 to 48 hours following the announcement of the tender offer— to prevent selling to arbitrageurs.

- Halt trading. A listed company, particularly one with good relations with its listing officer, can sometimes arrange to have trading halted in its stock for a day or two in order to allow time to prepare a defensive statement. For an unlisted company, the SEC can sometimes be prevailed upon to do it. This serves not only to allow time to develop the defensive position, but to put the defensive plan into action as well. It also puts a severe crimp in the activities of the arbitrageurs.

- Anticipate defenses. Management should also anticipate all the legal defenses that might be available, such as an antitrust suit.

Still, the best defense of all is for a company to recognize both its attractiveness to others and its vulnerability before that attractive and vulnerable position is forced to become a defensive one. And the defense must not be structured in ways that may be construed in a lawsuit as having anticipated a takeover in ways that might diminish the benefit to the shareholder.

There is one other element to be considered that, while it is endemic to major corporations of the size of a Conoco or a DuPont, offers a clear moral for any company involved on either side of an unfriendly proxy fight. That element is the measure of who really owns the stock.

A study issued in mid-1981 by Corporate Data Exchange, Inc., at the peak of the Conoco fight showed that only 34 investors, predominately institutions, owned 22.89 percent of Conoco and 18.82 percent and of DuPont, *simultaneously*. In addition to these holdings, 35 percent of DuPont stock is owned by DuPont family members. "In effect," the report said, "the same shareholders will be deciding the fate of this merger on both sides of the transaction."

The moral, again, is to know your stockholders, no matter how large the involved companies are. This is as true in a very small company takeover attempt as it is in dealing with Fortune 500 companies.

The White Knight

More and more, in the real world of takeovers and tender offers, the white knight is sought for protection against raiders. And who awoke the white knight, and put him back into action? The courts.

Simply put, if somebody offers to buy 50 percent of your stock at a premium over market, the fact that you just don't feel like selling is not sufficient. If the raider's offer is good for the shareholders, particularly in terms of dollars, you've either got to have a good reason for fighting back, or be prepared for a suit from shareholders. When, a few years ago, American Express tendered for the stock of McGraw-Hill and McGraw-Hill fought back, it had to make a very strong case that antitrust and freedom of the press were at issue in order to fend off shareholders' suits.

And so one defense is to rub the bottle and summon up the white knight—a friendly company that is willing to top the offer by the raider.

Law does change corporate sociology, and as a result of recent court cases, both attitudes toward takeovers and defense techniques have changed. Richard E. Cheney tells this story:

> Several months ago, I was sitting in a law firm's offices with the president of one of our client companies. He had been approached by the chief executive of a foreign company who told him that he was going to take him over one way or another—peacefully or otherwise.
>
> Was our client bristling with indignation? Not on your life. He spent a whole morning rehearsing how he was going to say "no" at various price levels.
>
> First he was going to say, "What price do you have in mind? Because if the price isn't high enough—say only $30 a share—it isn't even going to be worth our while to get together with you to learn what the antitrust implications of a merger are. We'll explore them in court."
>
> If the price was a bit higher—$34 a share—he was going to suggest that they get together to explore the antitrust implications.

If the price was still higher—$38 a share—he was going to offer to mail the offer to the shareholders, but tell them he and management didn't plan to tender (and they had 24 percent of the stock). He was also going to say that he would be receptive to other offers.

And if the price was higher still—$40 or more—he was going to have a joint press party with champagne all around.

When Revlon attempted to raid Gillette, investor Warren E. Buffett functioned as the White Knight. Or, since he didn't buy the company outright or merge his company (Berkshire Hathaway, Inc.) into it, a White Squire. As a friend of Gillette management, and with an eye toward making a good investment, Buffet and Gillette management structured a deal in which Buffett bought convertible shares that gave him a substantial 12 percent interest in Gillette at a favorable price. That created a financial structure for Gillette that forestalled Revlon, and took them out of the picture.

And so as the game gets more sophisticated, the rules get more refined. The SEC gets into the act, and judges make rulings. For example, Cheney describes "the bear hug," in which the raider suggests that the company under attack advise the shareholders that the raider is willing to pay the same or higher price that he paid for the block of stock he bought at premium in the open market.

The Bear Hug

"The bear hug," says Cheney, "can be a powerful tool with today's directors. Class actions have made them skittish. They don't like to be placed in a position where a stockholder can sue them for depriving him or her of a good deal. This helps the raider. It warms up the market before he has to make a formal filing of a so-called 13D with the SEC."

In the forests of takeovers, the woods are full of strange beasts, hiding behind each tree. And since the object of everybody's affections is the shareholder, he or she is best won by being wooed in the sunshine, well before the raider comes.

The ESOP Defense

As used successfully by Polaroid to fend off a raid by the Disney family's investment vehicle, Shamrock Holdings Inc., the ESOP has become a major defensive tool.

An ESOP is an Employee Stock Ownership Plan, in which large blocks of stock are sold to employees. Where state law requires a large vote by shareholders to approve a merger—85 percent in Delaware, for example—an ESOP virtually precludes a hostile takeover. When the courts upheld Polaroid's ESOP as a legitimate ESOP, and therefore a legitimate defense against Shamrock's raid, the ESOP became very popular. The list of companies, formerly vulnerable to takeover, that installed them is extensive.

Shareholders and the Proxy Fight

Increasingly, shareholders are asserting themselves in interesting ways, and are being supported in their efforts by the SEC. New SEC initiatives (see Chapter 6) pave the way for greater shareholder participation in corporate affairs, and the shareholders are taking advantage of it. Institutional holders of stock, for example, are increasingly pressured to vote their stock, which is new for them. Activist institutions are lobbying, and some of them successfully.

The California Public Employees Retirement System (CalPERS), for example, has anti-poison-pill measures on corporate proxies for a number of companies each year, and is frequently successful. For example, it won about 40 percent of the votes cast for just such a resolution at Great Northern Nekoosa Corporation.

The SEC has allowed institutions to focus their tactics by a ruling that no longer prohibits shareholders from directly soliciting votes from more than 25 percent of other shareholders. This puts outside shareholders on a par with management in communicating to all shareholders. Clearly, this new trend will affect the future of corporate governance.

Holders in Street Name

Inherent in this whole situation is an area of stock market operation, the details of which seem to be a mystery to an extraordinary number of corporate executives. This is the holder in Street name, or trusteeship.

Many shareholders, for a wide variety of reasons such as the case of stock transfer, choose to have their stock held by their brokers. Other shareholders maintain their stock in trust portfolios, such as those administered by banks, or under discretionary management, where the manager has the legal power of attorney to buy and sell shares in its own name without consulting with the actual owner of the stock. The number of shares of stock held this way is vast. In some companies, as much as 50 percent of the stock may be in Street name. It constitutes a large body of shareholders that can be reached, often most unsatisfactorily, only through a third party. It is very difficult to build shareholder loyalty when you don't know who your shareholders are.

Holder of Record

When a broker holds shares of stock for an investor in Street name, it is the broker who is the holder of record for those shares, even though the shares are legally owned by the investor. The investor is the beneficial holder.

The beneficial holder may vote his shares only through the holder of record. Thus when a broker's name appears on the transfer sheets as the holder of a number of shares of stock, there is no way of knowing how many shareholders actually own the shares, or even how many of those shares are owned by the brokerage house itself in its own account.

Non-Objecting Beneficial Shareholders

The beneficial shareholder who does not object to his name being known is a non-objecting beneficial holder (NOBO). In the past, there was no obligation for the broker or banker to make lists of NOBOs available, and in fact, secrecy was the practice. Access to NOBO lists was by stealth. Since the institution is required to forward corporate literature to its holders in Street name, investor relations practitioners made a practice of including return postcards in the literature.

Now institutions are required to supply lists of NOBOs to corporations requesting them. Stock brokerage firms comply to direct requests. Banks, however, tend to require the written permission of the shareholder to supply the name to the company.

In any investor relations program, and certainly in a proxy fight, getting the lists of NOBOs is extremely important.

The Proxy Statement

When a proxy statement is sent to shareholder, the proxy department of a brokerage firm will request a quantity of proxy statements and proxy material to be sent to the beneficial shareholders. Since the request for this material is frequently made several weeks in advance of the time of mailing, the number is approximate because shareholdings can change overnight. The brokerage house then forwards this material to the beneficial holders, usually at the company's expense. Since brokerage houses cannot always be relied upon to make this request sufficiently in advance, it is a good idea to anticipate the request by sending a questionnaire to each broker in the transfer sheets. It can be a two-part business reply postcard, requesting information on the size of their holdings and the exact amount of proxy material they will need. This goes a long way to assure the distribution of this material to shareholders in Street name.

When the proxy material is received by the brokerage firm, its proxy department then sends it on to the beneficial shareholder. At least 30 to 45 days should be allowed for this procedure prior to the meeting at which the proxies are to be used.

The beneficial holder then designates the way his proxies are to be voted and returns the information not to the corporation, but to the broker. *Only the broker, as shareholder of record, may vote.* However, he or she votes on the instructions of the beneficial shareholder, combining his votes in one total number for, and another against. Traditionally, brokers assume that any proxy unreturned by the beneficial holder is a vote in favor of management's proposals, and usually votes accordingly. Moreover, a traditional ten-day "rule" applies. The broker has the option to vote all proxies for which instructions had not been received from the beneficial shareholder, ten days prior to the meeting. This is a general practice rather than a hard and fast rule, and normally does not apply in cases of proxy fights, where votes may be held until the last minute.

Cede & Co.

Cede & Co. is a name that appears frequently in the transfer sheets of listed companies and the more heavily traded over-the-counter companies. It is an unusual operation.

Cede & Co. is the name—the nominee—for Depository Trust Company. This is an operation established by the securities industry to facilitate interbroker transactions. When stock is bought or sold, it is deposited with Cede & Co., which then appears on the transfer sheets as the shareholder of record until the stock is transferred by Cede to the new shareholder or broker.

To reach the beneficial shareholder listed through Cede, the corporation must go to the broker who is the shareholder of record, then through the correspondent if there is one, and then through Cede.

Cede makes it simpler to some degree. If a corporation's shares are held by Cede, it should be receiving a monthly printout from them showing the names and positions of the brokers or banks that have deposited their shares with Cede. If the corporation does not receive these printouts, they can be arranged for directly with Cede in New York. Their address is 55 Water Street, New York, New York 10041. Since Cede is a transitory operation by its nature, any proxy material to be sent out should be established from a printout from Cede, dated as closely as possible to the mailing date of the material. Cede will supply a fresh printout for the exact record date required, as well as its monthly reports. To determine the exact number of shares held in Street name by any one broker, the number of shares listed by the broker as holder of record must be combined with the number of shares Cede records for that broker on its transfer sheets.

Remember also that when shares are held by Cede, even in behalf of a broker, it is Cede and not the broker who is the holder of record for those shares. For those shares held by Cede, the broker will turn over proxy instructions to Cede for forwarding to the corporation, although the broker may occasionally ask that Cede supply the signed proxy to the broker to be returned with the proxies he or she already holds.

Nominees

Nominees are firms that represent large shareholdings either held in trust, as by banks, or by other institutions. Nominees do not register under their own names; they take an artificially contrived name to designate their identity as shareholders of record. In passing along proxy material, they must be dealt with in exactly the same way as brokers, and they vote the shares they represent in the same way as well. The difference is that since they are predominately representatives with authority to act for the alternate beneficiary, they do not have to get the approval of the individual beneficial shareholders they represent in order to vote a proxy. They do not accumulate proxies, nor do they have a ten-day rule. The nominee merely passes the proxy material on to the beneficial holder, who can if he wishes, return the proxy directly. This is a matter of agreement between the nominee and the beneficial holder.

Since nominees use names that do not indicate their principal, it is sometimes difficult to distinguish brokers from nominees on the transfer sheets. Brokers can be identified in Standard and Poor's directory, *Security Dealers of North America.* Nominees can be identified from a directory called *The Nominee List,* published by the American Society of Corporate Secretaries, Inc., 1 Rockefeller Plaza, New York, New York 10020. It should be remembered, though, that nominees are also absolutely recalcitrant about identifying the individual shareholders they represent.

From the Street name and nominee structure it should become clear that it is virtually impossible to identify any potential raider who is quietly buying up a stock. Larger companies engaging in a takeover attempt frequently use several brokers or nominees to purchase holdings in smaller quantities. This is why it is extremely important to scrutinize the transfer sheets regularly to determine unusual buying trends. Watch for the sudden and frequent appearance of new brokers as holders of record or for new nominee names. While the attempt to fathom the meaning of unusual buying patterns or unusual stock activity can be tremendously frustrating, it is still worth the effort. It at least supplies a clue that something unusual is happening. And the first clue is sometimes unusual stock activity—a sharp rise or drop in volume or stock price may be a warning sign of something—even if it's only a rumor regarding the company. The corporate management that pays attention to these signs may not sleep better at night, but it retains control of its company.

Since most Street name holders do so for reasons not usually connected with aggressive takeovers or for other obtuse reasons, there is nothing untoward—it is even wise—in making an attempt to make contact with them directly. This is done by including a note in the annual report or in any other shareholder material that will reach them through their nominees, suggesting that the company will be delighted to supply additional copies of shareholder material, or to answer questions directly from any beneficial shareholder. This frequently works well, and in no way subverts the efforts or activities of either brokers or nominees.

The Proxy Solicitation Firm

Obviously, proxy solicitation, particularly under the pressure of a takeover fight, is a highly complex activity. Very few companies do it on their own, preferring instead to use the services of skilled and experienced specialists whose organizations are structured to do the job efficiently.

Typical of the activities performed by such organizations are:

- Shareholder list analysis
- Proxy solicitation in connection with
  - Annual or Special Meetings
  - Contested elections of directors
  - Management proposals
  - Adverse proposals
- Distribution of annual reports and proxy material
- Distribution of quarterly reports
- Assistance in tender offers
- Assistance in exchange offers

Organizations such as Hill & Knowlton—others are Georgeson & Col, and D. F. King—maintain an ongoing structure that includes constant liaison with shareholders, brokerage firm proxy departments, depository companies and banks. This allows them to move swiftly and efficiently in behalf of any client, particularly under the time pressures of a tender offer.

Whether it is to win a proxy fight or to garner votes from management on a controversial issue or merely to maintain good shareholder relations, communications with the large body of shareholders that holds stock in Street name is every bit as important to the company as it is with the shareholder of record who can be reached directly. Every feasible effort should be made by the company to reach every one of its shareholders as part of its investor relations program.

And if there is one large lesson to learn, it is that the tender offer, both friendly and unfriendly, is very much a part of corporate life. There are, of course, arguments on both sides of the question of whether the takeover is good or bad. And arguments within arguments. Are unfriendly take-overs good for the economy or bad for it? Does the economy benefit, or just the shareholders? And indeed, do the shareholders always benefit? Does the board of directors have a right to turn down an offer that might put money in the pockets of the shareholders? What are the responsibilities of the board to defend against a hostile takeover attempt? Thorny questions, all, even those tested in courts and for which some legal answers have been given. For the clever predator, there is always a loophole that can skirt a legal precedent.

Another question is whether anybody really wins in a hostile takeover, and especially whether the subject of the takeover ever wins even when he successfully fends off the attacker. The cost of defense is horrendous, including legal fees, investment bankers, and most significantly, the distraction from running the business. And the sigh of relief when the white knight wins out often masks the fact that the company didn't want to be acquired by anybody in the first place.

In fact, there would seem to be only one defense that works well in behalf of the company, and that is to take a large dose of preventative medicine by building a sound company. The place to cut 'em off is at the pass before they ride into town with guns blazing. The price of not taking defensive measures can be overwhelming.

12

Competing for Capital

Obviously, competing for capital in the world's capital markets is not solely a function of investor relations. Many more factors enter into it, such as the shifting sources of capital, the overall economy, the ability of a company to perform effectively, and so forth.

And yet, no company can be effective in raising capital without some kind of outreach to the financial community and its investors; without projecting, on one level or another, the ability to put that capital to good use. Whether this outreach is little more than a personal relationship between company executives and the sources of capital, or a full-fledged program including activities such as those described in these pages, an investor relations program it is.

It would be foolhardy to try to describe the nature of investor relations practices in the coming years. There are too many variables beyond the control of any individual or group, and so any significant changes in practices in the future will be either reactions to changing conditions in the marketplace, or to the yet-to-be-disclosed bright idea that somebody has in response to a perceived opportunity. It is devoutly to be desired, for the sake of progress, that such originality is forthcoming.

The Changing Capital Markets

Still, certain aspects of the economy, the markets, and the nature of business in the capital markets become clear for at least the immediate future.

It would be impossible, for example, not to realize that the effects of the changes in the USSR and the Eastern European Bloc will be profound. The failure of communism aside, the attempts to create market economies in

286

countries with no recent tradition of capitalism constitute an awesome effort. As of mid-1990, the rush by American business opportunists to find ways to participate has been overwhelming.

But how that will shake out, and affect the capital markets worldwide and in the United States, is anybody's guess. How it will affect Europe 1992, the unification of European markets that had been planned before the events of 1989 and the democratization of Eastern Europe, is also not yet clear.

Nor is it clear how the downturn of the economy, at mid-1990, will affect the capital markets in the long term. As of this writing, the Western world stands poised confrontationally with Iraq in what seems to be an insurmountable problem. How the insurmountable problem will be surmounted is not yet clear, beyond realizing that some things will never be the same again thereafter; some things will. Cassandra may know the answer. Wisdom doesn't help in long-term forecasting.

The problem is that all this comes about just as the internationalization of the capital markets has been accomplished. Capital, say the economists, knows no borders. But this is one of those economists' sayings that sounds good, but means nothing out of context. It really means that capital from the free world goes to any country in which opportunity exists. When the price of the dollar is right, and interest rates are right, money is invested here. This is why the 1980s saw so much foreign investment in the United States. The battle cry was that the Japanese and the English were buying up America.

Well . . . some of it, anyway. And a good thing, too, because who cares where investment capital comes from when you need it. And were the Japanese and the British really buying America? Actually, despite the apparent size of their investment, there's still a lot they didn't buy. But what they did buy fed a lot of capital into the American system.

Foreign investment posed some problems, too. Here we have the picture of Mr. Campeau of Canada buying up all the major department stores. Here we have another picture of Mr. Campeau overleveraged. Here we have yet another picture of Mr. Campeau on the verge of bankruptcy, despite the fact that some of the individual stores were doing well.

But on the same page in the newspaper of the pictures of Canadian entrepreneurs going into bankruptcy, we see pictures of the highly visible Mr. Trump, the highest flying billionaire ever, missing multimillion-dollar bank payments, and being put on a personal allowance of a mere $450,000 a month. In financial downfall, failure, like capital, knows no borders.

At the same time, we have the worst federal budget deficit in the history of the nation. It doesn't matter that this deficit is the gift of a president who got elected on a platform that included a promise to balance the budget. The fact of the matter is that the deficit of $2.3 trillion means annual interest payments of more than $15 billion. It means that the government is competing in the debt market with American corporations, which profoundly affects the capital markets.

The same administration that gave us the budget deficit also gave us the regulatory structure that led to the savings and loan crisis, in which the cost to the economy of the massive failures of savings and loan associations, via payouts to protect the investors and depositors, is so large that its magnitude hasn't yet been amply measured. The current estimation is that it's going to cost this country some $2,000 for every man, woman, and child within our borders. That money may eventually find its way into the economy, and therefore into the capital markets, but the route is remarkably circuitous. The company with vast market potential, and capability to serve that market but for capital, is going to have a hard time getting the recycled cash from the S&L rescue plan.

This past decade also saw the demise of a great deal of the onerous regulation that had, business complained, plagued business for so long. Some of the deregulation worked, as in aspects of the airlines, in which competition resulted in lowered prices on some air routes.

It also worked to allow savings banks to lend in areas of real estate that had heretofore been prohibited to them. And a lot of real estate got capitalized, but so did a lot of real estate developers to whom prudence extended only so far as the next loan check. As a result, we entered 1990 with an extraordinary number of banks with bank examiners sitting on their doorsteps, telling them that they could no longer run their own banks, because they had made too many imprudent and uncollectable real estate loans. This didn't—and won't—make it any easier for the manufacturer who needs a line of credit to keep his production lines going.

Calling the 1980s the decade of greed, as it became fashionable to do as we entered a new decade, was easy to do for several reasons, all of which affected the capital markets.

First, the tax structure favored the rich. Saying this is no longer a partisan political observation—the hottest book of 1990 on the subject said so, and it was written by a political conservative. In other words, if you made a lot of money, you got to keep more of it than if you made a little money.

The carnival on Wall Street, the fertile fields of the capital markets, produced almost as much grist for exposé writers as it did capital for industry. A whole new class of prisoner was developed at federal prisons, made up of inside traders, arbitrageurs who functioned illegally, brokers who colluded, and others of that ilk. If Chapter 5 talks conservatively of business news making the front pages of newspapers, it ignores, then, the events of the last part of the 1980s, in which so many millionaires and billionaires celebrated in the first half of the decade were indicted for fraud in the second half of the decade. If all you knew about the capital markets was what you read on the front page, there wasn't much to engender faith in the American economic way.

To further feed the concept of greed, magnitude held sway on page one of the newspapers. The word *billion,* once breathed with awe, is now spoken as freely, and as casually, as the standard dishes on a breakfast menu. More millionaires and billionaires were made in the 1980s than in any prior decade in history. And they were not all made the old fashioned way—by producing something. They became rich through capital market manipulation, buying and selling companies, using money to make money—all the tools of capitalism. The junk bond, remember, was king.

Also emerging in full swing was speculation—there's no other word for it—in intangible investments that have nothing to do with capitalizing industry except in the most ancillary way. These are the futures indexes—foreign exchange, commodity, stock exchanges, and so forth. They are merely wagers on action, and not investment.

A peculiar locution came into existence that says more about the period than it's supposed to. What happened is that the word *player* became popular. The participants in a deal were called *players.* The participants in a financing or a merger were called *players.* It seems a small point, but Freud would note that using this simple little word in this context says a great deal about how the participants view their actions—not as a responsible capitalization of business, but as a game in which they were *players.*

The problem with this sort of thing is not so much one of morality—is the junk bond immoral?—it's one of the effect on the capital markets. It complicates market activity, at the very least. It distorts the market, making it difficult to raise capital in an orderly way. Combined with the federal deficit, it fouls up the credit markets, raises interest rates, and makes the equities investor wary.

The Institutional Market

Perhaps the most important configuration to emerge from the activities of the 1980s has been the growth of the institutional market.

Until just a few decades ago, the retail stock buyer was at the root of the market system. It was not too long ago that the institutional pool of investment capital was limited to insurance companies, a few pension funds, a handful of mutual funds. But the individual investor was king.

All this has changed, of course, but the magnitude of the change is awesome. Thanks to some market crashes, both large and small, and some wide swings in the domestic economy, the individual investor has pulled in his and her oars, and like the Greyhound Bus ad, has left the driving to the mutual funds. While there are still individual investors to be wooed and won, the market is now institutional with a vengeance.

Thanks to ERISA—the Employees Retirement Income Security Act—the pension fund itself has become institutionalized in American industry. And while there was some early anxiety about the ability of corporate pension funds to grow sufficiently to meet obligations as employees retired, a strong economy resolved that question. Between 1985 and 1989, for example, pension fund assets increased some 55 percent, from $1.59 trillion to $2.47 trillion—all of which must be invested in one prudent way or another. This is a powerful force in the marketplace.

And to this, add the growth of mutual funds, of which there are more than $1 trillion in invested assets. The mutual fund industry burgeoned in the 1980s. On the one hand, it's a relatively safe and convenient way for the individual investor to participate in the market. On the other hand, the funds themselves, realizing the market potential, became sophisticated marketers. Telephone switching, which allows an investor to switch from one fund to another with a simple phone call, allowed the small investor to play tape watcher, without the burden of exploring the potential of the individual stock. Cable television and Financial News Network bring the tape into almost every home, and turn every homebody with a few bucks into a tape watcher. The funds themselves built *families* of funds—Fidelity's Magellan Fund, Fidelity's Growth Fund, and so forth. There were funds for every season and for every purpose under Mamon. There were growth funds and hedge funds and sector funds. Successful fund managers became as popular as baseball players, and when Magellan Fund's Peter Lynch retired, it had the same feeling, to the public, as when Joe DiMaggio hung up his uniform.

There also came into maturity, in the 1980s, the 401(k) pension fund. It differed from others in that participants are given investment options for their own retirement funds. A company might offer its employees, for example, a choice of investment opportunities that included a growth fund, a high-risk fund, and an index fund (one based upon the stocks in a standard index, such as the Standard & Poor's 500). This not only drove the mutual fund industry into a feeding frenzy, it made active investors of individuals whose prior financial dealings were rarely no more sophisticated than a mortgage.

Pension Funds and Economic Power

At the start of the decade, yet another new element entered the capital markets. The pension funds suddenly recognized the economic sway they held in corporate America. At the beginning of 1990, for example, the 20 largest corporate pension funds accounted for more than 25 percent of pension assets, which meant a vast concentration of power. Heretofore, the funds' large holdings in any corporation were simply an investment factor. Now, it dawns on many fund managers, they begin to recognize their voting power.

And they're using it. Texaco, for example, was forced to name a director proposed by the California Public Employees Retirement System, which held a large block of Texaco stock. Institutional holders voted their stock to defeat anti-takeover proxy proposals made by Honeywell, Inc. Who knows where the ramifications of this power may lead, and what effect it will have on the capital markets.

Clearly, then, the capital markets of the 1990s are emerging in very different configurations from the capital markets of the past. This means, of course, that the rules and structures for competing for capital must also change. The change will come, of course, not by fiat but by evolution, simply because the changes in the capital markets are dynamic and evolving.

The Changing Nature of Investor Relations

As we enter the last decade of the century, we see clear evidence of these changes. And not only in shifting sources of capital, and in new instruments of finance (beyond junk bonds). We see it most clearly in the changing nature of the practice of investor relations.

The history of investor relations as a technique for competing for capital is short, but dynamic. It started as a minor public relations function, in which the same public relations person who sent out your product press release sent out your dividend or earnings release. Then, as companies became aware of the competitive nature of the capital markets, investor relations campaigns began to take on more substance, and investor relations began to build a body of techniques all its own.

It took very little time for company management to realize that the more successful investor relations programs were those that had a strong base of financial sophistication, as well as communication skills. The emphasis of investor relations practice shifted, then, from public relations to a financial function. Investor relations practitioners began to be drawn from financial, rather than public relations, ranks.

In the 1980s, as the world economy grew and the competition for capital heated up, the element of marketing entered the picture. Marketing techniques began to be applied to financial and communications techniques, to shape investor relations as a new and singular profession.

As investor relations once split off from public relations, we now find the several specialties in investor relations splitting off, with some firms specializing in only one aspect of the investor relations practice.

While most companies are more than adequately served by a single investor relations function or firm, the magnitude of the capital markets, and the companies competing in those markets, warrants specialization.

For example, the distinctive nature of proxy solicitation, and the sheer weight of labor involved in it, has long warranted the proxy solicitation firm as a single entity. But the increasing complexity of the marketplace has made those firms even more viable. Gearing up for a proxy solicitation, particularly on a contested issue, requires many more hands, machinery, computers, and experts than are likely to be found in the average investor relations company or department. And so the proxy firm thrives.

Annual reports are another case in point. Normally the province of the investor relations firm or department, firms that specialize in annual reports have evolved that, for the most part, do a superb job. They understand the specific requirements of an annual report, and they have the experience and capability to fulfill those requirements. There is some weakness when the specialist is a designer rather than an investor relations expert, and the report is driven not by the needs of the capital markets but by design considerations. But the annual report is too important a document to be done casually, and so the specialist thrives.

Mailing list management is another growing specialty. Mailing list management is an arcane craft, frequently equated to witchcraft. Those with a turn of mind to do it have built it into an art form, as well as a specialty. Inherent in this is not only the output—using the mailing list house to move material to investors and shareholders—but the research aspect as well. All those names, intelligently and professionally analyzed, tell a story that makes marketing both possible and sophisticated.

There are other aspects of specialization that are springing up. Some firms are specializing in just the public relations and communications aspects of investor relations, or dealing with just press relations. Others are specializing by industry, such as computers or hi-tech, on the basis of understanding and being able to communicate the unique aspects of a particular industry to those who specialize in analyzing or investing in that industry.

The Street Work Specialist

Perhaps the most interesting kind of specialized firm that's evolving is the specialist in Street work—dealing directly with brokers, analysts, and others. While this area is not the first or most common to emerge in investor relations, it's the most interesting, because it offers a new approach to investor relations practice.

As you saw in Chapters 2 and 3, one form of dealing with the financial community is to work directly with brokers and other investment professionals to place large blocks of stock with them to resell to their customers. Some of these customers may be individuals, and others may be small institutions. It requires a keen understanding of how Wall Street works and of the company behind the stock, as well as a large measure of selling skill. This is particularly useful in representing a smaller company, usually in the over-the-counter market, with a smaller float and a stock price of under $10 a share. Every good investor relations practitioner has a network of such contacts, or knows how to approach brokers and investment professionals to accomplish this.

Now, investor relations firms specializing in broker networks that place stock are springing up. They don't do press relations, or analyst meetings, or corporate communications, or shareholder relations—just Street work.

These firms can, in proper context, be useful. But there's also a double danger, first in assuming that a segment of an investor relations program is a whole program that will achieve sustaining goals, and second in the opportunity for misrepresentation and other negative activities that can, in the long run, hurt the company.

The Future of Investor Relations

In looking at these specialized firms, and their role in the future of investment relations, a number of factors emerge.

First, in the growth and sophistication of a practice such as investor relations, and in competing in the capital markets, it's inevitable that growing complexity and magnitude should breed firms specializing in one aspect or another of the practice. An industry shapes itself to meet the needs of the market it serves, and if that market changes, then so will the industry serving it change. And as we've seen historically, no one can predict the ways in which the capital markets will change, even in so short a term as the next decade.

But second, there should be cautious consideration of the difference between focus and specialization. It's one thing to focus an investor relations program on one aspect or another of the program—meetings, mailings, shareholder relations, etc. As the demands of the program change, so then should the program. Specialization, on the other hand, too often freezes the program in that specialty. There are times when a broker network is a poor answer to the needs of a company competing in the capital markets; there are times when it's the place to focus. To substitute specialization for focus can sometimes make for a poor program.

There will undoubtedly be many other ways in which investor relations practice will change, in both the near and far term, but to predict beyond evidence is foolhardy. The evidence of change is always with us, as is sometimes the nature of change. But the ultimate of the future eludes us, as it should. Besides, if somebody told you tomorrow's stock market closing prices, would you believe it?

It is certain that there are dynamic, swirling changes in the capital markets, both domestically and internationally. But the very nature of competing successfully is to function from the strength of the change, and not the static; to lead the future wherever possible, and to bend with change as it occurs if it's not. To do anything, in this world, because that's the way it was done yesterday is to deprive oneself of opportunity.

Competing in the new capital markets of the 1990s is not only going to be different, and in ways we can't yet know, but it's clearly going to be more arduous and more demanding.

The chances are that it's also going to be more profitable—and more fun.

Appendix 1

Costs and Budgets

In a well-run investor relations program, there is no question that the greater and more extensive the effort, the greater the effectiveness. Nevertheless, the cost of an investor relations program is not a measure of its potential success. Programs that cost a great deal may be no more effective than programs that are moderately priced. The measure is the program—not the cost. Virtually every cost factor may be foreseen. And at least, a program should be budgetable.

Essentially, the fee and expense elements of an investor relations program are the following:

- Consulting fees
- Shareholder and Street research
- Design and printing
- Mailing
- Investor meetings
- Travel costs to meetings, major press interviews, and so forth
- Out-of-pocket and miscellaneous expenses, including phones, fax, Dow Jones and Reuters, entertainment, and so on
- Contingencies

Fees

For companies using outside consultants, the fee structure is determined at the outset.

Fee structures vary from one consulting firm to another, although basically there are only two types used by most consultants—straight fee and hourly rate. Fees for an effective full program are usually in the range of $36,000 to $60,000 a year for smaller consultants and $50,000 to $150,000 for larger consultants. This is predicated on the assumption, of course, that the larger firm offers more extensive programs and services—which is indeed an assumption. Talent, which is what you're really buying, doesn't necessarily reside solely in the larger, higher-priced firm, although many large firms have some extraordinarily good people. But then, so do many of the smaller firms. Although some programs can exceed these amounts, it's unlikely that an effective and well-rounded program can be performed professionally for less than $30,000. However, there are good consultants who might give you appropriate segments of a total program, which may well serve your needs, for $18,000 to $24,000 annually.

The straight fee basis is usually a simple fixed amount, paid monthly. This has the advantage of simpler budgeting.

The hourly rate functions much the same as with accountants and attorneys. Usually a basic minimum fee is agreed upon, with hours charged against that fee, also as agreed upon. The maximum allows for overall budgeting. The hourly basis functions best if there is a clear understanding beforehand of the hourly rate of each person who is to work on the account. Each month, the client is billed on a printout, which indicates each person who worked on the account, his or her hourly rate, and the time he or she put in. Each person's time is broken down in each of one to two dozen categories to the quarter hour. This allows the client the added advantage of seeing how the time was spent in each of the categories. Many firms also use the hourly rate to advantage by budgeting allotted time for specific tasks to each executive and each of several offices. The interoffice allocation makes it possible for the firm to function more effectively on a national basis by virtue of clear-cut, time-budgeted assignments from office to office. It also helps clients to know what they're getting for their money.

Most firms bill a month in advance. Those firms that use the hourly rate usually bill about half the agreed-upon minimum in advance. Because it generally takes at least a year to measure the effects of a program, most contracts are for that period, although some of the better firms can be flexible.

Considering the complexities of evaluating the effectiveness of a program, any fee structure, whether it be a monthly flat fee or the hourly rate, depends for its success on some kind of detailed annual plan and reporting system. Since much of the investor relations effort is done in the consultant's rather than the company's offices, only a sound plan and reporting system allows the client to know that the fee is actually going to effective effort.

Research

While research on both shareholder lists and professional investors is an inherent part of any sound program, and is usually included in the fee, there are times when more extensive research is warranted. Outside research firms will analyze lists, do research on shareholder attitudes, and so forth. These firms charge separate fees, which must be negotiated, and which are usually very large.

Design and Printing Costs

Printing, in investor relations, is primarily for annual and interim reports, reprints of speeches, and postmeeting reports. Other printing may be brochures, corporate profiles, and reprints.

The design of an annual report, the most expensive printing item in an investor relations budget, ranges from $100 a page to a total of $25,000 or more for the extensive report of a major company. Layout, typography, galley proofs, and camera-ready mechanicals may add another $5,000 to $25,000. Photography and other expenses attendant to the report, such as travel and research, are extra. Photographers generally charge $300 to $2500 a day for their services, plus expenses. The cost of printing the report depends, of course, on its size, the number of copies, the quality of paper, and so on. It's a good idea to get several bids from printers, selecting only those whose quality of work has been judged on the basis of samples. Printing costs vary from one locale to another, and price is not necessarily a key to quality. Printing costs in New York, for example, are likely to be higher than in Cincinnati, despite the fact that Cincinnati is one of several major cities with excellent printers. It can cost $2 to $4 per copy for printing a small-quantity report and $1 to $3 per copy on reports in larger quantities.

An element of cost enters into selecting the designer for a company located in a different city from that of its consultant. If there is sound reason for a New York consultant to use a New York designer, even if the report is to be printed elsewhere, then expenses for the consultant to deal with the designer are lower. Sometimes, however, a company will find it more convenient to use a local designer, in which case the consultant will have to visit with him once or twice to supervise the production of the report. Experience in multicity operations can do wonders to rationalize costs.

Design costs for interim reports and other material are usually considerably lower, not only because of the size, but because of the simplicity of the format. Interim reports normally follow the same format from one to the other, at least during the course of any one year. Speeches and similar printed matter, while usually just straight text, still require a measure of design and production expense, since they must be attractive in their appearance no matter how simple the makeup. Background reports generally follow a predetermined format with every little design factor involved. While they are usually offset from typed copy, there's frequently a measure of professional pasteup to be done, usually at negligible cost. Reprints are usually photo offset from pasteups of the original copy. Here, too, while the pasteup cost is negligible, it's still a factor. Offset-printing costs vary, but are easily determined. Brochures that may occasionally be part of an investor relations program are designed and produced in essentially the same way, and at essentially the same cost, as annual reports.

Mailing

The elements to be calculated in mailings to shareholders and the financial community include:

- Mailing lists
- Envelopes
- Paper
- Postage
- Labor for sorting, sealing, collating, stapling, inserting, stamping, and post office delivery
- Printing
- Return postage paid postcards

Mailing lists, it has been noted, are very difficult to maintain, and therefore consume a measure of time—whether it be internal or external. In mailings to the ever-mobile financial community, what often may seem to be an undue amount of time and attention go into a constant updating, checking, and changing mailing lists, including the return postcard technique.

When an outside mailing house is used, these costs are incorporated into the basic price of mailing, since it is assumed that the mailing house keeps its lists updated for all its clients. Mailing lists today are usually maintained on computer, and each computer listing changed is an expense. It's less of an expense, however, than the very high cost of mailing material to the wrong address.

The cost of envelopes must be considered as an additional expense of any mailing. Most consulting firms use their own envelopes for releases and may charge clients for exact cost or with a normal markup. Annual reports, quarterly reports, and so on are usually mailed in 9 by 12 envelopes, most often custom printed for the purpose, especially if a form of bi-pack is required by the transfer agent. In the design of any printed material, unusual sizes mean special and expensive envelopes. It's infinitely cheaper to design for a standard size envelope.

There's really nothing to be said about postage, except that it keeps going up.

As in any corporate effort, labor is an element that must be calculated in any budget, from stuffing envelopes to maintaining mailing lists. Except if it's broken out separately for mailing list maintenance, it's usually incorporated in the total cost of mailing.

Most financial consultants, whether they use an outside mailing house or their own internal structure, are able to supply a rate schedule for reproducing and mailing material. It's best billed as a separate expense item. More and more, rising costs have forced investor relations consultants to adopt advertising and PR expense-billing practices, and they now add a fixed percentage charge to many costs. Fewer consultants now rebill such expenses at exact cost.

Analyst and Broker Meetings

Large luncheon meetings are the largest expense in dealing with analysts and professional investors in an investor relations program. It's simply the cost of lunch for any group of people. Most investor relations consultants hold meetings in good restaurants and private clubs that are normally familiar with serving group meetings, and their costs are readily predetermined. All reputable firms should merely pass on the cost of these affairs, with no markup.

Expenses beyond the cost of meals and drinks are negligible, although they may include sound system and audiovisual equipment rental. Displays specially designed for meetings are usually arranged for with display firms, and are a separate expense.

The program may include visits by analysts, press, and others to the company's office, plant, or other facilities. Normally, the expenses involved are travel costs, housing, meals, and local transportation.

Major Travel Costs to Meetings

The cost of travel by executives to meetings held in other than their own cities must be calculated. A normal investor relations practice, designed to save expenses, is to arrange meetings to coincide with executive travel for other reasons. Thus it's sound practice to keep the investor relations consultant advised of out-of-town travel by management.

Out-of-Pocket and Miscellaneous Expenses

Normally, out-of-pocket and routine expenses include:

- Clipping services
- Photography and art work
- Telephone, fax, electronic transmission
- Wire services, such as PR Newswire
- News bulletins and other lettershop charges for stationery, printing, collating, and mailing
- Transportation
- Promotional expenses for meetings with press, analysts, and so on
- Postage (including return postage)
- Messenger services
- Photocopier and supplies
- Subscriptions to trade publications
- Dow Jones and Reuters newswires
- Travel expenses, local and out of town
- Secretarial overtime on special projects
- Miscellaneous minor expenses

Clipping services charge a monthly fee plus a cost for each clipping. Clipping services are necessary to determine the extent to which any publicity issued by the company is printed. Unfortunately, no low-cost method has yet been devised to mechanize what is essentially a human job—scanning thousands of publications. As a result, the number of clippings received is usually a small representation of any material that appears.

Telephones, facsimile, and other means of communications are sometimes billed at exact cost, determined from both records and bills. The larger the firm the more readily available these records should be through effective use of easily available technology and accounting codes.

PR Newswire and local, state, and city news services usually charge an annual membership fee, and then a use fee, predicated on the distribution and the length of the material. For example, PR Newswire charges $75 for a 12-month membership, and for distribution to its entire U.S. list, $375 for up to 400 words, and $95 for each additional 100 words. It breaks down its list by states and some major cities, and charges accordingly. It now has PRN Facsimile Service, which can distribute your release by fax to a predetermined list at a very reasonable price.

Transportation expenses usually include transportation within a city, such as cabs, and so on. Travel transportation and expenses should be broken out and listed separately.

During the course of an investor relations program, it's frequently necessary to conduct business with members of the press and the financial community over lunch, dinner, or cocktails. These expenses are usually documented by receipts.

In addition to postage for regular mailings, there is postage normally used in mailing letters, fulfilling analyst's information requests, packaging and shipping quantities of background material, including Federal Express, UPS, and so forth.

Costs for messenger service are usually incurred within one city, although occasionally messengers must be used to transmit important material between cities. These expenses are supported by copies of bills from the messenger service.

Photocopying and telecopying—faxing—are tremendous conveniences that are now part of every office operation. They are usually calculated on a predetermined rate based on costs and personnel time.

In order for an investor relations firm to function, it must keep abreast of the industry of which its client is a part, as well as the trade press for that industry. Subscriptions to publications necessary for that purpose are normally billed to the client, at cost.

Larger investor relations consultants usually maintain Dow Jones and Reuters tickers to monitor news releases and other material of importance to the client. The cost of this service is usually apportioned to each of the consultant's clients.

The costs of travel—indeed all expenses in behalf of a client—are usually allocated on the same basis as determined by the Internal Revenue Service. This includes transportation, meals, hotel expenses, transportation within a city, auto mileage, tips, and miscellaneous out-of-pocket expenses, and so forth. These expenses, traditionally, are not marked up.

While normal secretarial and office services are considered part of a consultant's or company's own internal operating expenses, special projects frequently require additional expense, such as secretarial overtime or the use of temporary office help. Consulting firms normally include these costs in expense billings.

In the normal course of a program, miscellaneous minor expenses are sometimes incurred. These include additional copies of publications, tips, phone calls made away from the office, and so on.

Contingencies

Even in the best-planned program, circumstances frequently arise, often in the form of opportunities, for special projects or activities. This may include an opportunity to participate as a panelist in a seminar, the need for a special brochure or pamphlet, and so forth.

While these occasions are normally unexpected, their value can sometimes be measured in terms of cost, and may be perfectly valid as additional expenses. It's a good idea to add 10 percent to the expense budget for contingencies.

Granted the flexibility of expenses that tend to be variable, it's still possible to review a program well in advance and generally estimate what the expenses relative to that program are likely to be. This should make it possible for any company or experienced investor relations consultant to budget appropriately for the cost of the program. By frankly discussing expenses and expense billing policies with an agency during an initial interview period, budget shocks can usually be avoided. And in checking references, expenses should be one of the items to be queried.

Appendix 2

Summary of Recent SEC Rulings Pertaining to Reporting to Both the SEC and Shareholders

---

The following material is abstracted from reports issued by the international accounting firm Ernst & Young, for the benefit of its clients. It is reprinted here with its permission.

During 1989, the SEC continued to focus its rule-making activities on the recommendations of the National Commission of Fraudulent Financial Reporting, referred to as the Treadway Commission, after its chairman.

The FASB and other standard setters also have issued other pronouncements and they have been considered, where applicable, in the example financial statements contained herein.

SEC Issues MD&A Guidance

In FRR 36, the SEC issued interpretive guidance for preparing *Management's Discussion and Analysis of Financial Condition and Results of Operations (MD&A)*. FRR 36 is a significant step in the SEC's continuing project to improve the quality of MD&A. The SEC plans to continue its focus on MD&A as it reviews future filings by registrants. While FRR 36 provides guidance in a number of areas, its principal focus is on the need for improved disclosures of prospective information. The SEC distinguishes between prospective information that is required to be discussed and voluntary forward-looking disclosure. MD&A requires disclosure of the effect of *currently known* trends, events, and uncertainties that are reasonably expected to occur. In contrast, optional forward-looking disclosures involve anticipating a less predictable impact of a known event, trend, or uncertainty.

Management must discuss the company's financial condition, changes in financial condition and results of operations. The purpose of the discussion is:

> . . . to provide to investors and other users information relevant to an assessment of the financial condition and results of operations of the registrant as determined by evaluating the amounts and certainty of cash flows from operation and from outside sources.

The SEC believes MD&A disclosures should reflect the general purpose of the MD&A requirements: "To give investors an opportunity to look at the registrant through the eyes of management by providing an historical and prospective analysis of the registrant's financial condition and results of operations, with particular emphasis on the registrant's prospects for the future."

Prospective Information

The discussion should specifically highlight known material events and uncertainties that would cause the reported financial information not to be indicative of future operations or financial condition. This includes discussion of both: "*(a)* matters which would have an impact on future operations and have not had an impact in the past, and *(b)* matters which have had an impact on reported operations and are not expected to have an impact upon future operations."

FRR 36 interprets the rules by indicating that disclosure of prospective information is required unless management (1) determines the known trend, event, or uncertainty "is not reasonably likely to occur" or (2) determines, assuming that the known trend, event, or uncertainty comes to fruition, that its consequences would not be reasonably likely to have a material effect on financial condition or results of operations.

It appears as if the SEC is increasing the pressure for an event to be disclosed at an earlier stage. Whereas in the past management may have been able to appropriately conclude that disclosure of an event is not necessary because it was premature to determine whether it may occur, FRR 36 now requires disclosure unless a positive assessment can be made that the event will not occur. Adding to this difficulty is the SEC's acknowledgment that it has and will continue to use the benefit of hindsight in evaluating filings by registrants.

Generally, discussion is required of:

- Specific information about the company's liquidity, capital resources and results of operations.
- Known material events and uncertainties which may make historical financial information not indicative of future operations or financial condition.
- The cause of material changes in line items of the consolidated financial statements from prior period amounts.
- The impact of inflation and changing prices on net sales and revenues and on income from continuing operations.
- Any other information the company believes necessary to an understanding of its financial condition, changes in financial condition and results of operations.

Other areas addressed in FRR 36 relate to the following disclosure areas:

Liquidity and Capital Resources—Registrants that have disclosed plans for future expansion should discuss prospective information regarding sources of capital to fund the planned expansion. Trend analysis also should be provided for expected material changes in the mix and relative cost of capital resources.

Regulation S-K defines liquidity as the company's ability to generate adequate amounts of cash to meet both current and future needs. We interpret "needs" as encompassing the company's need to pay obligations as they mature, to maintain capacity, to provide for planned growth, and to provide a competitive return on investment. The company must examine its individual circumstances and identify those balance sheet, income, and cash flow items that are indicators of its liquidity.

The discussion of liquidity is required to include:

- Known trends or demands, commitments, events, changes in circumstances or uncertainties that will result in, or are rasonably likely to result in, material increases or decreases in liquidity.
- Actions or plans to remedy any identified liquidity deficiency.

- Internal and external sources of liquidity and any material unused sources of liquid assets.

Material Changes—Registrants should disclose the reasons for material year-to-year changes in line items of the financial statements. This should be done to the extent necessary to obtain an understanding of the registrants' business as a whole.

Interim Period Reporting—Registrants should update MD&A in interim periods to reflect effects of significant events.

Segment Analysis—Registrants should provide MD&A disclosures in a segment basis where the various segments contribute disproportional amounts to revenues, profitability, and cash needs.

Preliminary Merger Negotiations—Preliminary merger negotiations could be viewed as required MD&A disclosure because these negotiations represent a known event or uncertainty reasonably likely to have material effects in the future. However, the SEC believes that the information needs of investors must be balanced against the risk of premature disclosure that could jeopardize completion of the transaction. Accordingly, where disclosure is not required and has not otherwise been made, the MD&A need not contain a discussion of the impact of such negotiations if management concludes that any discussion would jeopardize completion of the transaction.

High-Yield Financings—The SEC believes investments in high-yielding financings or non-investment grade loans offer potentially greater returns and pose greater risks than other investments. Thus, the SEC notes registrants should consider MD&A discussion of the impact of participation in these transactions.

The SEC believes that cash outlays for income taxes that are expected to exceed income tax expense during the next three years should be presented in management's discussion.

The discussion should address the financial statements and any other statistical data that the company believes will help in understanding financial condition, changes in financial condition and results of operations. However, the information provided ". . . need only include that which is available to the registrant without undue effort or expense and which *does not clearly appear in the registrant's financial statements."* The discussion should principally explain *why* changes occurred in the financial condition and results of operations. The numerical data in the financial statements and notes need not be repeated in the discussion. For example, from the comparative financial statements it is clear what the amount of increase or decrease in revenues is from the prior year and the respective percentage change is readily computable. In FRR 36, the SEC encouraged management to elaborate on the reasons for line item changes. The SEC makes the point that a mechanical recitation of numerical differences easily computed by a reader of the financial statements is not necessary or desirable.

The discussion generally should cover the most recent three fiscal years (i.e., the same period covered by the financial statements). The instructions suggest traditional year-to-year comparisons (e.g., 19X5 vs. 19X4 and 19X4 vs. 19X3), but other formats may be used if the company believes they would aid reader understanding. When trend information is relevant, it may be necessary for the discussion to refer to the five-year table of selected financial data. The SEC suggested in FRR 36 that management use the statement of cash flows for a source of MD&A discussion of liquidity and capital resources; this should produce discussion more comparable from registrant to registrant.

Capital Resources

Regulation S-K does not define the term "capital resources," but mentions equity, debt and off-balance sheet financing arrangements as examples. The following should be described:

- Material commitments for capital expenditures as of the latest year end, the general purpose of the commitments and the plans to finance them.
- Material trends, favorable or unfavorable, in the company's capital resources, including any expected material changes in their mix and relative cost.

The SEC notes in FRR 36 that registrants disclosing plans for future expansion should discuss prospective information regarding sources of capital to fund the planned expansion. Trend analysis should be provided for expected material changes in the mix and relative cost of capital resources. Again, the SEC also reminds management to look beyond the next 12-month period.

Generally, we believe it is difficult to separate the discussions of capital resources and liquidity. Companies may find it difficult to discuss the long-term aspects of liquidity without discussing capital resources. The rules permit these topics to be combined in the discussion when the two topics are interrelated.

Results of Operations

In discussing the results of operations, management should

- Describe any unusual or infrequent events or transactions or any significant economic changes which materially affect income from continuing operations, and the extent to which income was affected. Such transactions may include the sale of assets or operations, sale of tax benefits, early debt refunding, and LIFO inventory liquidations. It is not necessary to repeat the disclosures of these items in the financial statements. However, we understand the Commission believes companies should address the impact of these transactions on cash flow and reported profits and trends, the estimated effect on future operations, and whether it was a "one-time" transaction. In addition, SAB 74 requires that impending changes in accounting methods, such as pending adoption of FASB Statements, that are expected to have a significant impact on future financial information be similarly addressed.

- Describe any other significant components of revenue or expense necessary to understand the results of operations.

- Describe any known trends or uncertainties which have had, or are expected to have, a material impact on sales, revenues, or income from continuing operations.

- Disclose any future changes in the relationship between costs and revenues if events are known which will cause a material change, such as known future increases in labor or materials costs or prices.

- Discuss the extent to which material increases in net sales or revenues are due to increased sales prices. (Although not specifically covered in the rules, we believe material *decreases* in sales volume or prices, or the discontinuance of a product line, also should be discussed.)

If a company does not present segment information because it has a dominant segment and there has been a change in operations that is expected to continue and that is not obvious because the company does not present the segment separately, the SEC has warned that the discussion should address the impact of the change. And Section 209.03 of the Codification of Financial Reporting Policies states that management's discussion and analysis should address current year changes in idle facilities when such changes materially impact the results of operations.

Proposals Affecting Periodic Reporting

Report of Managment's Responsibilities

In 1988, the SEC proposed rules that would require registrants to include in the annual report to shareholders and in annual reports on Form 10-K, a report describing management's responsibilities for the financial statements and the system of internal control. The proposed rules are similar to a recommendation made by the Treadway Commission.

The rules, as proposed, would become effective for calendar year 1990 reporting and would require the management report to contain a statement describing:

- Management's responsibilities for the financial statements and the system of internal control.

- Management's assessment of the effectiveness of the system of internal control as of the latest balance sheet date.

- Management's response to any significant recommendations made by its internal and independent auditors concerning such controls.

The proposal would not require independent auditors to perform any procedures beyond existing responsibilities under generally accepted auditing standards (GAAS). So, independent auditors would be required to read the management report and, based on procedures performed during the audit of the financial statements, consider whether management's assessment of the effectiveness of its internal control structure is materially misstated.

The SEC staff has indicated that it plans to issue final rules in this area during 1990.

SEC Proposes Technical Amendments to Regulations S-X

The SEC published for comment proposed amendments to Regulation S-X. These amendments would conform many of the SEC's current requirements to disclosures required by recently issued FASB Statements on loan fees (Statement 91), consolidation (Statement 94), statement of cash flows (Statement 95), income taxes (Statement 96), and insurance (Statement 97). The SEC has characterized the proposed amendments as principally technical.

Of interest, however, are the proposed income tax disclosures upon the adoption of Statement 96. Responding to Statement 96's balance sheet focus, the SEC's proposal would have required registrants to quantify significant components of the deferred tax balance sheet amounts in lieu of analysis of the components of deferred tax expense. Based on comments received on this proposal, we understand that the SEC likely will not require such quantification when it issues final rules. Further, the staff has indicated that, pending the Commission's consideration of these proposed amendments, the SEC staff will not insist on disclosure of significant timing differences as required by Rule 4-08 (h) (i) (ii) (B) of Regulation S-X for those registrants that have adopted Statement 96. The staff believes that this requirement is inconsistent with the balance sheet orientation of Statement 96 and that registrants need only provide the disclosures required by Statement 96 and any additional disclosures the registrant concludes would be useful and meaningful in the circumstances.

Also relating to income tax disclosures under the proposed rules, the SEC's current disclosure requirements relating to the foreign and domestic components of income tax and separate disclosure of U.S., foreign, and other income taxes would be retained. Also retained would be the current requirement to disclose significant items separately in the reconciliation of the statutory rate to the effective tax rate.

The proposed amendments also include revisions of Items 17 and 18 of Form 20-F that would require foreign private issuers to provide a statement of cash flows or substantially similar information in filings with the SEC.

The SEC is expected to issue final rules relating to these amendments in early 1990.

Foreign Operations

Impact of Rate Changes—Companies are encouraged to present an analysis and discussion of the effects of exchange rate changes on the reported results of operations; the purpose of such supplemental disclosures is to assist financial statement users in understanding the broader implications of rate periods.

Companies that make such disclosures should take care that they are not misleading. For example, reported dollar sales of foreign operations might decline because of a change in exchange rates, but that change also might affect selling prices, sales volume, and cost structures. In that situation, it might not be sufficient to discuss only the effects of translation on reported sales. Companies that quantify the effects of translation at different exchange rates should evaluate the need to clearly explain that disclosure.

Cash Flow Implications of Functional Currencies—One objective of translation under Statement 52 is to provide information that is generally compatible with the expected economic effects of a rate change on an enterprise's

cash flows and equity. The functional currency decision and the resulting translation method generally should reflect that objective. One of
the functional currency indicators is cash flows. That indicator points to
a foreign functional currency when cash flows related to the foreign
operation's individual assets and liabilities are primarily in the foreign
currency and do not directly impact the parent's cash flows. It points to
the U.S. dollar (i.e., the parent's currency) when cash flows related to the
foreign operation's individual assets and liabilities directly impact the
parent's cash flows on a current basis and are readily available for remit-
tance to the parent. The SEC apparently believes that financial statement
users might consider the cash flow indicator to be paramount and that
they might draw conclusions, based on the functional currency, about
the availability of cash from foreign operations to meet the needs of
other operations.

The SEC has suggested it would like to see companies display net
investments by major functional currency and present an analysis of the
translation component of equity either by significant functional currency or by geographical areas used for segment disclosure purposes.

The SEC believes the presumption might be that cash is available from
operations with a U.S. dollar functional currency, but not from those with
a foreign functional currency.

Integrated Reports

The SEC permits the annual shareholders report and Form 10-K to be filed
as a combined report.

The report must contain all the information required by Form 10-K,
including the cover page and required signatures. A cross-reference
sheet should indicate the location of information required by the items
of the Form. When responses to certain items of the Form are separated
within the report, an appropriate cross-reference should be made.

If the information required by Part III of Form 10-K (see Instruction G)
is omitted, a definitive proxy or information statement shall be filed.

Information contained in integrated annual reports, other than that required by the Form 10-K instructions, is not deemed "filed" for purposes
of liability under Section 18 of the 1934 Act.

Before electing to prepare an integrated report certain factors should be
considered. Cost may not be a significant factor because the savings of

preparing only one document may be offset by its larger size and by additional disclosures required by the SEC rules. Some commercial companies will have to include audited financial statements of unconsolidated subsidiaries, investees and affiliates whose securities are held as collateral, as well as financial schedules.

Summary Annual Reports

In recent years, some companies have expressed interest in an approach to shareholder communication referred to as *summary annual reporting*. A summary annual report replaces the traditional annual report most public companies provide to their shareholders, but it does not include all of the financial disclosures required by the SEC's proxy rules. The proxy rules require that audited financial statements, management's discussion and analysis, a five-year table of selected financial data, and certain other information be included in an annual report to all shareholders when soliciting proxies for the annual meeting. Companies electing to issue a summary annual report must continue to provide this information to shareholders; an alternative some companies are considering is to include this information in an addendum to the annual meeting proxy statement. This alternative approach to annual reporting does not involve any waiver of SEC rules.

Since the summary annual report is not used for compliance purposes, there are no specific rules on its content. The only restriction on the information included in the summary annual report is the general requirement that corporate communications by public companies must not include false or misleading information or fail to disclose material information necessary to make the statements made not misleading (i.e., Rule 10b-5 of the Securities Exchange Act of 1934). A Financial Executives Institute research study suggested that, at a minimum, the summary annual report include a narrative financial review; a balance sheet, income statement, and statement of changes in financial position for at least two years; selected five-year data; a management report; and independent accountants' report; and certain other significant information from the audited financial statement footnotes. We believe the summary annual report also should include an offer to provide the company's annual report to the SEC on Form 10-K.

Style

The regulations provide that the Form 10-K should be produced on good quality unglazed, 8-½ × 11 inch white paper. If annual shareholders reports are larger than 8-½ × 11 inches, the copies filed with the SEC, including those incorporated by reference and those required to be submitted by the proxy rules, must be reduced prior to filing. However, if certain exhibits (e.g., contracts, leases, maps, plots, geological surveys, and computer-generated reports) are larger than 8-½ × 11 inches and reducing them is not practical or would make them illegible, they need not be reduced.

The body of Form 10-K must be in Roman type at least as large as 10-point modern type. The financial statements, including the financial statements sent to shareholders, and other statistical data also should be generally at least as 10-point modern type. However, "to the extent necessary for convenient presentation," Roman type at least as large as 8-point modern type may be used for financial statements and other tabular data. All type must be leaded at least 2 points.

Each copy of the report with the SEC must bound (without stiff covers) in the left side so that the reading matter is legible.

Impact of Inflation and Changing Prices

In December 1986, the FASB issued Statement No. 89, "Financial Reporting and Changing Prices," which rescinded the inflation accounting disclosures required by FASB Statement No. 33. Statement 89 was effective for financial reports issued after December 2, 1986. In August 1987, FRR 30 was issued and amended Item 302 of Regulation S-K by deleting references to the FASB's inflation disclosure requirements rescinded in December 1986. Companies were reminded, however, that Item 302 requires a discussion of the impact of inflation if it is material.

The instructions require only a brief textual presentation of management's views, and the discussion may be presented in whatever manner appears appropriate. This requirement calls for a *narrative* discussion, not a numeric quantification, of the impact of inflation.

Other Required Disclosures

The causes of material changes in financial statement items must be described to the extent necessary for users to understand the business as a whole. This requirement applied to all financial statements—not just the income statement. Determining which changes are material is left to the company. If the causes for a change in one item also relate to other items, repeating the discussion is not required. And the amount of the change need not be mentioned if it is easily computable from the financial statements. In fact, the instructions emphasize that the discussion should not be a recitation of numerical data from the financial statements.

SAB No. 29 stated that management's discussion should contain an explanation of material changes in earnings per share resulting from a change in the number of shares outstanding, such as that resulting from a large purchase of treasury stock. Although this guidance was deleted when the SABs were codified, the SEC staff believes the management's discussion requirements contemplate such disclosures. The SEC staff has indicated that management's discussion should address the impact of such transactions as they affect balance sheet and income statement captions, including earnings per share. Although some repurchases of outstanding stock may not have a material effect on other financial statement captions, discussion may be required to explain the impact on the trend of earnings per share.

The SEC staff indicated in Staff Accounting Bulletin No. 74 that registrants should disclose the impact of accounting standards which have not yet been adopted that are expected to materially affect financial position and/or results of operation when adopted (e.g., a change from the deferred method to the liability method of computing deferred income taxes that will be made in a future period). SAB 74 requirements include:

- A brief description of the new standard, the date that adoption is required, and the date that the registrant plans to adopt, if earlier.

- A discussion of the methods of adoption allowed by the standard and the method expected to be utilized by the registrant, if determined.

- A discussion of the impact that adoption of the standard is expected to have on the financial statements of the registrant, unless not known or reasonably estimable. In that case, a statement to that effect may be made.

- Disclosure of the potential impact of other significant matters that the registrant believes might result from the adoption of the standard (such as technical violations of debt covenant agreements, planned or intended changes in business practices, etc.).

Based upon the nature of the government's inquiry, disclosures also may be required in Form 10-K under "Description of Business" and "Legal Proceedings" as well as financial statement disclosure of loss contingencies.

Appendix 3

Sample Press Release

From: XYZ Company
           777 Sixth Street
           New York, N.Y. 10010
           (212) XXX-XXXX
Contact: Lucy Paul
           (212) XXX-XXXX

FOR IMMEDIATE RELEASE

RECORD FIRST QUARTER EARNINGS INCREASE
ON HIGHER SALES

REPORTED BY XYZ COMPANY

New York, N.Y., April 10 —— Record sales and earnings for the first quarter of 199– were reported today by XYZ Company. Sales for the quarter ended March 31, 199–, were $xxx,xxx,xxx, a gain of 15 percent compared to $xxx,xxx,xxx in the first quarter of last year.

Earnings for the quarter were $xxx million, or $x.xx per share, compared with $xxx million, or $x.xx per share in the prior year's quarter.

In reporting first quarter results, John A. Smith, XYZ Company chairman, said, "XYZ Company's earnings were higher than anticipated at the start of the year. We are especially pleased with these results in view of today's economic conditions. Although there are some soft spots in the rates of incoming orders, most areas should remain strong throughout the year.

"Most of the increase in earnings is due to improved operating profit margins on higher volume," said Mr. Smith. "Revenue gains came from higher metal sales and machine tool shipments during the three-month period."

Strong earnings improvements were achieved by the company's precious minerals division. Sales and earnings of fabricated metal products were off, due to industry dumping and a ten-day strike at the Rose Dam facility. Earnings from the ABC machine tool subsidiary were ahead of the 198– quarter largely reflecting in-plant operating efficiencies. ABC continues as the company's largest contributor to operating profits.

Overseas business in the fabricated metals segment was strong during the reporting period, but according to Mr. Smith, "the rate of new orders is declining, and we expect a down cycle for the next few months."

XYZ Company is the world's largest producer of all minerals, and a leading manufacturer of fabricated metal products principally to the auto industry. Its ABC subsidiary is a major factor in the machine tool industry supplying the pollution control, metalworking, and mining industries.

#   #   #

XYZ COMPANY

STATEMENT OF EARNINGS
FIRST QUARTER ENDED MARCH 31, 199—

| | ($ IN THOUSANDS) Three Months Ended March 31 | |
	199—	199—
REVENUES	$xxxxxxxxx	$xxxxxxxxx
COST OF SALES	xxxxxxxxx	xxxxxxxxx
OPERATING PROFIT	xxxxx	xxxxx
INCOME FROM OTHER SOURCES	xxxx	xxxx
TOTAL	xxxxx	xxxxx
INTEREST EXPENSE	xxxxx	xxxxx
INCOME BEFORE PROVISION FOR FEDERAL AND OTHER INCOME TAXES	xxxxx	xxxxx
PROVISION FOR FEDERAL AND OTHER INCOME TAXES	xxxxx	xxxxx
MINORITY INTEREST IN NET INCOME OF SUBSIDIARIES	xxx	xxx
NET INCOME	$ xxxxxx	$ xxxxxx
AVERAGE COMMON SHARES OUTSTANDING	xxxxxxxxx	xxxxxxxxx
EARNINGS PER COMMON SHARE	$ X.xx	$ X.xx

Appendix 4

Research Questionnaire

Market research is a crucial part of investor relations. The following is a questionnaire—or more specifically, an inventory of questions from which questionnaires are drawn as appropriate—used for many of its clients by the investor relations professionals of Burton-Marsteller, the international public relations firm.

XYZ COMPANY
SECURITY ANALYST RESEARCH QUESTIONNAIRE
GENERAL QUESTIONS

- Do you actively follow XYZ Metals Company? How often do you contact management? (visit, phone)
- Do you follow XYZ because:
    a. It is a major factor in the metals field?
    b. You think it has investment potential now?
    c. You need information to answer inquiries?
- When you go to an institution do you find that
    a. They are informed about XYZ?
    b. They are receptive to the story?
    c. They have built-in biases about XYZ?
    d. You've never discussed XYZ with an institution?
- What do you think is a reasonable multiple for XYZ today? Relative to other metals companies?
- What gives you the greatest difficulty in analyzing this company? Any specific business area? The way earnings are reported? Lack of information?

- What do you perceive to be XYZ's greatest strengths? Greatest weaknesses?
- Are the company's securities suitable for institutions? Why?
- Do you have an earnings estimate for 199—?
- What is your investment opinion of the company?
- What are XYZ's greatest strengths? Weaknesses?
- Which areas of the company's business offer the greatest potential growth over the near/long term? Which areas offer the least potential? Why?
- How would you rank XYZ relative to its competitors in terms of:

  a. Performance—last two years

  b. Potential—future ability to benefit from higher copper prices
- How do you assess XYZ's earnings in terms of:

  a. Visibility: Can you identify sources of earnings easily?

  b. Quality: Are accounting practices considered conservative relative?

  c. Predictability: Beyond economic cycles?
- What external factors are most likely to affect XYZ's revenues and earnings? Are they the same as those affecting other companies in the industry?
- What must management do or continue to do if earnings are to rise considerably over the next five years?
- What circumstances outside the control of management must prevail if earnings are to rise consistently over the next five years? What can management do to minimize the potential negatives? Exploit the positives?
- How would you describe XYZ Company's image in one simple phrase?

Management

- How would you rate XYZ's management compared to the other leading metals companies?
- How do they differ?
- What is XYZ's greatest management strength(s)? Weaknesses(es)?
- What is your opinion of XYZ's management depth? Who have you spoken to at the company? Who do you see as backup for Chairman Smith?

- Can you identify any competitive advantages ABC has over competitors? (e.g., better facilities?)
- How do you view prospects for over the next six months to a year? Next two years?
- How do you view prospects for ABC?
- What are the key factors that influence this business? Economic cycles? EPA regulations? Innovation? Energy?
- What problems do you see for ABC? Capacity undersupply? Technological obsolescence? Price competition?
- Do you see any major growth areas? Expansion possibilities?
- Can you identify what is unique and/or significant about ABC business?
  a. Competitive position
  b. Management controls
  c. Unique customer position
  d. Marketing expertise
  e. Product reputation
  f. Proprietary products
- How well does this business fit in with ABC product mix in terms of modifying cyclicality of earnings?
- What are your major printed sources of information for ABC?
  a. Trade magazines—which ones?
  b. Government publications—which ones?
  c. Machine tool industry association
  d. Other
- What key information do you need from ABC to properly assess this portion of their business?
- Do you think the recent ABC acquisition increased the company's earnings potential, predictability, quality? What would you have changed?

Communications

- How would you assess XYZ's communications with financial community?
  a. Quality of written reports
  b. Frequency/timing of reporting

c. Personal contact

d. Accessibility of management

e. Analyst meetings

f. Other corporate material

- What information would you like to receive about XYZ (mention here or wait until you discuss divisions)?

- Is there any area of the company's business that gives you difficulty in analyzing? Please explain.

- Would more information help? What do you want?

- How would you rate XYZ for credibility and consistency of corporate information?

- In your opinion, is there anything the company can do to improve its communication with the financial community?

- What are the key factors you use to analyze XYZ? What is the key information you use in analyzing XYZ?

Metals/Mining

- What do you consider the key factors to be in evaluating a metals/mining company? What factors determine its profitability?

a. Efficiency: mines, smelters, refiner production

b. Technological expertise: processes used

c. Equipment—Age

d. Engineering expertise

e. Reputation

f. Management

g. Present market position

h. Marketing capabilities

i. Volume

j. Product line diversity

k. Reserves

l. Other

- Which do you consider to be the outstanding companies on the basis of these considerations? Why?

- How would you rate XYZ relative to these companies on the basis of these important factors?
- What are you projecting for the economy for 198—? For specific metals prices? For demand? For supply?
- How do you view prospects for metals companies over the next six months to a year?
- Which of the companies are less vulnerable to changes in the economic cycle than XYZ? Why? More vulnerable? Why?
- Do you think the boom or bust cycles for metals are over? Would a metals policy help? How will government regulatory activity affect metals companies in the future? Affect XYZ?
- What do you see as the major problems in the metals industry? Energy costs? Lack of skilled labor? Cost of capacity expansion? Inflation and pricing problems? Government regulation?
- What are the most significant indicators used to project performance in the metals industries? Gross National Product? Industrial Production Capacity utilization/operating rates? In mining, refining?
- What are your major sources of information in this area other than company-generated information?

  a. Trade magazines—which ones?

  b. Trade associations

  c. Government generated information

- Where would you place XYZ relative to competition in terms of production costs? Why? What are the problems? How could they be solved?
- How do you break down sources of earnings?
- How do you rank the metals companies in terms of capital employed? What are the greatest growth areas for metals companies?
- Do you agree that acquisition of ABC was a smart move? Good acquisition?
- How do you assess XYZ's marketing and sales structure? Relative to competition? What could be improved?
- Does XYZ have any competitive advantages? Disadvantages?
- Are there any outside influences that constitute an important risk for XYZ government regulations, EPA public interest groups, water pollution, air pollution?
- What would XYZ have to do to have you recommend the stock?

ABC Subsidiary

- Who are the ABC's most important competitors in industrial products? Machine tools?
- How would you compare them in terms of market shares? Product quality?
- Have you ever had contact with the group division heads? If so how would you evaluate them in terms of knowing the business? Would you like to have an opportunity to meet with them if it could be arranged easily?
- Looking at the company as a single unit, how do you think its performance will respond to changes in the economy? What factors might offset negative trends in either the economy or specific industries? What can management do to assure this?
- Does the company have any competitive advantages?
- What factors differentiate this company from the rest of its competitors?
- How would you rate XYZ's operating efficiencies relative to competition?
- Is there anything that comes to mind that makes the company unique? Interesting?

Financing

- Do you think XYZ's financing is adequate at present? Do you see any need for outside financing in the near future? For what purposes?
- Do you have any questions or reservations about the company's balance sheet? How?
- Is return on investment satisfactory relative to expectations? Relative to competition?

Acquisitions

- Do you have a perception of the company's corporate goals/philosophy on expansion through acquisition?

Appendix 5

Fact Book and Corporate Profile Outline

As an aid to analysts and others, the fact book or corporate profile summarizes basic financial and other pertinent information about a company in one place. The following is an outline used by Burson-Marsteller, the international public relations firm, for many of the fact books prepared for clients. It is an inventory of information from which can be drawn outlines for other kinds of companies, as appropriate.

XYZ COMPANY
FACT BOOK OUTLINE

SECTION I: Introduction to XYZ Company
A description of the company by division
1. The number of types of properties
2. Important locations
3. Products
4. Major markets served
(Highlights only)

SECTION II: Business Strategies
A statement describing XYZ's future direction:
1. Where the company intends to go—major goals
2. Methods used to achieve goals
3. Show analysts how management views the business—current and future e.g. portfolio, a metals company
4. Discuss assumptions underlying plans
5. Policy statements on how investment decisions are made
6. Expected returns—time and dollar return

7. Planning and financial controls in place
8. Policies on diversification
9. How company measures progress—financial measurements

SECTION III: Organization: Organization Chart
SECTION IV: Minerals/Metals
A. Industry Profile
   1. Define the industry in terms of metals produced: aluminum, copper, lead, zinc, precious metals, uranium
   2. Discuss markets served, major uses (primary, secondary, and undeveloped) and product characteristics that provide competitive advantage.
   3. Growth—past ten years; look at the future potential
   4. Economic factors affecting future industry growth
   5. Economic factors affecting cost of production—look at this from the point of view of cost (industry-wide labor settlements, for example), Federal environmental controls
   6. Supply/demand patterns: availability of each metal in the short and long run
   7. Price history; characteristics during economic change; impact of inventories
   8. Influence of worldwide political events
   9. Governmental regulations—e.g. land use
   10. Profile of customers—e.g. wire mills, auto companies
   11. Distribution methods, costs
   12. Major competitors—who they are, what they produce
   13. Technology—e.g. recent changes in smelter technology
   14. Labor history
   15. Outlook and future trends
B. Commodities Exchanges: The Marketplace
   1. Comex and LME
   2. Warehousing
   3. Hedging
   4. Buying and selling forward
SECTION V: Mining and Minerals Operations
   1. Describe each property separately:
      a. Atlas
      b. Beulah
      c. Caesar

          d. Dog Patch
          e. Everyman
     2. Note metals and produced
     3. Include quantity produced (by mineral), historical and current grade, production statistics
     4. Describe facilities—smelter, refineries, transportation methods, distances
     5. Environmental requirements by state; describe status
     6. Capital expenditures: major expenditures made during the past five years and impact on productivity, expansion, health and safety
     7. Describe current and planned expenditures; describe project timing, projected income flow, reason for and projected benefits of the investment (where possible)
     8. Explain by-products impact on costs; account for relationship to production
     9. Describe marketing department, size, structure, and function
    10. Discuss specifics of sales, shapes, sold, price variations by shape, transportation, services offered, methods of pricing, contracts
    11. Exploration: companies by name and location, how program is planned and executed, where located, people, dollars

Section VI: ABC Subsidiary
    A. Machine Tools
      1. Industry Profile
        a. Size of market
        b. Growth of the market—past five years
        c. Economic factors affecting costs/prices
        d. Economic factors affecting industry growth
        e. Major competitors; market share
        f. Business indicators used to measure the market
        g. Major end use markets, growth factors, size
      2. Description of the Business
        a. Describe products
        b. Number of products in product line, descriptions, uses
        c. Where manufactured
        d. How distributed
        e. Product characteristics; advantages
        f. New product development; expansion of the line
        g. R & D expenditures

h. Capital expansion plans
i. Pricing strategy relative to competition
j. Strategy to improve profit margins
k. International operations—location, products, markets, manufacturing strategies
l. Outlook
B. Divisions: Pollution Control, Metalworking, Mining Machinery
1. Describe products by division
2. For each division—market size for products, growth
3. Factors that influence market growth, cyclicality
4. Major competitors
5. Product line, important uses, substitutes
6. Distribution
7. Outlook—future trends
8. International operations
9. Manufacturer facilities
10. R & D expenditures, new products

SECTION VII: Management
Biographical information on senior officers

SECTION VIII: History of XYZ Company
Discuss ABC acquisition, as well as origin and development of the company

SECTION IX: Financial Statements
1. Five-year balance sheets, income statement, sources/uses
2. Important ratios
3. Accounting policies
4. Notes

SECTION X: Appendix
1. World production/consumption of each metal
2. World prices for each metal over the last decade
3. Industrial Production Indexes
4. XYZ sources of earnings—table showing dollars of revenues derived from major sources: metals, industrial equipment

Appendix 6

Outline for Annual Meeting Presentation

The presentation given at a company's annual meeting of shareholders by its chief executive officer is more than a summary of activities—it is a position statement. As such, it should be tailored to meet the needs of the company. The following is a typical outline for such a presentation, prepared by Burson-Marsteller, the international public relations firm, for one of its clients.

XYZ COMPANY
ANNUAL MEETING PRESENTATION
CHAIRMAN JOHN A. SMITH

A. Report on Operating Performance
   I. Quantitative (Corporate Results)
      a. Earnings, Revenues, Returns, Dividends, Comparisons to previous years
      b. Explanation of quarterly results, particularly deviations from standard performance
   II. Qualitative (Highlights of individual operating units)
      a. Minerals and Metals
         1. Product extracted, refined and sold; increases or decreases from prior year and reasons
         2. Overview of market prices for various minerals during the year
         3. Expenditures: capital employed for maintenance of facilities & new capacity
         4. Management change: new president named in 4Q

   b. Fabricated Metal Products
      1. Industry Conditions: Automotive
      2. Labor Relations: Strike at Rose Dam
      3. Change in Market Share: Reasons
      4. Expansion plans overseas
   c. Machine Tool Division
      1. Market conditions: Pollution Control, Metalworking, Mining
      2. Backlogs
      3. Productivity Gains

B. Outline for Coming Year
   I. Economic Environment
   II. Corporate Plans/Goals/Major Projects
   III. Financing Requirements/Sources

C. Miscellaneous
   I. Dividend Policy
   II. Corporate Office Move
   III. Senior Officer Promotion
   IV. Board of Directors: Additions/Retirements

D. Question & Answer Period

Appendix 7

Outline for Security Analyst Presentation

The presentation before security analysts is a significant opportunity to present the company in its best—and most accurate—light. The following is typical of an outline of a presentation prepared by Burson-Marsteller, the international public relations firm, for one of its clients.

XYZ COMPANY
SECURITY ANALYST PRESENTATION OUTLINE

   I. Five reasons to consider investing in XYZ Company
   A. Strong financial position
   B. Low price/earnings ratio
   C. Successful growth over past 7 years
   D. Share of market in growing fabricated metal industry
   E. Strength of management
  II. Strategy for coming year
   A. Continue to tighten financial controls
   B. Increased R&D
   C. Expand geographic market
   D. Strengthen sales staff
   E. Upgrade facilities
   F. Sell selected properties
   G. Enter joint ventures
 III. XYZ Today
   A. Minerals Business
      1. Remains basic business
      2. Foundation of corporate earnings/consistency
      3. Outlook for minerals prices

B. Objective Cited:
   1. Balance business through diversification
   2. Improve efficiency of fabricated metals business
   3. Strengthen financial position
C. Success with each objective
D. Acquisition—AVC Subsidiary
   1. Business description/market position/business fit
   2. Historical returns, earnings
   3. Facilities
   4. Management depth
   5. —% of total XYZ investment in ABC
   6. Potential: Growth Markets/Robotics
   7. Plans:
      a) invest only in products with potential in excess of market
      b) increase R&D by —%
      c) refinance short-term debt
E. Fabricated Metal Products Division
   1. Productivity Improvements: Revenue per Employee 198— versus today
      a) new equipment
      b) alternate fuel sources
      c) close of Rose Dam Facility
   2. Shipments: down/reasons: economic or internal
   3. Overseas Expansion Plans
F. Strengthened XYZ Financial Position
   1. Two years ago
      a) financial ratios below goals: Long-term debt —%; cash flow —% debt; Pretax interest coverage —
      b) required cash resources: $XXXX
   2. Strategy
      a) sold Bass City plant for $XXX
      b) equity offering: net $XXX
      c) capital spending reduction —%
      d) improved inventory control equal to $XXX in added cash
   3. Today
      a) cash $XXX
      b) working capital requirements $XXX
      c) financial ratios improved/debt ratings higher
   4. Projected Requirements and Sources of Cash
      a) sources—internal generation; outside financing
      b) requirements—capital projects, working capital, debt retirement

Appendix 8

Institutional Investor Record

With the growing importance of institutions in the stock market, an effective investor relations program depends upon keeping up-to-date data on each institution that's a potential or actual investor in a company's stock. These records can be kept on paper or in a computer, and must be updated frequently. Here are two forms used successfully by the international public relations firm, Burson-Marsteller.

Name: PORTLAND MANAGEMENT COMPANY

Address: 1400 N.W. Tenth Avenue
                          P.O. Box 1350
                          Portland, Oregon 97207

Telephone: (503) 555–6666

Total Assets: $7.2 billion

Percent equity: 67%

Portfolio Manager: John Portland

Analyst: Harry Berk

Holdings of SCI as
of 3/31/90:   200,000 shares

Fund SCI is in: Portland Growth

Comments:

Columbia Management is an independent investment counselor, wholly owned by its employees. Manages 6 funds.

They use a variety of investment approaches in decision making: top down, asset allocation and sector rotation; emphasis is on growth. Each portfolio has been 40–45 stocks with moderate turnover rates, generally in the 50% to 100% range.

They do not work from an approved list but ideas are approved by all twelve members of the investment committee. Employs 12 portfolio managers/analysts and 9 portfolio managers. Only 25% of research is generated internally; 50% is Street, 25% consultant/other.

*   *   *   *   *

Shore Drive Management
9 Shore Drive
Greenwich, CT 06836

Telephone: (203) 555–1990

Shore Drive is an independent investment counselor, owned 100% by five individuals. 95% of assets are pension funds invested in equity accounts and an equity fund called the Shore Drive Fund. SCI is one of their largest holdings. Manages approximately $705 million, all U.S.

Investment approach is value: low P/E. Has about 33 stocks in each portfolio; follows approximately 50 stocks regularly. Average account turnover is moderate (50%–100%); 80% in-house research, 20% Wall Street.

Takes a bottom-up approach, mixed with fundamental research to find high-quality out-of-favor stocks, with low P/Es relative to historic norms and the market. Looks for companies that have lost their Wall Street sponsorship.

SCI is held in Shore Drive Fund

The portfolio manager is Lee Wallace
The analyst is Earle Brown

Holds 1,234,000 shares

Appendix 9

Electronic Information Services and Databases

Today's investor, professional or otherwise, has access by computer to an extraordinary amount of information. For the serious investor, or investor relations professional, access to this information on a timely basis may be crucial. The following list is abstracted, by permission, from The Individual Investor's Guide to Computerized Investing, *8th ed., published by the American Association of Individual Investors, 625 North Michigan Avenue, Chicago IL 60611*

Argus On–Line
Argus Research Corporation
17 Battery Place, New York, NY 10004
(212) 425–7500

$50/annum plus $1/minute usage time. Also available on a flat-fee unlimited usage basis.

Provides research reports from 20 Argus economists and analysts.

BTC–64 (formerly MI–64)
Bonneville Telecommunications
19 W. South Temple, Suite 200, Salt Lake City, UT 84101–1503
(800) 255–7374, (801) 532–3400

$297 plus monthly data and exchange fees.

Provides market news and real-time quotes on grains, meats, petroleum, precious metals and currency from U.S. and selected exchanges.

Cadence Universe Online
CDA, Investment Technologies, Inc.
1355 Piccard Drive, Rockville, MD 20850
(800) 232–2285, (301) 975–9600

$100 setup charge; $45/hour connect via Telenet; from $5–$50 per specific report.

Provides instant on-line access to CDA's vast library of comprehensive mutual fund, bank and insurance company and investment advisors data for performance comparisons and analysis.

Citibase
Citicorp Database Services
77 Water Street, 7th Floor, New York, NY 10043
(212) 898–7200

$65/hour on-line, $100 start-up fee; diskettes also available.

Provides historical U.S. macroeconomic and some financial information.

ComStock
ComStock
670 White Plains Road, Scarsdale, NY 10583
(800) 431–5019, (914) 725–4271

$295/month and higher

Real-time price quotation service for stocks, option, futures, and currencies from over 45 U.S. and international markets.

Daily Pricing Service
Street Software Technology, Inc.
40 Wall Street, Suite 6003, New York, NY 10005
(212) 425–9450

$400/month

Provides closing bid-and-asked quotes for a comprehensive list of U.S. Treasury notes, bonds, bills, agencies, strips, mortgage-backed securities, and interest rate futures/options.

Dialog Business Connection
Dialog Information Services, Inc.
3460 Hillview Avenue, Palo Alto, CA 94304
(800) 334–2564, (415) 858–3785

Price varies depending upon information retrieval. Menu-driven, applications-oriented service which offers on-line access to data on over 2 million public and private companies.

First Release
Dialog Information Services, Inc.
3460 Hillview Avenue, Palo Alto, CA 94304
(800) 334–2564, (415) 858–3785

$1.60/minute

Provides access to the latest news from 4 major newswire databases, updated within 15 minutes of transmission over the wire.

Disclosure Database
Disclosure Incorporated
5161 River Road, Bethesda, MD 20816
(301) 951–1300

Price varies by vendor.

Contains financial and textual data extracted from documents filed with the SEC on over 12,000 companies.

Disclosure/Spectrum Ownership Database
Disclosure Incorporated
5161 River Road, Bethesda, MD 20816
(301) 951–1300

Price varies by vendor.

Contains detailed stock ownership information for companies extracted from documents filed with the SEC by corporate insiders, 5% owners, and institutional owners.

Ford Investor Services
Ford Investor Services
11722 Sorrento Valley Road, Suite 1, San Diego, CA 92121
(619) 755–1327

$300/month for monthly or $600/month for weekly updates and actual computer charges alternatively–$96/hr with no fixed fee.

On-line data available for all computers or disk based data and options analysis software (Epic) for IBM PCs.

FutureSource Technical
FutureSource (formerly Commodity Communications Co), a division of
Oster Communications, Inc., 955 Parkview Boulevard, Lombard, IL 60148
(800) 621–2628, (708) 620–8444

$340/month plus exchange fees.

Combines real-time futures and options quotes with technical analysis.

Insider Trading Monitor
Invest/net
99 N.W. 183rd Street, Suite 237, North Miami, FL 33169
(305) 652–1721

$1/minute

A database of all securities transactions of officers, directors, and major
shareholders of all publicly held corporations required to file under the
Securities Act of 1934.

Institutional Brokers' Estimate System (I/B/E/S)
Lynch, Jones & Ryan
345 Hudson Street, New York, NY 10014

Standard CompuServe connect charges plus expanded report, $2/com-
pany; brief report, $0.50/company.

Provides consensus earnings estimate on over 3,400 publicly traded corporations.

Investext/Plus
Investext, Division of Thomson Financial Networks
11 Farnsworth Street, Boston, MA 02210
(800) 662–7878, (617) 345–2000

$75 for starter kit (includes account number and password, user's manual,
terminal software, and $50 worth of connect time).

InvestorNet
InvestorNet International, Inc.
15560 Rockfield Boulevard, Suite B-1, Irvine, CA 92718
(800) 535–5321, (714) 587–1912

Contact InvestorNet International for price information; 10% discount for
AAII members.

Nationwide interactive computer network that brings together buyers and sellers of fixed income securities.

Lexis/Nexis Financial Information Service
Mead Data Central, Inc.
9443 Springboro Pike P.O. Box 933, Dayton, OH 45401–0933
(800) 227–9597, (513) 865–6800

Connect time, $26/hour; telecommunications time, $13/hour; search $6–$35/search ($1 for each real-time quote requested); printing, $0.025/line

Offers the full text of research reports written by top analysts at dozens of major investment banking and brokerage firms; the full text of 10-K and 10-Q reports; abstracts of more than a dozen other key SEC filings (available within 48 hours of filing); and information on limited partnerships, companies and plants by SIC code, data on corporate directors, and hard-to-find information on privately held and OTC companies.

Lotus One Source
Lotus Development Corporation
55 Cambridge Parkway, Cambridge MA 02142
(617) 577–8500

$7000 to $20,000 for an annual subscription.

System of business and financial information products delivered in CD–ROM.

Market Center
Bonneville Telecommunications
19 W. South Temple, Suite 200, Salt Lake City, UT
(800) 255–7374, (801) 532–3400

$350 plus $10/month maintenance fee plus monthly data and exchange fees.

Provides real-time quotes on stocks, options, commodities, mutual funds, corporate and government bonds.

Market NewsAlert
Comtex Scientific Corp.
911 Hope Street, Stamford, CT 06907
(800) 624–5089, (203) 358–0007

Price varies

Offers coverage of the corporate arena including news, press releases, and SEC filings on listed companies as well as OTC companies.

Media General Databases
Media General Financial Services
P.O. Box C-32333, Richmond, VA 23293
(800) 446–7922, (804) 649–6587

Price varies.

Provides detailed statistical information in all NYSE and AMEX listed common stocks and NASDAQ National Market issues.

NIS Equity Research Service
Northfield Information Services, Inc.
99 Summer Street, #1620, Boston, MA 02110
(800) 262–6085, (617) 737–8360

$16,500 annually, 20% discount for AAII members

A stock market database. More than 4,500 companies are analyzed each month by a series of 24 quantitative models.

OECD Main Economic Indicators
Doan Associates
1800 Sherman Avenue, Suite 612, Evanston, IL 60201
(800) 822–8038, (708) 864–8772

$600–$3700 depending upon update schedule

A compilation of macroeconomic data on the principal Western economies.

OmniNews
Comtex Scientific Corp.
911 Hope Street, Stamford, CT 06907
(800) 624–5089, (203) 358–0007

Price varies.

Combines real-time coverage of corporate news and SEC filing information with the political, economic, and market developments that can affect business.

OTC NewsAlert
Comtex Scientific Corp.
911 Hope Street, Stamford, CT 06907
(800) 624–5089, (203) 358–0236

Price varies.

Provides information on the OTC marketplace. News on over 10,000 large and small NASDAQ and unlisted "pink sheet" companies is available hours, and sometimes days, before it is available elsewhere.

PC Quote
PC Quote, Inc.
401 S. LaSalle Street, Suite 1600, Chicago, IL 60605
(800) 225–5657, (312) 786–5400

$395/month plus exchange fees.

Delivers last-sale, bid/ask, open, low and volume quotations via satellite from 23 major exchanges.

ProQuote
Automated Investments, Inc.
3284 Yonge Street, Suite 401, Toronto, Ontario, Canada M4N 3M7
(416) 489–3500

$495 plus exchange fees

Holds data for 5,000 to 10,000 symbols on a regular IBM PC, and an unlimited number of symbols on an IBM PC with expanded memory.

Quotdial
Quotron Systems, Inc.
5454 Beethoven Street, Los Angeles, CA 90066
(800) 366–5050, (212) 898–7148

$50 one-time registration fee; Plan A: $10 monthly minimum, $30/hr prime time, $10/hr nonprime plus exchange fees; Plan B: monthly minimum, $175, High density location, $19/hr, Medium density location, $12/hr, Low density location, $17/hr.

A dial-in financial information service that accesses Quotron's price and market database. The service provides real-time, 15-minute delay and after-market data on stocks, bonds, mutual funds, options, commodities, and market indexes.

Vickers On-Line
Vickers Stock Research
226 New York Avenue, Huntington, NY 11743
(800) 645–5043, (516) 423–7710

$50/year; $1/minute usage.

Provides access to the continuously updated institutional holdings and trading activity of stocks and corporate and convertible bonds.

*   *   *   *   *

The following list of electronic data services, supplied by the international research firm, FIND/SVP, are those most popular with nonprofessional investors, although many are sufficiently sophisticated to be used by professional investors as well.

Vendor	Key Databases	Contains
DIALOG 3460 Hillview Ave. Palo Alto, CA 94304 (800) 334–2564	Trade and Industry ASAP	Full text of over 300 trade journals
	Management Contents	Abstracts, 700 journals
	Computer Database	Abstracts, 600 journals
	ABI/Inform	Abstracts, 800 publications
	PTS Promt	1500 mostly trade publications (including 200 non–U.S.)
	PTS Mars	110 marketing journals
	Investext	Wall Street analyst reports, over 60 major research firms
	Disclosure Financials	Corporate financial results, 13,000 companies
	Disclosure Management	Management biographies
	Moody's Corporate Profiles	Overviews of 3600 corporations
	Dun's Market Identifiers	Directory of over 6.6 million companies
	Dun's Financial Records	Financials for 750,000 companies—mostly private
	D&B Business Credit Reports	Credit histories—11 million companies
	PTS Newsletter	Full text of over 250 business and industry newsletters

XYZ COMPANY *(Continued)*

Vendor	Key Databases	Contains
	PR Newswire	Updated every 15 minutes; Press releases from over 12,000 companies
	Business Dateline	Full text of over 180 regional business publications
	IDD M&A Transactions	Includes data on all partial and completed merger, acquisition, or divestiture transactions valued at $1 million or more, or with undisclosed value
DOW JONES P.O. Box 300 Princeton, NJ 08540–0300 (609) 452–1511	News/Retrieval	Stock quotes; *Wall Street Journal*; *Barron's*; corporate performance data
	Tradeline	15 years price history on 150,000 issues
VU/TEXT 325 Chestnut Street Suite 1300 Philadelphia, PA. 19106 (215) 574–4100	VU/Text	Regional newspapers
NEWSNET 945 Haverford Rd. Bryn Mawr, PA. 19010 (800) 345-1301	NewsNet	Full text of over 450 newsletters
	TRW Business Profiles	Payment history—8 million businesses
REUTERS 61 Broadway, 31st Flr. New York, NY 10022 (800) 426–4318 or (212) 493–7100	Textline	Full text and abstracts; over 1,000 periodicals, many foreign
	Equities 2000	Securities prices
COMPUSERVE 5000 Arlington Center Blvd. P.O. Box 20212 Columbus, OH 43220 (614) 457–0802	Business Information Service	General and business articles, brokerage reports, stock quotes

XYZ COMPANY *(Continued)*

Vendor	Key Databases	Contains
	Compustat	Historical data on over 5000 U.S. and Canadian companies
TELERATE One World Trade Center 104th Floor New York, NY 10048 (212) 938–5200		Securities prices

There are, of course, other uses of the computer in investor relations. PR Newswire, Business Wire, and other services now accept material transmitted by computer. Their output is accessible by computer as well. Other networks exist, such as *First Call,* an international network established by the brokerage houses to transmit directly to institutions, and now available to the public.

Telescan Gateway (Telescan Incorporated, 2900 Wilcrest, Houston, TX 77042) is a service for investors and investor relations professionals that simplifies database searches by taking your information request and supplying your answer from its own search of more than 700 databases.

In addition, there's the growing use of email—electronic mail systems that function to allow computer users to communicate with one another. These include MCI Mail, Telescan, AT&T, Prodigy, and a growing number of both public and private email systems. Technology has entered full force into the world of investing and investor relations.

Appendix 10

Investor Relations Checklist

In keeping track of the activities and priorities of investor relations clients, particularly for its foreign-based clients, the international public relations firm, Burson-Marsteller, maintains the following checklist.

Communications Activities

Resident Investor Relations Spokesperson

Research/Focus Groups

Message Development

Audience Targeting

New York Analyst Meeting

Boston Analyst Meeting

Regional Analyst Meetings

Roundtable Meetings

Two and a Half Day Meeting

One on One Meetings

Fact Book

English Annual Report

Interim Reports

Portfolio Managers Summary

Analyst Newsletter

Broker Fact Sheet
Teleconference/Audio Conference with Analysts
Press Materials
Business & Financial Media Publicity
Trade Media Publicity
Editorial Board Backgrounding
Spokesperson Training
News Distribution
Media Monitoring and Analysis
Stock Watch

Appendix 11

The Initial Public Offering

The investor relations aspect of the initial public offering can be complex, particularly because of the SEC strictures on communication and disclosure. The rule is that until the issue is out of registration, no activity may be undertaken that might be construed as selling stock. The following checklist is used by Burson-Marsteller, the international public relations firm, in dealing with IPOs.

PREREGISTRATION

One year before

- Develop message/position
- Establish name recognition
- Create industry visibility
- Identify analysts/competitors

Three months before

- Do not introduce new publicity, advertising programs

60 days before

- Issue release announcing intent to file
- Enter quiet period
- Continue existing communications:
  - Marketing and sales
  - Financial/business
  - Keep press inquiries factual

REGISTRATION OFFERING

- All activities reviewed by legal counsel, underwriter
- Begin prospectus
- Develop short video tape
  - Based on prospectus
  - File with SEC
  - For brokers, road show
- Distill prospectus for broker fact sheet
- Issue release at filing

QUIET PERIOD

- Now 25 days
- Prepare basic IR program
  - Assign IR official
  - Develop media, analyst list
  - Prepare disclosure guidelines
  - Coach internal team on disclosure, analysts' needs
  - Design 1st quarterly report
  - Create press kit
  - Write fact book
  - Review advertising options, needs
  - List in directories
  - Develop internal communications guidelines
  - Review release procedure, schedule
  - Prepare shareholder welcome letter, survey, guide
- Develop action plan, schedule

FIRST-YEAR PUBLIC

- Meet with sellside analysts
- Mail information to regional firms
- Seek regional newspaper listings
- Meet with market makers
- Plan meetings with buyside

- Start publicity support
- Consider stockwatch program
- Begin annual report
- Prepare for annual meeting
- Measure program impact through research

Appendix 12

Major Business and Financial Publications

While it would be impossible to list here all of the business and financial publications that serve as outlets for company publicity, the following are the major publications in the field:

Barron's National Business and Financial Weekly 200 Liberty St., New York, NY 10281

Black Enterprise 130 Fifth Ave., New York, NY 10011

Business Month 488 Madison Ave., New York, NY 10022

Business Week 1221 Avenue of the Americas, New York, NY 10020

CFO 268 Summer St., Boston, MA 02210

Chief Executive 205 Lexington Ave., New York, NY 10016

Crain's New York Business 220 E. 42nd St., New York, NY 10017

Crain's Chicago Business 740 North Rush St., Chicago, IL 60611

Corporate Finance 810 Seventh Ave., New York, NY 10023

Dowline Magazine P.O. Box 300, Princeton, NJ 08543

Entrepreneur Magazine 2392 Morse Ave., Irvine, CA 92714

Equities (formerly OTC Review) 37 E. 28th St., New York, NY 10016

Financial World 1450 Broadway, New York, NY 10018

Financier Magazine 420 Lexington Ave., New York, NY 10170

Forbes 60 Fifth Ave., New York, NY 10011

Fortune 1271 Avenue of the Americas, New York, NY 10020

Harvard Business Review Soldiers Field, Boston, MA 02163

Inc. 38 Commercial Wharf, Boston, MA 02110

Industry Week 1100 Superior Ave., Cleveland, OH 44114

Investors Daily 1941 Armacost Ave., Lost Angeles, CA 90025
Institutional Investor 488 Madison Ave., New York, NY 10006
Journal of Accountancy 1211 Avenue of the Americas, New York, NY 10036
Journal of Commerce 110 Wall St., New York, NY 10005
Management Review 135 W. 50th St., New York, NY 10020
MBA Magazine 18 North Main St., Chagrin Falls, OH 44022
Money 1271 Avenue of the Americas, New York, NY 10020
The Money Manager 1 State St. Plaza, New York, NY 10004
Nation's Business 1615 H Street N.W., Washington, DC 20062
National Business Woman 2012 Massachusetts Ave. N.W., Washington, DC
   20036
Pensions and Investment Age 220 E. 42nd St., New York, NY 10017
The Wall Street Transcript 99 Wall St., New York, NY 10005
U.S. News and World Report 2400 N Street N.W., Washington, DC 20037
USA Today 1000 Wilson Blvd., Arlington, VA 20044
United States Banker Ten Valley Dr., Greenwich Office Park, Greenwich, CT
   06831
Value Line Investment Survey 711 Third Ave., New York, NY 10017
Wall Street Journal 200 Liberty St., New York, NY 10281
Wall Street Reports 120 Wall St., New York, NY 10005

Wire Services

Associated Press 50 Rockefeller Center, New York, NY 10020
Dow Jones News Service 200 Liberty St., New York, NY 10281
Reuters News Service 1700 Broadway, New York, NY 10019

Appendix 13

Directories

Bacon's Publicity Checker—Annual publication analyzing publicity requirements of almost 7600 business, trade farm, and consumer magazines (Bacon's Clipping Bureau, 332 S. Michigan Ave., Chicago, IL 60604)

Bacon's Publicity Checker—Newspapers—(Annual) A comprehensive directory and placement guide to more than 9000 dailies, weeklies, weekly multiple publishers, news services, syndicates, and Sunday supplements in the United States and Canada. (Bacon's Clipping Bureau, 332 S. Michigan Ave., Chicago, IL 60604)

Broadcasting Yearbook—(Annual) Broadcasting Publishing Co., 735 DeSales Street N.W., Washington, D.C.

College and Military Contacts—Listings of more than 850 alumni publications, more than 1000 student publications, more than 500 military publications. Includes college and military affiliations, format, target readership, number of pages, photo usage, ad rates and contacts, college student enrollment. (BPI, 1515 Broadway, New York, NY 10036)

Directory of Investment Research—(Annual) Nelson Financial Communications, One Gateway Plaza, P.O. Box 591, Port Chester, NY 10573

Directory of Pension Funds and Their Investment Managers—(Annual) Money Market Directories, Inc., 300 E. Market St., Charlottesville, VA 22901

Directory of Security Analyst Societies, Analyst Splinter Groups, and Stockbroker Clubs—(Annual) National Investor Relations Institute, 1730 M St., N.W., Suite 806, Washington, DC 20036

Editor & Publisher International Yearbook—(Annual) A state-by-state and city-by-city listing of daily newspapers in the United States and Canada with information on their circulation and names of executive personnel (Editor & Publisher Magazine, The Editor & Publisher Co., Inc., 850 Third Ave., New York, NY 10022)

The E–Z Telephone Directory of Brokers & Banks—(Quarterly) An alphabetical listing of the New York financial community, with addresses and telephone numbers (E–Z Telephone Directory Corp., New York)

351

Financial Analysts Federation Membership Directory—(Annual) Financial Analysts Federation, P.O. Box 3726, Charlottesville, VA 22903

Financial 1000 Yellow Book—A directory of those who manage the leading 1000 U.S. financial institutions (Monitor Publishing Company, 104 Fifth Ave., 2nd Floor, New York, NY 10011)

Gale Directory of Publications—A complete directory of 1900 daily newspapers, 8200 weekly, and 3000 trade and consumer magazines, all listed alphabetically by state (Book Tower, Detroit, MI 48226)

Hudson's Washington News Media Contacts Directory—A directory of Washington, DC, area news media, including editors (Hudson Associates, Rhinebeck, NY, annual)

Institutions—(Three times a year) A directory of portfolio managers, analysts, and traders at major financial institutions in the United States and Canada (Technometrics, Inc. New York)

Investment Newsletter Contacts—A directory of more than 900 investment newsletters, including subject matter, price, publisher, circulation and other pertinent data. (BPI, 1515 Broadway, New York, NY 10036)

Middle West Publicity Media Directory—(Annual) A directory of Chicago area publications and news media, including key editorial personnel (St. Clair Press, Chicago)

Military Publications—Describes over 600 American military publications, listing circulation, advertising rates, and other data. (Public Relations Publishing Co., Inc., New York)

New York Publicity Outlets—Directory of New York City, metropolitan area, and major national publications, including personnel and deadlines (Public Relations Plus, P.O. Box 1197, New Milford, CT 06770)

News Bureaus Contacts—A directory of the locations and personnel of all news bureaus in the United States and their branch offices (BPI, 1515 Broadway, New York, NY 10036)

News Media Yellow Book of Washington and New York—A directory of those who report, write, edit, and produce the news in the nation's government and business capitals; contains six specialized indexes (Monitor Publishing Company, 104 Fifth Ave., 2nd Floor, New York, NY 10011)

Nominee List—A directory of nominee names and their identification (American Society of Corporate Secretaries, New York)

O'Dwyer's Directory of Public Relations Firms—(Annual) and *O'Dwyer's Directory of Communications Executives*—(Annual) J.R. O'Dwyer Company Inc., 271 Madison Ave., New York, NY 10036

Professional Guide to Public Relations Services—Describes and evaluates 1000 products and services, including names, addresses, fees, phone numbers, and personal observations; includes suggestions on techniques (AMACOM 135 W. 50th St., New York, NY 10019)

Professional's Guide to Publicity—Public Relations Publishing Co., Inc., 1633 Broadway, New York, NY 10019 (published 1978)

Security Dealers of North America—(Annual) A complete directory of all brokers, dealers, underwriters, investment bankers, exchanges, and so on, arranged by states in the United States and Canada, including key personnel (Standard & Poor's Corp., New York)

Simon's Editorial Offices in the West—A directory of western media and editorial personnel (David H. Simon, Los Angeles)

Syndicated Columnist Contacts—Complete information on where to find columnists, plus history and operation of newspaper syndicates (BPI, 1515 Broadway, New York, NY 10036)

Ulrich's International Periodicals Directory—Information on 50,000 periodicals from all over the world; almost all major language publications with information on publisher, personnel, rates, circulation, frequency of issue, languages of text, where indexed or abstracted; plus money exchange table with conversion rates and formulas (R. R. Bowker Co., Ann Arbor, MI)

The Working Press of the Nation—A reference to basic communication media in the United States in four volumes: Newspaper Directory, Magazine Directory, Radio & TV Directory, Feature Writer and Syndicate Directory; presents names of personnel, addresses of publisher, subjects covered, phone numbers, titles, etc. (The National Research Bureau, Inc., 424 N. Third St., Burlington, IA)

Writer's Market—Annual directory for freelance writers, listing over 4000 publications, including a section on trade, technical, and professional (Writer's Market, Cincinnati, OH)

Newsletters

While not directories, there are several newsletters that may be of interest:

Boardroom Reports—General business information (Boardroom Reports, 330 West 42nd St., New York, NY 10036)

Investor Relations Newsletter—(Monthly) Reports current thinking on problems in investor relations, as well as new regulations (Enterprise Publications, Chicago, IL)

Jack O'Dwyer's Newsletter—A weekly comprehensive report of activities in the public relations and financial relations fields (Jack O'Dwyer, 271 Madison Ave., New York, NY 10010)

PR Aids Party Line—A weekly newsletter of current placement opportunities in all media (Morton and Betty Yarmon, 35 Sutton Place, New York, NY 10010)

PR Reporter—A weekly newsletter of activities of public relations and investor relations practitioners, including frequent discussions of current public relations problems (PR Reporter, Meriden, CT)

Public Relations News—A weekly newsletter of activities of public relations and investor relations practitioners, including frequent case histories of successful programs (Public Relations News, New York)

The Corporate Communications Report—(Bimonthly) Reports and discusses latest problems in corporate communication with the financial community (Corporate Communications Services, Inc., New York,)

The Corporate Shareholder—A semimonthly inside report on investor relations (Corporate Shareholders, Inc., PO Box A–I, New York, NY 10025)

Clipping Services

Bacon's Clipping Bureau (332 S. Michigan Ave., Chicago, IL 60604)

Burrelle's Press Clipping Service (75 E. Northfield Road, Livingston, NJ 07039)

Luce Press Clippings (Box 379, Topeka, KS 66601)

Suggested Readings

GRAHAM & DODD'S SECURITY ANALYSTS, 5th ed., by Sidney Cottle, Roger F. Murray, and Frank E. Block. New York: McGraw-Hill, 1988. 656 pp.

THE INTELLIGENT INVESTOR, by Benjamin Graham. New York: Harper & Row, 1973. 340 pp.

THE ANATOMY OF THE FLOOR, by Leonard Sloane. New York: Doubleday, 1980. 228 pp.

TRADING, by Susan Goldenberg. Orlando, FL: Harcourt Brace Jovanovich, 1986. 263 pp.

MANICS, PANICS, AND CRASHES, by Charles P. Kindleberger. New York: Basic Books, 1978. 271 pp.

CRASHES AND PANICS, ed. by Eugene N. White. Homewood, IL: Dow Jones-Irwin, 1990. 260 pp.

THE STOCK MARKET, by Richard J. Teweles and Edward S. Bradley. New York: John Wiley, 1987. 526 pp.

INVESTMENT ANALYSIS AND PORTFOLIO MANAGEMENT, by Jerome B. Cohen, Edward D. Zinbarg, and Arthur Zeikel. Homewood, IL: Richard D. Irwin, Inc., 1987. 738 pp.

CORPORATE FINANCIAL ANALYSIS, by John D. Finnerty. New York: McGraw-Hill, 1986. 566 pp.

MODERN PORTFOLIO THEORY: PRINCIPLES OF INVESTMENT MANAGE-MENT, by Andrew Rudd and Henry K. Clasing, Jr. Homewood, IL: Dow Jones-Irwin, 1982. 578 pp.

THE DOW JONES-IRWIN GUIDE TO MODERN PORTFOLIO THEORY, by Robert Hagin. Homewood, IL: Dow Jones-Irwin, 1980. 353 pp.

QUALITY OF EARNINGS, by Thornton L. O'Glove. New York: Free Press, 1987. 204 pp.

THE NEW FINANCIAL INSTRUMENTS, by Julian Walmsley. New York: John Wiley, 1989. 454 pp.

THE TECHNIQUES OF FINANCIAL ANALYSIS, by Erich A. Helfert. Homewood, IL: Dow Jones-Irwin, 1981. 285 pp.

MORE DEBITS THAN CREDITS, by Abraham J. Briloff. New York: Harper & Row, 1976. 453 pp.

UNACCOUNTABLE ACCOUNTING, by Abraham J. Briloff. New York: Harper & Row, 1972. 365 pp.

THE FINANCIAL REVOLUTION, by Adrian Hamilton. New York: Free Press, 1986. 268 pp.

DOW THEORY REDUX, by Michael D. Sheimo. Chicago: Probus, 1989. 176 pp.

THE DOW JONES INVESTOR'S HANDBOOK 1990, ed. by Phyllis S. Pierce. Homewood, IL: Dow Jones-Irwin, 1990. 185 pp.

THE HIGH YIELD DEBT MARKET, ed. by Edward I. Altman. Homewood, IL: Dow Jones-Irwin, 1990. 306 pp.

THE CFO'S HANDBOOK, ed. by Richard F. Vancil and Benjamin R. Makela. Homewood, IL: Dow Jones-Irwin, 1986. 642 pp.

MARKETS: WHO PLAYS . . . WHO RISKS . . . WHO GAINS . . . WHO LOSES, by Martin Mayer. New York: W. W. Norton, 1988. 303 pp.

INVESTOR LINES: FINDING AND USING THE BEST INVESTMENT INFORMATION, by Michael C. Thomsett. New York: John Wiley. 207 pp.

SUSAN LEE'S ABZS OF MONEY AND FINANCE, by Susan Lee. New York: Poseidon Press, 1988. 219 pp.

WEBSTER'S NEW WORLD DICTIONARY OF MEDIA AND COMMUNICATIONS, by Richard Weiner. Englewood Cliffs, NJ: Prentice-Hall, 1989.

THE VEST-POCKET MBA, by Jae K. Shim, Joel G. Siegel, and Abraham J. Simon. Englewood Cliffs, NJ: Prentice-Hall, 1987. 300 pp.

THE DOW JONES-IRWIN GUIDE TO USING THE WALL STREET JOURNAL, by Michael B. Lehmann. Homewood, IL: Dow Jones-Irwin, 1987. 282 pp.

THE DOW JONES-IRWIN GUIDE TO BOND AND MONEY MARKET INVESTMENTS, by Frank J. Fabozzi. Homewood, IL: Dow Jones-Irwin, 1987. 298 pp.

THE HANDBOOK OF FIXED INCOME SECURITIES, ed. by Frank J. Fabozzi and Irving M. Pollack. Homewood, IL: Dow Jones-Irwin, 1983. 1101 pp.

THE INVESTOR'S GUIDE TO CONVERTIBLE BONDS, by Thomas C. Noddings. Homewood, IL: Dow Jones-Irwin, 1982. 250 pp.

THE MONEY MARKET, 3rd ed., by Marcia Stigum. Homewood, IL: Dow Jones-Irwin, 1989. 1252 pp.

THE COMPLETE GUIDE TO SECURITIES TRANSACTIONS, ed. by Wayne H. Wagner. New York: John Wiley & Sons, 1989. 381 pp.

HOW CORPORATE AND MUNICIPAL DEBT IS RATED, by Hugh C. Krieger. New York: Sherwood, 1976. 180 pp.

STANDARD & POOR'S RATINGS GUIDE, by Standard & Poor's. New York: McGraw-Hill, 1979. 417 pp.

THE NASDAQ HANDBOOK, ed. by National Association of Securities Dealers, Inc. Chicago, Probus, 1987. 577 pp.

THE DOW JONES-IRWIN BUSINESS AND INVESTMENT ALMANAC - 1990, ed. by Sumner N. Levine. Homewood, IL: Dow Jones-Irwin. 739 pp.

BOND MARKETS, ANALYSIS AND STRATEGIES, by Frank J. Fabozzi and T. Dessa. Englewood Cliffs, NJ: Prentice-Hall, 1989. 347 pp.

THE ACCOUNTANTS HANDBOOK OF FORMULAS AND TABLES, by Lawrence Lipkin, Irwin K. Feinstein, and Lucille Derrick. Englewood Cliffs, NJ: Prentice-Hall, 1989. 627 pp.

THE HANDBOOK OF INTERNATIONAL INVESTING, ed. by Carl Beidleman. Chicago: Probus, 1987. 900 pp.

THE INDIVIDUAL INVESTORS GUIDE TO NO-LOAD MUTUAL FUNDS, 8th ed., by The American Association of Individual Investors. Chicago: International Publishing Corp., 1989. 459 pp.

HANDBOOK FOR RAISING CAPITAL, ed. by Lawrence Chimerine, Robert F. Cushman, and Howard D. Ross. Homewood, IL: Dow Jones-Irwin, 1987. 666 pp.

SECURITIES LAW COMPLIANCE, by Alan Pessin. Homewood, IL: Dow Jones-Irwin, 1989. 457 pp.

CORPORATE COMMUNICATIONS HANDBOOK, by Wesley S. Walton and Charles Brissman. New York: Clark Boardman, 1989.

WALL STREET AND REGULATION, ed. by Samuel L. Hayes, III. Cambridge, MA: Harvard Business School Press, 1987. 206 pp.

THE TAKEOVER GAME, by John Brooks. New York: Dutton, 1987. 390 pp.

SECRETS OF THE TEMPLE, by William Greider. New York: Simon & Schuster, 1988. 798 pp.

THE PREDATOR'S BALL, by Connie Bruck. New York: Simon & Schuster, 1988. 385 pp.

THE TAKEOVER DIALOGUES, by Edmund J. Kelly. Arlington, VA: Washington Network Press, 1987. 170 pp.

THE INDIVIDUAL INVESTOR'S GUIDE TO COMPUTERIZED INVESTING, 7th ed. Chicago: American Association of Individual Investors, 1989/1990. 468 pp.

Index